My
Strange
Love

My Strange Love

Selected Film Reviews
and Essays, 2001–2021

Stuart Klawans

Sticking Place Books
New York

Grateful acknowledgment is made to *Parnassus: Poetry in Review* for permission to reprint the essays "My Strange Love: Intimations of Stanley Kubrick Recollected from Early Childhood" and "Narcissus Sees Through Himself: Jean Cocteau and the Invention of the Film Poet," to *Film Comment* for permission to reprint the essay "Proportions Observed: Re-Viewing the Italian Neorealists," and to *The Nation* for permission to reprint selections from many years of reviews.

www.stickingplacebooks.com

ISBN 979-8-89976-060-0

For Bali, Jake and Ruby

Contents

Introduction

Film reviewers are the short order cooks of the arts and letters. Someone at the window bawls out the next item to be served, and we hustle to slap our words onto the counter while they're still hot and moist.

And after next Friday rolls around with its new releases, does anything remain of our previous week's labor, other than congealed scraps? Sometimes, maybe. Here are selections from some twenty years of film reviews and essays, presented in the hope that they might be of more than momentary interest, perhaps because they address films of lasting merit, or advance arguments that remain viable, or at least offer a phrase that can raise a smile.

The opening section, "Where I'm Coming From," talks about experiences and ideas that run throughout the rest of the book. These appear in autobiographical reflections, essays on two of my critical preoccupations (neorealism and auteurism), and an encounter with my spiritual advisor. An essay in this section from the 150th anniversary issue of *The Nation,* my main berth as a film critic, represents a conviction that the magazine has upheld significantly, if not consistently, over the decades: a left humanist belief that the arts can be liberating, though perhaps not through a key-to-lock method.

"Movies Are Better than Ever!" makes good on an ad slogan of my youth by praising some of the films that mattered most to me in the early 2000s, when the art of cinema was said to be dying yet again. This section makes no claim to being comprehensive. You will find that some of your favorite movies are missing from it. Mine, too. Freelance film criticism is a practice in which the one-time opportunity to preview a film might coincide neither with the magazine's deadline nor with the demands of a rent-paying job. Gaps are inevitable. But here is proof that the world's filmmakers, refusing to wither away, delivered at least forty memorable movies over the course of these twenty years.

"Nope," titled in honor of Jordan Peele, offers innocent merriment at the expense of some of the period's stinkers. I hope these slams amount to more than mere bullying. I've tried to direct my derision at films of an instructive rottenness, especially when they were puffed up by writers who ought to have known better. I've also included disappointing works by some of the filmmakers I most admire.

The themes of the other sections, some auteurist in focus, some more general, should be self-explanatory. One exception is "Wars and Rumors of War." The earliest piece in this collection, written when I returned to *The Nation* from a brief hiatus, dates from a moment when the Bush administration had only recently invaded Afghanistan and was preparing to move on to Iraq. My final review, written in late 2021, was about a Ukrainian film, which envisioned a war with Russia that had not yet started but (as it happened) would begin soon enough. Wars framed everything I wrote. Whether they were being fought in the Middle East and Central Asia, the former Soviet Union, or Israel and Palestine, they were a continual preoccupation of filmmakers and their audiences throughout the years this book represents.

That said, I could not bear to end this book with a pan across a killing field that stretches to the horizon. Chaplin would not have accepted that as a conclusion, nor for that matter would Tarkovsky. Looking over my notes, I saw titles of all sorts of lively, intriguing, sometimes trouble-making movies that I longed to include in the book but had failed to smash into any category. I picked twenty-six, many of them small films that had not gotten the attention they deserved, and arranged them in the favorite format of all writers: an alphabet. Elsewhere in this book, films are locked into a chronology. When they're in an alphabet, it's possible to think of how they can mingle, scramble and recombine in people's minds, leading to new statements that no one could foresee.

I am grateful to all the editors and colleagues who for so long helped me string films together into sentences. Curious readers can find selections from my first dozen years of this activity in a previous collection, titled *Left in the Dark.* The present selection brings the story to its close, when I resigned from *The Nation* in 2021. In assembling these pieces, I resisted the temptation to revise. You will find the original infelicities intact. I made an exception only for grievous errors of fact, where I let the mistakes stand but added notes of correction. I also updated "black" to the now-standard "Black" in reference to African American people. Other than that, I have done only as much cosmetic surgery as was necessary when severing the occasional review from an article where it had been connected to two or three others.

Special thanks to Laurence Kardish, friend and mentor, for his role in encouraging this collection, and to Paul Cronin, editor and publisher, for the stickiness of his courage.

Where I'm Coming From

My Strange Love: Intimations of Stanley Kubrick Recollected from Early Childhood

If we'd thought to name our afternoon's pastime, we might have called it Spot the Bomb. We made it up while rambling through the neighborhood one overcast spring day: a game whose first move was a shouted "I saw the flash in the sky!" Whoever called out the sighting would point east, across the Yates Avenue playground toward the steel mills' smoke, or west, from the schoolyard's asphalt toward the railroad tracks, or south, past 100th Street to the yellowish haze over Calumet Harbor. Whoever questioned the sighting would be told, "You have only *five seconds* from when you see the flash!" Then, screaming "Get down!", we'd all drop into the fetal position we knew as Civil Defense.

I don't recall any great anxiety in this game, apart from feeling that one of the kids was a missile bully. He bellowed us down, and did it for twice as many bombs as anyone else spotted. Besides, he prolonged the sport beyond the point where I would have preferred the swing set. But I couldn't have refused to play. Everyone knew that South Chicago was a prime Russian target, its round-the-clock industries scheduled for destruction right after the White House. For just that reason our teachers had educated us to cower beneath our desks, heads down and eyes closed. For that reason our television sets whined in the middle of programs—a test, we were told, of the Emergency Broadcasting System—and sirens practiced their howling each morning at 10:30. I can guess the year we invented Spot the Bomb because I know when those sirens set off a panic. It was autumn 1959, when the White Sox won the pennant in a night game, and the Fire Department blasted an off-hours salute.

Most likely, then, I'm remembering a pastime invented in spring 1960, when green elms were lined up along the streets and imported earthworms glistened under the bushes. (Worms and soil were both new to this place, built over acres of slag from the mills.) Winter left the houses bubbled and peeled; but with winter gone, our two-story duplexes looked moist and strange against a shifting CinemaScope of clouds. If we'd wandered east, we'd have come to the factories: Wisconsin Steel and International Harvester, vast and dark, brooding for miles along Torrence Avenue. And to the west, I'd discovered a stand of poplars at least eight feet deep, thick enough that you could pretend they were a wood. Step in, and you were suddenly out of the neighborhood, gazing in solitary peace at a marshland beyond, which stretched as far as 103rd and Doty and its colossal incinerator tower. I loved to look at the massings of flame and rusting metal that bounded us, just as I loved the raw, not-quite-domesticated nature in our midst, which a developer had thought would prettify our streets, but instead had made them poignant.

What a thrill I felt, a few years later, when I first came across *The Prelude*! It turned out that somebody else had grown up "Fostered alike by beauty and by fear." In Wordsworth's case, though, the faculty that awoke in childhood had natured into a poet's imagination. My power to refigure the world turned out to be no more than a critic's; and so, over time, I've found consolation both in the Romantics and the rationalists. Think of Hume, who refuted Wordsworth in advance, discovering nothing godlike in a "fancy" that was principally good for tossing out "winged horses, fiery dragson, and monstrous giants." These, Hume demonstrated, were the products of a "gentle force" of the mind, which busied itself by linking single ideas into compounds.

If I were to try to reconcile these two accounts of the imagination, I might propose that Hume was analyzing from the outside and Wordsworth experiencing from within. But that explanation says nothing about the motives of the writers, or the mindsets of the readers who found them persuasive. In 1739, in *A Treatise of Human Nature,* Hume demoted the imagination to something quasi-mechanical and semi-idiotic. In 1798, with the publication of *Lyrical Ballads,* Wordsworth launched the exaltation of that same faculty. Only sixty years had passed. Why the change?

Since Hume didn't believe in causes and effects, I won't pretend to establish any; but I do notice that this shift in attitude coincided with a shaking of confidence in the public sphere. England's empire endured its first contraction during those sixty years. In the same period, a newly, freakishly militant France began to threaten the security of all institutions and borders. Just when political and economic relations were growing unstable, imagination became individualized—more fastened on autobiography— and yet, paradoxically, more primordial. To simplify grotesquely: Hume and his first readers did not know the Terror; Wordsworth and his first readers did.

These thoughts, of course, were unavailable to a nine-year-old in that spring when John Kennedy invented the missile gap. I knew only that the majesty of my neighborhood stirred me, and that its obliteration would be mercifully quick. That was the happy meaning of our game's *five seconds*. No one in South Chicago would need to linger in a lonely underground shelter or waste away with radiation poisoning. According to our skeptics, we might not even experience the flash—for how could we see the white light that would pierce our eyes, when by definition it was blinding? We stretched our minds, trying to picture this sublime moment, and found that the effort calmed us, as did our newspapers when they spoke not of a Reign but a Balance of Terror. The phrase had a reassuring, middle-of-the-road tone.

The time was coming, though, when I would not be reassured. In the years just after Spot the Bomb, I became better acquainted with the Terror, largely because two "educational" films inadvertently moved me to doubt everything official. In so doing, these pictures also incited me to my first acts of film criticism. No movies ever affected me more—which is funny, since I don't even know their names.

The first one I saw in my grammar school's gym. Boastful Mrs. Fitzgerald, who read aloud from J. Edgar Hoover's *Masters of Deceit* and thanked herself for it on our behalf, one day announced an assembly and marched our seventh-grade class down the length of the building, through the wide double doors to the gym and into a buzzing gloom. The lights high overhead were dim in their cages; the walls were hung with the broad creepe of the blackout drapes. As I took a seat in the cramped ranks of folding chairs, I saw that, far ahead, the basketball backboard had been cranked to the ceiling and the screen unrolled at the rear of the stage. Had anyone bothered to explain this assembly? If so, the speech must already have been delivered. The gym abruptly went black, the kids all shouted, the teachers threatened indiscriminate reprisals. Then the projector's beam touched the screen and, by reflex, we all grew quiet again.

With that, I learned that the Luella Elementary School, from fourth grade through eighth, had been summoned to learn about Our Shield in the Sky. Nuclear bombs would never touch American soil, we were told, because the pilots of the Strategic Air Command were on duty day and night. A movie voice yawned and rang from all sides, booming from the speakers and bouncing around the gym. It took a second or two for the words to coalesce into sense; but they were clear enough that I could understand the film's climax. With the latest advances, the narrator said, our planes would soon outrace even an intercontinental ballistic missile. Here is a demonstration.

On the screen, a rocket shot upward, a plane took off, a rocket trailed across the sky, a plane zoomed higher, a rocket trailed across the sky, a zooming plane shot fire from its wings, a rocket trailed across the sky and suddenly splattered into a great white cloud.

"Yaaay!" shrieked the assembled kids, exulting as one—all except me. I sat silent and alone, thinking, "But there was no missile!" The man had said this would happen someday, not that it could happen now. Besides, this was a movie. The attack we'd seen didn't even come from Russia!

Now the A-bomb really had me worried. Through the agency of this movie, its cross-cutting so crude that even I saw through the technique, the bomb had instilled in me a new kind of fear: not that I would vanish in a flash, but that my life would be prolonged among the gullible. Worse still, I now saw that the people in charge of us knew all about gullibility and were ready to encourage it—clumsily, at that.

Just how clumsily, I was to learn a bit later, with a second cinematic technique.

My parents, ever generous, had bought me a television set, which sat before the window in my attic bedroom, up in the overheated skull of the house. I watched even on Sunday mornings. If nothing else was on, I would tune in to the educational channel, where a Japanese man would be teaching origami, or an unseen lecturer carrying on about Goebbels and his tools of propaganda.

So, while idling in my room, I got to see an example of Goebbels' work at its worst. The narrator sounded furious about it; and I was pretty shocked myself. This clip from a Nazi newsreel showed Winston Churchill carving up the world. Or, rather, the newsreel showed the image of a spinning globe, onto which the director had superimposed some footage of Churchill at the dinner table, doing the honors with a roast.

That the victim of this mendacity was Churchill seemed outrageous to me, but no more so than the method of the lie. How dared the Nazis *combine* images? They had made something happen on the screen that never took place in front of the camera. For the first time in my life, I had come to prize an essential truthfulness in movies, thanks to seeing it violated.

But that was only the first half of the shock. The second came on a Sunday morning a few weeks later, as I sat in bed in my pajamas watching a Pentagon-produced show called *The Big Picture*. The feature that day was a Signal Corps newsreel about the Communist menace. It was full of the usual stuff: maps being darkened by the encroachment of Soviet arrows, minor chords in the brass being blared *sforzando*. Then came the moment of revelation. The image of a spinning globe filled my TV screen. Superimposed on this toy world was footage of Nikita Khrushchev at the dinner table. He was doing the honors with a roast.

After that, I had a better handle on my dislike of Mrs. Fitzgerald. Ever prickly about my elders' self-satisfaction, ever ready to deflate it, I now understood her preening anti-Communism as a form of pride in being fooled. But what a strange thing to be proud of! Surely she knew—since even I knew—how our fear of Russia was being slapped together for us, with one ready-made picture pasted over another. (The imagination does not create; it combines.) Yet she pretended *not* to know, and thought her pretense made her superior. It was as if we'd let the missile bully scare us for real with Spot the Bomb; as if we'd formed a Bomb Watchers Gang and pressed other boys to join, when we all knew our founding member had been faking. I understood very well the sense of power you get from a gang; I'd helped form a few, and had been excluded from more. But in the Bomb Watchers Gang, you'd be a member and an outsider simultaneously, a liar and the willing victim of lies. And what pleasure would you get? Not the chance to brandish cap guns and celebrate triumphs, but only to duck and cover. Mrs. Fitzgerald, I saw, had agreed to live in perpetual fear. As recompense, she got to admire herself for planting fear in others.

So ended my grammar-school training in film studies and the Balance of Terror. A much larger field of inquiry now waited outside the bounds of the neighborhood, in the near-black Victorian hulk of Bowen High School. I was a child of twelve when I entered the place, in autumn 1963. I was still just 13 the next summer—but well prepared for the experience—when I went with a few friends to the Hamilton Theater on 71st Street and encountered *Dr. Strangelove*.

o   o   o

I think of it as my first art movie. By that, I mean it surpassed and defied expectations, which in this case were modest enough. Our group walked into the movie house with the notion that *Dr. Strangelove* would be funny and dirty, and that the Hamilton's management hoped never to hear from our parents. On all these points our wishes were fulfilled, from the cashier's grimace at our arrival to the world's annihilation at the end. No viewers could have enjoyed more hugely than we the dreamy, loving insertion of a fuel hose into the slitlike opening of a bomber's tank. (We'd all been tipped off what *that* was about.) None could have howled more happily at the mention of "precious bodily fluids." We'd even brought to the movie a rudimentary conception of "satire," having read this word in *MAD* magazine.

The more delighted we became, the less amused were the older members of the audience. With the typical bigotry of adults, they assumed we had no right to appreciate *Dr. Strangelove* out loud. They thought we couldn't understand it. We understood, all right—though at a distance. The attitudes we'd learned from *MAD* were our substitute for a first-hand knowledge of politics; our study of *Playboy* allowed us to savor the movie's dirty parts. Looking back, I think we weren't wrong to approach the movie through these impressions from magazines—though I regret that on the subject of women and what you could do with them, I, too, was readily gullible. I might have applied to *Playboy* and the sex jokes of *Dr. Strangelove* the same skepticism that I'd discovered in watching Red Scare propaganda; but I didn't. I came out of the Hamilton Theater a satisfied customer.

Yet I was also dissatisfied, in a way that was utterly new to me. I worried, as a fish worries at the hook, because of Dr. Strangelove's sudden ability to rise from his wheelchair. Of course I understood why the excitement of the moment might make his right arm shoot upward in a Nazi salute; I knew why, under pressure, he forgot himself and addressed the President as "mein Führer." These slipos testified to certain facts of post-war history, which a Jewish boy could register without recourse to *MAD*. As a movie-mad kid, I also could recognize Kubrick's parody of psychiatric melodramas, which always called for the climactic cure of one kind of cripple or another. But what was the meaning of *this* miracle cure? Why did it happen? What did it have to do with *anything*? The mystery nagged at me so much that a week later, riding home from a visit to Aunt Molly and Uncle Phil, I was still talking about it, at length, from the back seat of the car. "Enough!" my mother finally snapped from the front. "It's just a movie!" With that, I knew for the first time that I'd seen something more than a movie.

Something more: That is to say, I experienced my dissatisfaction as a surplus, which overflowed the ninety-three minutes of the film. My task, as I understood it, was to locate the hidden source, in which I would discover a truth that would explain not only *Dr. Strangelove* but also something of the world into which I'd emerged from the Hamilton, trailing clouds of puzzlement as

I went. I was thirteen. I thought art was embedded with secrets, which you could decode.

Reconstructing those feelings now, almost forty years later, I can analyze how the movie went about bothering me. One of its tricks was to ascribe great importance to Strangelove, who made nothing happen. He didn't build a Doomsday Machine; he didn't order a nuclear attack; he didn't climb into the bomb bay of an airplane to loose the all-fatal nuke. Strangelove scarcely even spoke until the final scene; and yet he was the title character. I couldn't see why.

Nor could I comprehend why the movie's high point seemed to be his liberation from the wheelchair. The immense clouds that erupted after his cure, blossoming across the whole planet, seemed to express his joyful recover. I understood, of course, that this healing could be interpreted in a straightforward way, as you would have read the editorial cartoon in a newspaper. Strangelove equalled the Nazis, with their heartless efficiency and brutal power. His mobility, regained, must therefore have edqualled the return of unencumbered fascism. This would all have been plausible enough, except that the moment bore no resemblance to editorial cartoons. It played more like something from the Gospels. Toss down your throw-weight and walk! Despite my being a Jewish boy, I wanted to know: Were we all saved in Dr. Strangelove?

And was Strangelove as irrelevant to the action as he seemed? He was played by Peter Sellers, who in the same film also portrayed a British officer and the President. It felt that some sympathy accrued to Strangelove from these other characters, just as a portion of Strangelove's suffering bled into them. Maybe the officer and the President, too, were crippled in some way. Maybe they, and we, would be redeemed with Strangelove when the world blew up.

Right then, had I known enough to search for feelings rather than answers, I would have had all the answer I required. Yes, Strangelove's cure was a miracle. He received it just before we were all granted our prayer for annihilation. Hadn't we once passed a happy afternoon anticipating the blast? Didn't the movie's most vital, exuberant character straddle the outsize phallus of a bomb and ride it, crowing, into the cataclysm? Weren't the finale's mushroom clouds so many puffs of orgasm, deferred since the beginning's refueling scene? We ached for the ultimate release. We wanted it bad.

This was the aspect of *Dr. Strangelove* that qualified as secret knowledge—secret only because I refused to know about it. *We* refused in 1964, when war was still officially unthinkable (despite being ongoing) and a celebrated television commercial, directed by Tony Schwartz, convinced most Americans that Barry Goldwater intended to nuke a daisy-plucking child. By this point in the development of my movie mania, I could inventory the parts from which Schwartz had assembled his fiery dragon, his monstrous giant. I could define his radically simple montage as an example of suspense editing; and what's more, I could enjoy the effect. This commercial was far more skillful than the propaganda that had inspired my first, lackadaisical skepticism. Besides, I agreed with Schwartz's propaganda, which made his cheating juxtapositions something to admire, not deride.

I was ready for such argumentation; but nothing had prepared me for Kubrick's imagination, which made room for ambivalence. I couldn't add up everything he cross-cut or superimposed, because so many elements of the mix were invisible on the screen, inaudible on the soundtrack. They were mental processes—memories and associations—which interfered subtly, unpredictably, with the more mechanistic operations of "fancy." Since I was too pious to own up to a big chunk of my thinking—the part that longed for the flash—I also was unable to fathom Strangelove's miracle cure. All I knew was that some bigger meaning had been opened: something too threatening to be called either funny or dirty, though it masqueraded as both and so was all the more troubling. I thought of the hint of vanity in Strangelove's wavy blonde hair, of his flirtatious smile and flattering, sibilant speech. I put those traits together with his apparatus of sadism: the tinted eyeglasses, the black glove, even the circular slide rule (a tool of domination, as any high-school kid would know). I combined the elements in my mind, but the sum kept coming out wrong. They yielded *more.*

I hadn't known this was something a movie could do. I wasn't sure, at this point, that I wanted it done. But the appetite for ambivalence, once aroused, turned out to be insatiable. At first it was reading, more than moviegoing, that fed and sharpened the hunger—though movies figured in it, too, once I pushed beyond 71st Street. Within a few years, I discovered filmmakers who were even more subtle and unpredictable in the way they played on my associations. Kubrick would not be one of my favorites.

But that doesn't matter. Like any lover in middle age, I still smile when I think of him, my first. I miss him, too, when I watch those movies today that are big-budget, bankable-star versions of *Our Shield in the Sky*, such as *Independence Day, Armageddon, The Peacemaker, The Sum of All Fears*. Week after week, I sit through these exercises in cross-cutting, which cater to our nihilism and our piety alike, but always in sequence, never at once. First some terrible destruction rains down; then the source of the destruction is destroyed. At both times, the kids shriek "Yaaay!" And I sit in the dark, alone.

o   o   o

Or rather, I would be alone at those times, except for my memory. Allied with Hume's "fancy," memory gives rise to a function of imagination of which I was ignorant when I first saw *Dr. Strangelove*, but which matters to me deeply now. Imagination allows us to converse with our dead.

The dead one at times might be my father, who helped train me in film criticisms, since he, like all good fans, was a critic himself. I often recall how he leaned toward me in the middle of one picture—a comedy not a thriller—and said, "You know what's coming next, don't you?"

The dead one can also be myself. The teenager who watched *Dr. Strangelove* still comes around to haunt me when the lights go down—though, more often, I'm visited by a slightly older ghost, the one who got out of the neighborhood and past the high school, to have his first encounters with subtitles. This is the kid for whom terror became a normal presence. He knew he would probably stay out of Vietnam and jail, but he could never be sure of it. He doubted he would be killed in a riot—or a full-scale race war—but he couldn't see why not. This kid had found himself in a nation of Mrs. Fitzgeralds, who wanted their government to incinerate Asians, to murder Blacks who complained too vehemently, to keep those bombs piling up. He didn't need to scan the perimeter at all hours, watching for harm; but he understood very well that most of his fellow citizens wouldn't have minded if it came to him.

When my imagination awakens in the dark, I sit with that kid, more than with anyone else. His discoveries remain fresh in me; I feel his fears, and (even more) his loves. That's why, when I search for beauty in the movies, I'm always happiest to see it in scenes that resemble the South Loop, where a narrow iron bridge crossed the brown trickle of the Chicago River, and the bays of the Polk Street Station stood abandoned and rusting alongside the water. I loved that place because my father worked there, in a loft building with the honorably tired appearance of a factory worker coming off an overtime shift. I loved the place because I thought Antonioni could have used it for a location.

During my first summer home from college, when Antonioni and daily terror were new to me, I worked there, at 310 West Polk Street, in a mindless job my father had secured for me. I loved him more for seeing him in this setting, where he was no longer my father but one of several paunchy, cigar-chewing men, who worked together and kibbitzed and nursed their resentments against a cool, disapproving boss. Because my father had become finite, localized, he was more precious to me; and I loved the silent car rides we shared each day—rides in the same direction that led to college and a bigger world of movies.

We'd leave at seven to beat traffic and go north on Jeffrey Boulevard until it turned into a highway, which stretched and curved along Lake Michigan's shore. To our left, the wooded edge of Jackson Park blurred past; to our right was a vast hemisphere of clouds, and silver waves as far as the horizon. My memory has retained no blue days over the lake; the scene is always overcast, so it seems we're driving by a bandshell as big as the world, built so that no orchestra is needed. The dome and platform are the music. I attend the performance every day of the week.

This is Chicago's sublime—in my experience, as much natural grandeur as most people ever get. In a dream from that summer, I stand on the rocky shore, at dawn, as a deep roar passes overhead. There is no flash. The sky darkens, and I see that the massed power of the Chinese air force is coming from behind me, from the lake, spreading west over Chicago. As soon as the planes reach the Illinois Central tracks, miles and miles of low slum dwellings and factory sheds burst into flame. The whole city is an orange panorama, and I am leaping with joy.

Parnassus: Poetry in Review, vol. 26, no. 2 (2002)
Written for a special issue on the theme of terror and imagination

A Radical Future: Films

I cried to Captain Kirk to save me, but he could not hear. I sought the Little Tramp as my companion, but Grumpy Cat hid him from view.

Cinema is gone; everyone agrees. And yet cinema also abides, if only so that Jean-Luc Godard can go on delivering valedictions to what it used to be. Like the history of which it's a part, the moving image has not finished its work, nor is it likely to end anytime soon. I think it's just gotten a little too much into itself.

It's a disconcerting situation, given that cinema used to be so expansive, with movies surfing over the world on the waves of modernity's Big Bang. That primordial explosion, which Eric Hobsbawm called the dual revolution, sent industrial capitalism and political liberalism bursting together across the globe from their point of origin in Western Europe, burning down, building up again and transforming whatever stood in their path. About a century into the process, in a rented room in Paris, the unstoppable conflagration flickered across a public screen for the first time.

The dual revolution's new medium was a relatively modest technical innovation—one "without a future," as Louis Lumière thought—tinkered into existence at the end of the 19th century's more impressive breakthroughs, such as the railroads, photography and electric light. Cinema was also a latecomer among the social and cultural innovations of the dual revolution: new forms of spectatorship and consumption that ranged, as Miriam Hansen has written, "from world expositions and department stores to the more sinister attractions of melodrama, phantasmagoria, wax museums and morgues." To this roster I would add panoramic paintings, including one of particular interest for a magazine founded in 1865: Paul Philippoteaux's *Cyclorama of the Battle of Gettysburg*, whose encompassing hyperrealism first astonished the public in 1883.

Many types of spectacle were available to a world in transformation; but it was film, especially, that the tremors of the 19th century carried along as they rippled into the 20th, turning a mere novelty into modernity's most all-consuming mode of expression. Soon everything had to be filmed: from scenes along the Nile to Shackleton's expedition to Antarctica, from a staged version of the coronation of King George V to the actual Passaic textile strike. So rapidly did movie cameras spread across the globe, in such an unceasing project of documenting and fabricating, that

André Bazin famously likened cinema to the art of mummifica-
tion, observing that both answered an urgent psychological need
to arrest and preserve transient reality.

I remain loyal to Bazin and will come back to him shortly. For
the moment, though, I will ask you to think of early cinema's best-
known images, which present a picture not of formaldehyde-laced
anxiety but unbounded dynamism. The train chugs into La Ciotat
station. The space capsule pokes the moon in the eye. The Little
Tramp stands on deck with his fellow immigrants, staring at the
Statue of Liberty. And so the images continued throughout the
20th century, from the stagecoach rolling across the valley to the
spaceship flying to Jupiter and Beyond. Film for most of its life
has projected the feelings of a society that believed it was going
somewhere.

This bustling, outward-looking aspect of the moving image
was more than a matter of appearances. Film became pre-eminent
in the 20th century not only by giving mass audiences what they
wanted to see but by adopting, and sometimes helping to origi-
nate, the new society's industrial and financial developments. By
the early 1920s, commercial cinema had become the first art form
organized on the principles of the assembly line and the cartel.
By the late 1940s, American studios were becoming pioneers in
outsourcing production around the world and shifting business
operations across borders, moving capital according to the needs
of trade agreements and currency fluctuations. Cinema even found
new opportunities for expansion when its main corporate rival,
radio, underwent the vast reorganization required for television.
The TV stations had air time to fill. Movies rushed in to fill the
void.

o   o   o

Then the shock waves of the dual revolution stopped moving
outward.

It's hard to fix a date for the turning point. You might
choose 1973 and the OPEC oil embargo, or 1975 and the end of
the Vietnam war. I tend to think that the expansive dynamism
continued beyond the fall of the Berlin Wall, as capital burst the
final barriers and flooded into the former Soviet bloc. The money
by then was already pouring into China; it had been doing so since
the early 1980s. During the 1990s it flowed more easily than ever
throughout the rest of the globe as well, bringing with it a triumphant neoliberal ideology.

At which point—too late—Wile E. Coyote saw that the boulder he'd loaded into his giant Acme slingshot had rocketed to the limit of the elastic and was sproinging back, straight at his head.

In Wile E.'s honor, we might title the recent history of the world and its moving images *The Great Rebound.* Two centuries of ceaseless outward movement have given way to collapse and recession and retrenchment, punctuated by moments of false prosperity. People multiply without having anyplace new to grow into, until the face of the earth is covered by the swarming of economic migrants and political refugees. Personal debt mounts; jobs, natural resources, ice caps and coastlines shrink. Our great cities, which once were bubbling cauldrons of artistic and social invention, have congealed into sparsely populated clusters of superluxury housing—storehouses for the wealth of absentee billionaires— serviced by a reserve army of the dispirited. The very language of progress has atrophied. The best-publicized adversaries of neoliberalism no longer speak of marching into the glorious socialist future but spiral backward, seeking to recover the purity of a vanished and largely imaginary caliphate.

As the world turns in on itself, the noisy, dirty, propulsive innovations that it once found fascinating have been replaced by germ-free technologies useful for control and surveillance: genetic and digital engineering. The former directs our thoughts toward the interior of the body, where life might be managed cell by cell; the latter, toward the continual monitoring of one another's activity. The selfie and the spy satellite photo are the close-up and long shot of the globe's real-time movie.

As for the movies that label themselves as entertainments, I can think of three visual tropes in particular that characterize the present era: the wormhole in space that proves to be a conduit into one's own mind; the digital gibberish that scrolls down a computer screen, showing us all that we can know of the world; and the violent act that is abruptly arrested in mid-air, permitting us to enjoy a 360-degree view of its superfluity. These emblems of stasis and self-enclosure were first brought together (to the best of my knowledge, and horror) in *The Matrix.* By now, I must have seen them all another thousand times.

We have left behind the era when Annette Michelson, writing about *2001: A Space Odyssey,* could propose that cinema in its essence is a kinesthetic voyage. Today, even if a movie is projected in 3D and is set aboard the *Starship Enterprise,* the picture rarely draws you into a journey (just the opposite—the images pop out at you, pinning you to your seat), and Captain Kirk goes nowhere except into his own past. That's the experience as it plays out in theaters. Outside the theaters, where most people now do their viewing, kinesthesia has become utterly impossible, since the screen is no bigger than your hand, or sits in the corner of the living room where you've spent eight hours binge-watching *House of Cards.*

Many observers describe this shift in the culture of moving images as an inevitable result of technological change, which has made it convenient and economical for producers and distributors to convert from a photographic to a digital format. Maybe so; but I think this deterministic analysis probably turns the story on its head. It certainly doesn't relate technique to content and preference, or attempt to explain, for example, why the eternally plucky Little Tramp has almost disappeared from sight, whereas 445,000 videos of a miserable-looking cat are posted on YouTube. It seems to me that we have hurried to embrace digital images in their most common forms not because they're all that's made available to us, but because we *want* to stare into our hands and sit inside all night. Is it any wonder? As we live through the Great Rebound, we retreat within, and the moving image comes with us.

o   o   o

Like all sweeping historical narratives, the one I've just sketched out takes account of everything except what's really interesting—the details. Still, there might be some truth to it, including the escape clause: our present situation is not mandated by technology, or anything else. We retain some freedom to choose our future. The question, as always, is what to choose.

I want to be cautious in proposing an answer. The most obvious wish to express in *The Nation* might be for the industry to welcome a rising proportion of women, queers and people from backgrounds other than European. This would certainly be a tremendous change for the better—but not, perhaps, a radical departure. The trend toward workplace diversity in the moving image, though far from complete and far too late in coming, has been ongoing. We might think of it as a rolling aftershock of the dual revolution, more than as the eruption of a new phase in history.

I also don't want to overstate the potential benefits of my choice for cinema's future. If I should sound as if the culture of moving images can have a solid effect on the world, rather than a wavering influence, I would fall into the peculiar form of exaggeration that substitutes artworks, and arguments about them, for political and social action. Encountered most often in universities and the art-gallery network, this swell-headed insularism seems to me to be another evidence of the collapse of our sense of possibilities, rather than an effective way to open the horizon again.

Finally, I need to acknowledge that the future of the moving image, radical or otherwise, is now being decided by a bunch of ten-year-olds. My ideas won't greatly affect what they like.

All that said, I offer my prescription anyway, in the conviction that my taste, and yours, can be important. They give us something we really care about to discuss with one another. They even help keep alive the old belief, articulated at the height of the dual revolution and still valid today, that we are not the objects of history but its subjects, who deserve a voice. What you and I want for the future of moving images will make a difference in the world, however uncertain in magnitude—and so I will say that I continue to base my preference on Bazin, and on his excitement about cinema as the approximate realization of a desire.

In our anxiety about death, Bazin thought, we are always trying to grasp at life: its surface appearance, its movement and texture, its abundance. The goal is unattainable, of course, but that doesn't matter. What counts is that we want to reach out. For this purpose, he wrote, film is especially useful, because its images are traces of the light that has bounced off of objects. Film gives us the reassurance of being in physical contact with the world we see on the screen, at however great a remove of space and time.

The transition to digital imagery has severed that contact; but it can't do away with the desire. Only we can stifle that. If we want a radical future for the moving image, then, and for our world, the first thing we might do is pick up our heads, turn our eyes outward again (however adverse the circumstances) and trust our urge to hold onto life.

We have held onto death more than enough. Visit that precursor of *The Birth of a Nation,* the *Cyclorama of the Battle of Gettysburg*—it's on view today, installed at the battlefield with a sound-and-light show—and you will see how a spectacle from the era of pre-cinema once satisfied the public appetite for funerary monuments. Countless movies, TV shows and video games today continue to cater to that appetite. Think of the raids and battles that are endlessly revisualized as if through a repetition compulsion, the defunct pop stars whose triumphs and demise are dismally "celebrated" over and over, the genocides that are mindlessly re-enacted as plot devices for adventure stories (set in the past or an alternative present, or on the future planet Mongo), the shooter games in which the only real action is to die and go back to the start. Using methods that may be more or less grandiose, with or without zombies in the story line, a long and ongoing line of image-makers has preserved and glorified only the things that are already dead. They've never even tried to touch the heart of life as it's beating.

In a radical future, though, the moving image will capture without mummifying. This is not a prophecy. It's an observation, drawn from the different possible futures that have already begun. When I started writing about films for *The Nation*—it was, by chance, around the time when the Great Rebound was making itself felt—I discovered that the people who made me most hopeful were working on, and smudging, the border between fiction and documentary. Chantal Akerman, Su Friedrich, Abbas Kiarostami, Mohsen Makhmalbaf, Hou Hsiao-hsien, Gianni Amelio—to throw out just a handful of names—made the last two decades of the 20th century an exciting time to think about the moving image. Did these filmmakers achieve anything beyond a negligeable market share? No. Would it be possible, in a cynical mood, to say that I bet on the wrong people, because nothing they did back then is now being felt? Of course. The one thing that cynicism is always good for is denial.

And yet the existence of an appetite for life—a large and widely shared appetite—became obvious in 2014 when Richard Linklater came out with *Boyhood*. Here was a new version of the impossible project, realized more vividly and popularly than ever: a record of the awkward, unpredictable, beautiful maturation of one person's life, presented within fictional circumstances but with the actual time of unfolding made as miraculously manifest as if a sweet puff of breath had come off the screen. Audiences were enthralled. Bazin might have wept with joy.

I won't call on others to copy what Linklater did in *Boyhood*, because nobody really can. (Besides, imitation is precisely what we don't need.) I will simply observe that *Boyhood* shows that a more outgoing, convivial, exploratory and humane future is now with us, and more than a few people want it.

Whether we pursue that desire is up to us. I say let's boldly go where no one has gone before.

The Nation, April 6, 2015
Written for the 150th anniversary issue,
on the theme of a radical future

Remembering Stuart Gordon

I have twice reviewed films directed by Stuart Gordon—his adaptation of David Mamet's play *Edmond* in 2006 and his gruesome fable about airheaded self-involvement and the will to survive, *Stuck*, in 2008—taking care to disclose that the filmmaker was a friend. This was fair notice but also a considerable understatement. Along with the other, far more prominent brothers, sisters, and whatevers of Chicago's Organic Theater Company, I used to call Stuart not just a friend but Fearless Leader, in three-quarters jest. This was in the 1970s and early '80s, before he got his hands on movie equipment, as he'd always wanted to, and made himself internationally famous with *Re-Animator*, the surpassingly grotesque, gory, and hilarious H.P. Lovecraft adaptation he devised with his old friend (and proto—Organic Theater conspirator) Dennis Paoli and William J. Norris. Given this information, you will not be surprised that I learned from Stuart how to make stage blood. (The best formula: McCormick red food dye titrated into Wisk laundry detergent, which imparts a lurid, purplish hue to the mixture and enables you to wash the costume in a sink between shows.) I learned a lot more as well; so much, in fact, that Stuart has loomed unseen over this film column since the day I began writing it. When I found out on the morning of March 25 that he had died—not of Covid-19 but heartbreakingly isolated from his family and friends because of the pandemic—the light of the present dimmed (not that it's bright to begin with, here in my social-distancing quarters) as I spiraled into the past.

Which is where I see a lot of us now spending our time. Despite many journalistic speculations about how life will change after Covid-19, in everything from the conduct of elections to the stuff you run into at art galleries, these visions of the future are all bluff and guesswork. Nobody knows anything quantifiable—how long the pandemic will last, the eventual death toll, the magnitude of the economic damage, the time that recovery will take—let alone such phantoms as qualitative outcomes. As I write, I don't even know when theaters will reopen or which film titles might be current as you read this, if you're among the people with access to streaming services. I do know that fresh streaming releases will be ongoing, with films originally planned for the theaters and those meant from the start for the likes of Netflix or Amazon. But to judge from the preponderance of articles in newspapers and magazines, as well as the personal comments that reach me, people for the moment are less interested in cinematic novelty than in finding comfort or distraction in movies from the past.

In this, too, Stuart remains my teacher. In many ways a traditionalist, more friendly toward 1950s Warner Bros. and comic book illustrations than to the formal conundrums he encountered in 1970s art houses and art museums, he would have been perfectly happy to see people enjoying the oldies—but despite his well-earned reputation as a genre-loving fantasist, I think he would have loathed any sign that people were using films to retreat from the world rather than engage with it. My thoughts go back to a fanzine writer who emerged with me from a preview screening of *Stuck*. Eyes glittering and voice throbbing with joy, he cried, "Stuart Gordon makes the violence so *real!*" And that, in my experience of his combined ethics and aesthetics, was always the point.

Stuart loved his actors when they threw themselves breakneck into their roles, not simply because he wanted to goose the audience (though his taste did run toward big effects, as suggested by the title he was contemplating for his memoirs, *More Is More*) but because he thought people ought to feel that something was truly at stake in every moment. He hated nothing more in a show or a movie than to see actors expertly shuck and jive instead of caring intensely about the situation they were in, even if it was a mental duel between Lord Cumulus, Avenger of the Universe, and Chaos, Prince of Madness. When Stuart added a section of audience engagement to one of his shows, the actors had damned well better be in people's faces, forcing an interaction and not miming their way through the house. When he watched other people's work, he would be scathing—in a genial, belly-laughing way—whenever a director blithely skated past an inconvenience of plot or character rather than work it through on the grounds of the premise.

As with Stuart's notions of how plays and films ought to be directed, so, too, with his sense of show business economics. He accepted grants for the Organic Theater when he could get them, but having begun his career at the University of Wisconsin baiting warmongers, censors, bigots, self-promoting local officials, violently repressive police, and any authorities who thought there was something wrong with running around naked, he distrusted government and foundation money. It could vanish easily, and if you depended on it too much, you were probably paying too little attention to the people who should have been persuaded to support your work: the audience. How honest were your defiant gestures—how *real*—if you expected an arts council to fund them?

Stuart preferred to safeguard the work by running the Organic Theater like an old mom-and-pop business, with his wife and perennial star, Carolyn Purdy-Gordon, sharing the risks and responsibilities.

Ma and Pa Gordon's attitude could hardly have been more different from the trends that had been taking hold in the East Coast avant-garde. By the mid- to late 1970s, the nickel-and-dime, grassroots experimenters of the previous decade's theater and film had begun to codify themselves into a semi-academic, grant-seeking, proudly anti-commercial circle, validated principally by themselves, their own press corps, and a growing team of institutional curators. I know I'm painting with too broad a brush, and I'm sure the scene didn't feel so insular from within, but viewed from the shores of Lake Michigan, much of the work being done then in New York was notable for its combination of communal self-approval and condescending irony. Conventions and themes familiar to a general audience were good only for being tossed into one of several versions of a cerebral yet inexplicable postmodern mélange, where they could be mocked, "interrogated," and turned into gibberish. The goal, as often as not, was admirably political, but the method amounted to an attempt to knock down existing power relations by semaphore, thanks to the breeze of your flailing arms. There was rarely any contact, just a shadowboxing battle royale among images and ideas, in which nothing was expected to be authentic except the status that the artists claimed for themselves.

By 1985, when *Re-Animator* staggered horribly into the world, this academic avant-garde lay helpless before Ronald Reagan and the resurgent Hollywood crudity that had triumphed with him. (For the full story of this dual ascension, see J. Hoberman's *Make My Day: Movie Culture in the Age of Reagan*.) It was possible in this context for critics to receive *Re-Animator* with excitement but also difficult for many to see that Stuart, too, was practicing avant-garde filmmaking, though of a different kind. His cinema was as opposed to *Rambo: First Blood Part II* as anything you could see at the Collective for Living Cinema or Millennium Film Workshop and yet was immediately accessible to anyone with a strong stomach and a sense of humor. The path of least resistance, though, was to type Stuart as a happy, irresponsible schlockmeister, serving up thrills to a niche audience. The possibility that he had something to say and meant it sincerely didn't much come into the conversation.

To be fair, people whose most important agenda was to break the death grip of patriarchy could be forgiven for thinking of Stuart's work as rearguard rather than avant-garde. As an artist talking to and about the dominant culture in terms it could understand, he risked keeping dominant terms in place and might have expected people to call him on it. But when works of art touch on reality—real emotions, convictions, and sensations, along with elaborations of premises as if they were solid and whole, if gonzo—you might give artists some credit for being right-acting, even if they're not explicitly right-thinking. Besides, what was so wrong-thinking in *Re-Animator*? It was a story about arrogance masquerading as benevolence, madness as a search for truth, and the gradual acquiescence of a well-intentioned, normatively thoughtless man in hideous crimes. Do you want to tell me that theme *isn't* real?

Much has been said over the past weeks about the prescience of Steven Soderbergh and Scott Z. Burns's 2011 *Contagion*, and with good reason. With *Re-Animator* in mind, though, I prefer to think about the Covid-19 movie that Stuart Gordon might have made, set in hospital corridors awash in body parts and bodily fluids, in the White House conference rooms where the situation is definitely under control, and in a corporate laboratory where someone is just *sure* of a lucrative solution. Much of it would be hilarious, except for the part that wasn't. As Stuart said after *Re-Animator* was released, "Violence should horrify. If it doesn't, there's something wrong with it. It should not be seductive."

Can I think of any recent movies in which something's wrong? Easily. Take Juliano Dornelles and Kleber Mendonça Filho's *Bacurau*, which has been much admired for using genre tropes (sci-fi, western, psychedelic splatterfest) for ostensibly political ends.

Give *Bacurau* a chance. Watch it on a streaming service for its tale of rural Brazilians fighting back against an invasion of extortionate, murderous creeps from the Northern Hemisphere. Then ask yourself if the filmmakers' attitude toward the country people is any better than paternalistic sentimentality; if genre mimicry should excuse a jolting, clunky visual style; and above all, if the film's violence horrifies. When I watched *Bacurau* at last year's New York Film Festival, I was appalled to hear the hall rock with cheers for each new butchery. Dornelles and Mendonça Filho gestured toward any number of actual social and political evils, but they clearly did not make the violence *real* to their audience.

Something similar might be said of Craig Zobel's recent US release *The Hunt*, which resembles *Bacurau* in a way that ought to unnerve the latter's fans. Both have plots that involve murder for sport, with the predators in Zobel's film being blue-state elitists and the prey red-state MAGA types. Well, bitter political animosities do divide the country, and Zobel (whose *Great World of Sound* is more deserving of your attention) has certainly pointed toward them. But his translation of this societal rift into a shoot-'em-up means what, exactly? Nobody can say, except that he's put himself into the marketing category of "controversial." The substance of his characters' lives, the motives of their beliefs, melt away in the blood and guts being spilled for fun. So it goes, too, with Dornelles and Mendonça Filho. They send out a semaphore of political struggle but deliver pornography.

I shelter in isolation and brood too much on the past—as perhaps you do, these days—and long to encounter other people once more in a common space. Movies can't spring us from this viral predicament, but now and at all times, the good ones can answer that need for connection. Even though they're just light, shadow, and sound, films can lead toward a form of human encounter, in an equivalent of shared space, but only if the artists behind them desire it. That, too, is something I learned from Stuart Gordon. Because of him, I can never be satisfied with a movie merely because it signals a message I agree with. I need it to be made in such a way that I imagine someone bent over a sink, squeezing the last drops of food dye out of the costumes.

He made the love so real.

The Nation, April 17, 2020

Narcissus Sees Through Himself: On Jean Cocteau and the Invention of the Film Poet

Having chosen at different moments of his career to rewrite *Antigone*, *Oedipus Rex*, *Romeo and Juliet*, *Beauty and the Beast*, the legend of Tristan and Isolde, and the myth of Orpheus, Jean Cocteau placed himself among those convention-breakers who believe the best-known stories are the ones worth repeating. In his name, I begin with a familiar tale.

It concerns that most ingenuously avant-garde of aristocratic Parisian couples, the Vicomte Charles and Marie-Laure de Noailles, who in 1929 began to dabble in film production. From Man Ray, they commissioned *Les Mystères du château de Dé*, a fine, half-hour example of the absurdist house-party movie in which everyone plays dress-up. (That included the Noailles. It was, after all, their house.) Soon afterward they became more ambitious in their patronage, putting up a million francs, with no conditions, so that an artist with very little technical experience of the cinema and no great chance of appealing to a mass audience could make a feature-length sound film. Although the man was already celebrated for his ability to summon up arresting images, any movie of his that might be labeled a *succès* was also likely to be trailed by *scandale*.

So it was, when the film had its premiere in November 1930 amid right-wing riots, police censorship, a threat of excommunication for the Noailles, and (most serious of all) the loss of the victome's membership in the Jockey Club. Yet for all the trouble the Noailles had caused themselves—quite innocently, according to the artist, who later described them as having been baffled by the uproar—they had given world cinema one of its greatest achievements: a work that continues to floor audiences today with its incomparable brashness, defiance, invention, and humor.

That film, of course, is *L'Age d'or* by Luis Buñuel.

The other film the Noailles commissioned in 1930, for an additional million francs—*Le Sang d'un poète*, by Jean Cocteau— got a much more polite reception upon its premiere in January 1932 (a decent interval having been allowed for after Buñuel's film was sprung on the world), then went on to attract an audience that was too large and too persistent to be dismissed as a cult following. In New York City, the film's run at the Fifth Avenue Playhouse lasted for almost two decades. In more recent years, though, *Le Sang d'un poète* has not held up well against its Noailles twin.

Like many of Cocteau's films (the most notable exception being *La Belle et la bête*), it is today more studied than enjoyed: a work largely of antiquarian interest, to be dropped as a passing illustration into syllabi on the evolution of queer identity or last century's French avant-garde.

A first-rate critic who was sympathetic to both of those subjects, Stephen Harvey of The Museum of Modern Art, sounded a valedictory note a mere twenty years after Cocteau's death. Writing for a commemorative anthology assembled on that anniversary, Harvey began by asking how much of a contribution Cocteau really had made to the history of film and then politely avoided giving an answer. He did find space to deride the avant-garde snobs who adore *Le Sang d'un poète* but would never bother to watch Cocteau's popular entertainments. And what would these people get, if they broke down and saw *L'Aigle à deux têtes*? "Enjoyable kitsch," according to Harvey. That was in 1982. Since then, only the Disney animators have boosted Cocteau's reputation as a filmmaker.

And yet if the cloud of artsiness around Cocteau's films can now seem cloying, the extent of his influence cannot be doubted. Begin with François Truffaut, who gave Cocteau pride of place in his epoch-making essay of 1956, "A Certain Tendency of French Film," in which Cocteau's portrait photograph came first in the gallery of filmmakers who deserved to be called *Les auteurs*. "Since 1945," Truffaut wrote, "he has given French cinematography five of its greatest films: *La Belle et la bête*, *L'Aigle à deux têtes*, *Les Parents terribles*, *Les Enfants terribles*, and *Orphée*."

People who mistakenly believe that Truffaut's *politique des auteurs* was simply an assertion of the primacy of the director over the screenwriter should note that Cocteau had not directed one of these films and for another had relied on help from the more experienced René Clément. If Cocteau was indeed the *auteur*—or, as he would have put it, the *poète*—of all these movies, it was surely in the nonprofessional sense of being the one who conceived the situations and characters (even if they were adapted from existing works), envisioned the imagery and tone (even if they were realized for him by hired craftspeople), and through his person drew together and inspired all the other collaborators. You might think there was something neo-Platonic in this notion of the *auteur* as soul to the movie's body, if it didn't correspond so realistically to Cocteau's actual role, over the decades, as the animator of various projects, beginning famously with *Parade* for the Ballets Russes:

a piece for which he was not the choreographer, the composer or the production designer, but that emerged as it did because Cocteau insisted it should.

Perhaps this idea of the *auteur* as animator was also on the mind of the teenaged Jean-Luc Godard, when in 1949 or 1950 the critic Alexandre Astruc ran into him in the Café de Flore and heard him declare his intention of becoming "the Cocteau for the next generation."

I take this to have meant something more than a desire to make his way as an independent artist within the French film industry and turn out a series of distinctive pictures. "The next generation" gave away the scope of the ambition, which Cocteau could embody for Godard in a way that Jean Renoir (for example) could not. Cocteau was more than a filmmaker. He was, in practical terms, the spirit of his age, seeming to know everyone, to connect everyone, and to set the tone for many other people's work.

Even Buñuel said as much, despite having inadvertently showed him up. The big influences on Buñuel during his student years in Madrid in the early 1920s, he recalled, were Apollinaire, Cocteau. And who got him the commission from the Noailles to make anything he wished, even *L'Age d'or*? Again, Cocteau. As Buñuel told the story, Cocteau went to Charles de Noailles after having seen *Un Chien andalou* and urged him to finance Buñuel's next movie. In a sense, then, *L'Age d'or* owed its very existence to Cocteau—who nevertheless claimed, not very plausibly, that he did not see *Un Chien andalou* until after he completed *Le Sang d'un poète*.

The precise sequence of events may no longer be recoverable, having vanished in a haze of opium smoke and Surrealist fabulation; but here too, it's clear that Cocteau appears as an ideal. He is the film poet *par excellence*, the rare and brilliant individual who animates, imagines, and inspires.

The only difficulty is that this notion clashes with Cocteau's own presentation in his films of what it means to be a poet.

o   o   o

Actually, there are two such presentations, in *Le Sang d'un poète* and the 1949 *Orphée*, and they also clash with each other. "*Orphée* orchestrates, twenty years later, the theme that in *Le Sang d'un poète* I played clumsily with one finger," Cocteau wrote—which is true, as far as it goes. The works are so entwined that he might even have claimed that his original *Orphée*—a one-act play written in 1925 and first performed in 1926—contained a song that he had later felt compelled to pick out on the piano of his debut film. Still, *Orphée* the film diverges radically from *Orphée* the play, and both differ from *Le Sang d'un poète* in ways that can't be explained by the challenges of manual dexterity or the addition of tuba and xylophone.

The rupture is even remarked upon in the spoken words of *Le Sang d'un poète*, when a taunting, teasing piece of classical sculpture (played by Lee Miller under a coating of plaster) urges the poet to escape from his doorless room by stepping into a mirror. "You wrote that it was possible to go into mirrors," she tells him, referring to the central action in the play *Orphée*, "but you didn't believe it." In *Le Sang d'un poète*, then, Cocteau (or his sleek-haired and muscular stand-in, Enrique Rivero) takes up in earnest a challenge he had posed for himself but evaded in the play. There, the poet had entered the realm of Death through the surface of a mirror but had done so without any self-reflection. Here, an extended and ultimately violent exploration of the poet's fears, weaknesses, and desires awaits him on the other side—the other side of the mirror, or of the face he shows to the world and to himself?—with repercussions that will continue after he has returned.

Twenty years on, when we get to the film *Orphée*, we find that the poet (now played by an even more magnificent stand-in, Jean Marais) also undergoes an ordeal by passing through the mirror. But this trial turns out to entail a different self-discovery from the one in *Le Sang d'un poète*, and has different repercussions.

Whatever else this summary might reveal, I hope it brings out the most prominent feature of the films' terrain: Jean Cocteau. He was a celebrity when he wrote the play *Orphée* (and wrote his persona into it); and he is, without embarrassment, the celebrity who welcomes viewers at the beginning of *Le Sang d'un poète*, where he is half-disguised and half-revealed by a patchy plaster mask over his features and a set of classical robes draped over his 1920s clothing. At once laughable and oracular, this incompletely eternal Cocteau gestures mutely toward the apparatus of film production arrayed behind him, as if ushering us into the setting where the famous man creates. Once there, we will find his instantly recognizable head at one moment dangling from the ceiling like a mobile (having been rendered as a wire sculpture, in the style of Calder) so it can oversee events, and at another appearing in much more finely detailed modeling (like a life mask in bas-relief) to accompany a title card that reads "How I got trapped inside my own film. — Jean Cocteau."

For the truly inattentive viewer, there is even an introductory text in which the author explains that the images in his film are like heraldic symbols, signifying the costly battles through which he has suffered.

Viewers less interested in Cocteau than he was in himself may be excused at this point if they feel like running off to catch the next showing of *L'Age d'or*. But if the antiquarian may be indulged, just a little, I think it is helpful to put the seeming narcissism of *Le Sang d'un poète* into the context of the French avant-garde films that preceded it.

Works such as Man Ray's *Les Mystères du château de Dé*, *Emak-Bakia* and *L'Etoile de mer*, Fernand Léger's *Ballet Mécanique*, Marcel Duchamp's *Anemic Cinema*, and (best of all) René Clair's *Entr'acte* (made with Cocteau's *Parade* collaborator Erik Satie) may be described as personal in some sense; but none of them is concerned with an actual person. Instead, they are non-narrative (or barely narrative) *jeux d'esprit*, full of puns and anagrams, harmless burlesques, charming stop-motion animations of mundane objects, and (in the case of Clair) a few ooh-la-la peeks up a ballerina's tutu. It's entirely in keeping with the spirit of these films that in more than one instance they use an amusement park as a location. Visually à la mode, they are full of optical stimulation for its own sake, deploying such up-to-the-minute techniques as allover abstraction, solarization, kaleidoscopic superimpositions, upside-down and sideways views, and disorienting swings of an unmoored camera.

Le Sang d'un poète, by contrast, is visually much more old-fashioned: Harking back to the bygone era of Georges Méliès, it relies on simple editing tricks and staged tableaux within discrete and otherwise static scenes. (These are augmented by shots where the camera points down at the floor—which has been made to look like a wall—so that the actors seem either to struggle against gravity or else to defy it. Cocteau in effect invents Méliès's methods for him, thirty years after the fact.) To anyone who frequented the movies in 1930, whether the popular cinema or the avant-garde, *Le Sang d'un poète* must have looked deliberately quaint—except, of course, that the archaic film technique was put in the service of incidents more disturbing than even Buñuel had imagined.

Although he was much more savage than his French counterparts, Buñuel too was grandly impersonal, with his mockery of the Church, the nation, the moneyed classes, the normal sorts of things that happen between men and women, and (for the finale) Jesus. Many people could find much to object to in *L'Age d'or*; but I doubt that anyone has ever detected a confessional note in the film, or felt a sympathetic twinge of anguish, alienation, guilt, despair, or longing while watching it. Not so with *Le Sang d'un poète*.

Cocteau's cinematic debut stands out from other art films (and anti-art films) of its period in being a Romantic outpouring, set loose in an age of Surrealism. It dares to ask the audience to take seriously the emotions of its author—including, but not limited to, his selfpity and self-aggrandizement—even while visualizing those feelings in scenes that scramble historical periods, conflate incongruous settings, and flout the laws of physics. Perhaps the autobiographical impulse accounts even for the combination of this startling imagery with an outmoded film technique. In many ways, *Le Sang d'un poète* looks like movies that Cocteau might have remembered from his childhood.

Perhaps Cocteau had in mind this uneasy persistence of auto-biographical content within quasi-Surrealist form (uneasy, because to the Surrealists nothing was more disgusting than personal expression) when he described *Le Sang d'un poète* as "a realistic documentary of unreal happenings." On the unreal side of things, we have the nameless poet's struggles, in an eighteenth-century garret, with a willful and parasitic piece of art that invades his body; the uncanny peep shows he watches in the corridor of a cheap hotel, as he crawls from keyhole to keyhole; and the game of cards he plays, in modern evening dress, in a snowy Parisian courtyard, with a dead schoolboy lying under his feet, a clique of wealthy theatergoers watching from boxes overhead, and a dismissive clas-sical statue sitting opposite him at the gaming table. As for the first half of the phrase—"a realistic documentary"—it perhaps implies that the emotions represented in these scenes have been observed objectively, as facts with their own existence in the world.

This insistence that an author's inner experience can provide worthwhile subject matter will not be novel to today's audiences, and might not be all that welcome to them, either, given the long ascendance in our era of confessional poetry and memoir-writing. But then it's neither sporting to blame other people's excesses on Cocteau nor possible to identify him personally with all of the images in *Le Sang d'un poète*. The schoolboys' lyrical snowball fight at dusk in the courtyard, where a bully named Dargelos makes his brutal but alluring appearance, certainly comes from Cocteau's life. So too do the shadow-play of the opium pipe, the dumbshow of the hermaphrodite, and the drama of the self-inflicted gunshots to the head. (Cocteau's father died this way.) But what is the viewer to make of the little girl who is thrashed to teach her to fly? Or of the Mexican man who is endlessly shot at dawn by a firing squad? These latter scenes might have some oblique reference to the life of Jean Cocteau. Then again, they might be the sort of thing that could happen to any poet, if he's hunky and dislikes wearing a shirt.

Enough of these ungrounded allegories float through the film to undo any assumption that *Le Sang d'un poète* is exclusively about Cocteau. He is of course the specific case, who gives the film its circumstantial details. (As a semi-notorious figure whose fame was carried into the picture, he is also the Peggy Hopkins Joyce of his own production, making *Le Sang d'un poète* one of the odder contributions to the tradition of celebrity movie culture.) But as the film's title acknowledges, Cocteau sees himself as one poet among many; and as the incidents suggest, he does not necessarily have an exalted notion of that status.

"*La gloire—toujours la gloire*," Cocteau jeers on the soundtrack, as the poet on screen gives himself a laurel-leaf crown made of his own blown-out brains. This is the first of two suicides in the film, committed after the poet has peeked into tableaux of his life that are shameful, tawdry, or violent, and yet have an aspect of the ridiculous. This first suicide, too, is at once horrid and burlesque, taking place in the Hotel of Dramatic Follies according to step-by-step instructions, recited as if from a user's manual. Bathetic guilt and suffering, bathetic self-destruction, a bathetic desire for glory: This is all a poet finds inside himself when he goes into the mirror.

And when he emerges from his introspection, into present-day society, he kills himself again. This second suicide is the climax of the final episode, titled "The Profanation of the Host" after the medieval legend of a desperate Christian woman who allows a Satanic Jewish pawnbroker to wheedle from her a consecrated wafer. I leave it to the reader to figure out each parallel between the legend (as Uccello painted it) and the events of the card game in the film; but I don't doubt that the role of the Christian woman is taken by the poet, whose blood-stained if glacially paced act of remorse wins the momentary applause of *le tout Paris*.

So ends Cocteau's first monumental depiction of what it means to be a poet. I can't say it's a vocation that would recommend itself to many people. A poet is passive in the face of his creations. He catches them like a disease; he yields helplessly to their calm and knowing demands. When he looks at himself as he is, rather than as the medium through which these works come into the world, he sees an object of derision. Alone in his room, he feels guilty and appalled. Out in the world, he enjoys the company of splendidly bejewelled people, on the condition that he betray for their brief amusement his most tender and painful memories.

Whether this is a faithful representation of a poet's life, a prose writer should not pretend to judge. All I know is that a viewer who uses a little historical imagination, and is willing to be patient with a novice filmmaker's missteps—his self-indulgence in prolonging shots, his clumsiness in editing them—will find that *Le Sang d'un poète* is intriguing as a puzzle and startlingly harsh as self-portraiture.

One of the first works to propose that the basic elements of film—images, words, sounds—might be arranged into a coded message, *Le Sang d'un poète* might not be as noble as a heraldic shield (the type of cryptogram to which Cocteau compared it) but at least deserves credit for being a devilishly complex rebus. You can see why aspiring
filmmakers would have been excited by the possibilities it revealed. What isn't so clear is why they would have wanted to be film poets at all, if the message of *Le Sang d'un poète* was to be believed.

Fortunately, they would read something different in *Orphée*.

o   o   o

It is one of the great hairstyle movies. Under the assumed name of "the Princess," Maria Casarès keeps her dark tresses pulled back in severe self-control, as befits a hypnotic, aristocratic Death. François Périer as her chauffeur Heurtebise wears his hair shiny and slicked back, in a style that hints at obedience but is a little oily, a little unreliable. In the role of the feminist leader Aglaonice, sworn enemy of Orphée, Juliette Gréco whips around her loose black existentialist hair in freedom and anger. She is an independent spirit, and a dangerous one, compared to her former companion Eurydice, played by Marie Déa, whose head is a garden of childlike domesticity, sprouting with light, well-mannered curls. Edouard Dermithe, as the doomed, drunken young poet Cégeste, sports the late-1940s version of a hipster's blonde pompadour. It peaks from his forehead and sweeps back aerodynamically; but it is clearly the hair of a very minor poet, compared with the grandeur that caps our Orphée. If a seraph were to fold all six of its wings over this man, the beauty of their arrested motion would not equal the waves that rise and billow around Jean Marais's head.

The mere fact that *Orphée* can be described in such terms establishes that it is no cryptogram. Words, sounds, and images have returned to their usual place in support of a narrative—a story that is full of fantasy but still develops in the normal way, through the interaction of characters with each other, rather than through the absorption of a single character into a series of visions. Cocteau's directorial technique, too, has become suavely conventional. He now moves the camera and edits to create a coherent cinematic space, where the comings and goings of characters always make sense (even when an exit is effected magically, by Heurtebise) and the most eerie of all the events (Death's nightly visit to Orphée's home, to stand silently at the foot of his bed and watch him sleep) requires only that she walk forward into an ordinary room.

This is filmmaking that the broad public can understand and enjoy, and did: After opening on the Champs-Elysées, *Orphée* went on to win a large audience. It seems fitting, then, that the poet in this film does not struggle with his feelings, memories, and creations but instead contends with society—that is, with a world divided between his fans and his detractors, both of which drive him to hissy fits.

Though his poetry has made him so famous that policemen tip their hats at the mention of his name and young women mob him for his autograph, Orphée writes nothing and imagines nothing throughout the course of the film. He merely transcribes, having become fascinated by the strange phrases emitted by the radio of Death's Rolls-Royce. Orphée does not yet understand, of course, that the car belongs to Death; nor does he guess that the radio's words (which resemble the coded messages broadcast during the war by the French Resistance) are in fact meaningless, having no purpose other than to hold his attention. As passive in his way as the protagonist of *Le Sang d'un poète*, he lets himself be drawn in by these mating calls from the other world. He will not turn them off, despite the protests of his clinging, cloying, inconveniently pregnant wife (the most persistent and irritating of all his fans). He is determined to publish the broadcasts as his own work, at the risk of further outraging his most violent critics.

No one but Orphée himself, it seems, likes these nonsense verses—though he cares far less about them than he does about the irresistible, dark woman who seems to be their source. A female Death is the active figure who drives on the poet in this film, much as a female statue drove on the protagonist in *Le Sang d'un poète*, the difference being that the statue was devious and indifferent, whereas Death in *Orphée* is not only chilly and imperious but also faithful and loving. As for the mirror world into which Death entices the poet, it is not a dowdy small hotel occupied by strangers who never meet, but rather a nocturnal setting of grandiose architectural rubble.

The great discovery that the poet makes about himself in this place (in actuality, the ruins of the bombed-out military academy at Saint-Cyr) is that he loves Death more than life—and that his love is returned.

To be a poet in this film, then, is to be a much bigger figure than the one in *Le Sang d'un poète*, just as Marais is leonine compared to Rivero's house cat. Orphée turns his back on public opinion, strides outdoors through the wreckage of history, takes Death in his arms, and makes her swoon. Despite his celebrity, he is not in the least like Jean Cocteau.

That is to say, Cocteau has given him none of the autobiographical trappings that the protagonist of *Le Sang d'un poète* brandishes, as if they were the attributes of a saint martyred for art. Orphée hardly even drinks; and although many commentators interpret the animosity between him and the young people of the Café des Poètes as reflecting an aging Cocteau's strained relationship with a new generation on the Left Bank, no wireframe portrait bust of the writer-director spins over these scenes to confirm the identification. Orphée remains a fictional character—or, to be more precise, he is a movie character, whose traits overlap only with those of Marais, not Cocteau.

Just at the moment when a real café-dweller of the younger generation, Godard, was seeing him as the very spirit of personal filmmaking, Cocteau had removed his persona from the main character of *Orphée*. Perhaps this is a paradox; but it is no self-contradiction. I think it was precisely because *Orphée* avoided Romantic confession that it could nourish the ambitions of Godard and his fellow would-be film poets.

From *Le Sang d'un poète* they could get a notion of the artist at work, pursuing *la gloire, toujours la gloire* while stuffing the sausage casing of his creation with the greasiest bits of his own life.

This image of the poet was encouraging, if a little messy, since it led young artists to believe they didn't have to search far for their subject matter; and the movie that conveyed the image was intellectually flattering, suggesting that filmmaking could be a form of writing.

But the image was also discouraging, in that the poet was someone cut off from other people. His final apotheosis, which did him no good, was a cruel joke; and the film that had been realized about him was destined to be seen by a relatively small audience.

From *Orphée*, by contrast, the aspiring *auteurs* could get a notion of the poet as someone who is grander than his world—so grand that he can turn his back on it and literally court Death. This notion involved its own measure of bewilderment and suffering; but then it also offered the encouragement of a non-ironic glory, and even a happy ending (if you are willing to believe Orpheus could ever be truly happy with Eurydice). Perhaps best of all, a poet of this type was suitable to play the hero of a popular film.

Imagine them facing each another, these two representations of the experience of being a poet. Imagine them as mirrors, each of which reverses the writing in the other. If you could stand between them and be invisible—if you could look into them and see not yourself, but their mutual, opposing reflections—you would be at the point of origin for the endlessly contested, endlessly influential idea of the filmmaker as *auteur*.

It is an imaginary point of origin, of course. But then, the imaginary was Jean Cocteau's specialty—and for all of his narcissism, he did somehow vanish into the mirrors he had gathered around himself.

Parnassus: Poetry in Review, vol. 32, nos. 1-2 (2011)

Proportions Observed: Re-Viewing the Italian Neorealists

Whether you think of Italian neorealism as the Jesus of world cinema or its Count Dracula, you cannot deny that it has shown a remarkable talent for coming back from the dead.

Born in 1945 in the sudden explosion of Roberto Rossellini's *Roma città aperta (Open City)*—all observers agreed at once on the date, the film and the eruptive metaphor—neorealism seemed like the promise of a fresh beginning: not for Italian film alone, nor even for international cinema, but for the shattered world in which it had appeared. Critics and publicists rushed to identify its features almost before the films themselves had materialized. Neorealism was to be an urgent cinema of contemporary social problems, allied with a humanistic strain of Communism (although not programmatically Red), which used quasi-documentary means—authentic locations, non-professional actors, fact-based incidents and a steady gaze—to reveal truths about humble people that the mainstream film industries had suppressed.

These expectations were met, even though the Italian neorealists themselves had no explicit program until their greatest screenwriter, Cesare Zavattini, composed one after the fact. By the time he did, though, the movement was already suffering its first murderous betrayals, which appropriately enough came from the apostles themselves. Rossellini moved on from apparently political interests toward a concern with abstraction, spirituality and Ingrid Bergman. Luchino Visconti, with *Senso*, became an opera director not just at La Fenice and La Scala but on the screen. Vittorio De Sica, with *L'Oro di Napoli (The Gold of Naples),* reverted to his lifelong impulse to entertain, on both sides of the camera.

Within a decade of its birth, neorealism was so moribund—or had been altered so thoroughly—that its St. Paul, André Bazin, could think of no better way to preserve the movement than to dissolve it. "Neorealism as such does not exist," he asserted in 1955 in an essay in *Cinema Nuovo*. "There are only neorealist directors," who could no longer be identified by any shared subject matter, ideology, method, tone or style but only by "a consciousness disposed to see things as a whole."

If this was now the definition of neorealism, then Bazin might as well have been writing about the Holy Spirit, which could manifest its saving power in any place and form. And so it has done over the years: in virtually every country that's had a film movement called New, in virtually every developing or post-colonial nation where artists have struggled to create an indigenous cinema, in virtually every era of American independent production (from the days of Morris Engel and Ruth Orkin to those of Kelly Reichert and Rahmin Bahrani), Neorealism has been resurrected in so many forms and places that it has even been able to return in Italy, thanks to the likes of Gianni Amelio.

And all the while people have been driving stakes through its heart, as if neorealism were not an animating spirit but a monster of false consciousness, sucking the life out of filmmakers while it gloomily dominates their audiences' minds.

To cite only a few murder cases, and their motives: Jean-Luc Godard declared in 1958 that "All roads lead to *Roma città aperta*" but then went on to kill neorealism, freeing himself from its seductive representations of reality (as Brecht might have advised) the better to provoke with the reality of representations. Bernardo Bertolucci killed neorealism on behalf of a generation of young Italians, bringing to the surface of *The Conformist* everything that their overbearing fathers had repressed: baroque style, polymorphous sexuality, past complicity with fascism. In *Camera Buff*, Krzysztof Kieslowski acted as an avenger for all the Soviet-bloc film students who'd had neorealism stuffed down their throats, when he showed how many ways a filmmaker can muck up reality by presuming to record it innocently. Even Aki Kaurismaki had his turn at the slaughter. In *The Match Factory Girl*, for example, he made proletarian suffering and an observational style yield gallows humor instead of pathos, and so killed neorealism on behalf of moviegoers who neither want to be victims nor expect the world to care much if they are.

We have now had half a century of these deaths and revivals. By this point, even those of us who feel committed to neorealism in its contemporary forms must think of it as one of several persistent tendencies in filmmaking, not as a moral and historical imperative. As for the way people experienced Italian neorealism in Year Zero, when it seemed as if these films could change the world: we can only read about the moment and use our imaginations.

Where does that leave us in relation to the canonical works? Maybe it puts us in a good position to try watching them again, not as testimonies of their time and not as material for polemics but as movies, in the ordinary, Saturday-night sense of the word. I understand that it's perverse to take such a light-minded approach to the masterpieces of Italian neorealism, when nothing less than the revelation of truth is supposed to be at stake. But why not see what's left on the screen, after the tide of history has receded and the debaters have fallen silent? How does Italian neorealism look at life size, when it's no longer blown up to the scale of a savior or a succubus?

o   o   o

To my eyes, Rossellini's all-but-instant dramatization of life under German occupation, *Roma città aperta,* still has the power to shock, but mostly because it bears so little resemblance to our received idea of neorealism. It's "full of old ingredients," as Rossellini himself said. Even the indelible scene that announced something new in world cinema—the one of Anna Magnani, as the everyday heroine Pina, being shot to death by the Germans as she runs down the street—recalls a well-known precdent, since Rossellini (in a departure from his usual practice) filmed and cut it like an exercise in Soviet montage.

At least that scene happens outdoors, which locates it in the least convention-bound and most convincing of the film's three visual zones. The second of these is made up of borrowed interiors, notably the staircase and rooms of the dilapidated apartment building where Pina lives (a place of unforced dramaturgy and naturalistic performances). The third zone, which is no less prominent than the others, is comprised of soundstage constructions: impoverished approximations of Gestapo headquarters and a music hall's dressing room, where *Roma città aperta* regresses not so much to melodrama as to the artifice of silent film. At best, when Aldo Fabrizi (as the partisan priest Don Pietro) pronounces a curse on the Gestapo chief, you get a close-up that might have come from *The Passion of Joan of Arc.* On a middling level, when this same Gestapo chief gloatingly explains how he surveys all of Rome photographically, without having to leave his office, you seem to enter the world of Dr. Mabuse. At worst, when the flaming sadist and his vulpine, drug-dealing lesbian moll entertain themselves, you get the impression that the Italian resistance was fighting queers, not Nazis, and that Rossellini had dipped into a dramatic tradition too debased to deserve any individual citation.

Among the handful of absolutely decisive works in film history, perhaps only *Roma città aperta* is so ill-matched with itself—a result not only of the poverty of means so famously imposed on Rossellini, but of his clashes with the principal writer and co-originator of the film, Sergio Amidei. Contrary to Bazin's definition, very little in *Roma città aperta* now looks to have been seen as a whole: perhaps only Pina's death (whose critical moment is shown at a distance, almost indifferently, from the back of a departing truck) and the finale—the execution of Don Pietro—which is staged in a grassy field with matter-of-fact clumsiness, and witnessed by a band of boys who then walk off silently down the road, scarcely noticing the vista of the city below them.

It's only with Rossellini's next film, *Paisà,* that sustained evidence becomes visible of drama, reportage and a litter of circumstantial facts being fused into an approximation of the urgent truth. Here, too, the pieces of the film are ill matched; but now they've become discrete episodes, separate in geography and chronology, from the landing of the Allies in Sicily in July 1943 through the final days of partisan fighting in the Po river delta in April 1945. The gaps between episodes are intended; and so are the gaps within each episode, which for the first time bring to the foreground a fundamental trait of Rossellini, his embrace of elliptical storytelling. The more ellipses you encounter, as a rule, the stronger the episode feels.

The Roman episode, for example, dribbles away into pat dramatic irony, with its negligeable tale of a disillusioned prostitute and her drunken GI. The filmmaking in this section is smooth, and it's also forgettable, except for the patches of archival footage of the liberation. The Sicilian episode, though disablingly bound to the conventions of a platoon movie, is more robust, its irony more brutal; but here, too, little sticks in the memory, except for the sullen, ferocious face of the girl who takes up arms, impulsively and futilely. *Paisà* comes into its own—bringing Italian neorealism to life with it—in those episodes where elements of the story are allowed to stand alone. The continual motion of the crowds in Naples—not the press of people, but their turbulence—becomes almost an independent character in the episode. The street fighting in Florence rages on with its own desperate life, in the distance, but like a magnet draws you closer and closer. The monks in the Romagna episode, puttering about as themselves, are embedded in the film like a narrative conundrum; they're characters and setting in one. Most powerful of all, and most unforgettable, are the shimmering, glaring light and far horizons of the concluding Po delta episode, where there is no hiding in drama and no hiding from death.

The temptation is to call *Paisà* unprecedented—and the final episode certainly comes close, in the way it gives you an emphatically material experience that is at once explicitly pointless and deeply meaningful. But an important precedent did exist, in Luchino Visconti's *Ossessione*.

Released in May 1943, two months before the Allied landing and the fall of Mussolini, *Ossessione* was greeted rapturously by a circle of cinephiles, before various figures of greater authority had it condemned, banned, hacked to pieces and finally burned. But Rossellini managed to see it; so did De Sica. If they did not take *Ossessione* as an example to be imitated, they surely looked to it as a challenge to be met.

Film historian Mira Liehm catalogues what you could see in *Ossessione* that had been programmatically excluded from Italian films of the fascist era: "bumpy roads with cracked gas stations, pubs with greasy tables, the endless banks of the Po river with dirty grass and troubled water, the apathetic, indifferent, and tired faces of people…" Even with eyes long accustomed to the cinema of abjection, you can guess at what the impact must have been—although the jolt for audiences today may come less from witnessing sociological details than from being able to sense the dampness of a clinging undershirt, the musk of crumpled sheets, the whiff of sulfur from a match struck in an airless room. *Ossessione* remains truly filthy as a tale about marginal people and their passions—lust, greed, jealousy, guilt—and compelling in the way it plays out the borrowed plot of *The Postman Always Rings Twice,* drawing out the suspense despite having eliminated the planning of the murder, and even the killing itself. Visconti, too, was practicing an elliptical storytelling, long on situations and short on plot points. But whereas Rossellini would prove to be most himself when he stripped bare his visual style, Visconti was from the first draped in the mastery of every directorial flourish. Witness, for example, the prolonged introduction of the fatal and ill-fated drifter: how he's shown in long shots, then medium shots, always from behind, until Clara faces him for the first time—at which moment there's a sudden reverse shot, with the camera dollying into a close-up.

After the war, when neorealism was in the air and money from the Communist Party became available to Visconti, he stayed true to his elegance. In *La Terra Trema*—the only completed film in his projected trilogy about labor struggles—Sicilian fishermen and their families act out a drama about their own chronic impoverishment, using their homes and waterfront as the set; and in Visconti's hands, this material becomes a film of unsurpassed beauty. As agit-prop, of course, it's a complete failure. Classically structured with rising and falling action, the story (based on a novel by Giovanni

Verga) permits young 'Ntoni to stand up for himself in the movie's first half, only to get slapped down in the second. The gorgeous images—photographed by Aldo Graziati in long, highly mobile takes, with deep focus and infinitely nuanced light—reinforce your impression of lives held in equilibrium, if not stasis. They're perfectly poised; and yet, at the same time, they lend monumentality to a theme of heartbreaking pessimism, making *La Terra Trema* perhaps the most extreme of the classic neorealist films, and the most unrepeatable.

Not that *La Terra Trema* was in danger of being imitated, having cost 121 million lire to produce and earned back 36. But the quick conversion of neorealism from an intuition to a marketing category was already evident scarcely a year after the premiere of *Roma città aperta*. In late 1946, several of the people who had been involved in that film conspired to bring out something they called *Roma città libera*: a grotesquely chipper account of thievery, prostitution, illicit gambling and attempted suicide, all happening on one long night, all taking place right on the authentic streets of Rome. Gar Moore, the drunken GI from the Rome episode of *Paisà*, was on hand to play a drunken GI. The innocent, childlike perspective—already a convention of neorealism—was provided not by a kid but by De Sica, playing a distinguished gent who'd been knocked silly.

You can dismiss, or enjoy, *Roma città libera* as a strange one-off; but it's hard to laugh about the commercial normalization of neorealism when encountering something like Luigi Comencini's *Pane, Amore e Fantasia* (*Bread, Love and Dreams*). Here are all the acceptable ingredients—real village streets, a scattering of non-professional faces, a protest (useless, of course) against the decline of rural life. Prostitution casts its shadow, as always, and life is seen through the eyes of a child—though in Comencini's moralized version of neorealism, these latter two aspects of the story are fused in the singular flesh of Gina Lollabrigida, here playing a pigtailed donkey-girl who has a bad reputation but is really pure. All problems are wrapped up neatly, and De Sica himself presides over the resolution, as a grinning, slightly dirty-minded carabiniere.

If De Sica had not played a much more critical role behind the camera, just when it counted, then stuff like this stuff might have been the principal legacy of Italian neorealism. If the eruption of 1945-46 was to become a movement and not just an exploitable moment, then someone had to figure out an honest resolution (much more honest than Comencini's would be) between narrative convention and the facts at hand, With Zavattini as his indispensable partner, De Sica worked out the synthesis—one that could be adopted by others, and that still has the power to persuade and to move.

It took some time, though. The first De Sica — Zavattini experiment, *I bambini ci guardano* (*The Children Are Watching Us*), is considered to be another precursor of neorealism, having been produced at the same time as *Ossessione* and having suffered a similar launch in 1943. But unlike *Ossessione*, it has lapsed into the condition of a period piece: intriguing for its supposedly anti-fascist overtones (which will pass right by most viewers, unless explained) and notable mostly for what it foreshadows. Within a rather gauzy bourgeois tearjerker, De Sica and Zavattini for the firt time view a troubled world through a child's eyes.

With the postwar *Sciuscià* (*Shoeshine*), the gauze is suddenly gone—and the innocence of young eyes becomes questionable. Betrayed by their elders and dumped into prison (where the fascist salute is still an ingrained habit), boys who had started out as best friends wind up betraying one another. Compared to the world-historical action of *Roma città aperta,* the story is no more than an anecdote. But it's an anecdote about step-by-step moral corruption—a process that Rossellini's film had scarcely acknowledged, let alone investigated—set in locations far more devastated than any in *Roma città aperta,* or even *Paisà.* If some atmospheric studio sets are mixed in with the real places, professional actors with the kids, crane shots with the straightforward eye-level views, this is done so seamlessly that it can almost be ignored.

But with *I ladri di biciclette* (*Bicycle Thieves*), the entire world at last seems to be in plain sight, and nothing has to be ignored. As we reach this crucial moment, maybe I should practice my own version of elliptical storytelling and pass on. There is really nothing left to be said about *I ladri di biciclette*, except perhaps that it demonstrates how to perform the supremely difficult feat of achieving life scale in a movie. Neither monumentalizing their wandering father and son into archetypes of misfortune nor shrinking them into mere examples, De Sica and Zavattini perfectly judge their distance from the characters, always, and so create a cinema in which individuals are placed, in precisely human dimension, within a whole society. This is the situation that the father already understands, and that the son painfully comes to recognize: they belong to the multitude but somehow must live their own lives. The inherent tragedy of this situation becomes fully visible when Ricci, at the climax, has the opportunity to grab any of a thousand bicycles parked outside a stadium but instead, self-deafeatingly, chooses the one that sits by itself.

What De Sica and Zavattini gave to Italy's new fact-based, exploratory cinema was not a formula but a sense of proportion. Incurious filmmakers (the kind who shouldn't have been pretending to be exploratory in the first place) could imitate the outward characteristics. Others could press on with testing the proportions, as De Sica and Zavattini did with their last masterpiece together, *Umberto D.* The process, as they learned to their chagrin, was not surefire. *Umberto D* was such a commercial disaster, and aroused such opposition from the government's film-industry overseer, Giulio Andreotti, that it marked the close of the heroic era of Italian neorealism. And yet in *Umberto D*'s daring use of real-time sequences, its willingness to venture into a more middle-class level of society, and its candor about the protagonist's contributions toward his own downfall, you can see not an end, but a push toward still another new beginning.

As Bazin had hoped, there would in fact be many fresh starts. In *Accatone,* his contribution to the youth-adrift movie, Pier Paolo Pasolini would open up previously unseen locations (in Rome's outlying slums) and previously unacknowledged subjects (not just prostitution but the beating of prostitutes, by men who enjoy one another much more than they like women) and would alter the ratio between individual and society, never showing a group of people without presenting their portraits one by one. In *Salvatore Giuliano,* Francesco Rosi would turn a true story of Sicily's endless corruption into a bravura action movie, a courtroom drama and a political thriller, building a web of relationships around a title character who is virtually unseen. In *Il Posto,* Ermanno Olmi would tell a story about a first job and first love that would have been too uneventful to come to Zavattini's attention, since no newspaper would have bothered to use it as filler; and yet the film would be large enough for the thoughts and feelings not only of the protagonist but of the people all around him.

Italian neorealism had died. Italian neorealism would come back. Life, you see, begets life.

Film Comment, September-October 2009

Constantine

About two-thirds of the speaking characters in *Constantine* are either demons or angels. The paraphernalia of exorcism abound, and Keanu Reeves wears a sick and weary look, like someone whose adventure has not been excellent. When I left the screening, my soul cried for succor. I hurried toward Congregation Anshe Tsurres and my spiritual adviser, Rabbi Simcha Feffeferman.

"Rabbi," I cried, bursting into his study, then halted on the threshold in confusion. The low, dim space was crammed with leotard-clad women, so many that they rubbed against the sloping spines on the bookshelves and pressed the rabbi to his desk. Each wore around her wrist a thread that was as crimson as her perfect manicure. In the sudden hush, I heard steam pipes. Then, from the desk, came the familiar hoarse voice: "You don't write, you don't call, a fax you don't send. At least you could knock."

Stammering apologies, I began to back away; but the rabbi held me in place by the crook of a finger, saying, "So, we were finished today anyway, yes? Go, be well." The visitors, obedient, lifted from the carpet a heavy burden of Prada and filed past me, trailing the varied odors of Saks.

"What?" I said when the last had gone.

The rabbi shrugged. "Kabbalists. You think the mortgage pays itself? Listen, better you should close the door and explain what's the aggravation."

"I have just seen a movie," I said, "*Constantine*, about Keanu Reeves's struggle for faith. He chain-smokes and coughs up blood and gets photographed as if in appalling fluorescent light, and why? Because he spends all his time punching demons in the face and sending them back to hell."

"And from this he makes a living?"

"No, it's not clear how he gets his money. He occupies about 50,000 square feet of prime real estate in downtown Los Angeles—an abandoned bowling alley, with a retro Sam Spade office-studio on the second floor—and he can afford to keep his own car and driver, but a job? No."

"And this makes him unhappy?"

"He's unhappy because he's doomed. When he was a teenager, he committed suicide and then was resuscitated. And because the experience taught him that all the scary parts of Catholic doctrine are true, he knows that the next time he dies, he'll go to hell forever. Keanu has seen the place—it looks like Century City viewed from the freeway, only all busted up and red—and he doesn't like it. So he goes around fighting creepy demonic tempters, in the hope that good works will buy him into God's grace."

The rabbi frowned, but only because he was now standing on tiptoe before a bookcase, trying to push a paperback copy of *The Time Out Guide to Kabbalah* into concealment on the third shelf. "Good works, grace. From this, I don't know."

"Well, let me tell you, it's a losing proposition. The angel Gabriel, who in this case is Tilda Swinton dressed in a suit and tie, tells Keanu that he won't get into heaven unless he stops being selfish and learns to serve others."

"Ah!" the rabbi grunted, plopping into his chair. "*Topper*. You remember—Cary Grant and Constance Bennett die and can't go to heaven because they never did anything good. So they have to haunt Roland Young and make him happy. Not a great movie, but there's this joke about his wife's underpants—"

"Please, I beg you. I need you to help me understand this movie. The sorrowful LA gumshoe who has seen too much is no longer uncovering the schemes of licentious tycoons, or even of sci-fi companies with interstellar operations. No more social corruption. He now confronts pure evil, which is simultaneously personal and cosmic. That's why, when Keanu is approached for help by a devoutly Catholic police detective, Rachel Weisz—"

"How am I supposed to understand something like this? Rachel Weisz is Catholic like I am."

"Just because she's got that name—"

"And face. You need I should tie a red thread on her wrist?"

"She's *playing* a Catholic! The same way she played the skirt role in *The Mummy*, I might add. A police detective, sure, but for the whole last reel, she's pretty much supine, while the ultimate battle is fought over, around and in her inert body. And yet—did I tell you?—she gets to visit the infernal Century City, too, so she can prove to the audience that she's a true soulmate of Keanu."

"Rachel *Weisz*?" the rabbi said.

He lifted his palms, as if this improbability had freighted the atmosphere and he had to guess by how many ounces. Then he rose and shuffled to the dimmest corner of the study, where he creakily lifted a box from a low shelf and brought it back to his desk. It was a Ouija board.

"This," I said, "is idolatry."

"And *this*," he said, "is giving me a headache, the way you're banging me a tea kettle over *Constantine*. Have I seen this movie?

No. Do I know from you what it's about? No. So now, before the migraine starts, we're going to get some answers. Here, put your finger."

I protested; but the rabbi grabbed me by the wrists and pulled my fingertips onto the plaquette. He added his own. We held our breath. We heard steam pipes.

After a minute, I said, "The camera angles—"

"Shh! Do you feel it?"

I didn't. Then the plaquette jumped under our fingers. It clacked onto the board, remained still for a second, and then began hopping faster and faster in a syncopated staccato.

"What's going on?" I asked.

"Eleanor," said the rabbi.

"What?"

"Eleanor Powell. Wonderful talents she had. By me, she's always the first to visit. But we need someone for *you*, boychik. Eleanor! Listen, dollie, young Klawans here needs advice about a movie. A new movie. You know anybody?"

The plaquette rattled out a coda and stopped cold. Nothing. I waited now, with real anticipation, and at last felt the plaquette glide toward the crescent of letters. In rapid succession, it spelled out WE WANT POMES OF SILENCE.

"Yow," I said. "I think we pulled in James Merrill."

"Have I met him?" the rabbi asked.

KEENING MY DEARS WE CRY FOR KEANU—

OUR EYES ADORE BUT THE EARS DON'T WANT TO

"You have now," I said. "Mr. Merrill? A great admirer, and I'm sure our feelings about Keanu are not wholly dissimilar, but if I might discuss this movie with someone more, more—"

I FLY UP YRS

The plaquette wrenched to a halt. "I didn't mean to insult him," I said.

The rabbi shrugged. "More than he can say about you."

But it seemed that the invective had only begun. The plaquette started to move again, with a new brusqueness. It had bustled its way through "fathead dope sap sucker" before I realized a fresh force had taken charge.

"Pauline," I said. "Long time."

"Well anyhow you wait around thinking they can't drain all the fun out and then when you get to it you find it's like a used-up winesack just a big limp empty shaggy bladder about as attractive too."

"This is someone you know?" the rabbi said.

"Pauline, are you talking about the afterlife now, or *Constantine*?"

"He had that loose goofy pleasure in himself a mind as comfortably floppy as the hair over his face that's what made him so attractive at first not just the teenage Gary Cooper body or the Sabu eyes and even when they made him an action star in *Speed* he remained the careless one Dennis Hopper seemed to do all the worrying Keanu could slack off while defusing a bomb but then Bertolucci had to go and turn him into a holy man and worse was to come *The Matrix*."

"Even though I despised the whole trilogy, I thought Keanu had some nicely underplayed comic moments in the first picture."

"Well he's no Brendan Fraser when you see Fraser underplay it's a choice Keanu has no alternative that's why he got into trouble when he got stuck being a cyber god by the end of *Matrix Revolutions* he was blind and bloodied and ready to sacrifice himself for the sins of the world if you can believe that and that's where he picks up in *Constantine* still long and lithe but the face is hangdog now he mumbles to himself and squints at his cigarette smoke as he performs an exorcism for a Mexican family who could sue for defamation on behalf of their whole country."

"Let's not get into that, or the fact that the one Black man in the film, Djimon Hounsou, is cast as a witch doctor, or the suggestion that the minions of evil tend to be a little limp-wristed. Keanu is the only character, Weisz included, who isn't squashed down to an ethnic or gender stereotype, and so, despite his psychic troubles, he's the only one who seems normal. Makes me glad that *Constantine* doesn't have any Jewish characters."

"She's Jewish, this Pauline?" the rabbi asked.

"You see the Brentwood religiosity in *Constantine* and you understand what Mel Gibson was making *The Passion of the Christ* against well that and the Jews he can't distinguish anyhow a good director can get away with a little stereotyping it's like a little salt but the director of this one Francis Lawrence throws in the whole box him and his screenwriters Kevin Brodbin and Frank Cappello they're counting on the audience to want only known quantities a Rachel Weisz who's still courting the Mummy a Keanu who's still Neo from *The Matrix* only crossed with Humphrey Bogart a visual style full of forced closeups and dizzy perspectives so it's equally recognizable as film noir and comic book a booming score that's like *Carmina Burana* heard through a cough syrup hangover the only novelty proposed is the special effects and that offer has become pretty old hat."

"Of course I agree with you. What bothers me most, though, is the hedged Manicheism. *Constantine* preaches that humans are mere pieces on a game board, and that God and Satan are the evenly matched players. I don't know what's worse, the way the movie abandons its conceit at the end and tilts toward the standard hosannas, or the way it implies that our lives here don't really matter, except if we give up smoking."

"Matter I'll tell you what matters you die and they turn you into Molly Bloom how's that for indignity."

But she was cut short. The rabbi, his face even more pale than usual, had lifted his fingers from the plaquette and was walking toward the bookshelf. He dragged from it *The Time Out Guide to Kabbalah* and threw it into the trash. "This is what my students want from the movies now? No. Better the bank should foreclose."

"Congratulations, rabbi. You're doing the honorable thing."

"And you, Mr. Film Critic? What have you pulled out of this spiritual hooey that's maybe a little honorable?"

"Me?" I said. "Notice that not once have I talked about Bush."

The Nation, February 17, 2005

Movies Are
Better Than Ever!

The Royal Tenenbaums

Though it's choked with dead bodies and disappointments, *The Royal Tenenbaums* comes before you with a smile. It wants you to know it's a whimsical film: the kind of story you might check out of the young-adult section of the library, where the books have funny line drawings at the chapter heads. An unseen narrator speaks, in tones that remind you of afternoons spent tucked into an armchair, and the characters pop up on the screen, as if called from the pages of some latter-day E.B. White. Here is the family of eccentrics; and here is their big, comfortable house—limestone and turrets outside, dark wood and burgundy walls within—set on a cozy New York cul-de-sac. Everything's a little too charming: from the pet mice that skitter through the frames to the straight-on, photo-album views of the characters, who are shown complete with captions. At this early point, of course, you haven't begun counting the casualties.

Even within the opening moments, though, you might guess that the pink icing has been layered onto a brick. "Is it our fault?" ask three children, when their father informs them he's moving out. No, replies Royal Tenenbaum (Gene Hackman), speaking from the very far end of a dining-room table. Then, with a candor that's as absurd as the table's utter bareness, he adds, "Of course, your mother and I made some sacrifices to have you."

What could fill such a paternal void? Etheline Tenenbaum (Anjelica Huston) pumps it full of ambition. Her children must all become geniuses; and so, with a briskness that's well summed up by the pencil she keeps stuck in her hair, she programs the kids until they're famous for their success. The effect, again, is only too charming: In quick succession, you see little Chas standing at his desk, running a business empire; little Margot typing away at award-winning plays; little Richie stringing his tennis racket, on the way to the pros at the age of 8. You may smile to see these half-size people behaving like grown-ups; but in that corner of your mind reserved for unease, you may also wonder whose fantasies they're living out. Their father (that good-for-nothing) chases after big money, bright lights and the sporting life; and so the children turn themselves into whatever he desires in the big city of Gotham.

Not that anyone in the movie uses that name; but what else can you call this place, where a man can live on credit at the Lindbergh Palace Hotel? *The Royal Tenenbaums* is set in the romantically dowdy city of John O'Hara's stories and Charles Foster Kane's side-street love nest: a New York that, despite being imaginary, has drawn so many millions of real people. It's here that the movie actually begins, twenty-two years after the parents' separation, when a broke and aging Royal is evicted from the hotel, and the child prodigies come face to face with the futilities of impending middle age.

Through a combination of lies and sexual longings that I needn't detail, everyone moves back into the old family house, which still flies a ragged pennant emblazoned with a T. Royal apparently means to reclaim this flagship property, and Etheline with it—goals that can best be achieved, he thinks, if he claims to be dying. Never mind the illogic. (It will reach its height later, in the woozy report of another character: "I wrote a suicide note as soon as I regained consciousness.") The main point is, Royal takes everyone on a visit to the cemetery, during which sequence each of his offspring unearths a buried injury. We're reminded in quick succession of how Chas (Ben Stiller) wound up with a BB pellet lodged in his flesh, as a permanent grievance against Royal; how Margot (Gwyneth Paltrow) lost a finger of her right hand, in yet another incident that can be blamed on the father; how Richie (Luke Wilson) played his final, disastrous tennis match, on an afternoon when disillusionment led him to make seventy-two unforced errors. Unlike his siblings, Richie hasn't bled yet; but he knows how treacherous, how funereal, love can be. It's a lesson he shares with Etheline's new suitor, Henry Sherman (Danny Glover), who by this point in the film has proposed marriage and fallen into an open grave.

I shouldn't make too much of these elements that are literally underground (the film doesn't); but there they are, underlying the whimsy, which meanwhile keeps your eyes busy with surface effects. They're clever enough, these effects, such as the reduction of the characters' wardrobes to a single outfit apiece. Richie still wears the sunglasses, headband and long hair of a late-seventies tennis pro. Margot, with her kohl-rimmed eyes, mink coat and little striped dress, comes across like an 11-year-old playing dress-up, or a grown woman pretending to be a little girl. As for Royal, he's a lounge lizard of the tweed-jacket era, trying to dignify himself with a pair of Henry Kissinger's eyeglasses—which is to say he's a disbarred attorney and looks it. And all the while, as you're occupied with these little conceits, the film's geologic strata are shifting into place.

The Royal Tenenbaums is the work of director Wes Anderson, who wrote the screenplay with his regular collaborator, Owen Wilson. Since their previous picture was the utterly brilliant *Rushmore*, expectations have run high for the *Tenenbaums*, and disappointments have been voiced. I, too, felt let down at first. The fantasy version of New York City seemed arch to me. (Taxis are always instantly available, and invariably bear the logo of the Gypsy Cab Co. The only place to exercise is the 375th Street Y.) I also wondered whether some of the characters, such as the perpetually pissed-off Chas, were absolutely necessary to the story, and whether the redemption of Royal wasn't too much of a foregone conclusion. The second viewing hasn't moved me to play a mug's game and compare *The Royal Tenenbaums* to *Rushmore*; but it has convinced me that a strong imagination is at work in every part of the picture.

The talent is easiest to see in the performances that Anderson has elicited, beginning of course with Gene Hackman's Royal. He's a man without an internal censor—whatever pops into his mind comes out of his mouth—who nevertheless tries to con people. A hopeless ambition; yet astonishingly, he has moments of success, which Hackman somehow makes plausible and transparent, sleazy and endearing, in a single gesture. It's a big performance by a big actor; and it's matched, paradoxically, by Gwyneth Paltrow's infinitesimal gestures as Margot. In one of her best scenes, where she's reunited with Richie after many years' absence, she almost smiles. Then she doesn't. That's it; and it's enough to make Margot into a booming echo chamber of hurts and longings.

Just as memorable are Luke Wilson, whose Richie tries so hard to be sane and responsible, from within a body that seems anesthetized; Bill Murray as Margot's husband and father-surrogate, an Oliver Sacks-like neurologist who snickers openly at his weirdo subjects; Danny Glover as the gentlemanly and inept Henry Sherman; and Owen Wilson, who plays the most desperate of the characters and the most successful, the popular novelist Eli Cash. Residents of the imaginary Gotham need someone to supply them with fantasies of other nonplaces, such as the primitive, authentic West. Eli does the job, and pays the cost of having bad mescaline dreams leak out of his head.

It's clear enough why this theme of dreams and disappointments should appeal to Anderson and Wilson, who themselves achieved a precocious success. You might read *The Royal Tenenbaums* as a film by bright young people who are brooding too much over their next move; and you wouldn't be wrong. But early triumphs and long slides into mediocrity have long played their part in the myth of Gotham. So, too, has the occasional late redemption.

The second time I watched the *Tenenbaums*, the young-adult archness seemed to me like Eli's prep-school outfit, which he wears until far too late in life. When you realize why he's changed it for a preposterous Western get-up—something that only makes him look more like a kid—you understand he should have stayed in the blue blazer. He might not like what it symbolizes, but it suits him.

The whimsy suits *The Royal Tenenbaums*, too. It's the smile of two filmmakers who seem to feel sad, but can't hide their delight in what they do. It's the dirty grin of Gene Hackman, shoplifting his way into your heart.

The Nation, January 7, 2002

A Grin Without a Cat

What date shall I assign to Chris Marker's magnum opus, *A Grin Without a Cat*? This rugged oak of an essay-film, whose gnarls trace the growth and withering of decades of leftist politics, is now playing for the first time in the United States, where it's being shown in the form Marker gave it after the demise of the Soviet Union. I might say it's a film from 1993; and yet the version we now have is the revision of a work completed in 1977, when Communism was still alive, and anti-Communism was more than the hungry zombie it's since become.

Communism was still alive, but even then Marker perceived a change. The last major event he incorporated into his essay was the 1974 election of Valéry Giscard d'Estaing to the presidency of France. In the film, this election represents the end of a period of turmoil that had begun in 1967: the year of campus uprisings in the United States against the Vietnam War, increased union militancy in France, bloody student protests in Berlin against the visiting Shah of Iran, the death in Bolivia of Che Guevara. It's fair to say that the main body of *A Grin Without a Cat* deals with these years, so I might date the film 1967-74.

But then, the historical marker slips back even further. To explain why Che perished as he did, to account for his prestige in death, to suggest how that martyrdom shaped the period that followed, the film revisits 1962, when Douglas Bravo launched a guerrilla war in rural Venezuela. Believing that a few militants could spark revolution on their own, Bravo and his followers abandoned the discipline of the Communist Party. That was the good news. The bad news was, they also abandoned the party's political base. In Marker's words (which are spoken throughout the film by several voiceover narrators), the guerrillas made themselves into "a spearhead without a spear, a grin without a cat."

The phrase brings to mind Lewis Carroll, and maybe Gogol, too. I will have something to say about the rude adventures of this grin. First, though, a question: Assuming there was once a whole cat, what did it look like?

Marker gives a filmmaker's reply: He goes back in time to *The Battleship Potemkin*. His picture begins in that other movie—begins twice, in fact. As his first gesture in *A Grin Without a Cat*, Marker shows us Eisenstein's celebrated vision of the *Potemkin* mutiny, in which a sailor faces a line of riflemen and wins them over with a single shout: Brothers! Out of that moment, Marker develops a great, thrilling montage sequence of his own, spanning half a century of conflicts in the streets and ending on Eisenstein's Odessa steps, more or less in the present day. There, as if to begin the film again, Marker shows us a pleasant young woman who sits in the sunshine, chatting with an offscreen interviewer. She is a French-speaking Intourist guide, and she can testify that this site is very popular. She brings people to it two or three times a day.

We might conclude that the not-quite-mythical cat was on the prowl sometime between these two historical moments, the first of inspiration, the second of nostalgia. We might decide that *A Grin Without a Cat* is dated 1925-93.

During those years, was anything left unfilmed? To watch this picture is to be astonished at the world of footage that's been piled up here, some of it shot by Marker himself, most of it recorded by others, both known and anonymous. The raw materials of *A Grin Without a Cat* include images of a US pilot bombing Vietnam, as seen from the cockpit; scenes of carefully staged party congresses in Havana and Beijing and of an unscripted, on-the-run congress in 1968 Prague; views of the festive Cat Parade in Ypres; broadcasts of the Watergate hearings and of the Shah of Iran's grandiose party for himself in Persepolis; raw footage of Communist and Trotskyist workers getting into a fistfight at a factory gate; interviews in the jungle with Douglas Bravo, in the Pentagon with a counterinsurgency expert, in the Citroën headquarters with that firm's managing director; Soviet newsreels from World War II; a student collective's newsreel from 1967 Berlin; shots of Giscard d'Estaing playing the accordion and of The Who destroying their instruments; behind-the-scenes pictures of training sessions at the School of the Americas; and the usual amalgam of flaming automobiles, flying tear-gas canisters, descending truncheons and human beings lying in pools of blood.

So complete is the filmed record on which Marker draws, and so associative is his method of using it, that he can show us a statement made in 1968 by a Czech national hero, Emil Zatopek, just before he was stripped of his military rank for protesting against the invasion; Zatopek at the 1952 Helsinki Olympics, when he famously swept the distance running events; and Zatopek in 1972, when he was released from the mines and trotted out to look solemn at the Munich Olympics, when the games continued despite the murder of eleven Israeli athletes. But then, Marker comments, "I had been in Mexico City in 1968, when 200 people were killed so the games could begin," and we have that footage, too.

This sort of thing can make your head spin; but since it should also make your head clear, Marker's montage is not only associative but diagrammatic as well. *A Grin Without a Cat* is divided into two main sections. Part One, "Fragile Hands," concentrates on the events of 1967 and 1968, up to the fizzling of the May revolt in France. Part Two, "Severed Hands," begins with the Soviet invasion of Czechoslovakia, continues with the rise and fall of Salvador Allende (and the Gang of Four) and concludes with the fading of the cat's grin, late in the 1970s.

Marker tends to present these events in big loops. He'll jump from source to source, place to place, to develop an argument (about the concept of a revolution in the revolution, for example); he'll digress to examine the way people gestured with their hands, or how they either filled or did not fill the space between striking workers and police; and then he'll swing back to close the loop, concluding one phase of his essay and moving on to the next. At each phase (at least in the earlier part of the film) he also introduces elements that I might as well call dialectical. When he shows a group of war protesters preparing to burn their draft cards in 1967, he also shows a rally of the American Nazi Party. When French student leader Daniel Cohn-Bendit comes into the picture, so does Giscard d'Estaing. We watch the New Left rise in tandem with the New Right. In Marker's view of history, the development of the New Right may have been the New Left's greatest achievement.

If so, then the Old Left contributed ample help. Marker makes the point with stunning force during his section on Czechoslovakia, when he unexpectedly closes one of those big loops of montage. Citizens of Prague have surrounded a Soviet tank driver and are berating him—"How could you, a Communist, be doing this?"—when that intertitle from *The Battleship Potemkin* pops onto the screen again, in a way that's now heartbreaking and futile: Brothers!

And since Marker is a moviemaker above all, *A Grin Without a Cat* also makes its point as a movie should, through the actions of its star. Yes, there is a lead actor in this film: Fidel Castro, whose many performances, interspersed throughout the picture, amount to a little drama of their own, complete with a nasty plot twist. Here is Fidel on the podium, addressing a night-time rally with wit, vigor and good sense. Here he is again, sprawled casually on the grass for the benefit of the camera, giving a very good impersonation of a man speaking spontaneously, sensitively, about popular militancy and his comrade Che Guevara. And here, giving a radio broadcast, Fidel appears to work himself into a fury against the invasion of Czechoslovakia, as a dramatic overture to praising the Soviets for their tanks.

This is dense, complex, allusive filmmaking, encyclopedic in ambition, profound in understanding, playful enough in form to make you smile sometimes at the tricks of history. Though Marker has made an elegy to the left, he would prefer that you leave the theater invigorated, feeling that power is still abroad in the world, and that you and your friends might still disrupt its dirty work.

My only complaint is that the film could have sent you home feeling even better. During the period Marker covers, the feminists got a few things done, often without bothering to define their relationship to the Communist Party; but feminism shows up very late in *A Grin Without a Cat*, as a mere afterthought. Africa doesn't show up at all; yet activists from around the world made some changes there too, such as ending apartheid and establishing a new democratic state. You may choose to add to the list a third or fourth victory. We've had a few, despite all of history's tricks.

The Nation, May 13, 2002

Russian Ark

While going about their business, great artists often make monkeys of the people who write about them. Look at what happened to one chatterer, who not long ago was playing the critic in the *New York Times*. "There are two kinds of tough-minded, morally uncompromising artists in today's film world," he wrote, "those who want to make musicals and those who don't... Pre-eminent among the wallflowers is the Russian master Aleksandr Sokurov."

Unknown to this monkey—me—the Russian master had just shot one of the most splendid ballroom scenes in film history. It's the thrilling climax to *Russian Ark*, a movie that has absolutely no precedent, except for *The Scarlet Empress*, *Gone With the Wind*, *The Leopard*, *Doctor Zhivago*, the agglomerated screen translations of *War and Peace* and all other costume epics. *Russian Ark* sums up and surpasses these pictures in the sense that it's nothing *but* feathers and pearls and epaulets and gold braid, music and color and figures out of the past. By cutting these things loose from the moorings of a plot—or even a single time period—Sokurov has allowed his sumptuous pleasures to flow freely, purely, without troubling you to remember which archduke is in debt to whose cousin.

But then, being tough-minded and morally uncompromising, Sokurov has also made *Russian Ark* into a haunted meditation on the disasters of history, and on our precarious efforts to rescue something from the flood. The melancholy that has pervaded many of his previous films—*The Stone*, for example, or *Mother and Son*—also seeps delicately through *Russian Ark*. It's as if this picture wanted to hold still and be quiet, even as it launches into the longest tracking shot ever made.

Imagine a black screen, with no sound except for sparse, quiet, atonal music that sounds like someone's nerves being re-strung in a neighboring galaxy. "I open my eyes and see nothing," says a man's voice in the darkness. "An accident. I can't remember what happened." Then, in a wan light that mutes the colors, figures appear in a small courtyard: women flushed with excitement, young officers laughing and hurrying forward in a light flurry of snow. The voice on the soundtrack remarks on what you've already noted: The costumes belong to the nineteenth century. But what is this place, the voice wants to know? Who are these people? The camera plunges after them, into a doorway, down a dark stair, through a confused hallway and up again, pressing on through the maze like the eye of the ghostlike narrator.

And for the next ninety minutes, this motion will never stop, as the camera eye wanders through what proves to be the State Hermitage Museum. No second camera will add its point of view; no cut will suddenly carry you into a different time or place. *Russian Ark* will turn out to be a single Steadicam shot, threading its way without interruption through dozens of different spaces and lighting conditions, while being threaded through itself by hundreds of choreographed performers. Some are in contemporary dress and some in costumes of earlier eras. Some represent historical figures (Peter the Great, Catherine the Great, Nicholas and Alexandra) or nameless soldiers and aristocrats, while others appear as themselves: Hermitage director Mikhail Piotrovsky, for example, or the artistic director of the Mariinsky Theatre, Valery Gergiev.

Considered just as a stunt, this single, feature-length shot is superlative, if not utterly mad. Think of the months of planning and rehearsal it required. Then picture the anxiety-racked day of the shoot: the assistants whispering frantically into their headsets, the grips trying to duck unseen past the camera (there were almost as many grips as credited performers), the heroic Steadicam operator Tilman Büttner carrying on long after his thighs must have turned to lead. Had anything gone visibly wrong in those ninety minutes, the whole movie would have been ruined.

Get beyond your astonishment at the magnitude of this feat and you begin to notice the directorial skill that sustains it. To give only two examples: When Sokurov wants to make a sudden jump in space—an effect that would have been easy to achieve, had he allowed himself any cuts—he cagily has a pair of hands intrude into the frame. You assume you're seeing a close-up of the lead actor's body; but unless I'm mistaken about this Wellesian trick, the hands actually belong to a stand-in. That's how the lead actor can suddenly, magically be standing far away, in a place you've never seen before, when the camera looks up again. Here, Sokurov literally uses sleight of hand. Elsewhere he relies on something like the blocking traditionally practiced by good theater directors. A throng is flowing down the great stair of the Hermitage, carrying along the camera, when a man in the foreground seems to recall that he's left something upstairs. He turns and begins to push his way back up, against the crowd; and so the camera turns, too, to follow him, allowing Sokurov to direct your attention to a different view of the architecture.

But even though it took daring to shoot a film in one take—daring, and awe-inspiring skill—what does the stunt mean? Sokurov has explained that he wanted to insert himself into the flow of time—a comment that strikes me as enigmatic and incomplete because there is more than one flow of time in this movie, or perhaps no flow at all. Since the Hermitage of *Russian Ark* is inhabited by the ghosts of three centuries, time stands still; since the historical period changes as you pass from room to room, time moves unpredictably. Maybe I can rephrase Sokurov's statement: By taking place in real time, the shot becomes like a steady searchlight cutting through darkness, while the imagined eras are like eddies that pass intermittently through the beam.

This is something new—and its novelty goes deeper than the invention of machines that can record a feature-length take. It even goes beyond an artist's determination to use this technology and his discovery of an appropriate purpose for it. *Russian Ark* alters the nature of cinema.

There have always been single-shot movies, starting with the Lumière brothers' brief scenes of railroad stations and factories. But even when such films have been longer and more self-consciously artistic (as in the work of Michael Snow), they have revealed themselves to us as artifacts made by a machine, which mindlessly captured whatever was put in front of it. The people and settings were really present before the camera—that much we knew—but by the time they had appeared before us, they had become phantoms. Events staged for the camera are therefore more absent than present to the audience—except when filmmakers create choreographed tracking shots. Then the machine becomes less important than the intelligence that manifests itself, as we recognize that a mind is telling the camera and the actors where to go. Now the shot is more than the record of a performance. The passage through space and time becomes a performance in itself.

Such shot-performances have always had a fragmentary character, as contents of a greater whole—until now, when Sokurov has made the accomplishment of the shot exactly congruent with the movie. *Russian Ark* embodies, in its totality, the performance that his cast and crew carried out. The thing itself is now present before you, and will be present again each time you watch the film.

And yet, as I've said, *Russian Ark* is full of ghosts. (It sums up and surpasses all haunted-house movies.) Most notable among the spooks is a nineteenth-century French aristocrat (Sergey Dreiden): a long-faced, frizzy-haired phantom, trim in a tight black coat, who strides about with his arms clutched behind his back, dropping amused, condescending remarks about Russia and its people, and arousing some irritation from the camera-eye character. Though unnamed, the Frenchman is surely Chateaubriand—an ideal ghost for Sokurov's purpose, since he is the author of *Memoirs From Beyond the Grave*, and also a sharp, disillusioned witness to the first age of revolution. With his celebrated sensitivity to fragrance, Chateaubriand goes through the Hermitage sniffing at paintings; and that's as much respect as he'll pay to the formal and material qualities that are so important to museumgoers today. Catholic and premodern in his understanding of art, Chateaubriand thinks only of iconography. He's shocked that a painting of Cleopatra (half-naked at that) should be installed right next to a picture of the Virgin; he's incredulous, and outraged, that a boy of our era, someone who is ignorant of the Bible, should pretend to understand an image of Peter and Paul.

That the Hermitage should have been built and decorated on Italian models seems to Chateaubriand the height of folly. "Italy is a warm country," he reminds the camera-eye. But then, of course, the czars had to import architects and sculptors: "You Russians don't trust your artists." This is a particularly cutting remark, assuming that the camera-eye represents Sokurov, a Russian artist whose works were all shelved during the Soviet era. And yet, despite what he's gone through, the camera-eye keeps defending the Russians to his smug interlocutor. He defends them until a change comes over Chateaubriand, who by the end of the great ballroom scene is no longer so mocking of his hosts. Everyone is leaving, the camera-eye says, as the aristocrats begin to pour down the stairs, toward the end of their era. Aren't you coming?

Chateaubriand shakes his head and steps back. "There's nowhere to go," he replies. "I'll stay."

It's a gorgeous moment—although, if *Russian Ark* has a fault, you might locate it in this nostalgia for aristocratic splendor. The film might have benefited from one, just one, of those title cards that clutter *The Scarlet Empress*: "Under the despot's heel, the poor cry for bread and freedom," or something like that. But Sokurov gives no hint of goings-on outside the palace walls. The film not only repudiates the Soviet past (by abandoning all montage, for one thing, and so pissing on the grave of Eisenstein) but also remains shut up inside the Hermitage—the ark—as if the whole twentieth century had been a flood, from which a few precious remnants of imperial culture have been saved. I won't disagree politically with this sentiment—it's Sokurov, not I, who has to live with this history, so let him think as he pleases—but I question the way its pessimism clashes with the movie's spirit. Everything about *Russian Ark* is ingenious, exuberant, risky, bold. I find it strange that Sokurov should expend such tremendous energy, such genius, in making the film and then pretend, at the end, that we're all just holding on.

Let that be a topic for further discussion. I prefer to close with a comment on another form of pessimism, peculiar to those Americans who have learned to disdain art. It's the conviction (recently expressed in a number of newspaper articles) that film festivals have no reason to exist, unless they help studios to market their pictures. Just what the world needs: more sales opportunities for Hollywood products.

So I note that *Russian Ark* will be shown in one of the most severely curatorial of these supposedly useless events, the New York Film Festival, which begins September 27. When I endorse the festival, readers ought to know that I am not a disinterested observer; I have spent some time on its selection committee. And I say, even so: If the festival had done nothing in its forty seasons except launch *Russian Ark* on US screens, it would have justified its existence for all time.

The Nation, October 4, 2002

Corrections: A second viewing revealed to me that the trick of passing the camera over a pair of hands in order to conceal movement in the background was actually just a trick of my memory. My identification of the film's interlocutor as Chateaubriand was imaginative, if you're being generous, or if not merely ignorant. It's generally accepted that he's meant to be Astolphe-Louis-Léonor, Marquis de Custine.

Punch-Drunk Love

Although I'm mad for Paul Thomas Anderson's new picture, *Punch-Drunk Love*, I also suspect it's made me a little crazy. Why else should I fall, and fall hard, for the world's first one-character romantic comedy? The tale of a wheezing, withdrawn young man in suburban Los Angeles and the woman who unaccountably redeems him, *Punch-Drunk Love* bursts with music, color, movement, wit, passion, suspense—everything you might want, except for the woman herself.

Her absence can't be an accident. In previous pictures such as *Boogie Nights* and *Magnolia*, Anderson has put dozens of actors onto the screen and given each a delectable moment to play, or more often a chewable monologue. So it's not just a change in scale that makes *Punch-Drunk Love* seem a departure from his earlier movies, which ran longer than this one by an hour or more. The deeper difference lies in the way Anderson's worldview has contracted, so that the movie seems to take place in the head of only one man.

Like Anderson's earlier characters, Barry Egan walks into the movie with a résumé suitable for realist fiction. He's got a defining occupation (as a wholesale merchant of novelty toilet plungers), a vivid family background (he cringes before seven bullying sisters) and a behavioral pattern that hints at psychological depth. Barry practices a craven politeness, except when overcome by the sudden need to smash; and since he's being played by Adam Sandler, a comic actor known for his wise-ass shleppiness, this side of the character comes before us pre-interpreted.

By contrast, Barry's love interest is so thinly conceived as to approach the wraithlike. She, too, is played by a performer with an established screen persona—although not *that* established, since the movies in which Emily Watson has appeared, wrapping her suffering in a high-strung, sensuous embrace, have reached a mere fraction of Sandler's audience. Watson's presence puts some flesh on the character of Lena Leonard; but without the detail that's been lavished on Barry, Lena threatens to melt back into the sunlight from which she seems to have materialized.

Lena is, in fact, the third unexplained phenomenon to manifest itself in *Punch-Drunk Love*. The first is a doomed car, which goes crashing, shrieking, tumbling through a warehouse district of the San Fernando Valley just after dawn, with no cause for this catastrophe other than Barry's having glanced down the street.

The second apparition, which follows immediately, is a red van, which pulls up in front of Barry as if in continuation of the wreck. Unseen workers remove a harmonium (Barry will call it a "little piano") and place it at his feet. Then, soon after the van speeds off, Lena saunters down the alley to Barry's warehouse with the sun glaring behind her, so that you make out very little except her red outfit. You might say that Lena personifies the surprises that have preceded her. She sums up an experience of unforeseen, bone-shaking loss of control, and a promise that music might come from a small, still-mute crate.

If Barry were played by a standard leading man, you would be justified at this point in resolving never to see *Punch-Drunk Love*, and also in ripping to shreds this page of the magazine. The movie would be just another feature-length projection of male fantasy; but then, there is nothing standard about the choice of Sandler for the lead. An infant clomping around in the body of a long-faced, mouth-breathing adult, Sandler seems in *Punch-Drunk Love* to have no padding on his feelings. His Barry shields his eyes at every light, shrinks back from every noise. Emotions register in him immediately, in a performance that's as beautiful and unself-conscious as it is unexpected. What registers most in Barry, as he stands before Lena, is something like the sense of astonishment, awe and pain that babies feel when they learn that the mother is a separate person.

To suggest how magically this emotion plays out in *Punch-Drunk Love*, I must now say something about the words, the suit, the music and the shot.

The words, very often, sound like impromptu poetry of the Ashbery school. A typical Barry utterance: "I have a lot of pudding, and in six to eight weeks it can be redeemed." This actually means something, though you could almost wish that it didn't. More to the point, though, are the words that pop out of Barry's mouth when he appeals to someone for psychiatric help, and is asked if his feelings seem normal to him. "I don't know," Barry answers on a rising tone, "how other people are?" A perfect self-diagnosis, which I fear applies to each of us.

The suit worn by this unwilling solipsist is blue. In interviews, Anderson has explained this costume as a tribute to MGM musicals; think of Fred Astaire in *The Band Wagon*. But I note that Fred's suit is a grayish, sophisticated blue. Barry's is the blue that your mother used to spread on the other half of the peanut butter sandwich. Though Barry tries to dress as a grown-up, the color shows he hasn't yet got it right.

Music thrums relentlessly through *Punch-Drunk Love*, as if it were the pounding of blood in Barry's temples. Anderson has always liked a busy soundtrack; but this time I thought he'd overdone it, until he launched into a sequence scored to a Harry Nilsson song: "He Needs Me," sung by Olive Oyl in Robert Altman's *Popeye*. Only a true movie-lover would have chosen this tune, which was the first thing about it that won me over. The second was the experience of being carried out of Barry's head at last. Presumably he's the one imagining this sproingy two-step, whose scrawny waif of a melody keeps spiraling upward until it gets dizzy. But in the rapturous babble of the lyrics—"He *needs* me he needs *me* he needs me *he* needs me he *needs* me he needs *me*"—Barry seems to be guessing his way into Lena's mind; and what he guesses turns out to be right.

Which brings me to the shot: the climactic moment you may have seen excerpted in TV commercials or frozen in newspaper ads. As the song approaches its high point, Lena flings herself onto Barry. The two are silhouetted, in medium long-shot, against a doorway that opens onto a beach. For a second, they're alone: two black outlines against a blue rectangle, in the middle of the CinemaScope frame. Then, from the left and right, other silhouettes begin to cross the screen, as Lena and Barry go on embracing. Barry finally knows, a little, how another person is; and now that he does, multitudes of people come rushing in—people of every description—as if Barry were being released into the world.

Or maybe the audience in the movie theater—a multitude of figures in the dark—is released into the movie. As the shot filled up, I felt as if I, too, might walk right through this movie, which had abruptly opened into gregariousness. Here was a moment of pure happiness, discovered at the violent, innocent heart of *Punch-Drunk Love*. Whether it's delirium or sanity I can't say, but I'm very glad to have been included.

The Nation, November 11, 2002

Friday Night

Let's say you're one of those funny people who tire of the movie industry's summer dinosaurs—the booming tread of their feet, as they announce their commercial heft and shake the theater's seats—and feel it's enough if pictures and sounds are sensuous and smartly put together, even though nothing much happens by way of a plot. Maybe you also feel relieved if the character to whom nothing much is happening is a woman. For you, Claire Denis has created a wonderfully fleet little mammal called *Friday Night.*

I might say that *Friday Night* takes you through the stages of a near-anonymous one-night stand in Paris; or, to interpret the film more freely, that it brings you into a woman's fantasy of such a fling, as she imagines it on the night before she moves in with her boyfriend. Either way, what really matters is that the rooftops slowly darken until the Eiffel Tower becomes a beacon against the rose of sunset, and that Laure (Valérie Lemercier) drives out into the night and gets stuck in an impossible traffic jam. "The city is choking, everyone is exhausted," a traffic reporter says on the radio in strangely cheerful tones. "We must be generous. Try carpooling." As if called into being by this advice, a man appears and asks to sit in the car. Laure says yes, without hesitating. Jean (Vincent Lindon) then takes the wheel, and the traffic miraculously disappears. By mutual though almost wordless consent, Laure and Jean proceed from this speed derby to a hotel—or rather, according to the glowing, truncated sign, a HOT—which turns out to be entirely empty. Images of hands, clothes and parts of faces flash across the screen, as the couple satisfy themselves the first time. The second time, they get undressed. Then they go out to a near-empty restaurant for a pizza, across the surface of which the anchovy wriggles like a goofy smile.

When the night is over, Laure is happy, and Jean has not turned out to be what an American filmmaker would have made him: a serial killer, thief, sexual freak or disease-bearer. I'm glad about that, and I'm glad that Lemercier, as Laure, looks like the writer Emmanuèle Bernheim (on whose novel the film is based) and also like one of Claire Denis's artistic forebears, the filmmaker Maya Deren. She, too, might have dreamed such a movie, in which things get good for a woman after she lets a man take the wheel: a fantasy of abandoned control, realized in this case by a virtually all-woman crew that includes cinematographer Agnès Godard and editor Nelly Quettier. Another reason to like the French.

The Nation, July 7, 2003

Lost in Translation

A *Love Affair* for the postcollege, flirting-with-Buddhism set, Sofia Coppola's *Lost in Translation* is a travelogue of the emotions, concerned with the deepening relationship between a playful, bored, world-famous roué and an edgily intelligent woman who doesn't keep busy enough. The roué is all-American Bill Murray, rather than *Love Affair'*s excitingly Gallic Charles Boyer; the woman, Scarlett Johansson, is considerably younger than was Irene Dunne; and the meeting place, where these voyagers temporarily float free of their attachments, is not a trans-Atlantic steamship but the Park Hyatt hotel in Tokyo. With those adjustments taken into account, though, and with the crucial substitution of color film for black and white, you might say that Coppola has done something remarkably improbable for a young filmmaker who is cool by birth. She has dreamed up a close contemporary analogy to the Leo McCarey classic, right down to its chapel scene. *Lost in Translation* turns out to be a relaxed and surprisingly chaste character study, in which a difficult-to-impossible romance takes place in a luxurious setting full of music and spiritual longing.

Spiritual longing might in fact be the film's defining element, even though Coppola has begun with a shot of Johansson's recumbent tush, which in the soft green light looks like a panty-clad hill, all lush and vernal. You know at a glance that someone will want a leisurely climb; and even without having seen the trailer, you can be sure that the someone is Murray. Economy of means: With a single image, Coppola signals that *Lost in Translation* will grow tense around the question of when and how Murray will get into bed with Johansson. And more: Since all but the most untutored moviegoers know that the age difference between these actors nearly matches that between Coppola and her father, Francis, the answer to the question would seem to entail not just plot complications but also legal issues, or maybe atavistic horror.

Who could be so clean-minded as to ignore the implications? Not Coppola. She brings the daughter-father theme right to the surface by making parenting the core subject of her characters' deepest conversation. As Johansson lies next to Murray—I will confirm that she's in bed, although I won't reveal when or how she got there—he gives her the kind of common-sense advice that a drifting twentysomething might want from a father. In an act of ventriloquistic wish-fulfillment on Coppola's part, Murray even tells her that his children are the most delightful people he could ever hope to meet. It's a lovely sentiment under any circumstances, and all the more touching when the father is horizontal beside his nubile daughter-surrogate.

But, that said, who could be so dirty-minded as to insist on an incestuous Sofia-Francis reading of *Lost in Translation*, when the characters spend less time in bed than they do riding the Park Hyatt elevators? Johansson and Murray also visit karaoke bars, game arcades and Buddhist temples, contemplate flower arrangements and neon signs, sit around in still more bars and then wonder aloud about how seriously to take a book titled *A Soul's Search*. Of course the possibility of sex continues to hover as they do these things; but the opportunity is also continually edged aside, since these characters are smart enough to know that sex is a way to lose themselves, and what they really want is to get their bearings from each other. *Lost in Translation* is about the dislocation of these two people—in Tokyo, but also in the course of their lives.

The dislocation seems all the more absurd for Murray because of his superior height, which makes him stand out like a landmark in every scene. Like a landmark, he is pointed at, photographed and gathered under, not just because of his size but because he is playing the role of Bob Harris, a Hollywood star who has come to Japan to endorse a brand of whiskey and collect $2 million. This circumstance would make some men feel secure in the world—and yet Murray spends most of the film gazing down with muted, baggy-eyed astonishment. Already weary from travel when he comes onto the scene, then further undermined by insomnia and drink—"The good news," he says, "is the whiskey works"—he greets most situations with a reptilian blink, a swallow (as the initial wisecrack slides down his throat) and then a quietly voiced rejoinder, the import of which is generally "Get me out of here."

Johansson is more vocal. As Charlotte—a woman who has been left on the loose while her husband works day and night—she weeps over her confusion, treats her husband's friends as idiots and marvels aloud at what a *pathetic* midlife crisis Murray is having. Most actresses would be insufferable in the role; but Johansson, whose plush-lipped smile can be wide and knowing at once, has a way of softening Charlotte's aggression, whether it's directed at others or herself. She lets you see that she teases people, or flat-out insults them, mostly out of despair about herself; you see that she lets herself despair only to the point where she'd need to tease herself. Like other young people who are getting a late start in life, Charlotte has good reason to feel troubled; but her sense of the ridiculous prevents her from becoming fully engaged even with her own unhappiness. How bad is she allowed to feel, when she's got a Yale degree, a five-star hotel and the hippest bars in Tokyo?

So there's a delicacy, a reserve, to Johansson's character, which melds beautifully with Murray's air of reluctant resignation. (He knows the Buddha's Four Noble Truths require him to abandon his desires—he knows his body is starting to make the same demand—but the devil in his ear keeps whispering, "Not yet.") *Lost in Translation* is the unexpectedly involving story of how these two people start to play with each other—and play seriously—in a wonderland of colored lights, pop music and indecipherable writing that they find incomprehensible.

As a director, Coppola is especially good at the colored lights and pop music part. With the help of cinematographer Lance Acord (who also shot *Being John Malkovich*), she makes her tourist's Tokyo into a true floating world. She is less good when the characters need to come back to earth. Coppola has the bad habit of cutting scenes short just when the actual decisions would have to be made—when Johansson, after a distressing phone call, would need to figure out how and why to stop weeping, or when Murray would need to accept or reject the slapstick advances of a prostitute who has come to his room. *Lost in Translation* suffers from too many such magical nontransitions; but it's rescued because Johansson and Murray carry through the thought, even when Coppola fails to.

She is, by the way, 32 years old and has succeeded beyond all reasonable expectations in making a movie that's droll, wistful, dreamy and (in its last moments) bracingly sober. It's as gorgeously strange as Tokyo itself that someone of Coppola's generation should want to make such a picture. It's as heartening, and as sweetly melancholy, as *Lost in Translation* that she should feel nostalgic while doing so. "I wanted the movie to feel…like a memory," she has said, and so she chose to shoot on film rather than digital video. "Film might not be around that long, so we wanted to shoot on film while we still can."

There, if you're searching for it, is the real daughter-father romance.

The Nation, September 29, 2003

Crimson Gold

About a third of the way through the long, long flashback that is *Crimson Gold*, someone mentions that the main character, Hussein, needs to work outdoors because of his claustrophobia. It's a throwaway comment—but like every other detail that's doled out in the film, it makes your stomach drop, as if the quicksand around you had given way another inch. Why hadn't you seen from the start that Hussein couldn't bear confinement? It should have been obvious from the first scene—the one where he died by his own hand, having botched the robbery of a jewelry store.

You think back to that beginning, or rather end, which was played out in a narrow, darkened space defined on the far side by a barred security gate and on the near side by the awkward, blubbery silhouette of Hussein himself. For something like four minutes, or eternity, this opening shot of *Crimson Gold* had kept you trapped with Hussein, by Hussein, while the camera's sole movement was a slow push forward, squeezing the lens toward the body, the body toward the bars. At last the only air left was outside, in an unattainable little slice of the Tehran streets. People on the sidewalk were milling about and shouting, since the store's owner (unseen by you) was already dead on the floor. Then, at the moment of maximum compression, Hussein's ski mask came off; his hand lifted toward the shadowed head, holding a pistol.

So—Hussein had been claustrophobic! If you think of *Crimson Gold* as a series of explanations for a desperate crime, then you might dismiss the film (wrongly, I think) as just another late-neorealist weepie: the portrait of an abject prisoner of circumstance. But it seems to me that the movie is concerned both with the shackles on Hussein and with the freedom of the more affluent people around him, audience members included. The deeper mystery of the film—for which *Crimson Gold* offers no easy solution—is that every new piece of information we get about Hussein turns out to be something we might have known.

Directed by Jafar Panahi (*The White Balloon*, *The Circle*) from a screenplay by Abbas Kiarostami, *Crimson Gold* is full of characters who think they understand Hussein, and who are never so insultingly wrong as when they pretend to be generous to him. A con artist in a cafe invites himself to Hussein's table and grandly puts the order onto his own tab—picking up the cost of one whole cup of tea—while addressing him as a fellow thief. (In fact, the fortyish Hussein has a job delivering pizzas.) A client in a fourth-floor walk-up—someone who turns out to have served with Hussein in the Iran-Iraq war—calls the deliveryman a saint, then tips under 3 percent and shoos him from the door. Another client, a wealthy young man who has spent time in America and despises Tehran, plays the unpretentious democrat with Hussein, inviting him into his apartment to share the pizza and then, preoccupied and indifferent, leaving him to wander alone through the vast, gilded triplex (no chance of claustrophobia here).

Then there's Mr. Vaziri, owner of a jewelry shop in the chic district, whose charity toward Hussein proves fatal. In the kindest, most sincere tones possible, the elderly jeweler advises Hussein and his fiancée to go down to the souk and buy some nice, locally fashioned gold, rather than attempt to purchase his fancy stuff. When Hussein zooms away on his motorbike into the thick traffic that is so common in Iranian cinema, he is furious both with Vaziri and with the fiancée, who clings to his back and keeps apologizing as if she'd done something wrong.

A hulking, overstuffed sausage of a man, Hussein speaks in intermittent rumbles and walks as if numb; but for all that, he's shrewd about people. He deplores his fiancée's meekness, his future brother-in-law's horniness (the young fellow can't believe that in Hussein's youth, women walked around with their hair showing and everything), his own slowness and corpulence. (The medicine he takes, evidently to treat a wartime trauma, has made him unrecognizable to himself.) Behind the drooping eyelids glints intelligence—damaged and outraged, but real—which saves Hussein from being merely a toy of the filmmakers. He's also saved by another, more important quality: true generosity.

This authentic kindness comes to the fore in one of *Crimson Gold*'s longest, most extraordinary scenes, in which Hussein attempts to deliver pizzas to a fashionable apartment building and is stopped by the vice squad. They're staked out in the darkness, waiting to arrest guests leaving a party where liquor is being served and men are dancing with women. To prevent Hussein from warning these miscreants, the police chief orders him to park his motorbike and stand to one side. Hussein can't make his delivery and he can't leave—which makes him similar to a young cop he talks to (a bored 15-year-old with a rifle) who will be on duty until near dawn, and to a number of curbside detainees who had come to pick up partygoers and now are stuck in their cars, waiting for the arrests. The situation, in a way, is a mirror image of the opening scene: exterior instead of interior, nocturnal instead of daylit, with the silhouetted criminals being shown not in the foreground but at the rear of the shot. (They're visible behind the shades of a second-story window, doing the frug.) The most important difference, though, is that here Hussein is not completely constrained. He can press for a little freedom of movement—and he uses it to hand out the undeliverable pizza to anyone who is hungry, cops and detainees alike.

Crimson Gold has scenes of even greater tension, pathos and outrageousness, but this one feels to me like the heart of the film. That's partly because it culminates in an act of kindness, carried out by the character who can least afford the expense; but it's also because the film's meticulous control of themes and visual forms is carried out here with such apparent casualness. Everything seems to happen on its own, with open-air ease—including the performance by the lead actor, Hussein Emadeddin (in real life a pizza deliveryman), whose utterly natural demeanor in the role can have been achieved only through hours of painstaking work.

Not that you think about Emadeddin's effort, or Panahi's, when you're watching the film. *Crimson Gold* conceals its considerable art. It wants only to draw you into its subject, so that you once more learn what you already knew about Hussein and his world. It's mysterious, how we perpetually need reminding. It's astonishing, how well Panahi and Kiarostami prompt us. In *Crimson Gold*, we keep sinking and sinking into a quicksand of recognition—which is merely to say, this is one powerfully absorbing movie.

The Nation, February 2, 2004

Eternal Sunshine of the Spotless Mind

Not wanting to curse Charlie Kaufman with too much praise, I'm tempted to say that his nonexistent twin Donald is the best American screenwriter since Preston Sturges. Donald won't let the comparison upset him. As you may recall from *Adaptation*, he is not the type to fret about living up to his reputation, or anything else; and besides, he's nonexistently dead, having been murdered in the last reel of his only film. Let Donald be the genius; or say that some random puppetmaster is responsible for what Kaufman writes, controlling him from within as in *Being John Malkovich*; or pretend that his scripts, though outwardly witty and inventive, are in fact damnable instruments of violence, like Chuck Barris's TV shows in *Confessions of a Dangerous Mind*.

Better yet, wipe all praise for Kaufman from your memory, after the example of his unforgettable new film, *Eternal Sunshine of the Spotless Mind*.

Even Sturges couldn't have gotten away with that title. It's from Alexander Pope: "Eloisa to Abelard," a poem that previously worked its way into *Being John Malkovich*. In that Kaufman script, the puppetmaster performed Eloisa's story for a streetcorner audience, and got popped on the nose for his trouble. In *Eternal Sunshine of the Spotless Mind*, Kaufman's character Clementine (Kate Winslet) aspires to the pristine oblivion that Eloisa desires; and like Eloisa—like Kaufman's character Joel (Jim Carrey)—she, too, gets popped on the nose (figuratively speaking), not by any outside force but by her own "loose soul unbounded." Pretty fancy stuff, for a sci-fi romantic comedy.

The sci-fi element is a new medical procedure, performed out of a suspiciously shabby second-floor office somewhere on Long Island. Clementine visited this clinic after breaking up with Joel, so she could have him erased from her memory. Upon learning that she dumped him so radically, the outraged Joel now decides he'll do the same to her. "Is there any risk of brain damage?" he asks during his consultation. "Technically speaking," the doctor replies, "the procedure *is* brain damage." To make the patient more comfortable (or to save on office rent?), the actual erasing is done at night in the victim's home, by a couple of slacker technicians whose behavior, in other movies, would be construed as felonious entry and assault. Although some computers are in evidence, the main equipment turns out to be a metal helmet that resembles a colander, and that makes the supine, unconscious Joel look like a little boy playing Flash Gordon.

The methods to which Joel has resorted may seem crude and desperate, but they're nothing compared with his behavior. As the action shifts to the inside of his mind (where much of the movie will now play out), you watch him live again through a series of fast-fading moments with Clementine, each of which turns out to be dominated by his own nastiness. The walls of rooms fly apart around him, faces melt into unformed wax, rows of book covers turn a uniform white; and as these things vanish, so too does Joel's memory of his brutal coldness toward Clementine, his unforgivable insults. The effective target of the brain-wipe, apparently, is not the pain that she caused him, but his knowledge of the suffering he inflicted on her. It's no wonder, then, that he begins softening toward her, as guilt loosens its grip; and when, by way of plot complication, the dreaming Joel hears his technicians talk about Clementine, it's no wonder that their spookily echoing voices move him to resist the procedure.

Now one track of the story is taking place inside Joel, as he struggles to hold on to a memory of Clementine; and one track takes place in the world outside, where Clementine puzzles over a residue of feeling that keeps troubling her, a nameless and unaccountable spot on her mind. This set-up provides Kaufman with the challenges he revels in (don't ever let him sucker you into a game of three-dimensional chess); but it also offers an occasion for the more fundamental movie pleasures. Kaufman himself takes advantage of the structure by delivering thrills in the *Lonedale Operator* tradition, with Joel involved in a prolonged chase sequence and Clementine starring as the feisty gal-in-peril. For Michel Gondry, the film's director (and a co-author of its story), the script serves as a great excuse for a magic show (among my favorite tricks: the Amazing Shrinking Joel, crouched under a kitchen table at age 4). And for a couple of quick-change artists like Winslet and Carrey, the screenplay is an invitation to perform, perform, perform.

Winslet is especially chameleonic, since Clementine is changeable even when she isn't popping in and out of Joel's memories and fantasies. She's a lush young woman of variable hair color, sometimes walking around under something called "Blue Ruin," sometimes wearing a shade that goes with her name and favorite sweatshirt. Carrey's Joel, by contrast, is a somber, inward type, who wraps dark clothes around his meatless frame and hides his eyes behind an awning of loose hair. If you're stuck with an image of Carrey as hyperactive goofball, you will find his performance here to be astonishingly nuanced and restrained. In fact, you'll make that discovery even if you've got a clearer idea of him, and know how well he can tap into both vulnerability and an intense spitefulness.

What I love best about *Eternal Sunshine of the Spotless Mind* is the way Joel abandons that spitefulness in the end, if only provisionally, and Clementine lets herself settle down for once, so the two can share a persuasive, deeply moving moment of forgiveness. I also love how this ending prompts you to return, in your own memory, to the daringly lengthy prologue to the film, re-evaluating the meaning of its dialogue and key events. You revisit something Clementine had said to Joel—"Right now, I'm glad you're nice"— and you understand it in a devastatingly new way. You recall how Joel had found a dent in his car, and you now see the justice of the note he left for the driver in the next parking space. Joel himself didn't see it; when he scrawled "Thank you" on a scrap of paper, he was merely being sarcastic, in a hopelessly passive way. But a dent is a kind of memory set in metal; and by the end of the movie, you know why Joel has reason to feel grateful for this one.

I'm grateful, too. Thank you, Donald Kaufman. Thank you.

The Nation, April 4, 2004

Kings and Queen

She has the face of a mermaid—a real one, not a Disney blonde. The wide undulant mouth drinks in her world like oxygen; the hazel eyes reflect a bent and wavering light. The hair is wavy, of course, but also dark, weighty, enveloping, so that it looks more drenched than flowing. The luminous skin must be cool to the touch. No one with any sense would call this woman pretty; she's too beautifully unsettled for that.

He, on the other hand, is almost handsome, in a pinch-faced, unkempt, rodent-eyed, moss-toothed, dithering, vituperative, abandoned kind of way. You wonder that such a trim little man should persist in treating the entire world as a locked door, and himself as a battering ram. You marvel, once you've grown accustomed to his base level, that he never looks much worse for the blows. At times he even manages to dress with dash—although then, too, he overdoes things, alarming people by wrapping himself in the red cloak of a Renaissance duelist.

She is Nora (Emmanuelle Devos), the tragic heroine of Arnaud Desplechin's *Kings and Queen*. He is Ismaël (Mathieu Amalric), the film's comic hero. That two such characters should be able to coexist tells you most of what you need to know about Desplechin's uncontainable talent. His mind operates in bursts: unpredictable, overlapping flares of realism, fantasy, slapstick, pathos, poetry, suspense, which light up a broader emotional terrain than you'll find in any ten other movies this month. As with his mélange of genres, so too with his visual style—the way he cuts quickly, jumps through multiple views of a subject, pores over faces with a hand-held camera, changes the lighting in midscene. This abundance, which at times seems no more discriminating than life itself, impresses you at once. How could it not, when the musical score encompasses Anton Webern, Henry Mancini and a crew of French hip-hoppers?

What's not immediately apparent in all this is that Desplechin's bursts are orderly. They fall into patterns. With the credible improbability of life itself, they give Nora and Ismaël a shared past and the hint of a conjoined future.

Nora, who narrates her part of the story in an incongruously wispy voiceover, first comes before the camera looking like the capable, responsible one. Beautifully groomed, 35 years old and the manager of a Paris art gallery, she is a woman who is used to having men wait on her—including the roughly handsome, wealthy fellow who is about to become her third husband. At this early stage in the film, only the slightest faults disrupt the surface calm, as Nora takes the train to Grenoble to visit her father (an elderly professor of classics) and her vacationing 10-year-old son (the product of her marriage to a man who died young). When her father suddenly has to go to the hospital, Nora remains controlled (or is able to pull herself quickly back to order), even as she finds herself charged with the care of a dying man.

Ismaël, who turns out to have been Nora's second husband, is clearly the incapable and irresponsible one. He, too, goes into the hospital at the start of the film—a psychiatric hospital in his case, to which he is committed by an unidentified third party. Given that Ismaël lets his phone ring off the hook, distributes bad checks like confetti, owes hundreds of thousands of francs in back taxes and keeps a footstool positioned under the noose in his living room—not to use, mind you, just to clarify his thoughts by showing himself it's an option—you may imagine that a little observation is called for, perhaps some adjustment of meds. Granted, Ismaël is a professional musician, the violist in a quartet, and so may indulge in a little aggression against bourgeois norms. (Or maybe not. His parents, who smilingly decline to untie him from his bed, keep him company in the hospital by reciting Guillaume Apollinaire's "Zone"—and yet they manage to live as grocers in a provincial town.) But even by artists' standards, or those of his dope-fiend lawyer, Ismaël is a wreck. How did Nora last six years with him?

The answer is that the cracks in Nora run deeper than you would have supposed from those subtle, early infelicities: the odd pause in the action, the momentarily blank response. Pretty soon, to your astonishment, you see her trying to put her one treasure, her son, into the adoptive care of Ismaël, who is still padding around the loony bin in his bathrobe, so she can go unencumbered into her new marriage to a man she frankly does not love. This is far from the worst that Nora has done, or is yet to suffer—but by this point *Kings and Queen* has drawn you so thoroughly into her emotions that you almost expect her to succeed in her desperate plan, and almost want her to.

As for Ismaël, he has no plans. He will put his lawyer in the clear, rescue a suicidal young woman, heal a rift in his family, resume a challenging musical career and set Nora's son on the path toward adulthood, all while behaving as if his pants are on fire. Blundering has seldom accomplished such a full and useful agenda.

A woman's story of guilty memories, sudden death, emotional violence, self-suppression; a man's story of pranks, pratfalls, sex and double talk. How does Desplechin make them one? On the most superficial and least satisfying level, he glues them together with imagery. Everywhere you look in *Kings and Queen* you see pictures from art history—reproduced as posters or calendars, framed in Nora's gallery or her father's home—all based on classical mythology. Through them, you are to understand that Ismaël is a laboring Hercules, though much smaller in stature, and Nora is a type of Leda, ravished by the terrible god who is her father. This doesn't get you very far—nor does Desplechin much advance your feeling for the characters by naming one after a defiant Ibsen heroine and the other after Melville's shipwreck survivor. I write off these frills to Desplechin's exuberance. His mind is so busy he can't stop himself from applying ornament to every surface.

Fortunately, though, there is a deeper unity to *Kings and Queen*, which comes from Desplechin's understanding of people's moral possibilities—an understanding that deserves to be called classical. He sees that Nora and Ismaël might be able to free themselves from their circumstances but not from their own natures. Hope therefore lies in their becoming more fully themselves, however frightening or absurd that may be. Ismaël must refuse yet another responsibility, the biggest of his life; Nora must burn something more out of herself, from the core. Then they may arrive at as happy an ending as life's troubled, ceaseless flow ever allows.

Desplechin describes *Kings and Queen* differently, of course. As a screenwriter and director, he thinks of how the film plays out in time: "A woman's destiny in an hour and five minutes. Another hour for the labors of Hercules. And ten minutes to save a child. We charge as fast as possible along all the fairy tales from which our lives are woven." Humans are fast, all right—blink and we're gone—but in naming the stuff of our brief lives, Desplechin does too little justice to himself, and to everything he's miraculously worked into his movie. Far more than most of his contemporaries, he knows we are woven of both story and substance, our old fables perpetually crossed with new blood, breath, spit, bile, song.

Ismaël, who quotes Yeats, might remind him of that. Ismaël would describe *Kings and Queen* as "the uncontrollable mystery on the bestial floor," in less than two and a half hours.

The Nation, May 30, 2005

A History of Violence

Women and children everywhere live with men who are killers. A slight exaggeration; they live in fact with modest, decent men, who killed at some point in the past as soldiers. My father was one of them. He had fought in Patton's infantry in World War II; and though that service was a source of pride to him, the experience of it was something he kept very quiet. From hanging around when he was with his veterans' group, I learned (under a child's cloak of invisibility) that some men separate themselves from war by talking a lot about their soldiering, and some do it by talking little. In neither case, though, are they likely to own up to killing. Someone else must have pulled the trigger.

Our books and movies and television shows are heavily populated by those others: the heroes who did what they had to do. Every nation adores them, although few countries do it so piously as the United States. We Americans believe, as an article of faith, that every front door opens onto a frontier, where the law can't protect women and children. Liberty Valance is always at large in our imaginations, and a big, suffering man is always around to shoot him.

But what if that defender were not a solitary gunman? What if he were instead the quiet, loving dad who had killed in his other life? How would we feel if that man, today, proved to be good at slaughter? These are the exaggerations—slight, of course—that bring shivering life to David Cronenberg's *A History of Violence*.

At the film's core are Tom and Edie Stall (Viggo Mortensen and Maria Bello), a couple who love each other so intensely, and are so tender toward their kids, that you ache for every moment of their doomed happiness. As a brief yet unendurable prologue shows you, two drifters are making their way cross-country, robbing and killing with a leisurely, irritable indifference. Soon the back roads must lead them to the Stalls' Indiana town. An autumn chill has started to settle on the landscape, which you might sense is readying itself for death. For a long time, though, the Stalls innocently believe that turning leaves are just signs of a new school year.

Their teenage son currently faces nothing worse than a locker-room bully; their little daughter sometimes worries about monsters, but only the kind that lurk in closets. Edie practices law, manages the house and flirts with her husband; and Tom, day by day, goes mildly about the business of running a Main Street diner—chatting with his handful of customers, joshing with the grill man, tidying up the two pieces of litter that are the sum of the town's sinfulness. Every flash of the little gold cross around Tom's neck testifies to his simple goodness, and to an imminent crucifixion.

When Cronenberg can at last wring no more foreboding out of these scenes of ordinary life, the murderers stalk into the cafe. What happens next turns the gentle paterfamilias into "American hero Tom Stall" (so the newscasters say). "I just did what anybody would do," mutters Tom, mouthing the formula with rather less conviction than is customary. You can see from the way he flips through TV channels that he is impatient for this episode to end—which it won't, of course. With the inevitability of a Kafka story, and with a comparably grotesque and funny precision of detail, new killers are soon replacing the old ones at Tom's counter stools. These fresh murderers are more numerous than the first batch, more jeering and expert. Worse still, they insist they know Tom.

I'm not sure how much of this story comes straight from the source (a graphic novel by John Wagner and Vince Locke), how much was invented by screenwriter Josh Olson and how much is pure Cronenberg; but I know that *A History of Violence* develops with the singleness of purpose, and the rigor, of a mathematical demonstration, one that begins with a commonly accepted truth and ends with brains spattered across the floor. The style (as in *Crash*) is distanced, composed and lingering at first, until it gains speed and force with the story's momentum. The action is both balanced and outrageous. Edie Stall, in happier days, plays dress-up for Tom, but later she is stripped bare; young Jack (Ashton Holmes) starts out by using his self-deprecating wit as a defense, but later he turns into an attack dog of sarcasm. Even the performers who are given scope to misbehave—Ed Harris and William Hurt, playing wise guys from one of hell's more laughable circles—fit neatly into the film's symmetrical equations.

Tom, of course, is the character who goes through the biggest reversal, which is all the more astonishing for being effected through Viggo Mortensen's body. When first seen, Mortensen's Tom is the Honest Abe Lincoln of coffee shops; the flesh clings so tightly to his bones, you'd think there'd be no room to conceal anything. He speaks with a patience and simplicity that are just this side of aw-shucks; and his eyes, though set far, far back from you, seem amused rather than distant. Later, when this man begins to change, Cronenberg bets the movie on Mortensen's ability to bring depth to a face that you thought was all surface. The camera tends to stay fixed on him, in close-up; and with little more than a curl of the left side of his mouth, Mortensen seems to sneer, snarl, gasp in despair and prepare to weep, all in the space of a few seconds.

And he does it without talking. Although there's a lot of good, sharp dialogue in *A History of Violence*, many of the strongest scenes are wordless, as if the movie had emerged from silence and sought to return to it as the natural state. In retrospect, you can see this trait, too, as a matter of balance. At the beginning of this fable of male bloodiness, and of the women and children who live with it, a little girl stands speechless before the man who will kill her. At the end of the story, it's Tom's daughter who is silent as she admits him back into the home, setting a plate at dinner for the man who has killed.

She has no need to talk, there being no alternative to her father's return; and he's got nothing he can say for himself.

The Nation, October 24, 2005

The Death of Mr. Lazarescu

Honey, let's go see that three-hour Romanian movie, about the sick old man who's lying on a gurney! Oh, you mean the new Ion Fiscuteanu picture—the one where he spits up, mumbles and falls asleep? Sure, darling, but we'd better buy our tickets online. *The Death of Mr. Lazarescu* is going to sell out!

May it be so—because however drab and draggy it may sound in synopsis, *The Death of Mr. Lazarescu* is a great movie.

Granted, it really is a three-hour ride with a dying man, portentously named Dante Remus Lazarescu: a 62-year-old engineer (played by the grizzled and blubbery Fiscuteanu) who is trucked this way and that through the Bucharest night, leaking confused words and bodily wastes at a series of unhelpful hospitals. You might say the film proceeds by subtraction. It progressively takes away Lazarescu's energy, mobility, command of language, control of bowels, tongue, clothes, hair and autonomy, until the complete man you saw at the beginning—pained and panting but still furnished with a home, habits, neighbors, family and sarcasm—is reduced to a slab of flesh under a sheet.

But *The Death of Mr. Lazarescu* also proceeds by addition, which perhaps explains one small part of its greatness. While Lazarescu is descending on his nighttime journey toward zero, the film builds up an entire social world around him—one that is harrowing, funny, infuriating, outrageous and sometimes profoundly moving.

The pileup begins in a hideaway typical of an aging widower: dirty dishes clustered next to the sink, towers of old newspapers stacked in the living room, voices yammering incessantly on TV and cats sprawled on every stick of furniture. Lazarescu doesn't live in this apartment so much as wear it, like his snug knit cap or polo shirt. You can sense the space clinging to him, permeated by his humidity and odor. Except for the cats (which seem to multiply every time the camera turns in a new direction), he is on his own— alone and waiting. Complaining of a persistent headache and vomiting, he has phoned for an ambulance; and while his request is going unanswered, minute after minute, there's nothing for him to do but pour a drink of some nasty caramel-colored stuff, rub his stomach, call the ambulance service again, take some medicine, grouse to the cats, put on a fresh polo shirt (he's vomited on the old one) and call his married sister to argue (with a certain eloquence, an intellectual keenness) about money. The light is dull and waxy, even in the kitchen. When Lazarescu settles down for any length of time, halting the hand-held camera in its wanderings, the image trembles slightly, as if palsied.

You and Lazarescu are allowed to steep in this woozy isolation until the director and co-writer, Cristi Puiu, is good and ready to introduce other people—starting with a big, booming neighbor and his pincushion wife. When interrupted by Lazarescu, who has ventured across the landing to ask for help, these two exemplars of the philosophy that "Life goes on!" scarcely bother to listen to the sick man or look closely at him, so intent are they on continuing their chronic warfare over his head—also around him, and in front. While his legs suddenly turn to water and the lights on the landing keep blinking off, the neighbors interrupt their self-absorption only to admonish Lazarescu about his drinking, or to offer a little pork moussaka (just the thing for someone who can't keep down an aspirin). Monsters of comic invention, these Bickersons would be enough in themselves to kill off poor Lazarescu, except that the paramedic finally enters, with a worried frown at all she sees.

This is Mioara (Luminita Gheorghiu), the film's other central character, who will soon take Lazarescu on a ride that unexpectedly lasts all night—or into eternity, if you prefer. A compact, middle-aged woman, redheaded and down at the mouth, she conforms at first to the film's pattern by ignoring Lazarescu. It's a routine, the practice of which, I believe, is not confined to Bucharest: When a slovenly, reeking old guy complains of vague ills, you excuse yourself as soon as possible. Yet some urging of professional pride— or some remark dropped by Lazarescu, who at this stage remains voluble—prods Mioara awake, to do more than treat Lazarescu symptomatically for alcoholism. She examines him and realizes he needs attention.

For the remaining two hours of the movie, attention is exactly what he won't get.

Between 10 o'clock on Saturday night and dawn on Sunday, Mioara carts her patient to four hospitals, each of which has its own atmosphere, rhythm and manners, and its own way of dismissing Lazarescu. At the trauma center, everyone orbits warily about a tall, rail-like doctor with the beard of Abe Lincoln and the attitude of an aggrieved prophet. He condemns Lazarescu on sight as a worthless drunk and excoriates Mioara as an idiot for having brought him into the emergency room; then, almost as an afterthought, the doctor writes an order for Lazarescu to get a CAT scan, at a different hospital.

On to the brighter, more modern University Hospital, where the usual insults soon give way to collegial interplay and gallows humor, carried out over Lazarescu's supine form. The neurologist, who tramps around in a belted red nightgown, flirts with the ER doctor. The radiologist, biting snappily into his chewing gum, issues a continual stream of grim wisecracks, among which is a fatal judgment on Lazarescu.

At the next stop, a harsh and shadowless hospital for neurosurgery, the doctors are interested only in themselves. Mioara is of insufficient rank to be allowed to speak to them and must be so informed, loudly and repeatedly. As for Lazarescu, he figures to these doctors as a hairy, obese procedural inconvenience, who is therefore to be disposed of procedurally. Just before daybreak, Mioara delivers her charge to the final hospital: an anteroom, you'd think, either to the next life or to nothingness, deserted, echoing, dimly lit, staffed by women doctors who speak in dreamy murmurs.

So *The Death of Mr. Lazarescu* arrives at last at a place of exhaustion and quiet, where the human animal is revealed in its bare material essence: a place of mystery. Every moment along the way has been vivid and convincing; every interaction, emotionally charged. And the deepest, most sustained of these interactions—the last relationship Lazarescu will ever have—turns out to be with Mioara.

At first, when he is still talking, she lets him converse with her only grudgingly, killing time on the road to the trauma center. She just wants someone to take him off her hands. But the more the doctors push her around, the more she pushes back, claiming this case as her own. The more Lazarescu weakens, losing contact with the world around him, the stronger grows Mioara's emotional bond with him. At the climax, in the neurologists' hospital, she rises to a level of heroic defiance against the doctors and their arrogance—while Lazarescu summons the last strength of his life to make a grand refusal, not only for himself but also, I suspect, for her.

Co-written with Razvan Radulescu, *The Death of Mr. Lazarescu* is the second feature to be directed by the 39-year-old Puiu, and the first in his projected six-film series on aspects of love, inspired by Eric Rohmer's *Six Moral Tales*. After winning a prize at the 2005 Cannes Festival (despite a reported defection at the press screening of all but a dozen viewers), *The Death of Mr. Lazarescu* provided last fall's New York Film Festival with a peak experience and is now opening for a theatrical run at New York's Film Forum, billed as a comedy.

It is funny, sometimes. But what really makes me throw back my head and laugh is not the film itself but the joy of seeing this magnificent picture now playing in a movie house.

The Nation, May 8, 2006

Pan's Labyrinth

Imagine your bad, false father as a giant toad, lazy and arrogant, that squats in the mucky depths of a dead tree, fattening on foot-long bugs. Or imagine this same monstrous father as something closer to human but faceless, hairless, sexless and naked, with dead-white skin hanging in folds. This sluggish, forked biped slumbers before the fire in a subterranean banquet hall, oblivious to the rich décor or the magnificent feast spread on the table. It wants to eat *you*, little girl, and comes at you when roused with eyeballs fixed in the palms of its hands. To see, for this thing, is to grab and kill.

Now think of a fully human stepfather: a fascist military officer serving in Franco's victorious army. The gloomy lair of this Captain Vidal is an old mill, set in the woods and mountains where he has been sent to hunt a few remaining partisans. Your widowed mother has married this man—why, you can't understand—and so you must either live under his power or else, like the partisans, find a way to rebel. But Vidal is harder to vanquish than a giant toad, harder to elude than a cannibal slug. He, too, sees only to grab and kill, but he doesn't hunger for you. He wants to consume your mother, by pulling a baby son from her womb.

If I write that you must undergo this trial—you, rather than young Ofelia, the heroine with the rosy face and unpromising name—it's because the magic that many films promise actually works in *Pan's Labyrinth*. Beginning with the dizzyingly hypnotic opening shot—or, even before there's an image, with the evocative sounds of the wind stirring, a lullaby sighing, a child gasping for breath—writer-director Guillermo del Toro succeeds in submerging you in Ofelia's memory and imagination, where grown-up threats and struggles turn into fairy tales.

Gliding through the woods at night, del Toro's camera discovers Ofelia lying on the ground, then tilts and comes closer as if it were an intelligent winged creature, curious and sympathetic. It approaches her bloodied face. Then it plunges into one of her eyes—the first of many eyes in this movie—and so into the volumes of her mind, which pulse with firelight and shadows. The interior of this child's skull is part puppet stage and part Piranesi engraving, reverberating with a basso narrator's fable about a princess who lived in a kingdom underground, and who ventured fatally into the world above. The camera rises on cue through a domed stair hall, toward an oculus that blazes with light. By the time a flash blanks out the screen, allowing the shot to continue (without seeming interruption) into a forest scene, the camera has you magnetized. You are going to be drawn along on all of Ofelia's adventures—but despite appearances, you have not been drawn entirely outside her thoughts. This daylit forest, too, lies partly within the maze of the little girl's consciousness.

Moviegoers who are just catching up with del Toro should know that this is not the first time he has told a story of the Spanish Civil War, or put a child's thoughts at the center of his movie. He did both in a 2001 release, *The Devil's Backbone*; and if you want to go even further back in his career, into his ostensibly pure genre movies, you might note that his insect-fear masterpiece, *Mimic*, is at heart concerned with the world of an autistic boy.

In *Pan's Labyrinth*, you may note the recurrence from these earlier pictures of favorite del Toro motifs: the intervention of a large, clacking insect, for example, which welcomes Ofelia to the woods and guides her through the movie, or the great importance that Captain Vidal assigns to chronology. (Not only does he devote himself obsessively to a cracked pocket watch; he dwells in a room dominated by the mill's old wooden wheel, as if he were living inside the mechanism of an enormous timepiece.) If these deliberate recyclings are evidence in del Toro of a heightened auteurist self-regard, then I say he's earned it. Everything he's done to date reaches a new stage of maturity, beauty and depth of feeling in *Pan's Labyrinth*.

I can credit much of the film's impact to Guillermo Navarro's cinematography, whose storybook palette is rich enough to encompass everything from the deep violets of a nocturnal scene to the soft, fluttering white of seeds drifting through shafts of sunlight. Thanks to Navarro, the images are more than clear and more than tactile. You can almost smell them: the worn stone of a Celtic carving, the smoke of the partisans' abandoned campfire, the blood that trickles over a tongue or (most of all) the moist odor of dirt and leaves clinging to Pan, the towering, obsequious yet not quite trustworthy faun who appears to Ofelia and instructs her on what she must do.

All this is compelling, but the deepest power of *Pan's Labyrinth* lies in the actress playing Ofelia: 12-year-old Ivana Baquero. One of the challenges of her role is that she gets to assert herself only with characters who aren't really there. These are the film's various computer-generated critters, plus the faun (who is a creation of actor Doug Jones, a hidden puppeteer and a ton of makeup). Baquero's scenes with live actors, though, require her to be almost exclusively reactive. In a moon-besotted movie that continually contrasts the true time of the lunar cycle with the false time of clocks, she is herself a kind of satellite, reflecting the light of stars. And what stars: Sergi López at his coldest, most brutal and slicked-back as Vidal; Ariadna Gil as Ofelia's drooping flower of a mother, clinging tenderly to a final hope; Maribel Verdú (Mercedes) as Vidal's sunken-cheeked housekeeper, whose head is bowed, whose eyes are lowered, whose voice is an acquiescent murmur, until suddenly they're not. You might think that Baquero would fade compared with these presences; but through sheer attentiveness (which is to say, the talent of a born actress to forget herself) she shines as much as anyone.

What is it, though, that shines through *Pan's Labyrinth* as a whole? I'd say it's the power of imagination—not imagination as Vidal misunderstands it, as a capacity for soothing self-delusion, but as the will to say no. Ofelia has the imagination to ask questions and disobey. Vidal, who knows how to be fanciful only with a straight razor, fails to imagine that someone—a woman, even— might find the strength to disrupt his monstrous order.

I don't know how you will value the imagination of *Pan's Labyrinth* against the quasi-documentary realism of the only film I know as a touchstone, Victor Erice's great *The Spirit of the Beehive*. It's a question of the season, I suppose. There is a clear, wintry light to Erice's film (which also concerns a fugitive hiding in the Spanish countryside and a child's dreams of wonder)—an observational style and dramatic irony that may suit the chillier times in your life, and that were fitting to the film's era. *The Spirit of the Beehive* was made and released when Franco still held power. Del Toro's lunar, springtime fabulism, by contrast, is appropriate to another era, when the people of Spain know that dictators don't rule forever. There is comfort in his film; but there is also a determination to remember, to keep faith and to encourage.

The beauty of *Pan's Labyrinth* exists for its own sake. The magic has a purpose.

The Nation, January 22, 2007

Syndromes and a Century

Life isn't a meaning, said Chaplin, but a desire. I may be quoting inaccurately, but given the sentiment, who cares? Chaplin was so precise in his art that he could roller-skate blindfolded to the edge of an abyss; and yet, true to his words, he seemed to love the audience's giddiness a little more than his own supreme poise, the image of an open road more than the certainty of "The End."

Giddiness, openness, poise, desire: These words may do as well as any to suggest the life you find everywhere in the inexplicable but wondrous *Syndromes and a Century*. Written and directed by Thailand's Apichatpong Weerasethakul (or Joe, as he's often called in the West), *Syndromes and a Century* is a work of immaculate craftsmanship, but one that is impossible to summarize, any more than a wind-sown arboreal orchid (one of the film's main props) could be brought to ground. All you might say, in a pinch, is that the movie consists of scenes in and around two present-day hospitals, one somewhere in the countryside and the other in Bangkok.

No story links these two places; and since a separate stretch of movie is dedicated to each—first the rural hospital, then the urban one—you might even say that the running time sets them apart. Nothing crosses this divide except a Cheshire-cat smile. A woman called Dr. Toey (Nantarat Sawaddikul) and a man called Dr. Nohng (Jaruchai Iamaram) appear in both halves of the film, but I can't say whether these figures are meant to be the same people working in different places or whether the hospitals are staffed by identically named look-alikes. Incidents recur, too— a soldier awkwardly declares his love for Dr. Toey, an elderly monk recounts a troubling dream about a chicken, a young monk undergoes dental treatment—but with variations that alter the tone of each encounter. (The outcomes can't be changed because there aren't any, cause and effect having been suspended as airily as the orchid.) On a higher level of variation, motifs including exercise classes, public recreations and renditions of pop music are enacted in rural and urban versions, cheerfully but to no apparent purpose.

Do these doublings mean anything at all? In statements and interviews, Joe has spoken of them as expressions of his belief in reincarnation. But since the film's monks have the best lines about that topic, I will concentrate on Joe's explanation that his parents were doctors "who raised us kids in a house provided by the small-town hospital where they worked." This place has now changed so much, he says, that "the landscapes and hospital buildings that

I remember simply don't exist anymore." Unable to recapture his memories of the past, he has taken pleasure in recapturing the feelings evoked by his memories. Beyond that, he says, *Syndromes and a Century* is "an experiment in re-creation of my parents' lives before I was born," with the movie's first half focused on a figure ostensibly representing his mother and the second half on the father figure.

Plausible. But if Dr. Toey and Dr. Nohng are supposed to become Joe's parents, they don't make any progress on it in this movie, where their sole encounter is charming, brief and entirely official. There's plenty of desire in part one, but it flows from a love-sick soldier (Nu Nimsomboon) toward Dr. Toey, who can respond only with a diagnosis; from Dr. Toey toward a botanist (Sophon Pukanok), who seems in recollection to have been more interested in the arboreal orchid than in her; and from a pop-singing dentist (Arkanae Cherkam) toward an object of romantic interest who is unattainable, being a monk (Sakda Kaewbuadee).

In part two, desire is better satisfied, since Dr. Nohng gets to neck in the hospital corridor with his girlfriend (Jarunee Saengtupthim) before slipping with her into a basement office. Yet gratification, O Noble Siddhartha, may not add up to happiness. The girlfriend wants Dr. Nohng to relocate to some Brutalist development zone (she's got construction photos, which are not encouraging), as if his hospital were not sufficiently cold and fluorescent. In Part One, by contrast, even though love goes unfulfilled, the characters live in a lush and sunny place that is itself both solace and sweet mystery.

The notion that the jungle can spring beautiful surprises on you just as readily as it tosses up tigers or sorcerers has been a part of Joe's work since his first feature, *Mysterious Object at Noon* (2000): a quasi documentary in which he began telling a story and then went around Thailand having different individuals and groups continue it, at one point in full-scale folk opera performance. As in any *cadavre exquis*, the gaps, incongruities and wild transformations could strike you by turns as humorous or grotesque, suggestive or uncanny. The difference in *Mysterious Object* was that they also seemed communal and revelatory: glimpses into a startling inner life shared by people all over Thailand.

So, too, in *Syndromes and a Century*, unexpected marvels keep popping up in everyday circumstances. That charming meeting between Dr. Toey and Dr. Nohng, for example, is a personnel interview, which she conducts when he reports for work at the hospital. It's a perfectly normal occasion, except for her asking questions such as, "Which do you prefer to draw, circles or triangles?" The answer, in this movie, has got to be circles. Dr. Nohng delivers it with the same quiet thoughtfulness that he accords all of Dr. Toey's non sequiturs, and she accepts his response in the same spirit, as if nothing he says could be wrong. "What do the initials DDT stand for?" she asks, apropos of nothing. After a moment's hesitation, he replies, "Destroy Dirty Things," and she, following a pause, writes the words down.

This spirit of acceptance seems to me to be the key to the movie's doublings. However Joe might explain them, they come off simply as alternate possibilities, which arise in no particular order and need be given no absolute value. Of course, you might prefer some to others—there are plenty of disappointments in the film, along with aggravations, failures and disabling maladies—but since all of them could be real, they all seem equally alive, and miraculous.

How so? Look at the endlessly delightful compositions that Joe gives you, with the characters often grouped toward one side and the other left unpopulated, so the frame is ripe with potential. Look at the light, which can be paradoxically strong in the distance and shadowed in the foreground. (Nature, in this movie, makes no assumptions about which part of the picture is important.) Watch how freely your point of view changes—now showing you one angle on a scene, now (for no special reason) a different angle that's just as good, and now wandering off to study something irrelevant but lovely.

Or listen as the crooning dentist gets closer to his beloved. Standing on a veranda in the night, the dentist recounts the tragic death years ago of his brother, then wonders if that long-lost boy could have been reincarnated as this monk.

"No," says the monk, with a broad-mindedness typical of *Syndromes and a Century*. "In my last life, I wasn't human."

The Nation, May 7, 2007

Paprika

The plot is a molasses coat hook, a cobweb parachute, a steam shovel made of butterflies. The story won't hold up in Satoshi Kon's *Paprika*—nor should it, this being an animated psychoanalytic sci-fi thriller—and so you hold on to what you can, which above all is your first impression of the title character. She comes before you as a Tokyo girl with bobbed hair the color of spice, a flirt who plants lipstick kisses on her business cards, a motorbike rider and night-cafe talker with a wardrobe that can change in the blink of an eye. She crosses rooftops by flashing from one neon sign to the next, as if every famous face were hers. But back on the ground, if anyone pays her more attention than she wants, she escapes by simply fading from sight.

Paprika is the young woman of everyone's dreams; or rather, to take the movie's plot as literally as it allows, she is a psychiatrist who somehow can enter people's dreams at will. It's a lot more fun than sitting in a chair and listening to patients drone, though also considerably more dangerous. By the end of the movie, nothing less than the whole waking world will be at risk; but whatever impossible complications this wonder-doctor may encounter during her very intimate, boundary-dissolving interventions, those first, high-flying images of her will carry you along. *Paprika* stays in your mind as pure freedom and pure exhilaration.

That can't be said of the straitened character for whom she serves as the inner self. The *Paprika* whom people meet in their dreams is a projection—maybe even a wish fulfillment—of the unsmiling Dr. Atsuko Chiba, a pale and angular woman who invariably wears a suit and keeps her hair pinned up. Unlike her magical alter ego, Dr. Chiba doesn't romp through the night sky. She deals with the day's business as experienced in a corporate tower: troublesome colleagues, a blood-chilling boss, political interference with her research.

But even though cold, controlled Dr. Chiba dwells in the world of the reality principle, she nevertheless faces problems that go beyond the mundane. A device for mind infiltration has vanished from her lab, having been stolen, perhaps, by a dream-terrorist; and as if that's not bad enough, her institute's chief of research has suddenly gone insane. You will not be surprised to learn that these two events are related. After the chief lifts his arm in an imperial salute and marches about stiff-legged while spouting nonsense—like a Dadaist in the Café Voltaire, you'd think, bent on world domination—he falls into a sleep from which he cannot be awakened. With her computer, Dr. Chiba taps into his mind and sees that he's dreaming of a parade, with confetti (though nobody's around to throw it) and music (performed by a band of marching frogs) and a float on which the chief sits enthroned, surrounded and cushioned by thousands of dolls.

Is this the chief's own dream? Or is somebody sinister dreaming it for him?

The answer, of course, is number two; and you won't need to steal an experimental psycho-gizmo to figure out who's the culprit. Despite *Paprika*'s continual melting of one narrative into another—despite its hypnotic swirl of stories within stories—Kon preserves the predictable outlines of each of his genres, including the one that explains whodunit. If you are the sort of moviegoer who insists on being surprised by a plot, then you may be disappointed that you can identify *Paprika*'s mastermind by sure and familiar signs. But surprises abound everywhere in this movie, not just on the level of "Who made that happen?" I'm not sure I know why *anything* happens in this picture; but I'm confident that as you tick off the conventions, Kon will keep startling you with their new and mysterious possibilities.

In fact, Hollywood clichés turn out to be integral to one of the two main categories of dream that Kon proposes in *Paprika*—the good category. Throughout the film, Dr. Chiba/*Paprika* is engaged in treating one Detective Konakawa, a square-jawed, mustached he-man straight out of a thousand hard-boiled police procedurals. The curious thing about Konakawa is that his dreams are a collage of American-style films: a circus picture, a Tarzan adventure, a spy thriller, a police procedural (of course). Konakawa keeps insisting to Dr. Chiba/*Paprika* that he doesn't like movies and never watches them; but an expert psychoanalyst recognizes denial when she hears it. The cure for Konakawa's crippling anxiety must lie in the kind of collective dreaming practiced in movie houses.

This kind of dreaming is shared, but it's also democratic and voluntary and unfolds over time. (First you watch a circus picture, then you watch a Tarzan adventure.) The other kind of dreaming in *Paprika*, the parade dream in which the chief is trapped, is also shared, but in the wrong way. It's dictatorial, coerced and locked into space. Instead of scenes succeeding one another, objects pile up in one place into a mad, random accumulation. The trappings are celebratory—like so many parades, this one pretends to be marching toward triumph—and yet there's a horrific mirthlessness to it. So much of the jumble consists of toys, as if your joining this procession (or being joined to it) were a matter of infantile regression.

But in Konakawa's movie dreams, there's always a tinge of adult regret, and the whiff of grown-up sexual desire.

If all of this sound complicated, I can tell you that Kon's source material, a novel by Yasutaka Tsutsui, is said to be even more convoluted. You can, if you like, simplify still further by watching *Paprika* just for the pictures, secure in the knowledge that you're getting the best damned delirium your moviegoing dollar can buy. (True to his love of genre, Kon bases his drawings on a classic style of comic-book graphics—then compacts and intensifies, as if pressing ten frames into one.) If you're feeling ambitious, though, and want to interpret and not just dream, you can watch *Paprika* as a cartoon feminist *Civilization and Its Discontents*, and Kon will reward that reading, too.

How might the movie be watched by its own resident psychiatrist? I suppose that depends on whether you ask the outer Dr. Chiba or the inner *Paprika*. They sometimes disagree—but that's another swirl in the story.

The Nation, May 24, 2007

Forever

Everybody in Heddy Honigmann's documentary *Forever* visits the dead, but nobody grieves. As the characters come and go in the principal setting—Paris's Père-Lachaise Cemetery—they stroll, relax on benches, scrub the marble or even sing, and the air remains clear and mild for them, as if Honigmann had made time pause at 10 o'clock on a spring morning. In the trees' shade, a speck of life shines on weathered stone: a ladybug creeping across a graveside sculpture. Views of incised symbols fill the screen, one after another, alongside rows of letters, some formally chiseled, some scrawled by a passing hand: random pages, you'd think, in an illustrated book of consolation.

Which of the dead do the living come to see? Frédéric Chopin, Marcel Proust, Oscar Wilde, the husband of an elderly Spanish woman, Maria Callas, Georges Méliès, Amadeo Modigliani, an Armenian man who designed shoes, Yves Montand, Simone Signoret, a forgotten poet of the nineteenth century, Guillaume Apollinaire, Jean-Auguste Ingres and, repeatedly, Jim Morrison (though his many admirers never seem to get to him). Sometimes, little more than curiosity has drawn the visitors. "Have you read his books?" asks Honigmann, unseen behind the camera, of a group of French people paying their respects to Proust. The reply comes with a shrug: "It takes a lot of time to read *À la recherche*." More often, though, the people Honigmann encounters feel they share something with the dead. They show it by offering gifts: a pen for Proust (so he can go on writing), a lipstick kiss for Oscar Wilde, a flower in Poland's colors for Chopin. They also talk about this bond, telling Honigmann of their losses.

"Why did you leave Iran?" she asks a lanky middle-aged man whom she's found by the tomb of the writer Sadegh Hedayat. The man thinks for a moment, then quotes a passage from Hedayat's *The Blind Owl*, about going abroad because of weariness with other people. "I was also a bit tired of everything," the man says of Iran, with a sad grin that tells more. And now that he's in Paris, how does he make his living? He drives a taxi—"but my real reason for living, what keeps me alive, is singing Persian classical music." Will he sing something now? No, the man says. It's not the time or place; but Honigmann waits, with the camera running. No, the man says again, trying not to look at her. His voice isn't warmed up; but Honigmann still waits, pulling in for a tighter shot. "What would you like me to sing?" he asks at last. Sitting next to Sadegh

Hedayat, the taxi driver takes out his notebook, chooses a poem by Hafez and begins to sigh and sob the lines, and his mournful cry continues even after Honigmann has cut from him to a detail of a memorial statue: the face of a shrouded woman, weeping into her hand.

From this small episode, you may begin to understand that the encounters in *Forever* aren't random at all, even though they're as unforced as the rustling of the leaves. So many of the subjects Honigmann chooses, such as Hedayat and the taxi driver, are people who have left home: the elderly widow who fled Madrid during the civil war; the young man from South Korea who found time to read *À la recherche* (but can't explain why it means so much to him, unless he says it in Korean); pianist Yoshino Kimura, of Japanese ancestry, who plays Chopin (another expatriate) in memory of her father. Like the taxi driver, these people have come to Père-Lachaise to feel closer to someone, most often a celebrated artist; and yet the monuments in these quiet lanes, like the visitors' favorite artworks, represent only what's gone.

"This is the tomb that moves me most of all," says Bertrand Beyern, a white-haired man who gives tours of Père-Lachaise, as he stands beside the memorial to Elisa Mercoeur. When Mercoeur died at age 26, in 1835, her mother had her poems inscribed on the gravestone. They were to be her immortality. "But now," Beyern says, "it's completely faded." The camera lingers over a pitted surface, haunted by the ghosts of indecipherable letters. "Soon there won't be much left but a few broken stones."

Forever is an essay about how people may abide with such loss—seeking it out, savoring it, instead of turning away. If they were artists, perhaps they played with absence, as Georges Méliès did. (Honigmann cannily represents him through one of his trick films, in which he showed himself juggling with his severed head.) If something is continually missing from their lives—the sense of sight, for example—they may make an art out of making do. (Two blind men, visitors to the grave of Simone Signoret, return home with a DVD of *Les Diaboliques*, which they listen to with chortling, speculative delight.) As for Honigmann herself: Toward the end of *Forever*, she demonstrates how a filmmaker may do well to cling to the little she's given, and ignore the vastness that escapes her, by recording one of Kimura's performances of Chopin. Shooting straight across the top of the piano, Honigmann frames a close-up of Kimura's face and simply leaves the camera there for the duration of the nocturne. A lesser filmmaker might have cut away to the hands, the expression of a listener, a photograph of the pianist's father; but Honigmann knows that the information you need, and all the emotion, are present in Kimura's intent features, which don't even stay in the frame. They sway in and out—and this corporeal ticking, this swing between here and gone, feels like climax enough.

It's been a long summer, my movie friends. Diversions, reports, polemics, come-ons and a plentiful supply of time-wasters have filled the theaters. Now, at last, comes a film that was made for love. I'd almost forgotten what I was missing until Honigmann reminded me—but that, of course, is what *Forever* is all about.

The Nation, September 24, 2007

There Will Be Blood

By the time the boy lies moaning on the floor, spooned against a father who is helpless to soothe him, the earth has blasted open, fire has whooshed up through an oil derrick and a dozen roustabouts, dwarfed by their handiwork, have raced in all directions across the stony Central California hilltop, trying to contain the immense forces they'd set loose. When at last they could do no more than wait, some had stood silhouetted before the tower of flame, marveling as it raged against an indigo sky. Others had watched from a distance, the glow flickering over their faces, while greasy black clouds spread into lingering daylight to the west. After night fell, around the time the derrick toppled, the boss's assistant had asked if the boy was all right. "No," the boss had calmly said of his son, "he's not," then went on watching the fire. All this, to a clattering on the soundtrack like a gamelan of pots, pans and mixing bowls, beating out insistent variations on lub-dub; and still the gargantuan sequence wasn't over. A fresh day had to break, and wagons loaded with dynamite shoved into the mouth of the fire, before Daniel Plainview could at last lie on the floor of his shack, to caress and restrain his damaged son.

Grim and gleeful, mechanistic and demonic, this tremendous set piece stands out as the most elaborate segment in Paul Thomas Anderson's *There Will Be Blood* but is only one of the film's half-dozen great dramatic eruptions. All of them are instantly recognizable as classic. Each is distinct in setting and style: the Wild West showdown, filmed in a panoramic sweep beside a rising lake of oil; the faith-healing service, in which the camera tracks a preacher's dance back and forth through his pine box of a church; the scene of Daniel Plainview's public humiliation, shot in steady, pitiless close-up beneath a cross of sunlight; the final confrontation between Plainview and his son, executed as an intricate pattern of cross-cutting within an office that's all carved mahogany and shadows. There's even a mad scene that rivals the big oil-strike sequence for virtuosity and violence, despite being shot with just two actors within a basement bowling alley.

You have, of course, seen other movies about the lawless West and the making of American fortunes. You've seen Charles Foster Kane, self-isolated and half-mad, tearing up his Xanadu. (You might as well know: that's where this is going.) But in the aptly titled *There Will Be Blood*, Anderson tells the familiar story not as he's received it from earlier films (much as he's studied them) or even from his putative source, Upton Sinclair's 1927 novel *Oil!*, but as a kind of social realist peyote vision. Utterly fluid yet coming at you in flashes, based on events of a century ago yet intensely present, the film seems as tangible as its desert hills and steam-powered machines but as unfathomable as Daniel Plainview: a rumbling abyss of a man, who will tell you he doesn't like to explain himself.

In this, as in other ways, he is true to the historic character of America's self-made men. As Eric Hobsbawm wrote of the nineteenth century's industrial millionaires, "None had noticeable scruples or could afford to have in an economy and an age where fraud, bribery, slander and if necessary guns were normal aspects of competition. All were hard men, and most would have regarded the question whether they were honest as considerably less relevant to their affairs than the question whether they were smart."

Though Plainview makes his great strike a little later than Hobsbawm's subjects, in 1911, he too is a hard man, who will stake a mining claim even at the expense of dragging his smashed bones across a landscape of bleached rocks; a lying man, who despite his roughneck past affects a gentleman's cooing, round-voweled manner to tell "plainspoken" truths, which aren't; a ruthlessly smart man, who knows of no graver insult than "fool" and is at his most dangerous when he finds he's been played for one.

Where he breaks from type—a departure that makes all the difference to the film—is in his disgust at that cruelest of hoodwinkers: the man of God. The old robber barons could abide the forms of religion when necessary, here dropping an endowment into a strategically advantageous church, there nodding to a sermon that blessed the accumulation of capital. But as much as Plainview aspires to hypocrisy, his one irrepressible, honest impulse is a physical revulsion toward the Almighty and His spokespersons. Reality to Plainview comes down to mechanics, and mechanics in his experience always threatens to become a chain of catastrophes: pulleys that malfunction at the worst moment, beams and hardware that fail to support enough weight, heavy drill bits that slip loose and fall until stopped by somebody's skull. So in this universe of accident and calculation, it must be one more damned trick of chance when Plainview comes snooping for oil in Little Boston, California, his boy H.W. in tow, and winds up negotiating for mineral rights with smooth-faced Eli Sunday, a goat farmer's son who has founded the Church of the Third Revelation.

Sunday, too, is self-made in his way, having anointed himself the evangelist of a new gospel that apparently is still coming in. That this young promoter bargains over the price of a lease doesn't much bother Plainview, who expects as much in business and also expects to win. But the oilman rips himself away with barely concealed anger when Sunday tries to seal the transaction by clasping his hand in prayer. That's too ambitious; that presumes Plainview could be merged into a cozy fellowship ruled by another man's say-so. Never mind that Plainview himself delivers orations on friendship, family and community when he's speaking in public, to sell his services or smooth the way for his operations. In private, he trusts and loves no one but H.W.; and when his relationship with the boy is ruptured—call it fate or another catastrophe of mechanics—Plainview's scorn for Eli Sunday turns into violent hostility.

For all its detailed attention to the building of an industrial fortune—the competition to acquire property, the management of men and equipment, the drive to control both production and transport—*There Will Be Blood* develops into a contest of wills between Plainview and Sunday, and so resolves unexpectedly into an argument about faith. Or, to judge from the malefic exuberance of the final scene, perhaps it's an argument against faith.

So where, you might ask, is the revolution? Admirers of *Oil!* and *Nation* readers may be disappointed to find that Anderson has chucked out the people's soviets, along with the rest of the novel's politics: the labor agitation, the factional debates, the translation of generational conflict into class struggle. If *There Will Be Blood* had pretended to give an accurate picture of its era, this would have been a fatal omission.

But few things can be as useless as a historical drama of historical interest—which is what Anderson would have risked making had he incorporated material that's wholly outside the experience of most of today's viewers. Instead, he's reasonably used his period characters to suggest contemporary political meanings. In Plainview's speeches, you hear a forecast of the present-day public entrepreneur, with his promises that the market (meaning himself) will shower bread, sunshine and good schools wherever he makes a buck; while in Sunday's preaching, you hear the voice of every modern fundamentalist election-broker who declares that Jesus alone (meaning himself) can set our society right.

In reality, as you may have observed, these two figures have been allied for decades. Anderson's twist is to set them against each other, in an imaginative reordering of society so radical that it almost qualifies as political in itself. He distorts history, the source novel and your sense of the contemporary scene. And what do you get in exchange? Just the invigoration of seeing God and Mammon going for each other's throat.

Of course, if Plainview and Sunday were allegorical, there would be no satisfaction in the spectacle. The antagonists have to be fleshed-out vessels of the promised blood; and so I come to Daniel Day-Lewis's performance as Plainview.

You can see how Day-Lewis pieced together the outward elements of the characterization: the slight stoop and limp that testify to old injuries suffered in the pit; the huffing and wheezing that suggest years of breathing rock dust and oil fumes; the grand, baritonal way of forming words, which Plainview must have copied from the era's classiest stump speakers; the habit of pausing and working his jaw, which betrays the agitation simmering beneath every show of patience. Other actors, too, could have figured out such signs. Day-Lewis establishes them and then makes you forget their presence, much as you ignore the scaffolding of the oil derrick once the forces of nature come blasting through. The emotion that Day-Lewis taps seems so spontaneous, and so volcanic, that his performance ought to be listed in the end credits as a special effect, along with the computer-generated imagery used for the fiery gusher. Even here, of course, there must have been calculation. I imagine that in preparing the performance, Day-Lewis might have worked backward from his biggest moments, planning when to hint at restrained fury, when to release a note of sarcasm or contempt and when to let loose an outburst, always increasing the magnitude toward the climax in the final scene. But this still says nothing about the complexity of the characterization—for example, the way Plainview will pet and imprison H.W. in a single gesture—or the wonderful paradox of an actor's displaying such power while being attentive to everyone else in the scene. Instead of blowing away his fellow players, Day-Lewis makes them all better by the sheer intensity of his focus on them. To mention only the most obvious case: the admirable Paul Dano, who could have played Eli Sunday opposite any Plainview and been memorable, meets the challenge in Day-Lewis's eyes and makes himself uncanny.

If there had to be one word for *There Will Be Blood*, in fact, I suppose "uncanny" would do. The score, composed by Jonny Greenwood of Radiohead (with a major assist from Johannes

Brahms), wraps you in a brooding, unnerving, exhilarating atmosphere in which massed strings can swarm like uneasy flies or shriek like a siren. The cinematography, by Robert Elswit, confronts you with a high, desolate terrain that sometimes, in the shifting light and color, resembles a crouched and breathing beast. Plainview wants nothing to do with the otherworldly, and given the screenplay's construction, he emphatically gets the final word on that subject; but the sounds and images contradict him.

There was something uncanny as well in the season's other downward-spiraling western, *No Country for Old Men*—that Calvinist horror show stalked by Javier Bardem as God's own bogeyman. Why the Coen brothers should believe in the total depravity of humankind and the need for grace (withheld more often than given), I really don't know; but they turned this worldview into an exceptionally well-made movie. It's so immaculate, it will provoke anxiety in you for two hours straight without so much as mussing your hair.

There Will Be Blood, by contrast, is flamboyant rather than immaculate, not just well made but brilliantly and intuitively expressive; and it leaves you feeling shaken but also a little stronger. Maybe Plainview wins his argument against faith, but he loses a deeper argument with H.W.—one about trust and kindness. His loss; your gain.

The Nation, January 28, 2008

24 City

When the full effect hit, about twelve hours after I had seen his *24 City* at the New York Film Festival, it occurred to me that Jia Zhangke must now be the most important filmmaker in the world. Whether he's the most inventive, entertaining, moving, thoughtful or visually enthralling is another question. I think he might well be in the running in all those categories; but among other first-rate filmmakers, he clearly surpasses everyone in the scale of his subject matter, which is nothing less than the biggest economic, social and physical transformation taking place in the world today, in the most populous of all countries. When you see the earth from outer space, it's said, the only visible human artifact is the Great Wall of China. When the early twenty-first century is someday viewed from a comparable distance, the main artifacts to be seen may be the films of Jia Zhangke.

In *24 City*, he addresses his great subject by recording the decommissioning and demolition of a vast munitions plant in the city of Chengdu, in Sichuan province, after the property has been sold to a private developer. In place of Factory 420 will stand an upscale, glassy, mixed-use complex, with only a couple of the old brick structures retained to lend a touch of picturesque nostalgia. Jia's documentation of this development is the panoramic side of the film, with tracking shots that sidle through the echoing sheds, long-focus shots that fill the screen with a sea of workers' faces, crane shots that rise over acres of rubble where the foundations of the new complex are dug. The intimate side of the film, conceived as a series of interviews between subjects and an off-camera questioner, gives you the stories of middle-aged people who once worked in the factory and of young people who grew up in its dormitories and schools—and these segments, by and large, are fictional, scripted by Jia and Zhai Yongming and performed by professional actors.

You might think of these pseudo-documentary monologues as half a dozen self-contained melodramas—so ripe is each with heartbreak and disillusionment—if it weren't for the utter naturalism of Jia's mise-en-scène and the tact with which he places his camera, making sure not to crowd his subjects and then taking one more step back. The weary but enduring Hao Dali (played by Lu Liping) sits before the casement window in her bedroom, where potted plants are arranged prettily on the ledge, and recounts how decades ago the government shipped her to Chengdu to work in the factory—during the voyage, she explains, she was forced to leave behind her son. For Little Flower, by contrast, the abiding loss is her hope of marriage. Posed gracefully in the chair of a beauty parlor, with the bustle of a street passing outside the window, she explains the long sequence of accidents, misunderstandings and hardships that have led her to face middle age alone, even though everyone in the factory used to say she looked just like the star of *The Little Flower* and *The Last Emperor,* Joan Chen. No wonder—she's played by Joan Chen.

The youngest of the fictional characters, Su Na (played by Zhao Tao), has escaped factory life entirely, having set herself up as a personal shopper for rich women. She's modern, fashionable, confident about making money—but the bottom drops out of her voice when she remembers her sole experience of industry, on the occasion when she went looking for her mother amid countless, seemingly identical workers on a deafening factory floor. Su Na tells this tale while standing against the windows of an abandoned schoolroom. A vista of skyscrapers and highway ramps stretches into the distance behind her; and as her story pours out, twilight begins to gather.

But then, darkness is always falling in *24 City*. Monologue scenes keep fading to black and then resuming, as if the whole world had shut its eyes for a moment to concentrate; daytime sequences keep alternating with lonely nocturnal excursions through the city. This is the rhythm of things being made and unmade, of lives being gathered and scattered—and in the grand sweep of Jia's documentary, it's a fifty-year pulse: astounding, ironic, futile, cruel. Yet in the stories that make up Jia's fictions, going in sequence from the oldest character to the youngest, each moment is full in itself—often with sadness, certainly, but also with pride, resilience and (most of all, most astonishingly) love.

The Nation, October 27, 2008

Wendy and Lucy

Toward the end of Kelly Reichardt's *Wendy and Lucy*, a security guard at a Walgreens presses $6 worth of kindness into the hand of the main character, a young woman stranded in a small city in Oregon. By this point in the film, you know how much money is left in the woman's pocket (a couple hundred), how much it would cost to fix her broken-down Honda (thousands), how far she needs to travel to get that cannery job she wants in Alaska (too far) and how much help she can expect from her family back in Fort Wayne (none). The six bucks aren't going to be much help, either. But the elderly guard is the closest thing to a friend that the woman has in this town, and the shot of the money, lying in her hand in the crisp early morning light, is so vivid that you can almost feel the moisture of the crumpled bills.

As in her previous feature, *Old Joy*, Reichardt advances a subtle, observational style of realism in *Wendy and Lucy*, keeping the lead performance by Michelle Williams restrained and inward, lingering on immaculately composed views of side streets or rail-yards, concentrating the action on a single problem. (Will Wendy find her missing dog?) Given the slight sentimentality of the screenplay (co-written with Jon Raymond), which underscores the hapless victimhood of Wendy and the callous piety of the people around her, I might describe the film as a contemporary American *Bicycle Thief*, if it had a bicycle or a thief. What it does have, in ample measure, is a clear eye, a patient heart and a much-needed respect for material facts. *Wendy and Lucy* will open on December 10 in New York at Film Forum, where it will shine in quiet valor among the award season's bigger, dimmer pictures.

The Nation, December 22, 2008

Gomorrah

The natural world makes infrequent appearances in Matteo Garrone's *Gomorrah*, showing up most notably as a box of rotten, stinking peaches dumped by a road near Naples. The peasant grandmother who has picked this unwanted fruit is not so much simple as senile, and doesn't know enough to come in from her rainy orchard. The old farmer lies ill in an antique wood-frame bed under the family crucifix, able to wheeze just one word— "Euro!"—to his visitors, who came to buy land to poison.

So much for the countryside and its traditions. The zone where rural and urban life mingle is represented in *Gomorrah* by two or three perpetually overcast beaches, all but devoid of people but littered with construction equipment and decaying block-houses. That leaves the city as the site of the main action—and by "city" I mostly mean a Neapolitan housing project that from the outside resembles a concrete ziggurat and inside is a stack of walk-ways suspended under a cloudy, peaked skylight. The walkways run between rows of apartments that are decaying at best, and at worst have had their facades ripped away, exposing a damp and crusted back wall that is reverting to the condition of a cave. There are exposed, dribbling pipes in the building and pools of ground-water; garages filled with rubble but no cars; vast, high enclosures that seem to have been abandoned by the builder before they got their interior walls, or ceilings, or any source of light except for a rip in the building's shell.

Monumental Italian ruins, in the contemporary version. But even in them, paradoxically, nature still asserts itself. You unex-pectedly hear bird song on the soundtrack, and in the background you see trees that rustle surprisingly green leaves, just before you witness the most heart-wrenching of the film's countless murders.

This, according to *Gomorrah*, is what the world looks like when it has been remade by gangsters.

The facts that justify this horrific vision have been established in a book of the same title by the journalist Roberto Saviano, who so vividly exposed the workings of today's Camorra—the Neapol-itan mob—that he's been living under police protection since 2006. The characters who inhabit the film's wasteland are the quasi-fic-tional creations of Saviano, Garrone and four more screenwriters, who have conceived *Gomorrah* not as a unified drama but as a continuous, intensifying bloodletting that touches the lives of five distinct clusters of people.

The youngest are willingly implicated. One plotline follows 13-year-old Totò, a watchful, fox-faced, freckled kid in a soccer jersey, who delivers groceries in and around the ziggurat but soon works his way into a job delivering drugs. A second line follows two older adolescents—mature enough to visit a strip joint when they've grabbed a little money but young enough to get their skinny asses kicked out for sheer ignorance—who have memorized De Palma's *Scarface* and imagine they, too, can become bosses if they deploy their sole assets: idiot bravado and a cache of stolen weapons.

By contrast, the stories that focus on middle-aged characters are concerned with people who live inside the Camorra only because the outside seems not to exist. Don Ciro, with his comb-over and beige zip-up jacket, looks like any unhappy accountant who is waiting for retirement, except that instead of working in an office, he shambles about the ziggurat, delivering cash to half the resident families. Pasquale, a master tailor, is a livelier figure, who might be happy anywhere he could exercise his talent; but the only place he can work is in a Camorra sweatshop, where he supplies the skill needed to manufacture haute couture on the cheap.

The fifth plotline, the only one in which anybody ponders a moral choice, combines young and old in the characters of Roberto and Franco: a recent university graduate apprenticed to a senior waste-management executive. Their story provides a moment of relief from the oppressive landscape by taking *Gomorrah* to Venice, where Franco shows Roberto how to negotiate with big companies. (Lesson one: assure the client that the disposal will be "clean," and offer a bid so low that he pretends to believe you.) Back in the south, this plotline also brings the film into some of its most grandiose settings, such as the towering cliffs of an abandoned quarry, where Franco dumps his toxic sludge.

Meanwhile, a gang war is raging.

Put this all together and you get an impression of the Camorra that feels comprehensive because it shows a multilayered, omnipresent organization in the act of destroying a variety of people, one by one. What you don't get is the coherent overview that Saviano provides in the book. He takes pains to show how the Camorra has made itself indispensable in today's mercantile economy, where producers of goods labor in workshops dispersed everywhere in the world, or seemingly nowhere at all, while consumers find that their disposable income is forever shrinking. In this system, costs have to be driven down relentlessly at both ends of the chain—and people who are not overly gentle can make good money doing it.

In short, Saviano's book is more than a harrowing underworld exposé—it's a study of globalization. Moviegoers who have read *Gomorrah* will recognize a trace of this argument in the film's story of Pasquale, who risks working with an upstart Chinese competitor to the Italian sweatshops. Those who haven't read the book will have to figure things out by themselves. Proceeding more like a Robert Altman than a Francesco Rosi, Garrone omits as much explanatory material as possible while allowing his plots to move forward with few interconnections, or none. He gives you sensation, not exposition. This might have been cause for complaint, if Garrone had romanticized even one of his characters; but *Gomorrah* is as unglamorous a gangland movie as anyone has ever made.

Its scenes abound in the uncanny, the outrageous, the grotesque, rendered huge in the widescreen compositions but at the same time invested with a harsh realism. Scrawny youths dressed only in sneakers and briefs tramp through an estuary, test-firing automatic rifles and grenade launchers. Boys wait in line to face their gangster entrance exam: taking a bullet in the chest. Kids who are too short to see over the steering wheels drive trucks in circles, carting toxic chemicals. A sedan barrels along a highway at night, with a man's disembodied head poking up behind the back seat.

At first, it appears that Garrone is using a limited visual repertory to present these monstrosities. Either the actors' faces bobble in the foreground of underlit settings, through which a hand-held camera closely tracks them, or else the figures shrink to the relative size of bugs, in steady long shots of gigantesque locations. The intimate mingles with the far-reaching. But as *Gomorrah* pulls you in more deeply, Garrone's technique becomes steadily more complex. He splits the frame into jagged areas of light and impenetrable shadow; he pulls in or extends the depth of field, sometimes making the middle distance dissolve and sometimes sending your eye zooming clear to the end of a long perspective; he executes vertiginous crane shots (of a character picking his way through carnage) or lets you fly at thirty miles an hour over the city streets (as when the two *Scarface* enthusiasts ride a motorbike toward their final showdown). The camera's performance, like that of the actors, keeps growing in scale and expressivity, even as life gets worse and worse.

Perhaps the most horrible moment of all comes in the closing shot, in which an earthmover rumbles across a beach and into the distance, its shovel raised like a metal hand toward a cold, opaque sky. Cupped within that hand are two corpses. To me, that was the worst of it, in this endlessly compelling, endlessly violent movie— not the sight of dead bodies being lifted like a sacrifice but the realization that I had just witnessed order being restored.

The Nation, February 23, 2009

The Beaches of Agnès

The things that you lose in the course of a long life, and the things you might somehow hold on to, are the stuff of Agnès Varda's latest essay film—"stuff" being a clunky word to apply where this innately elegant artist is concerned but also inescapable, since she likens her method in this film to dumping the contents of a purse.

Out tumble lint, valuables, makeup, mementos, business receipts, scraps of notepaper and pieces of identification, official and otherwise. Some of this accumulation, such as the family snapshots, might belong to any grandmother, as I think Varda would admit. Having dedicated a significant part of her work to making common cause with other women, she readily counts herself among their company. That said, though, she knows her career within this collectivity has been singular, and so are most of the odds and ends she pours out before the viewer. Founding member and sole woman of the French New Wave, witness to radical social movements and sometimes their abettor, entrepreneur, traveler, friend to a long list of artistic geniuses, she in effect brings out of her purse more than fifty years' worth of assorted and idiosyncratic film clips, portrait photographs and snatches of music, not to mention some recently gathered views of places she's known.

"A puzzle," she calls her life's materials as she sorts and arranges them, "with a hole in the center." Or, to switch to the metaphor of her new film's title, the assemblage she makes looks like a meeting place of the elements, continually forming and slipping away: *The Beaches of Agnès.*

You see her, in a prologue set in Belgium, tromping barefoot on one of the North Sea beaches she enjoyed as a child. "If you opened people up, you'd find landscapes," Varda explains. "If you opened me up, you'd find beaches." Meanwhile, her assistants are setting up a multitude of mirrors on the sand, as if to prepare the filmmaker for her self-portrait. "Show me in an old spotted mirror," she advises, looking into one that almost completely obscures her face, "or with my scarf blowing like this," as she studies the effect of having her head completely covered. For the most part, Varda makes the reflections show only her young helpers and the waves, sky and dune grass. Things drift away and things abide, but the self who mourns and retains is elusive—perhaps willfully so. Varda scratches into the sand her original given name—Arlette—and watches the letters wash away. She speaks of the lone recording of classical music she heard as a child, and fragments of the piece rise on the soundtrack over the view of the North Sea: Schubert's Unfinished Symphony.

Playful, quizzical, at times deliberately clownish, Varda claims the status of enigma in *The Beaches of Agnès*, saying in this prologue that she is only pretending to be eager to tell about herself, much as she's "playing at being an old lady" (this, at 79). "It's other people who move me," she declares. Considering the many characters who then figure in the film, and the love she lavishes on them all—from the baker down the street from her house to her late husband, Jacques Demy—I can believe her.

But permit me a little skepticism too. This short-statured, long-nosed woman with the mushroom-cut hair that keeps changing color throughout the film and the clothes that might have come from the trunk of a regional theater company is too compellingly intelligent a commentator, and too engaging a companion, not to be the star of her own life story. By the end of *The Beaches of Agnès*, you will know a lot about what she's achieved and how she's done it. You just won't learn this material in any order except the one in which she's been pleased to dump it out.

A surrealist of the tender and discursive sort (except when enraged), she enjoys curious juxtapositions and chance events and is willing to organize them if they don't produce themselves. In the seaside town of Sète, for example, where she spent her adolescence, she hauls out an old-fashioned handcart like the one seen in her first film, *La Pointe Courte*, and converts it into the platform for a little movie screen, so that two of her old friends can push it through the twilit lanes while watching a projected image of their long-dead father. It is an image, perhaps, of film as a humble funerary rite; by contrast, Varda also gives you an impression of film as a busy if accident-prone game. To represent the office of her production company, Ciné-Tamaris, she has a few tons of sand dumped into the middle of a Paris street and then installs her staff at desks on this "beach." A rainstorm blows in on the second day of shooting and destroys the set, but Varda greets the reversal with perfect equanimity. Her aesthetic, poised between mourning and play, has room for incompletion and happenstance. Besides, she's endured worse than the loss of a location.

As evidence, here are some of the photographs she took at the beginning of her career, in the late 1940s, when the actor and impresario Jean Vilar commissioned her to document his Avignon Festival. She was mortified, Varda recalls, when Vilar's gesturing right hand came out blurred in one picture of *Richard II*. Now, she says, she likes to see blurs in photographs, especially in the foreground. She lets the screen fill with a few examples of such incidentally messy images, with their evidence of a life too ongoing to be fully captured. Then she shows herself walking through an exhibition of her Avignon photographs—immaculately printed, blown up to more than life size, installed within the serene symmetry of a chapel—as she breaks down and weeps for all these beautiful people who are gone.

"All the dead," she confides to the camera, "lead me back to Jacques."

Her long relationship with Demy dominates her account of her filmmaking career. She credits him with getting her the opportunity to make *Cléo From 5 to 7*, discusses her visits to film festivals in the context of his triumphal progress, explains the course of her work in the 1960s in terms of her life with him on Noirmoutier Island and later in Los Angeles. But Demy is strangely absent from much of this narrative. Other family members, friends and colleagues appear prominently on the screen, in new or archival images—her children, Jane Birkin, Chris Marker (disguised as a cat)—but rarely Demy, except as a figure glimpsed through a courtyard window or a blurred white spot at the back of a production still from *The Umbrellas of Cherbourg*. He doesn't really become a presence in *The Beaches of Agnès* until Varda recounts the end of his life: his illness with AIDS, his composition of a memoir about his youth and her efforts to make this piece of his writing into the film that has stood for nearly the past twenty years as her final narrative feature, *Jacquot de Nantes*.

There's a production still that shows Varda at work in her director's chair, meanwhile reaching back to clasp hands with the husband she knew was dying. What slips away, and what you hold on to: to which did she dedicate *Jacquot de Nantes*? She would show Demy the scenes she was setting up, she recalls, and ask if they were accurate, and he'd tell her, "Yes. I can see myself in that." So it was important to her to have these re-creations of his life—unlike the re-creations of her own life that she inserts into *The Beaches of Agnès*, calling them "just a game." Varda says she doesn't quite get the point of dressing up a little girl in a swimsuit like the one she used to wear. For that matter, she confesses that she feels no connection to her childhood experiences and no emotion when revisiting the house where she grew up. (The retired physician who now owns the place, and who wants to show off his collection of model trains—he's something. "But the childhood home part is a flop.") I might guess, then, that the surrealist play of turning life into images becomes urgent for Varda mostly in retrospect, when the subject has gone or is going. If she doesn't take very seriously the images she creates of her past, it's perhaps because she's never lost herself.

And yet she turned 80 while making *The Beaches of Agnès.* Surely she felt her own mortality.

I'd say she did; and the wonder of this late masterpiece is that she acknowledges her mortality in it in three different ways, as everywoman, as a singular woman and as the hole in the puzzle—no woman at all.

As everywoman, she shows herself at the end posing happily under a tree with her children and grandchildren, dressed in white and standing a little apart from the others, as if already moving toward the next world. As a singular woman, she tacks a coda onto the film: a record of her raucous eightieth birthday celebration, with well-wishers trooping into her Paris headquarters to salute the aged great lady. But it's as no woman at all that she composes the third and most moving finale of *The Beaches of Agnès,* which consists of a view of a shack she constructed near the beach on Noirmoutier Island: little more than a frame enclosing an empty space.

You might say that Varda is the void in that shack, whose rippling, fragile walls, suspended from the frame, are strips of celluloid unspooled from a print of her mid-1960s film *Les Créatures.* There's nothing in the shack—and nothing to it, either—except for light, color and ghostly images of Catherine Deneuve and Michel Piccoli: something that's lost and preserved at the same time.

"I live in cinema," Varda concludes. "I feel I've lived here forever."

The Nation, July 13, 2009

35 Shots of Rum / Bright Star

Claire Denis's just-released *35 Shots of Rum* takes place on the tracks of Paris's regional train lines, in the rooms of suburban apartment blocks, along streets populated mostly by Black and brown French people, between the glances of family members and lovers. Which of the characters are family and which are lovers is not immediately obvious. For a while you just know that these people watch one another, and watch for one another, with patience and concern, overlaying the network of the big city's movement with an intimate and still geometry of their own.

Lionel (Alex Descas) stands beside the tracks from afternoon until nightfall, smoking and watching the trains go by: a middle-aged man with the physique of a heavyweight fighter but not the vanity, solid, pensive, reliable. Joséphine (Mati Diop) rides a train, goes shopping, comes back to her apartment. She's a slim young woman with the long, serenely sad face of an African sculpture; and when Lionel comes home, she hurries to look after him, bringing him his slippers, serving his supper, noticing his every gesture and mood. Round and smooth-haired Gabrielle (Nicole Dogué) has a way of seeming bundled up in herself as she smiles at nothing and waits, and waits, sitting on the stairs in the apartment building or gazing out her window at the tracks. As for Noé (Grégoire Colin), the only pink-skinned character in the film, he shows up in the shadows of the building looking like a threat, with his long, greasy locks and muscle-boy clothes. A close-up, shot from below, lends him an air of menace; but his eyes turn toward Joséphine's door with a look of purest longing.

He is the neighbor who comes and goes, loving Joséphine but never letting her hear it. Gabrielle is the woman who is not Joséphine's mother, though she wishes she were. And Lionel is Joséphine's father—though the way she treats him, you could imagine he's her husband instead. *35 Shots of Rum* is the story of how you gradually figure out how these characters fit together. It's the quiet, profound, beautifully observed story of how they figure themselves out, and get unstuck, and at last find a new configuration for themselves—a little movement.

o   o   o

Denis risks everything on domestic emotions in *35 Shots of Rum*. Jane Campion, by contrast, dares to make emotion strange in the just-released *Bright Star*, her fact-based period drama about the love between a smart young dressmaker, Fanny Brawne, and the frail, impecunious poet who moves in next door, John Keats.

He's played by Ben Whishaw, whose face, when shown from its most characteristic angle, becomes a sliver of moon—waning, most likely, considering the film is concerned with Keats's last years. She is played by Abbie Cornish, who at her most characteristic angle is the moon in full. An artist in her own right, proud to have created the first triple-pleated mushroom collar in Hampstead, Fanny at first shines sociably on Keats, remarking that the quality she most enjoys in writers is wit. "Wit," he grimaces. "Things that make you start, without making you feel." Her initiation by Keats into poetry—his type of poetry—will teach her to feel deeply, until she's dressed in black and howling in a barren woods.

If the theme of *Bright Star* is the realization of oneself in natural emotion, the method is gorgeously unnatural. Campion knows that the early nineteenth century is alien to us and so makes the most of costumes that look like they've devoured the hapless wearers and customs that resemble the rites of far-off tribes. And then, having respected the difference between Fanny Brawne's world and ours, Campion collapses it by bringing out the physical texture of everything, from the touch of fabric against the skin to the peculiar timbre of a voice raised in song. Every sensation seems more immediate than it would be for us today—the quality of the air when the seasons change, the glow of the Vermeer light when it pours through a window. So the characters' education into love becomes immediate for us, too.

Here are two profoundly moving pictures that leave room for you to think, and discover, and feel for yourself. Their authors, being middle-aged women, have scant chance of being touted as cool. Their artistry, having little commercial oomph, has no chance of being cited by op-ed writers looking to give a little zing to the zeitgeist. All these films do is risk engaging your emotions instead of your memories of other films. They strive to deepen your experience of life, not substitute for it. Entertainment reporters would call them niche films. I'd say that niche is as big as all outdoors.

The Nation, September 16, 2009

A Prophet

Jacques Audiard has never made a bad movie, but neither has he made many of them. Five films in fifteen years: it's a pace that might make you suspect him of harboring eccentric ambitions, or just being fussy, if he weren't so obviously in love with genre storytelling. Four of his films, the new one included, are crime pictures; the fifth might be classified as a caper; and though all are stylish, they're realized with such swift story development and emotionally direct acting that they give at least an impression of spontaneity, as if Audiard and his protagonists had figured out the plots together, on the run.

Perhaps "figured out" is an exaggeration. Audiard's principal characters bluff, blunder and scheme their way through situations that have every appearance of being too much for them, given their patent frailties. Even the ex-con in *Read My Lips*, paroled into a flunky office job, could be overmastered by a copying machine—and he was played by the one real tough guy among Audiard's actors, Vincent Cassel. (The heroine in that film was profoundly deaf and so had problems of her own, for which the tough-gal attitude of Emmanuelle Devos could not entirely compensate.) In Audiard's other crime movies, his lead actors have been a neurotic, inward Romain Duris in *The Beat That My Heart Skipped* (a remake of James Toback's *Fingers*, and for my money a considerable improvement on it) and the unmistakably homoerotic pair of Jean-Louis Trintignant and Mathieu Kassovitz in *See How They Fall*: Trintignant looking as fragrant and winning as a leather jacket salvaged from a garbage can, and Kassovitz trotting after him wide-eyed as if the jacket had true outlaw allure. As for Audiard's caper, *A Self-Made Hero* (his satirical fable about a Frenchman who joins the Resistance on May 8, 1945), it was another project starring Kassovitz, this time as an upwardly mobile fabulist who so much wanted his profitable lies to be true that his girlfriends, and the audience, forgave him.

So too will the audience forgive the typically vulnerable and malleable protagonist of Audiard's latest film, *A Prophet* (*Un Prophète*), even though Malik El Djebena is by far the most blood-spattered in this line of characters, and lives in the most violent and claustrophobic of the movies. Claustrophobic, yet expansive—because this contemporary prison drama stretches out for two and a half hours (not a minute of which is wasted) while covering six years of its main character's life and a major portion of the National Front's nightmares.

At the heart of the film is the dilemma of a young French Arab—illiterate, unskilled, at home nowhere except in the house of detention—when he at last graduates into the adult prison system and cannot make a place for himself in its cliques. On one side are the other Arabs, whose devotion to daily prayer appears to be alien to Malik. ("Have any special religious needs?" asks a guard—one of the very few old-style French people in the movie—during his intake interview. "You eat pork?" To which Malik shrugs and says, more or less, "Why not?") On the other side are the members of a Corsican gang, who are more powerful, more alien and (worst of all) more interested in Malik.

This gang needs him to kill another inmate, Reyeb, a wary informant who will let no one but a fellow Arab get close enough to strike; and though Malik has neither the tools nor the temperament for this job, he nerves himself up for it rather than let the Corsicans kill him first. In exchange for the murder, he receives a sweater (cheap, but better than his other clothes), the privilege of serving the gang members their coffee (while being called a dirty Arab) and immunity from further bullying (except, of course, by the Corsicans). All this, plus a life-size guilty conscience (which moves into the cell with him, looking just like the man he killed) and a thirst for revenge that is so urgent that Malik must be very, very patient to realize it.

About that guilty conscience, and the film's title: Malik eventually proves to be a prophet in an ironic sense of the word by transforming himself from a lone outsider to a criminal leader. (He even passes through the obligatory "Forty Days and Forty Nights," as noted by one of the film's chapter titles.) But Malik is also a prophet in something closer to the standard sense, as a seer. Some of his visions are so vivid and glowingly colored that they seem physically present—like his murder victim, who can even talk to Malik, despite the gash in his neck. Other visions are gray and shadowy, tapering into darkness at their margins and flashing before Malik in discontinuous glimpses; and these sometimes allow him to anticipate what's going to happen. The paradox of *A Prophet* is that the moments of clairvoyance aren't clear at all but resemble the iris effect that Audiard uses when he wants to make visible the limits of Malik's consciousness.

The film actually begins with one of these effects. First there's darkness and the sound of a man loudly protesting that "You can't put handcuffs on me." (Evidently, he's wrong.) Then, as the sounds continue, a portion of the screen opens to a confusion of clouded views of a police station—they look as if they'd been taken with a handheld camera during a downpour of baking flour—in the midst of which you get your first look at Malik. He sits hunched over in a semi-juvenile condition, scrawny, ragged, bushy-haired and (despite his own handcuffs) silent. If it were not for the cut under his right eye, which is seeping blood, you might imagine this man to be chronically docile and abashed. Certainly he's bewildered. At this stage in the film—and only at this stage—you understand the forces arrayed against Malik a little better than he does. The dimness of the image, which later will signal uncanny insight, here testifies instead to partial blindness.

Soon, though, Malik begins to see the here-and-now in a flood of daylight bright enough to wash out all the colors. This is the condition of the prison yard when he is first summoned by the man who will be his user, oppressor, protector and inadvertent teacher, the Corsican gang boss César Luciani (Niels Arestrup)— as squat, white-haired and nutcracker-profiled a godfather as you will ever meet—whose first words to Malik, interestingly enough, are "Don't look at me." Of course. In *A Prophet*, it sometimes seems as if the whole art of prison governance—the actual governance, I mean, as distinguished from the official—is a matter of determining whose eyes get to see what information. For example, as Malik rises in the system, he gets to acquire video equipment for his cell, on which he can watch contraband porn and clandestinely recorded messages. When Luciani wants to discipline Malik, he does so with a very convincing threat to remove his left eye with a spoon.

You might say, then, that in addition to being a tough and suspenseful drama about crime behind bars, a frequently gleeful study of France's changing demographics and an absorbing portrait of an isolated victim studying to become a winner, *A Prophet* is an essay on different modes of vision. It's about the inadequacy of subjective viewpoints, the potential power inherent in a mundane, realistic perspective (what you might call surveillance-camera sight) and the occasional superiority of an inward vision, which can be indistinguishable from blindness. At the decisive moment in his ascension, Malik in fact can see nothing. He is on his back in the middle of a deadly chaos, covered by bodies, unable to lift his head and look around, and for the first time in the film he's laughing.

With that image in mind, it's time to pay tribute to Tahar Rahim, the young actor who in his first major screen role plays Malik, or the many different Maliks who evolve. With his long, narrow head balanced uncertainly on sloping shoulders, Rahim was an easy choice to embody the character's physical vulnerability; but then, any adequate performer could have conveyed the suffering of a man who is periodically left writhing on cement floors. What impresses me about Rahim, and what makes *A Prophet* work so well, is the lightness he brings to the role. There's a gawkiness that permits you to smile a little at Malik's moments of confusion; a bounce to the step (never a strut) that lets you enjoy his hustles; and a secret sassiness that invites you to participate in small triumphs that nobody else is supposed to observe. The ultimate sign of Malik's intelligence? It's the way Rahim sticks out his tongue.

So far as I know, Rahim's most notable previous role was in a French TV miniseries, *La Commune*, written by Abdel Raouf Dafri, who had the idea for *A Prophet* and brought it to Audiard. This doesn't seem to have been a package deal, but it does give evidence that a French Arab sensibility was present at the start of the movie and ran all the way through. Credit where it's due—but especially to Audiard, thanks to whom this hot rod of a movie jolts along on fuel that's equal parts adrenaline and ambiguity.

What expression plays across Malik's features, late in the film, when he finally gets his revenge? The question isn't rhetorical; I really can't say whether satisfaction, sorrow or shock predominates. All I know is that the sequence of long shots and close-ups, in shadow and washed-out light, is perfectly judged and reveals all these emotions on a face that Malik keeps carefully still. Audiard number five: excellent.

The Nation, March 22, 2010

Poetry

See the beauty in everything, Mija's poetry teacher has told her; and so, when she discovers apricots lying along a footpath, she imagines they were ready to start their next lives and hurled themselves to the ground. How pleasant it is to think of suicide this way, as something sweet and fecund. It's the kind of idea that Mija has been straining for, and not just because she has taken it into her head, late in life, to learn to write poetry. Inescapably, though by no fault of her own, she is involved in the death of a girl who drowned herself.

Mija has journeyed to this farmland outside her provincial Korean city to speak with the girl's mother. But the idea about the apricots diverts her so much, and she feels so relieved to have thought of it, that the purpose of the trip seems to slip her mind. Words do, too, nowadays. The doctors say it's Alzheimer's; and so, for the moment, nothing is more important to Mija than to pause in the shade and write down her line of verse, using the notebook she carries in her wide-mouthed woven handbag.

One of the more conspicuous props in Lee Chang-dong's *Poetry*, that bag might have struck you as being less of a purse than a basket, if Mija's manner didn't wrap it in an air of old-fashioned gentility—a somewhat deceptive air, as it happens. By the time you get to the apricot scene, you know that even though Mija habitually dolls up in flouncy, soft-colored outfits with long skirts and lacy collars, then tops herself with a broad-brimmed summer hat, she makes ends meet at age 66 by laboring as a housemaid and homecare attendant. She strips off her ladylike street clothes to do laundry, scrub floors, wipe the bottom of an elderly stroke victim and give him his bath; and then she trots back to her little apartment to labor some more, cooking and cleaning for her teenage grandson. These struggles cannot invalidate the determination of a slight, still pretty woman to carry on uncomplainingly with a traditional, feminine smile (and the occasional muttered sarcasm); but neither do they allow her to kid herself for long. See the beauty in everything, Mija's teacher has said; but he has also urged her to look at things as they are, and given what she knows about life, she does not understand how she can do both. By the time she has reached the dead girl's mother and braved a conversation, the line evoking sweet, purposeful suicide has failed one of its tests.

You may judge the fullness of *Poetry*, a film that is beautiful and truthful alike, by the fact that just these few moments of it can yield so much—and I haven't even touched on the narrative core of this scene. Here, as everywhere else in the movie, you find an abundance of drama, or perhaps (more precisely) catastrophe. Lee has stuffed the plot of this quiet, meditative film with rape, theft, extortion, corruption, violent death, borderline prostitution and (hanging over it all) the unthinking arrogance of men toward women—a longer list of crimes than you'll find even in Im Sang-soo's *The Housemaid* (another noteworthy recent release from Korea), though without Im's cheerful grotesquerie. Lee, who prefers to look at things as they are, constructs a deliberately prosaic world where Mija's employer can make a grand gesture out of tipping her the equivalent of nine bucks, and the life of a girl known as Agnes can be priced at $27,000, subject to negotiation and fees.

If powerless Mija, continually overburdened and condescended to, were to plot to get justice in this world, all the while keeping her mask of meekness in place, she would end up as a kind of Korean Pirate Jenny—and so she does. But the source of *Poetry*'s fullness lies in Mija's refusal to stop at justice. As she faces the inevitable slipping away of everything—her meager income, her loutish grandson, her words, her life, the life of a girl she never knew—she resolutely searches for a beauty that is dependable and can endure.

I have seen *Poetry* twice—once at the 2010 New York Film Festival, where everyone seemed to think it the finest selection on the slate, and once as I prepared to write this column and give the film the lengthier consideration it demands. Nothing much changed between those two viewings, except that my admiration for Yun Jung-hee as Mija deepened into awe.

Needless to say, Yun inhabits Mija. The critical issue is the way Yun inhabits Mija's own performance in life, which might be described as erratic. Sometimes Mija fulfills social conventions—giggling on cue at a token compliment, for example, with a modest evasion of the other person's eyes. Just as often, though, she loses track of her assigned role: forgetting all but the merest pretense of sweet good manners as she dares the registrar at the cultural center to keep her out of the poetry class; or wandering abstractedly out of a meeting—right out of the building, in fact—to gaze with outthrust head and slumped shoulders at an irrelevancy; or flailing about on the street, with little hops from foot to foot as she makes her grandson play badminton with her, to get the exercise the doctors say she needs.

Of course, there's a great tradition in Asian cinema of exposing the gap between a woman's feelings and the ritualized behavior expected of her. (To cite just one example, think of Naruse's *When a Woman Ascends the Stairs*.) Part of what makes Yun's performance in *Poetry* so stunning, though, is that she plays Mija as if there were no gap. Yun achieves her deepest moment of pathos, perhaps, in a monologue delivered in the poetry class, where she instills just one drop of loss and sadness into a recollection of getting dressed up prettily at age 3. (It's Mija's happiest memory.) Yun saves her biggest fortissimo for a scene with Mija's grandson, where her raised voice and frantic gestures crash uselessly against the young man's disrespectful silence. And when the moment comes to reveal a lighter, unsuspected side to Mija, Yun (who has appeared in more than 300 films) rounds out the character by abruptly singing a sockeroo karaoke number. From these examples, you can see the variety of resources Yun brings to her job—but, more important, you may understand how consistently she uses them, creating a character in whom vanity is indistinguishable from lifelong ideals; and ideals can either reinforce decorum or shatter it, as if these supposedly separate elements were her limbs, her breath, her heartbeat.

It is a classic performance—and it had better be, because Lee makes Mija the focal point of most of his shots and every scene. And yet the visual style of *Poetry*—as smooth-flowing and unhurried as the film's fatal river—never forces Mija on you and seldom isolates her. Shown often in middle-distance and long shots, she is usually seen as part of the life of a classroom, a grocery store, a neighborhood street, a restaurant gathering. You might say that Lee the director gets out of the way of Lee the screenwriter. For all the self-effacement of his style, though, its motifs run through the film as insistently as—again—that river.

Water is everywhere in the picture: at the scene of the girl's death, in the stroke victim's apartment (where it eventually makes things dirtier rather than cleaner), in the shower (where Mija at last breaks down and weeps), in the cloudburst that accompanies Mija's trip to the country. Stopping at the place where the corpse was discovered, she opens her notebook to try to write something, and we see a close-up of the blank page as it begins to receive marks—not from her pen, but from the raindrops spattering down.

Nature, weeping, writes when Mija can't. I suppose some viewers will dismiss this image as a pathetic fallacy (though whether that concept is at all germane to Korean poetry, I don't know). But I can tell you that the rain's writing, unlike the line about the apricots, is true to Mija's experience, true to the horror of what happened to the girl, and utterly beautiful. I hope I'm not giving away too much when I say that Mija, who is too strong to allow the rain to do her work for her, finds her own way to write at the end. You should see how.

The Nation, February 3, 2011

Cave of Forgotten Dreams

Hyperbole fails. "A movie 30,000 years in the making! Goes where no film has gone before—or will ever go again! Mysteries and wonders leap off the screen! In a lifetime of moviegoing, you will never see another film like this!" Such ravings become mere statements of fact with Werner Herzog's *Cave of Forgotten Dreams*, a documentary that demotes cries of "Awesome!" to the status of mere reportage. The proposition, quite literally, is this: you can pay your money, strap on your 3-D glasses (yes, 3-D) and witness what Herzog alone has been entrusted to show you, or else forgo seeing the most primal and profound evidence yet encountered of what makes us human.

That evidence lies buried in the cliffs overlooking the Ardèche River in southern France, where in 1994 a trio of spelunkers pushed their way through a crevice in the rock face and found the oldest known cave paintings in the world. The walls of the site, now named Chauvet Cave in honor of one of its discoverers, are covered with hundreds of images of animals, which most archaeologists believe to be approximately 30,000 years old. There is some debate; but no one doubts that the paintings are almost pristine, the mouth of the cave having been sealed by a rockfall ages ago. To make sure that the condition of the paintings remains stable, the entrance has been resealed, this time by a steel bank-vault door. Small research teams and their highly select guests enter the cave for only six weeks during the year, breaking up their time to avoid letting too much body heat and moisture build up. No other people are permitted beyond the steel door—except for Herzog and a skeleton crew, who received permission from the French Ministry of Culture to film in Chauvet Cave in the spring of 2010.

Some details of Herzog's experience during the shoot are unavoidably worked into *Cave of Forgotten Dreams*, since passages through Chauvet Cave are cramped, and everyone must remain on a narrow steel walkway that the researchers have laid down. The crew members, with their battery belts and flat lights, could not help getting into the shots. This was only fitting; people who come to Chauvet Cave to explore someone else's form of image-making do well to acknowledge their own. But Herzog also incorporates voluntary self-revelations. He chooses to narrate the film in voiceover and to make his presence felt during interviews. And the presence, as should be obvious from decades of his cinema, is far from bland.

Speaking with an archaeologist about the difficulty of understanding the cave painters from the marks they left behind, Herzog likens the attempt to someone's trying in the future to imagine the lives of New Yorkers based solely on a discovered list of their names. "Do they dream? Do they cry at night? We would never know from the phone directory."

Never mind that the paintings are far from being piled up in a matter-of-fact list. They were made to glide and veer, warp and scurry by firelight across the surfaces of their chambers, where thousands of years of calcite deposits glisten like pearl. Herzog knows perfectly well that the spectacle is stunning, and he's prepared to keep his implicit bargain by giving you plenty of it. (That's why he complicated an already challenging shoot by filming in 3-D, so you could see the paintings in their plasticity, as they curve with the walls. Given the chance, I suspect, Herzog would have added Smell-o-Vision.) But he is not content merely to record these traces, however beautiful, of a vastly distant, all but unimaginable communal life. He is also determined to confront that unfathomable collective experience with what we know in the present—the idiosyncratic, the concrete, the individual—as if trying to look through both ends of a telescope at the same time.

You sense Herzog's delight when one of the younger scientists he interviews—bearded, ponytailed and draped in a stylish scarf—turns out to have come to archaeology from a career in the circus, where he rode unicycles and juggled. A kindred spirit! The scientist recalls having needed to get away for a while after his first days of working in the cave, so overpowering were the paintings, but then feeling reassured and happy when the images of the Chauvet lions invaded his dreams. Then there's the experimental archaeologist who plays "The Star-Spangled Banner" on his reconstruction of a Paleolithic flute; the researcher who gamely trots back and forth in a field for Herzog, demonstrating the spear-throwing technique of prehistoric hunters (who must have been much, much better at it, he admits); the master perfumer who is sniffing his way through the Ardèche region, collaborating on a project to reproduce the scent of the caves. The personalities of the principal scientists are so important to Herzog that at one point he stops the film to record a gallery of them in close-up, deep underground, while everyone silently listens for "the heartbeat of the cave."

Herzog's personality is necessarily a part of this confrontation across the ages, and a part of the texture of the film. Only minutes into the movie, he and cinematographer Peter Zeitlinger are already asserting themselves, flying the camera up the wall of a cliff for a dizzying, seemingly impossible view of the landscape. From there, the signature gestures multiply. At one point the camera flips upside down to accompany a description of a rockslide. At another, the crew walks out the far end of a long, broad chamber, taking their lights with them, so that the cameraman is left alone in the dark, and you are left imagining the intense isolation of the cave. So it goes until the coda, when Herzog puts you eye-to-eye with an albino crocodile in an artificial jungle, for reasons that could be explained in a review but probably shouldn't be. Let's just say it has to do with the challenge of understanding the cave painters, and is something only Herzog would have thought up.

Is this arrogance on his part? No—humility, the point being that none of us, Herzog included, could have thought up Chauvet Cave or really know what to make of it. And so for long periods in *Cave of Forgotten Dreams* the narration drops out and the cinematic personality approaches zero while Herzog leaves you alone with the paintings, accompanied only by the wordless chanting of Ernst Reijseger's musical score. You see the lines that delicately mark out the nodding, lifting profiles of horses, four of them superimposed in a herd, with their jaws lightly parted as if panting. You see row after upraised row of rhinoceros horns, curving like multiple crescent moons; the snuffling, speckled muzzles of lions; a bison scrambling along on eight scrawny, busy legs. There are also scratch marks on the walls, looking like the work of bear claws; heaps of glistening, pearly animal skeletons scattered everywhere on the chamber floors (though no human remains); and on several walls the outlines of hands, including one that can be singled out, over and over, because of a missing digit. Traces of an individual presence, at a distance of 30,000 years.

Awe without sanctimony, uncanniness without mystification, a respect for the profound difference of other people, and other orders of beings, without any pretense of abandoning one's self: these have always been characteristics of Herzog's best work. These traits reach their height in *Cave of Forgotten Dreams* as he comes as close as we're likely to get to the unapproachable—our own beginnings. Because Chauvet Cave must be protected, he had just one chance to bring out of it a filmed experience, not only for himself but perhaps for all filmmakers. The greatest praise you can give him is to say he didn't blow it.

The Nation, May 16, 2011

Melancholia/The Turin Horse

I have to preface my remarks on Lars von Trier's *Melancholia* by confessing that I have always thought of von Trier as a buffoon and a charlatan, whose only good movie (*The Idiots*) was the one in which he owned up to himself. Now, after *Melancholia*, I write as a penitent convert. The long, glorious prologue to the film—made up of uncanny, quasi-still images that were lit and composed like dioramas, set to *Tristan und Isolde*—was inexplicable, evocative, aching, grotesque, surging and overpowering, unlike anything I had experienced before at the movies and indispensable to my response to the narrative that would follow. This story, set in some unspecified von Trier land where people speak varieties of English, fell into two parts. First came the expansive, fluid and often bitterly funny dramatization of an ultra-posh wedding reception, in which Kirsten Dunst (giving her career performance) began as the most radiant bride imaginable and ended in isolation and despair. This section was followed by a tight, episodic chamber drama focused on the bride's sister (Charlotte Gainsbourg) and brother-in-law (Kiefer Sutherland), who struggled with a science-fiction premise: the approach of a stray planet, which either would or would not destroy Earth. Perhaps the question posed by *Melancholia* was not so much whether we would welcome, fear or be indifferent to the death of everybody. The ultimate question, rather, was how we would want to address the feelings of others as the end approached. The wordless answer to which von Trier roused himself may have been futile—that possibility was inherent all along in *Melancholia*—but it was magnificent.

And now, on the subject of magnificence and futility, I will tell you about Béla Tarr's *The Turin Horse*, an allegory of the end of the world and a documentary of things just as they are.

The Turin Horse begins with a black screen and a voiceover relating Friedrich Nietzsche's breakdown in Turin in 1889, when he saw a cabman whipping a horse and stepped in to embrace the animal. The narration comments on Nietzsche's later years and ends, dryly, with the words, "Of the horse, we know nothing." Some commentators, taking this introduction too literally, have identified what follows as Tarr's vision of that particular horse's life; but this is nonsense. As the images begin, we see a horse pulling a wagon, not a cab, in a desolate landscape utterly unlike northern Italy. Soon we learn that the staple foods in this place are potatoes and fruit brandy, the local outlaws are Roma and the main characters—the wagoner and his adult daughter—speak Hungarian (when they bother to speak at all).

Tarr keeps you aware at all times that these scenes are an artifact. The droning, two-chord music on the soundtrack is deliberately warped; the black-and-white cinematography is subtly altered to give a faint yellow aura to the sky at some moments, the hint of a reddish blush to the woman's hair at others; the shot sequence (using Tarr's characteristic long takes) reminds you that you're seeing repetitive daily tasks from different angles; and the plot, though minimal, is nothing short of apocalyptic. A storm howls for five days, after which the abyss opens.

You examine an artifact; and meanwhile you are drawn toward suffering creatures who deserve an embrace as much as does any abused carriage horse. The documentary side of *The Turin Horse*: this is the weight of time, pressing on a man and a woman. This is how material things weigh on them. And this is the force of their resistance, as long as it lasts.

The Nation, November 14, 2011

The Bling Ring

Based on a report that Nancy Jo Sales wrote for *Vanity Fair*, Sofia Coppola's *The Bling Ring* is the more or less true story of five high school kids from the affluent northwest suburbs of Los Angeles who, in 2008 and '09, allegedly stole some $3 million in designer clothing and jewelry by breaking into the homes of celebrities. These were apparently crimes of emulation as much as greed, carried out by young people who aspired, if they could not rise to the eminence of their highest models in life, such as Paris Hilton, to at least own their stuff. The curve of potential mockery bends toward infinity, yet Coppola restrains her satirical impulse in *The Bling Ring*, shaking her head ruefully more often than she snickers.

The one target she finds irresistible among her fictionalized characters is Nicki (Emma Watson), a bubblehead who has been home-schooled on a diet of psycho-spiritual pablum. After her arrest, Nicki instantly disavows her consumerist orgies and, with the help of a team of publicists, issues statements about her commitment to an unspecified philanthropic mission. "Thank you for respecting my privacy," she drawls in dismissal to the TV crews that she hopes will never go away, her expression so self-righteously deadpan that you might think she herself had respected the privacy of her victims (or that her victims, all creatures of the camera, had a lot of privacy left to violate).

But these moments of acidic humor are an element of contrast in *The Bling Ring*, as is Watson's star turn. (She stands out in an ensemble of newcomers for her fame, and also for playing the one character whose realization demands a Cate Blanchett-like mutability.) For the most part, Coppola weaves the film's texture from the experience of the character who is Nicki's opposite: Marc (Israel Broussard), the only boy among the thieves. Shy, tentative, gay and too willing to please, he is the voiceover narrator of *The Bling Ring* and the principal focus of the film's dominant quality, empathy.

Judgment, as far as Coppola is concerned, can be taken for granted. Laughter is a given, and attempts at understanding would be just so many exercises in social stereotyping. What she wants is to get behind her characters' eyes, onto the surface of their skin, inside the rhythm of their breathing. That's the truth you ought to get, she thinks, in a movie based on a true story. So, even while making her most satisfyingly story-driven film to date, Coppola immerses you in scenes long after you've absorbed their narrative purpose, deprives you of transitions that would be merely informational, makes the color and intensity of the light feel like a constantly changing, pervasive influence on events, and never puts any music onto the soundtrack that the kids wouldn't be listening to right then.

The Nation, August 19, 2013

Gravity

Dorothy had it easy. When she at last understood she wanted to go home, all she had to do was click her heels and say the words. But when Sandra Bullock makes up her mind to go home in Alfonso Cuarón's entirely amazing *Gravity*, she can't get there unless she's willing to somersault through the void, bounce repeatedly off large metal objects, swim through fire, consult technical manuals in Russian and Chinese (languages her character doesn't read) and, not least, master her death wish. "What now?" she yells at one point, in a tone midway between exasperation and terror, as the latest of her challenges (many of which are razor-sharp) come zooming out of an indifferent cosmos. This is what a medical engineer turned rookie astronaut may expect when she's stranded above Earth without a spaceship: a very bad four or five hours of plot time. The audience, though, may experience Bullock's struggles in *Gravity* another way: as the occasion for ninety minutes of pure exhilaration.

It all depends on how strongly you respond to the way motion pictures move. Although the plot of *Gravity* presents the ultimate case of existential dread, and a harsh lesson in the economics of being alone in the universe (only so much oxygen to budget, only so much time), the style revels in overabundance, having joyfully left behind all constraints. Cuarón is now leading the post-graduate fellowship program of the look-ma-no-hands school of film-making; and in case any of the moms out there are inattentive, he cues them through the characters to notice that wonders are being worked.

As *Gravity* begins, with the shuttle *Explorer* orbiting gradually into sight, Bullock's character (improbably called Ryan Stone) is bent none too happily over a task outside the capsule, her eyes fixed on the piece of equipment in front of her, while around her two crewmates who enjoy taking the longer view are at play. Shariff (Phaldut Sharma), who is tied to the *Explorer*'s frame by a long cord, has made himself into a human tether ball and is whipping around while shouting "Whee!" Kowalski (George Clooney), who is of course the cocky but comfortingly reliable veteran, has cut loose completely from the ship and is performing acrobatics with the help of a jet pack. You might think of Cuarón's camera as an unseen fourth person moving among these characters and sharing their happier moods. It joins in Shariff's rapture at being freed from the struggle to bear weight; it emulates Kowalski's lighthearted professionalism in always choosing the right thing to do, when it seems as if anything at all could be done.

While you lose track of the compass points and the passage of time, the camera in this endless, seamless first scene dives and darts around and under and through the superstructure of the *Explorer*, coasts up to and over and past the characters, slips smoothly from outside Bullock's helmet to inside for a point-of-view shot and without a single evident cut keeps circling the objects in motion, all the while being circled by them. You could say, without abusing the term, that you are witnessing a revolution. It's the overthrow of your normal understanding of how films are put together, effected by the conspiracy of Cuarón, cinematographer Emmanuel Lubezki and visual effects supervisor Timothy Webber by evoking the abandonment in outer space of your normal physical senses. You know, for example, that if George Clooney floats out of sight on the left side of the frame, he is not supposed to float back into the same shot from the right. That's a fundamental convention of moviemaking, based on the sort of real-world experience that tells you that Earth should be below Clooney's feet and not above his head, and certainly never in both positions at almost the same time. Say goodbye to convention; so long, quotidian up and down. You may think you've seen Stanley Kubrick explore the systematic derangement of all the senses in *2001: A Space Odyssey*, but *Gravity* now makes that film seem like an exercise in fixed-camera sobriety.

This is not to say that *Gravity* is a better film than *2001*. I'll get to that question in a moment. For now, let me make one more point about the style of *Gravity*: although computer-generated imagery has enabled the film's innovations, it does not account for their impact. The long, continuous takes seem so thrillingly impossible, the weightless flights of the camera so liberating, only because Cuarón is careful never to disturb your ingrained notion that a big movie camera must somehow have been set up at the scene to record what you're seeing. You know better, of course. And yet, starting with an opening image that temporarily pretends to be a static establishing shot, Cuarón keeps lulling you back into a belief in the physical presence of objects, imparting a Newtonian force and momentum to his surprises by bouncing them off your immovable assumptions.

And so I come to the three-dimensional tears of Sandra Bullock.

During a brief lull in the action, just long enough for you to catch your breath, Bullock's character reflects on the pain that the script says she's borne for years; and as she mourns, a watery globe suddenly floats into sight, to hang suspended in the illusory space in front of the screen. This teardrop, which you could almost touch, is now the main focus of the scene, while Bullock blurs into an indistinct backdrop. It's a charming touch and probably not overdone (except for being repeated immediately, to make sure everyone catches on). Still, it seems telling that *Gravity* should concentrate however briefly on manifesting a material substance before your eyes, rather than allowing Bullock to continue connecting with you directly, as she knows very well how to do.

Maybe Cuarón forces the emotion here in the guilty knowledge that his screenplay (written in collaboration with his son Jonás) gives Bullock's character only the most banal past to go with her wildly desperate present. Without revealing more than I should, I can tell you that 10,000 movie heroines have suffered the sorrow that haunts her. It's practically the first thing that male screenwriters grab for when inventing a troubled woman, but not the only evidence of thoughtlessness in this script. The Cuaróns also fall back on a sentimental religiosity that is beneath Bullock, and demand nothing more from Clooney than another flash of the easy heroism that he's spent the past fifteen years trying to complicate or avoid.

Hence the superiority of *2001*. Kubrick simply offers you more substance; and in the future, when the wow factor of *Gravity* is diminished, as that of *2001* has faded now, the imbalance between the two films will be even more obvious.

Still, I would hate to make *Gravity* sound like nothing more than a technical achievement. The film does have a theme—call it the worthiness of human burdens, or the heroism of standing on your feet—and uses the marvels of its imagery to drive that meaning home, just as surely as it uses your reliance on ordinary thinking to make itself seem astounding. This dialectic even places *Gravity* in tension with Cuarón's previous films. Although he solidified his reputation by toying imaginatively with social realism in *Y Tu Mamá También*, his artistic instincts seem to go strongly toward myth and fable. His was the only Harry Potter film that actually felt magical, and his terrific *Children of Men* (whose long, mobile takes presaged *Gravity*) built a wonderfully paranoid apocalyptic thriller out of rubble and hooey. In *Gravity*, he has let loose his love of the fantastic with a freedom and exuberance that no one could have foreseen, only to put it at the service of the message "There's no place like home."

If Clooney might be said to articulate Cuarón's thoughts when he remarks on the beauty that can be seen only from outer space, at the far edge of responsibility, then Bullock speaks to Cuarón's heart. I have read that she was not at first available for the film and that several other actresses were considered, and can say only that if she had not been cast, there would have been no ground to *Gravity*. Her taut, straining face and body unfailingly persuade you that she's calling up miraculous reserves of will-power and vigor; her voice, so often pitched between a sigh and a rasp, is always the right instrument to cry defiance in the midst of extremity. Despite the tears floating around, despite the wheeling universe, she is the center of this movie. When Clooney says to her, "You're going to make it," you know she will, because that is what Sandra Bullock does, every time. And she makes *Gravity*.

The Nation, October 28, 2013

A Touch of Sin

Jia Zhangke has opened vast new areas of subject matter for cinema in a highly self-aware but bracingly confrontational style. His ambition is only slightly less grand than is implied by the title of his 2004 film, *The World*. He'll settle for representing all of China. In *A Touch of Sin*, he tours the country from north to south—Shanxi, Chongqing, Hubei, Guangdong—while telling four linked stories that he's based on real events. A middle-aged miner goes on a shotgun rampage. A migrant laborer carries out an armed robbery, execution style. The receptionist in a bathhouse-brothel slashes two customers. A young hotel worker takes a dive off a balcony. Everywhere these four characters turn, they encounter entrenched corruption, the arrogance of wealth and the threat of sanctioned violence. They respond with self-righteous vengeance or cold-blooded opportunism, an impulsive lunge to maintain a last shred of respectability or a desperate leap out of this life into the next, which might turn out to be better.

Much has been made of Jia's shifts, in *A Touch of Sin*, from social realist observation to neo-realist melodrama to action sequences that might have come from martial arts movies. (Or westerns, for that matter: the rampaging miner stalks through his scenes like Charles Bronson in a duster.) For good measure, Jia gives his stories the cultural resonance of traditional opera—shown in street-plaza performances—and the emblematic presence of animals from the Chinese zodiac, as if the events he shows were part of the eternal round. Some filmmakers (Godard, for instance) might present this abundance in fragments, but not Jia. He seems to believe that the world (or China, at least) is whole; and so, although his film is panoramic in settings and quasi-encyclopedic in styles, it unrolls as a single picture, sweeping, fluid and mesmerizingly clear.

The Nation, November 11, 2013

American Hustle

Never mind the cocaine. When I remember the 1970s, I think of roller disco: dense crowds of people jacked high off the floor on their four-wheeled boots, zooming, teetering, slipping in and out of control as they showed off for one another. That's the dizzying sensation that David O. Russell keeps spinning you into in his deliriously enjoyable *American Hustle*, a combo caper film, romantic comedy and political satire based on the FBI's 1978 Abscam operation. How loosely based, only a disco pedestrian would ask. As the opening title says, "Some of this actually happened."

So much garrulous energy comes spilling out of the movie that before the plot can get well under way, three different voiceovers are already competing for your attention. The first gives the viewpoint of Irving Rosenfeld, a Bronx-born con artist who deals in paintings that are fraudulent and usurious loans that somehow never get made. He also owns a chain of dry-cleaning shops. The second voiceover is that of Sydney Prosser, a former stripper from Albuquerque who moved to New York, got a job at *Cosmopolitan* magazine (hello, Burt Reynolds!) and rose high enough in society to be invited to a party on Long Island, where she and Irving lock eyes. Though Sydney has the luck to look just like Amy Adams, while Irving looks like Christian Bale with a prosthetic potbelly, an appalling comb-over and a pair of tinted aviator eyeglasses that keep slipping down his nose, she falls for him, and he for her. Soon they're running cons together, with Sydney (shades of *The Lady Eve*) putting on three-fifths of an English accent and calling herself Lady Edith.

The third voiceover comes from Richie DiMaso, an FBI agent who busts Sydney and Irving for loan-sharking but offers to have the charges dropped if they'll run some cons for him so he can catch a better class of criminal. Also, as soon as he saw Sydney he liked her, he means *liked* her, and wanted to help her get away from Irving, as he explains at 300 words a minute. That's because Richie looks like Bradley Cooper with a beard and Jheri curls and acts like Bradley Cooper during his manic episodes in *Silver Linings Playbook*.

I have not yet explained Irving's wife, Rosalyn, who does not get her own voiceover but arguably does not need one, having been graced with the looks of a bouffant-topped and intensively manicured Jennifer Lawrence, whose murderous conversational style casts her as a sort of female Gallipoli, standing helpless before Irving's naval assault. Rosalyn does not like Sydney. Sydney does not like Rosalyn. The fact that two such women should not just love but compete over a hunched, wheezing mess like Irving is both an unacknowledged joke in *American Hustle* and a complicating factor in the FBI sting operation.

There are plenty of complicating factors, including Irving's sympathy for the first target of the operation (the salt-of-the-earth mayor of Camden, New Jersey), Sydney's wavering conviction that she's merely playing Richie when she encourages his attentions, and Richie's self-image as a heroic rule-breaker, a delusion that is entirely functional in this setting and leads him to raise the stakes again and again. Did I mention that the bait in Richie's scheme, a phony Arab sheik (actually Special Agent Paco Hernandez), is supposedly going to invest in casino gambling? Would it surprise you if the prospect of casino gambling elicited an appearance from another member of Russell's growing stock company, Robert De Niro? The trouble escalates.

So does the joy. I don't think Christian Bale has had so much fun in a performance since *American Psycho*. He shrugs, spritzes, talks like Danny DeVito and seems twice as alive as he does in his other new movie, the dour, doom-laden *Out of the Furnace*. Jennifer Lawrence, as you may have heard, is also currently in another film. She serves as a solid tentpole in *The Hunger Games: Catching Fire*. In *American Hustle*, she lets her talent loose, taking everything she does a step too far and gleefully getting away with it every time. Amy Adams, a performer who can do no wrong in front of a camera, takes nothing too far. She executes her scenes like a high-speed racer on a flawless slalom run; you hold your breath and look on in awe.

I could go on as well about Bradley Cooper and Jeremy Renner (as the irresistibly boisterous Camden mayor) but want to reserve the last words for Russell's direction. Like that other time-traveler to the 1970s, Paul Thomas Anderson, Russell is a big, expressive moviemaker who seems willing to try anything. Unlike Anderson, he's even willing to swerve a little out of control, roller-disco style. (You never know what detail will momentarily distract his moving camera.) He's also convinced that his cheap con artists are not pathetic creatures but rather are fundamentally, winningly wholesome.

American Hustle, may it live forever, is the only film I know where eternal love between crooks is pledged in the twirling ecstasy of a dry-cleaning carousel.

The Nation, December 23, 2013

Boyhood

For such a quietly observant film, unhurried in pace and grounded in daily affairs, Richard Linklater's *Boyhood* makes a lot of threats to end in violence. Drinking and driving, horseplay with flying saw blades, inexpert handling of a shotgun, assault with a blunt but shattering object: this is only a partial list of the potentially lethal activities that are made to coalesce, or sometimes erupt, around the central character, a boy named Mason, as he grows up in present-day Texas. Functionally, the notes of menace are useful for ratcheting up the tension now and then in a story that otherwise flows smoothly along Mason's course, from city to city, school to school, parent to parent. It occurs to me, though, that a thematic purpose also animates these recurring moments of dreadful anticipation. They remind you, often obliquely but always with a pang, that it's no sure thing for anyone to reach 18.

Nor was it a sure thing that Linklater would finish *Boyhood*. Maybe the hints of fatality in his story are also subtle traces, left on the movie's surface, of an anxiety about the extraordinary way the film was made.

Linklater shot *Boyhood* intermittently over a twelve-year span, from 2002 through 2013, using a core group of performers whose central member, Ellar Coltrane, started as a 6-year-old and grew up playing Mason. The method made production as precarious as life itself. Money could have dried up at any time, or a key actor dropped out. Even the availability of the materials became doubtful, with the rise of video during these years making it increasingly difficult for Linklater to keep going with 35-millimeter film.

As you watch *Boyhood* and gradually catch on to its trick of honesty, realizing that there have been no substitutions in the cast—the 12-year-old on-screen is the same kid who was 10 before, and 8—and noticing that the actors playing the parents haven't been aged with makeup but really are older, you might conclude, as I did, that *Boyhood* is one of the most patient, modest acts of daredevilry ever achieved on film. The persistence that Linklater maintained behind the camera must have been heroic; but in keeping with the subject matter, he doesn't make a big deal of it. He just carries you through the story, as naturally and amazingly as an exemplary boy such as Mason reaches manhood.

When I call Mason exemplary, I mean he's occupied with the activities of a great many American boys of his era. He steeps himself in the Harry Potter world, clicks madly at video games, listens to Coldplay, eats burgers, gets bullied, sometimes chafes under his parents and teachers, and eventually learns to talk to girls. So much for his main business. As for discovering the larger world, he experiences its events as myopically and discontinuously as most kids do: through a father who campaigns for Obama, for instance, and a mother and stepfather who buy a foreclosed house.

Maybe that doesn't sound like enough to hold you rapt through a very long movie; but then, the exemplary is only half the picture. The other half is the characters' back-and-forth struggle, by turns deliberate and instinctive, to pull away from the norm or squeeze back in. It's this continually developing movement, more than any feint toward violence, that generates the deeper, more satisfying tensions in *Boyhood*.

In Mason's case, of course, it takes a few years for the idiosyncrasies to show up. He seems at first to be much like any other 6-year-old boy with an arrowhead collection and a drama queen of an older sister (Lorelei Linklater). He's just a little more full-lipped, perhaps, and more apt to spend the whole day staring out the window. It's up to the estranged parents to give *Boyhood* its initial jolts of particularity.

The custodial parent (Patricia Arquette), a bundle of bustling organization and ripe sensual promise, is in her mid-30s when the story begins and has a habit of scattering declarations of need like psychic bread crumbs from a Hansel-less Gretel. Heedless, or perhaps not, that her children overhear them all, she will round on her current boyfriend at one moment, ordering him to get out if he can't respect her for putting the kids first, and start wailing in frustration the next moment that she's gone from being a daughter to a mother, with no time in the middle to be herself. Seeking a way out of her spiritual woods, she decides early in the film to return to college and earn a degree; and so she packs everyone in the car and moves to Houston, demonstrating a strength of will that is instructive for the children, combined with an equally characteristic impulsiveness that will keep them off-balance through most of their childhood.

Houston is where the mother remarries, disastrously, for the first time. It's also where she rejects the advances of the Pied Piper: her dashingly scruffy former husband (Ethan Hawke), a would-be musician, who returns from a period of wandering in Alaska to play catch-up dad. He collects the children in his thrilling muscle car (no seat belts!), fills them with bowling, junk food and the patented Hawke jive-talk, and returns them late to mom, who is too infuriated by his irresponsibility (or just the sight of his face) to abide his shyly suggestive smile. Here, too, are lessons for the watchful Mason: grown-ups can try to correct for their mistakes (even if they're not very good at it), and they also can have some fun.

Just above the boy's head, the mother is repeatedly trying and failing to live as a good housewife but gradually succeeding in a modest academic career; the father is repeatedly trying to keep up his tom-cat image but ultimately succeeding (to his self-amused surprise) in becoming a chaste and gainfully employed married man; and all the while, young Mason is developing into—who? Someone just like his parents, of course; and also someone as unforeseeable as the elongation of his childhood moon-face into an adolescent trowel. (The physical changes in Ellar Coltrane are almost a plot development in themselves, perhaps worthy of a spoiler alert.) As Mason grows to occupy more and more of the center of his own movie, he remains as quizzical and easily bruised as when he was small but also develops something stubbornly independent out of his dreaminess—an artistic temperament that dislikes confrontation (he will move 600 miles to avoid an ex-girl-friend) but can hold out against conventional expectations and compromise.

Thanks to the astonishing consistency of Linklater and the cast, and the faultless editing of Sandra Adair (a heroine in her own right), all this happens in *Boyhood* much as it would in reality, as a continual unfolding, without on-screen titles or chapter breaks. Neither is there anyone to explain what's going on—at least, not from outside the frame. As in most of Linklater's films, though, the characters have ideas, which they express in wonderfully alert yet unforced walking-and-talking scenes or sometimes, as when Mason drops in on one of his mother's lectures, a formal setting. She happens to be teaching John Bowlby's attachment theory on a day when Mason swings by, and so he hears, in a single moment, both her nutshell version of evolutionary psychology and a covert confession about his own family's life: we survive through love.

Mason seems ready for love when we leave him. He's just wandered off from his first day at college, still acting a little feck-less but already (due to long experience) blending in with a new set of people, and is watching a sunset side by side with a potential girlfriend. With a wisdom that is either Ellar Coltrane's, Linklater's or a blend of the two—such is the seamlessness of the movie—he gazes ahead calmly, as if over the heads of the audience, and speaks the film's last quasi-explanation of itself. They tell you to seize the moment, he says; but really, the moment seizes us.

Another spoiler? Well, that's *Boyhood*. That's life.

The Nation, August 4, 2014

Mad Max: Fury Road

As if you needed further evidence of my faulty judgment, in my previous column I said I was waiting "like everybody else" to see *Mad Max: Fury Road*. Now the box-office results are in, and it's plain that only a minority of us had been impatient for kinesthetic delights to hurtle into the frame from every side and at all times, never as you'd expect, while dystopian horrors blast back out of the screen with an equally endless inventiveness, here clanking with a grotesquerie of jerry-rigged chains and motors, there roaring with the excess of a rock musician shooting flames from his guitar, as Tom Hardy in an iron mask is raised up on an armored dune buggy like a hood-ornament crucifix and a crew-cut Charlize Theron commands the churning desert with her cold blue gaze, glinting under a coat of crankcase grease, all so the film can incite women everywhere to rise up with her, our one-armed Imperator Furiosa, and overthrow war-loving, Earth-devouring, mechanistic patriarchy.

Other people wanted to see *Pitch Perfect 2*.

Without prejudice to that jaunty a cappella comedy, I will say that its commercial triumph over *Mad Max: Fury Road* shows that I've fallen onto the dark side of a generational divide. It's not just that the plurality of the theatergoing audience cannot recall the glories of George Miller's original *Mad Max* trilogy, the most recent of which was released 30 years ago. Research (meaning chats with my daughter and a random sample of her friends) demonstrates that kids today neither recognize nor desire a cinema like Miller's, which does to the methods and imagery of pop movies what Jimi Hendrix did to the old-style electric blues, and to a similarly outrageous purpose. Despite the robust overseas ticket sales for *Fury Road*, the domestic appetite for this kind of filmmaking seems to have withered, leaving us with a young mainstream audience that wants to see genre conventions fulfilled, not exploded. Have I mentioned *San Andreas*?

No—I don't want to talk about *San Andreas*. I'd rather dedicate two more paragraphs to *Mad Max: Fury Road*, knowing that few other films this year are likely to be as impressive. It's like a simoom, a conquering Amazon, a burning bush. You don't so much watch it as enter its presence—and once there, you find that it does not stoop to explain itself. After all of 30 seconds' worth of introductory voice-over, which is not so much an exposition as a groan of despair from Max, the action starts and the guidance ends. Where do they come from, all these dead-white, half-naked, shave-skulled men? Why is it a form of blessing for them to have their mouths sprayed with aerosol paint, while their leader intones, "You will ride eternal, shiny and chrome"? How would you translate "He's a crazy smig who eats schlanger"? What makes you think you've got time to ask? Unlike action directors of the plodding sort, George Miller doesn't ask you to understand the deliriously strange world into which he throws you headlong. He just wants to change the parts you recognize.

Mad Max: Fury Road has been skewing a little old in its audience—an inevitability, when a film is R-rated—but it's got more rebellious energy than anything else around, even though its writer-director is a septuagenarian and its totally kick-ass heroine is played by an actress who is pushing 40, the age at which Hollywood wants to stamp Expired on a woman's forehead. This is not to imply that *Fury Road* is an entry in the current cycle of geezerfests such as *The Expendables* and *RED*, which convene actors in middle age or beyond to prove that their stunt doubles can still blow things up. Miller and Theron have no time for such jokey self-congratulation. They're too busy actually ripping up the screen.

The Nation, July 6, 2015

Everybody Wants Some!!

Titled after a Van Halen song and a truth universally acknowledged, Richard Linklater's *Everybody Wants Some!!* follows a dozen members of a college-baseball team through a cloudless late summer in 1980. You know the clock is ticking for these specimens of boisterously healthy manhood, as it always does for young athletes; and yet Linklater, who made the *Before* trilogy and *Boyhood* (which could have been called *Before Consciousness of Mortality*), allows neither pathos nor urgency to intrude this time. The master of deadline cinema flashes a title at the beginning, telling you that classes will start in three days and so many hours and minutes. Then, when each section of the film has drifted by, he revises the tally downward, with a precision that grows more ridiculous in proportion to the mounting evidence that his characters just don't care. For as long as the film lasts, these blithe young men with their Burt Reynolds mustaches and torso-hugging T-shirts live in an eternal present of chasing women, drinking, partying, making fun of each other, chasing women, dropping by the swimming hole, lounging about their off-campus houses, and talking nonsense. One afternoon, they even practice a little baseball.

For as long as the movie lasts, you too have nothing more pressing to do. It's only afterward, when you look back on this comedy of jock manners, that you marvel at how economically Linklater has wafted you along, using little more than breezy moods, plotless good spirits, and the rhythms of an encyclopedically eclectic pop sound track. Compared to the difficulty of sustaining a whole movie on such wisps, you might think, the creation of weighty masterpieces must be no trick at all.

That said, if you're determined to do it, you can wring a story, some themes, and even a moral out of *Everybody Wants Some!!* A freshman pitcher named Jake, played by the charmingly long-faced and gangly Blake Jenner, drives into the fictional Southeast Texas State University on surges of "My Sharona" and brings the camera with him to explore, with rapid efficiency, the old wood-frame houses where the baseball players live and to get introduced to the other characters. Thoughtful and a little quiet, but also poised and adept at blending in, Jake understands that the days ahead will be about transforming a gathering of highly competitive egotists into a functioning team.

Stupid bets, practical jokes, and the intense pursuit of victory in darts, table tennis, and Nerf basketball are some of the methods by which the characters test one another, developing a give-and-take and resolving their hierarchy. Skirt-chasing is another. Even though the frenetic nightly pairings-off are ostensibly done just for pleasure (and seem to deliver plenty of it), success in soliciting the warm cooperation of young women is one more means by which the ballplayers decide how they rank in relation to one another. In their muscular encounters on and off the diamond, McReynolds (Tyler Hoechlin)—dark-haired, gruff, and unbelievably strong—reigns as the man you shouldn't even try to beat. In the discos, roadhouses, and parties, Finnegan (Glen Powell)—blond, pipe-smoking, and drolly grandiloquent—reigns as the acknowledged leader in chatting up women. You might say that *Everybody Wants Some!!* is the story of how Jake meets the challenge of McReynolds, accepts tutelage from Finnegan, and then has enough wit and soul of his own to fall in with a woman he actually likes: an open-faced, sassily earnest performing-arts major named Beverly (Zoey Deutch).

Of course, this is an unrealistically rosy image of life, and it's clearly meant to be. You can recognize the paradisiacal aspirations of *Everybody Wants Some!!* by the fate of the one character who is not allowed to linger in its sweetness: a late-hippie pitcher named Willoughby (Wyatt Russell), who resigns himself to expulsion in the film's only plot twist. By sending Willoughby off, Linklater in effect confirms that everyone else remains within the gates of Eden, where the colors of Shane F. Kelly's cinematography resemble Valentine's Day candy hearts and the musical options—from disco and punk, from funk to country—unite rather than divide America's tribes.

Toward the end, the ballplayers are even granted a college student's vision of heaven on earth, when the team tags along with Jake to the performing-arts majors' start-of-school party. It's held in the off-campus house called Oz, which is as good a name as any for this panchromatic wonderland of fairy lights and $1.98 exotica. In truth, it's gorgeous, especially after you've been staring for so long at the ballplayers' bland quarters.

The moral—I promised you one—is that the athletes, like the rest of us, might intuit whatever grace they enjoy in their lives but have trouble recognizing it on their own. It takes the performing artists to show it to them. As for the climax—or as much of one as you're going to get—it involves Jake's being recruited at the party to play the White Rabbit in a skit where Beverly appears as Alice. "I'm late!" he cries, in the film's first and last expression of temporal anxiety. But his reading of the line is hopelessly, hilariously inept, not so much for want of theatrical training but because he lacks all conviction in the role. He's game enough, for Beverly's sake, but it's clear that he still hasn't heard the clock ticking.

Linklater hears it, though. Among his agendas in *Everybody Wants Some!!* is to revisit an important moment in his quarter-century-long career (this being a sequel of sorts to his first commercial hit, *Dazed and Confused*) while also thinking about his own college-age defection from baseball to theater arts. In many writer-directors who have reached their middle years, such self-reflection might be a bad sign. But I think that Linklater—arguably the highest-grossing experimental filmmaker of our time—has more than earned the right to work a few autobiographical musings into a picture; and besides, you're free to disregard them. All they do is lend this lighter-than-air contraption enough gravity to keep you skimming within safe reach of the ground. You will have to touch down eventually: You know it, and Linklater knows it. For a while, though, the two of you may as well enjoy the time of your life.

The Nation, April 25, 2016

Toni Erdmann

A large, shaggy something called *Toni Erdmann* got loose at this year's New York Film Festival, loping at will through the aisles of Alice Tully Hall while bellowing mournfully and tickling the patrons. People who had spotted the creature earlier, in Cannes or Toronto, had predicted the rampage; but as an experienced festivalgoer, I was skeptical about reports of a seven-foot-tall, pointy-headed movie that would jump out from behind a seat and try to hug me.

"Wait and see," I thought. The main slate already promised plenty of unruliness. Then the festival let *Toni Erdmann* out of its cage, and I, too, started jabbering that Bigfoot roamed Lincoln Center.

Written and directed by Maren Ade, *Toni Erdmann* is the story of an estranged daughter and father who are both going through life in disguise, the main difference being that hers is respectable. Slender, blond, and thirtysomething, Ines (Sandra Hüller) keeps her hair smoothed in a French twist and her body sheathed in black pantsuits as she plots her rise in the men's world of management consulting. Despite being assigned to the capitalist backwater of Bucharest, she maneuvers sharply against her colleagues, seeking to outdo them in the task of masking their client's outsourcing goals. It's cold-blooded work—and so Ines does not want to be distracted by her father Winfried (Peter Simonischek), a shambling, shabby, sixtyish German music teacher whose idea of fun is to play dress-up with fright wigs, Jerry Lewis—style false teeth, and an occasional application of ghoul makeup, the better to joke about, oh, mailing letter bombs and shooting people. Other than that, the old card seems harmless, except that he springs himself on Ines in Bucharest, unannounced, and begins to burlesque her profession. Disappointed that his daughter doesn't melt at once into reconciliation, Winfried starts pretending to be a management coach named Toni Erdmann, having donned for this purpose a black suit, black tie, and floor-mop wig. He looks like Neil Young in a remake of *Reservoir Dogs*.

From this rigorously concise summary, you will understand that a lot goes on in *Toni Erdmann*—and I've brought you only as far as the moment when Ines hurls spaghetti at her father and he responds by handcuffing her, after which things start to get disorderly. Wills are tested, competitions fought, more extravagant disguises assumed, and all possibility of disguise stripped away.

Should I say that Ines learns to loosen up in the screwball-comedy tradition thanks to an odd form of paternal care, or would it be more accurate to say that Winfried is pathetically, overbearingly needy, and Ines has to free herself before she suffocates? I can't decide—which is one of the great merits of *Toni Erdmann*. Here are two more: Sandra Hüller's performance, which proceeds from the tightest self-control to a recklessness destined for legend, and the delighted reaction of the audience. You'll want to see this one in a crowd when it opens in theaters, so you can feel the waves of laughter crashing over each other.

The Nation, November 28, 2016

Arrival

I couldn't wait to see Amy Adams talk to extraterrestrials in *Arrival*. Who else could make such a good first impression for us? The American president who evidently stills holds office in the movie—and is excoriated by talk-radio bullies for not declaring all-out war on space travelers—would certainly be a first-rate spokesperson for earthlings, but he'll soon be unavailable. And America's actual president-elect? I don't think he'd be the best choice in a situation that demands tact. The obscurity of purpose of our otherworldly visitors and the unfathomability of their minds would best be met by someone who's a human light source. Send Amy Adams to shine at them.

There's a climactic scene in *Arrival* in which Adams, as the linguist Louise Banks, stands in the immediate presence of an unimaginable being, with the floating red tendrils of her hair and marine blue of her eyes the only areas of strong color in a visual field transformed by cinematographer Bradford Young into an ophthalmologic aura, such as you see when your pupils have been dilated; and though the billows of light on-screen may cloak the alien, it's the unclouded surface of Adams's face that spreads the glow. Write off the effect, if you like, to mere cinematic technique combined with cultural prejudice, which sees in Adams's physiognomy a storybook princess or well-scrubbed hometown girl. You'd still need to account for the surplus of illumination—candor and intelligence made visible—that Adams can project the way Aroldis Chapman pitches fastballs. Her professional capability saves this scene from being just another episode of sci-fi transcendence. Her force of personality makes you proud to see the hand-lettered sign she holds up, earlier in the movie, to identify herself: "Human."

Adams is directed in *Arrival* by the Quebecois filmmaker Denis Villeneuve, who has previously alternated between artfully brutal suspense pictures (*Prisoners*, *Sicario*) and narrative conundrums (*Enemy*). Here he works in both modes at once, giving a bang-up staging to the military and popular response to the alien landing (high alert, total panic) while also evoking the increasingly odd psychological effect of the visitors on Dr. Banks. She already appears to be drifting emotionally at the start of the movie, holed up alone in a tasteful waterfront house (nice woodwork, picture windows, and wine glasses) and brooding over dreamy, discontinuous scenes of the life and death of her daughter. Banks's inner state becomes even more unsettled, understandably, when the US

Army shows up in the form of Forest Whitaker and whisks her away in a helicopter to an impromptu base in Montana, where she's expected to interpret the rumbles, booms, and crackles that presumably serve as speech among the recently landed aliens.

A conventional theme of humanism versus hard science labors into the film during this sequence, announced loudly through a rivalry between Banks and a new colleague, Ian Donnelly; and because this physicist is played by the studly Jeremy Renner, the extraprofessional destination of the characters' sentiments is also thuddingly obvious. These stumbles are the exceptions, though, in a picture that usually moves lightly and with refreshing subtlety. Villeneuve uses only a few economical strokes to establish the mood after the extraterrestrials appear: the sound of unseen fighter jets roaring across the sky, while in an almost deserted parking lot, one car backs into another. Villeneuve is similarly understated in the setting he constructs for Banks once she reaches Montana: a labyrinth of low, narrow, dimly lit military tents, which looks realistic enough but also seems like the outward, visible sign of the heroine's inner maze.

When Banks and her team proceed into the alien craft—the galaxy's biggest skipping stone, you'd think, which stands upright while hovering 20 feet over the ground—Villeneuve continues his labyrinth and elaborates on it. The investigators enter another tunnel, which is longer, darker, and even more suffocating than the ones in the tent city. It's more disorienting as well, since it starts out being vertical and unitary but then branches out by overcoming gravity and multiplying the possibilities of "up" and "down." There is light at the end of this tunnel: a bright rectangle with the unmistakable proportions of a movie screen. Just like you, Banks and her new colleagues are going to a show.

What they see when they get there is familiar enough to qualify as a traditional viewer attraction. The aliens who put themselves on view are variously reminiscent of tentacled monsters in horror movies, creatures floating behind the glass of a giant aquarium, and (in Donnelly's opinion) Abbott and Costello. At the same time, they so impressively defy expectations—especially in their means of communication—that I should cut short the description. It's enough to say that Banks has to work, mentally and physically, to follow the show she's watching, and can't succeed without instilling her own feelings into the production.

So is *Arrival* just another movie about watching movies—another roundabout trip through a self-enclosed system that ends at its own beginning? Yes, and no. We count on films, if they're any good, to be about something beyond themselves; and although the "sci" half of the sci-fi is thoroughly pseudo in this instance, and the linguistics more attuned to Robert Heinlein's dopey fantasies than Noam Chomsky's research, *Arrival* nevertheless succeeds in making terrestrial contact. It does so partly by deploying the unfailing Adams; partly by using aliens to direct our attention toward a real problem (the political division of Earth into competing national interests); and partly by treating the screen as a space for displaying continually changing possibilities—some that a smart, ethical woman would resist and some that she might joyfully embrace, whatever sorrow comes with them.

That's the agenda: Confront xenophobia, save Earth from itself, elevate movie-watching into intellectual struggle, and attain the peace that passeth all understanding. From these goals, you get artsy mishmash, which is how I'd characterize *Arrival* at its worst. At its best, which is considerable, you also get astonishment, awe, and tempered optimism (which is always good to have), along with respect for the female *Homo sapiens* and pleasure in the filmmakers' powers of invention.

It was purely by accident, of course, that *Arrival*'s release immediately after the election brought these qualities into theaters at a time of great darkness. What the movie offers is so valuable, though, that you might almost choose to take the story on its own goofy terms and pretend that someone, somewhere, knew we were going to need this picture.

The Nation, December 5, 2016

Get Out

Given that Jordan Peele's indelible horror movie *Get Out* has been in theaters for a while, you probably know that it's the story of a young African-American man who ventures into the wealthy suburbs for a weekend with his white girlfriend's family. There, he begins to feel even more assailed by creepiness than he'd expected—teeth-grindingly overwhelmed, as if every time these people try *not* to make him uncomfortable they sprinkle sour, powdery candy on his molars.

White liberal journalists, knowing that Peele got his start in comedy, have tagged *Get Out* as a satire on the racism that persists among their own groups. Permit me to say, no. In the first place, although Peele calculates just the right titration of comic relief for the film, he allows not one drop more. Satire implies the provocation of laughter, even if it's harsh or mocking. The truly disturbing *Get Out* seldom raises so much as a smile.

In the second and more important place, the subject of *Get Out* is not white liberals. The subject is the emotional world of the film's protagonist, Chris (the unfailingly sympathetic and convincing Daniel Kaluuya); and the primary intended witnesses to that world, sitting in the movie house or on their couches at home, are other African Americans. How else should I interpret the film's mode of address? At a critical moment in the plot, another Black character furiously shouts the title's imperative at Chris. Peele, by extension, might be said to yell the same directive to every Black person in the audience: Get out!

Get out of what? Let's say the illusion that you can trust white people; the delusion that you can risk loving one of them.

Being the pale type myself, I don't for a moment accept as literally true the premise of permanent, endemic white treacherousness. But Peele doesn't ask that belief of me, or anyone. What he does is scream in terror that this premise might be true; he howls at the nightmare vision of white people exerting their dominance not just around him but inside his body.

I see very few movies that express an emotion with such intensity, or set their uncanny images like barbs in your brain. Black people who are curious about the awards hoopla may find that *Get Out* speaks to them. Those who are not Black are free to eavesdrop. That's the great advantage Peele gives himself by choosing this genre as his vehicle. Everybody knows how to watch a horror movie.

The Nation, December 21, 2017

Sorry to Bother You

No sooner had the Greatest of All Time firmly established his reign as champion than he abandoned the name Cassius, as the world's most glorious butterfly might have shucked its cocoon. But in Boots Riley's *Sorry to Bother You* (which is, in part, a tale of metamorphosis), the scuffling and frequently scuffed protagonist clings to his given name of Cassius, often shortening it to Cash, which goes well with the surname Green. Amiable, imaginative, and at first seemingly none too energetic, Cash is all about getting that green, as he has to be, living in a garage in Oakland on which he owes four months' rent. To make money, he will sell whatever he needs to, including himself. For a considerable stretch, he does well at it, too, though with shameful consequences for his soul—which is the only part of this movie I could have predicted.

How many parts are there? It's hard to say. *Sorry to Bother You* bears some resemblance to the car that Cash, in his original state, impels through Oakland on pocket change and willpower: a vehicle banged together from so many spare panels that it's a five-tone. Working with much the same ingenuity and disdain for elegance that would have ruled in that auto-body shop, Riley has made a fable about union organizing and worker solidarity—astonishing to see such a thing nowadays—and then welded it onto a satire about the ways in which people perform race, a diatribe about contemporary media as a culture of humiliation, a critique of art-world critiques of global capitalism, and a horror movie. How all this fits together, I'm not sure; but I'm content to have muttered "Now what?" during the screening far more often than "That again!," and I'm delighted to have staggered a little on the way out, having had all that subject matter dumped on me in a little under two hours.

To the extent that *Sorry to Bother You* holds together, the person doing the binding is Riley's lead actor, Lakeith Stanfield. Best known for playing the kind, hapless, and obliquely brilliant stoner Darius on *Atlanta*—and for having shouted the title in *Get Out*—Stanfield begins the film holding his body like a question mark. The shoulders are hunched within an unfortunate sweater vest (just the thing, Cash apparently thinks, to impress the white people doing the hiring at the RegalView Telemarketing boiler room). The head is thrust forward, with eyes sometimes vaguely downcast, and it's topped by a possibly inadvertent hairstyle, whose protrusions echo the old ornamental fringe that dangles from the ceiling of his car. Everything about Cash at first seems puzzled, tentative, and dubious; everything overwhelms him. When he takes up the telemarketer's craft, he feels as if each call brings him crashing down from his workstation to a site he can picture on the other end of the phone, where people are going about their lives with no need of him. Each time, as you laugh, you see the mute apology that Stanfield puts into Cash's eyes.

Then the old hand at the next workstation (Danny Glover) lets Cash in on the secret of successful telemarketing: Use a white voice. No, not merely nasal, but also unconcerned, unpressured, unrushed—the voice of someone who has never been fired but only laid off. It's not the way white people actually talk, the mentor explains, but the way they think they ought to sound. Cash tries it (the abruptly high-pitched, singsong tones that emerge from Stanfield's mouth are voiced by David Cross), and it works too well. It's not just that Cash begins to rack up sales. It's that you see him straighten up and start to smile, with pride and pleasure brightening his face for the first time. And worse: Now that he's using his white voice, Cash no longer feels the slightest empathy for the people he's got on the line.

A man who has freed himself from empathy might be all set to make money, but he will no longer be a reliable help to the friends and fellow workers (Steven Yeun and Jermaine Fowler) who are struggling to unionize RegalView Telemarketing. Nor will he have an easy time holding on to his girlfriend Detroit (Tessa Thompson), given her anticolonialist, anticapitalist, Africanist ideals. Detroit earns her living on the streets as a kind of human billboard, holding aloft the products of a sign-making company, and at night creates performance art—which is another way to turn her own body into a sign. In one of the movie's more disturbing twists, she uses the performance not to recuperate from the day's indignities but to intensify them by calling abuse onto herself—whether in masochistic identification with Cash or to repudiate him violently, it's impossible to say.

We come to the theme of injury. For reasons that are too thickly determined to explain here, Cash spends the movie's second half with a length of white gauze wrapped around his head, its surface perpetually oozing a blot of red. You might interpret this bandage as an outward sign of the wound he has inflicted on himself within, especially as the plot gets weirder and a Bay Area gazillionaire white-bro disrupter (Armie Hammer) persuades him—in the film's most scabrously funny scene—to proceed from marketing artificial whiteness to acting out a confected Blackness. But then, Cash isn't alone in yielding to self-humiliation while telling himself that money cures all. In the world of *Sorry to Bother You*, TV's most popular game show has people compete by taking a massive beating, which also seems to be the prize.

Is that supposed to be amusing? The people in *Sorry to Bother You* generally think so. Having grown accustomed to taking blows, they positively bubble over at the sight of somebody else getting it for a change. I might complain that this analysis of our callousness is a little too pat and familiar, except that it isn't an analysis at all but one more dented panel on this jolting, fuming, ridiculously transporting jalopy of a movie.

"Stick to the script," the bosses at the telemarketing firm keep telling their workers. Cassius, who is no champion, does just that for the longest time; but in his first feature film, Boots Riley pretty much shreds the script, or several of them. Nothing in this movie happens the way it's supposed to, from the non-hero's discovery of his special gift (which turns out to be the opposite of empowering) to the valiant exposure, on live TV, of Armie Hammer's nefarious plans (which only helps move them along). The one unifying statement you could make about this burlesque is that it's a lesson in the virtue of disobedience—which, by the end, Cassius has learned. Unwillingly.

The Nation, July 6, 2018

Roma

Nothing I've seen recently—in years—can match the clarity of vision and intensity of feeling, expansiveness and intimacy, breadth and breath of Alfonso Cuarón's *Roma*.

Set in Mexico City in 1970-71 and based on events in Cuarón's childhood, the story in simple terms is about two women and the complementary troubles that bind them: the pregnancy of the unwed Cleo, a domestic servant of Mixtec background (Yalitza Aparicio), and the abandonment of Cleo's high-bourgeois employer Sofía (Marina de Tavira), whose husband has walked off. But, of course, nothing is simple here: not the love between Sofía's children and Cleo, the ignorance of the children about the events over their heads, the desperate anger that Sofía sometimes lets splash onto Cleo, or the current of violence that runs between poor and rich, country and city.

Roma is a film about private life, and a private home, that keeps moving into the public realm, with Cuarón's wide-screen, black-and-white camera continually traveling, tracking, exploring, revealing. It's not just ostentation. Cuarón makes good on the old notion that the moral purpose of camera movement is to show that the world is whole; that there is always something beyond the edge of the frame, and then something beyond that. And because Cuarón is faithful to the continuity of the world, he also has a way of letting the world pour into his shots, adding more and more action to the image whenever the camera does happen to pause. Without even stirring, he can unite a puddle on the floor with the blue sky above, and allow you to feel what both mean to the maid who does the scrubbing.

The Nation, October 23, 2018

Parasite

Bong Joon-ho opens *Parasite* like a devilish chess master pretending to play along conventional lines. Here, crammed into a semi-basement apartment in Seoul, is a comic family much like others you've seen—gruff father, blunt mother, hip and attractive adult daughter and son—all scuffling to stay fed. Here, too, is the sort of scheme you've often followed, in which sympathetic rogues lie and cheat their way into the graces of the rich. The son sees an opportunity to gain employment in the home of a wealthy family; the others soon follow, deploying ruse after ruse, until you flatter yourself into thinking you've understood the position and are a little ahead of Bong.

Sucker. He's planted traps all over the board. He's thought up complications that will squeeze you until you squeal. As soon as the middle game starts, you realize you're helpless before his onslaught, and happily so—even though happiness is exactly what this exquisitely devious movie will deny its characters. Call *Parasite* a satire of high and low, if you like—it's certainly concerned with hierarchies of class and their embodiment in the architecture and geography of Seoul—but don't imagine you'll escape untouched. That's the real story of *Parasite*, in two words: Nobody escapes.

Not that the Parks' tastefully magnificent home looks like any kind of dead end when Ki-woo Kim (Choi Woo-sik) shows up to claim a tutoring job under slightly false pretenses. An immaculately detailed International Style box set behind a substantial wall and a glistening lawn, the house is all free-flowing, open-plan space and floor-to-ceiling windows: perfect as a showplace for the Parks' immaculate lives and Bong's ingeniously unfolding choreography. By the time you reach this ostensible Eden, you've already seen a more likely site of confinement: the bug-infested coffin of hopes where the Kim family abides in the narrow, crowded streets far below. There, the windows are no more than a grimy band set at pavement level, admitting the stench left by drunks who use this cul-de-sac as an open-air pissoir.

No wonder Ki-woo wants to get into the sunlight and a cushy gig with the Parks, alternately educating their teenage daughter and flirting with her. No wonder his sister Ki-jung (Park So-dam) bluffs her own way into the luxury of a job with the Parks, as an art therapist for their 9-year-old son. (Ki-jung knows all about art therapy; she Googled it.) So it goes, through one underhanded trick after another—until one dark and stormy night, when the

Parks have left on a camping trip and the Kims think they're alone in paradise.

As Ki-woo likes to say whenever he comes upon a striking turn of events, "It's so metaphorical!" What happens next in *Parasite* is metaphorical, all right. It's also metonymic, symbolic, allegorical, and terrifyingly out of control—for the Kims, I mean, but not for Bong, who puts his scam-artist family through a breakneck sequence that gives you great filmmaking not by the moment or minute but the solid half-hour. It starts with the unexpected ringing of a doorbell, proceeds through alternating episodes of Grand Guignol cruelty and dirty-minded farce—imagine a treacherous staircase, a noxious peach, some not-so-private sex, and a teepee, not to mention a mock North Korean newscast—and concludes, much later and far below the Parks' home, in an unstoppable deluge of filth.

Bong is by now an acknowledged master of continuous action. Think of the emergence of the monster from the Han River in *The Host*, the onward-driving battles through the train in *Snowpiercer*, the shopping-mall rampage of the giant pet pig in *Okja*. But he's never before created a sequence that's so uncanny and yet so grounded in the mundane. The contrast between high and low expands to become outsized and dizzying, but the social vertigo it represents is already built into the hillside topography of Seoul. The horrific deluge has been present in potential since the first shot of a drunk peeing on the street; the *Tales From the Crypt* motif is already implicit in the Kims' dismally ordinary below-grade apartment. The visual correlate of this merger of fact and fantasy glows in Hong Kyung-pyo's cinematography, which dwells obsessively on the surface of every material: stone, wood, glass, concrete. The images make even the shafts of light in the Parks' house seem tangible—and therefore bursting with a promise or threat beyond themselves.

You might say something similar about the dialogue, which remains plausible even while rising toward hyperbole, like the speech in comic books borne aloft in balloons. When the Kim family's patriarch, played by Bong's wonderfully rumpled signature actor Song Kang-ho, speaks about the wealthy, he does so as poor people may do at times, with a terrible forbearance that helps him live with himself. Mrs. Park, he comments, is rich, but she's nice. To which his wife (Jang Hye-jin) snaps back that Mrs. Park is nice *because* she's rich. Money's like an iron, she says: It takes out the creases. The son finds himself similarly at odds with his sister when he pauses in the midst of catastrophe to wonder what his affluent, college-educated friend Min would do in this situation. It's a reasonable question—to which the sister shouts, "Min wouldn't *be* in this situation!"

That's about three-quarters of the way through the dark and stormy night, with worse still to follow. But as morning comes, bringing sunshine that now seems jeeringly bright, and the characters move into place for the climax, you begin to feel once more as if you can see what's coming next. This time, you're not mistaken. *Parasite* has gone into the end game; the final moves feel inevitable.

But even as the logic plays out, Bong pulls a twist out of the position, this time startling you, paradoxically, by using understated observation rather than satirical excess. Having dramatized the struggle of rich versus poor in wildly lurid terms, he brings the conflict to its dreadful conclusion with the simplest, smallest, most everyday gesture possible. One man sniffs disapprovingly at another.

And that's mate.

The Nation, October 8, 2019

Nope

The Matrix Reloaded

In the film from which there is no escape and no going back, *The Matrix*, the writer-director team of Andy and Larry Wachowski presented a grim choice between truth and illusion. The truth: We are born and die as captives on a despoiled Earth, where intelligent machines keep us drugged and confined so they may tap our bioenergy. The illusion: We wake to an alarm clock, then drive to a tall building and work from 9 till 5, after which we return home and watch TV till bedtime—all of which is a mere computer simulation, wired into our nervous systems by the machines so we won't wither too soon.

On the one hand, a nightmarish reality; on the other, a deadly boring dream. Had *The Matrix* shown these to be life's only choices, I doubt that moviedom would now be supine beneath the boots of its sequel. But the Wachowski brothers offered audiences a third, winning possibility: being cool. They imagined that a small band of adventurers—the cool are always few—had learned to pass back and forth between the dismal, industrial horror of the real world and the pristine Vancouverishness of the simulation. I will give *The Matrix* this much credit: It defined coolness precisely as a matter of this crossing over, shucking both the agonies of creatural life and the time-killing daydreams of social routine.

Of course, coolness is also a matter of style and attitude. In *The Matrix*, the performers' fallback pose was studiously unexpressive—or unstudiously so, in the case of Keanu Reeves—in the manner of people who feign indifference even to their own disaffection. Dark sunglasses added to the masklike effect. (To cite a deep student of the subject, Norman Mailer: The person who wears shades is signaling, "I can look at you, but you have *no right* to look at me." Or, in *Matrix* terms: "I'm just passing through your lousy idea of reality.") The clothes were African-American in inspiration—lots of black leather and tight black vinyl—and the fisticuffs Chinese, showing that cool people take an interest in a variety of cultures. (I mean, they enjoy turning ethnic associations into mix-'n'-match fashion statements.) The firepower? Cool to the extreme.

Lastly, I mention the special effects, about which I'll need to give some history. In spring 1998, The Gap startled television viewers with its "Khaki's Swing" commercial, featuring a 180-degree pan around jitterbug dancers who stopped motionless in midair. A full year later, *The Matrix* was released, making prominent use of this same so-called stereoscopic freeze. Considering the lengthiness of movie production schedules, I would guess this was coincidence, not copycatting. The Wachowskis must have been composing their effect when "Khaki Swings" first aired and were perhaps upset to have been scooped—but that's what can happen when a new technology becomes available and different companies find purposes for it. The innovators in this case, who deserve credit for the public breakthrough, were The Gap's then-creative director, Lisa Prisco, and commercial director Matthew Rolston; but it was the latecomers who developed the more influential use of the technique. Before you could blink, the Wachowskis' stereoscopic freeze was being imitated, even in *Shrek*.

I make this point merely to exorcise the technological determinism that haunts so much writing about film, whether in magazine articles or in the publicity handouts on which they're based. To grasp the appeal of *The Matrix*—as you should, since *Nation* people are among the most uncool on the planet—you ought to understand that this particular effect in the film dazzled people not just for its novelty but also for its meaning. Here was a computer simulation of utterly free movement, achieved within the fiction of a neurodigital prison. Like the characters' leather-clad, sunglass-guarded detachment, the stereoscopic freeze boldly dramatized the state of being neither inside nor outside a situation—more specifically, of being able to employ a technology while owing nothing to its principal controllers. An untenable fantasy, when you examine it; and the Wachowskis chose not to do so, until now.

With their new film, *The Matrix Reloaded*, the Wachowskis take on the theme of choice, or the lack of it. I draw this conclusion tentatively, since the movie is uncommonly talky yet incomprehensible. Very long, mostly wordless fight and chase sequences alternate with scenes in which characters explain what's been happening; and these expatiations sound like, "Abba gadda choice. Hava zacha power taya. Understand kala mana, anomaly sa'ah." Listen with your ears out of focus, and you almost catch the drift: The cybermessiah known as Neo (Reeves) may fight against the machines' domination, but all the while he's dependent on machines for his food, his water—even for the air he breathes. What's more, he wonders whether his rebellion has been anticipated and countered in advance, by an opponent who comes to the chessboard with far more computational power than he'll ever muster. Could the enemy in fact be playing with both sets of pieces? Is Neo's revolt a part of the system?

Not wishing to slight the world's late-night dorm-room philosophers with unseemly comparisons, I will merely note that this theme imparts a certain claustrophobia to the Wachowskis' images. In one of the film's major set pieces, Neo is encircled and smothered during a fight in a tenement courtyard. (His opponents come in an endless supply and are perfectly identical, which makes the effect grotesquely funny but all the more suffocating.) Much later in the film, Neo is again hemmed in by a dismayingly small set of possibilities: He is brought into a low, windowless room, whose curving walls are made of video monitors all displaying his face. Other characters who suffer confinement include the Key Maker (Randall Duk Kim), a meek but knowledgeable figure who has been kept in a closet, elaborately surrounded by his wares; and Trinity (Carrie-Anne Moss), Neo's love interest, who takes off on a high-speed car chase only to be shut into close quarters with half of a deadly pair of twins.

As these few examples suggest, the sense of claustrophobia in *The Matrix Reloaded* has to do with more than physical enclosure. Repetition, too, makes the world seem to close in on the characters, sometimes deliberately (as when the Wachowskis multiply a villain) and sometimes inadvertently (as when they run out of fresh kung-fu stunts but keep the fight going anyway). A third limiting factor, familiar from the first *Matrix*, is imitativeness. Maybe the Wachowskis didn't mimic "Khaki Swings," but they've borrowed heavily from many other sources. *Metropolis* figures prominently among them in the present film: In the image of an underground industrial city (put together, apparently, from pieces of old merchant marine freighters) and of a cavernous temple, where throngs of worshipers gather amid the stalactites and stalagmites. The Wachowskis have also rummaged carelessly through sacred texts and compendiums of myth, since religion—any kind of religion— seems useful to them when they want a proper noun. The people, places and things in *The Matrix Reloaded* include Zion, Niobe, Nebuchadnezzar, Logos, Persephone, Seraph, Osiris and just plain Oracle, making you feel like you're scanning the name tags at some trade show in the Joseph Campbell Convention Center.

My point is, *The Matrix Reloaded* moves more heavily than its predecessor. At times, the picture even grunts with effort, as when it builds up to the sex scene between Neo and Trinity. The whole first act of the movie seems devoted to getting the two of them naked, a process that requires the Wachowskis to intercut a full-scale orgy, featuring thousands of people bumping and grinding in the Temple of the Stalactites. Dreadlocks are flung about; piercings are flaunted (by "piercings," I mean the jack-plugs that are *Matrix* cyber-equivalents); and a group of primitivist drummers bangs away like the road band of *Stomp*, until slowly, slowly, Neo pushes himself toward Trinity's bed. As the close-ups loom, you might notice that Trinity has a long face, with thin lips and a pronounced chin—not unlike Neo's. Another instance of repetition: Keanu Reeves seems to be kissing himself.

More laborious still is the scene in which Neo must approach Persephone, played by the international sex goddess Monica Bellucci. In an episode that is noticeably awkward and protracted, Bellucci demands that Reeves kiss her as if he means it. I suppose the filmmaker Mark Rappaport will make much of this moment some day, when he puts together *Keanu Reeves's Home Movies*. He will note, as I do now, that the Wachowskis were fully aware of what they were doing. In fact, they're always too knowing by half. For the boys of whatever age who are the primary ticket-buyers, they supply PG-13 sex in an R-for-violence context, with the act coolly performed by a character who is neither in nor out of the situation. For more worldly-wise ticket-buyers, they provide a wink and a nudge. (Hey, we told you—it's all a simulation!) But to people who want passion and expansiveness from a movie, and ideas that are fresh rather than recycled, the Wachowskis have become an obvious drag.

They will make a gazillion dollars anyway and soon will tread moviedom under their boots once more, when they release the third and final *Matrix*. Necessity, more than choice, now rules the process (to cite for the last time the film's argal-bargal). The truly cool are few, but multitudes flock to a winner—as you may learn from Mr. Bush, another leading marketer of simulated liberation.

Do you think I've lost proportion, comparing an entertainment to a war? Then consider how *The Matrix Reloaded* continues and worsens the most disgusting feature of the original. At the end of this picture—I rejoice in spoiling the plot—human beings are murdered by the thousands, off camera. You hear about the massacre in passing; your sight is untroubled by anatomical details. A quick report is given, as "collateral damage" might be mentioned on the evening news, while the film's attention remains concentrated on the only people who matter: the stars.

Cool.

The Nation, June 2, 2003

The Passion of the Christ (Part One)

From the moment when Mel Gibson began promoting *The Passion of the Christ*—was it only ten years ago?—he has insisted that his goal was to be true to the Gospel text. Words are crucial to his project, so crucial that the film's dialogue is spoken principally in Aramaic and Latin; and words have consistently tripped him up.

Remember that for his initial, highly publicized attack against his critics, Gibson seized on the actions of an ecumenical group, which had obtained a bootleg copy of his script and expressed strong misgivings. It's unfair to judge a film by its screenplay, Gibson said, and he was right—assuming, of course, that in shooting *The Passion*, he had behaved as filmmakers ordinarily do and departed from the written word. If, on the other hand, he really had translated the Gospels to film, then the gap had presumably been closed between source and screenplay, screenplay and image. In that case, the ecumenists could easily have judged the picture by its shooting script, or (even more efficiently) by the Bible.

Gibson fell over his words for the second time when he circulated an endorsement from the Pope, reportedly obtained at a preview screening. "It is as it was," said the Pontiff, confirming the film's fidelity to Scripture; but then authorities in the Vatican disowned the remark, leaving the filmmaker with an embarrassing lacuna in his text. Is the incident as Gibson said it was? Or had John Paul never uttered the papal blurb?

Now, as the film is about to open, Gibson falls for the third time. While maintaining that *The Passion of the Christ* must be seen to be discussed, and seen in its integrity as a work of art, he has declined to let film critics watch the picture in advance. I make no special claims for reviewers. We may do our jobs well, or we may do them poorly; but all of us, however foolish or fallible, are dedicated to the very task that Gibson claims to want performed, although he'd rather not help us carry it out. I can assure you, we have had many more opportunities to preview *Eurotrip* than to see *The Passion of the Christ*, which has remained unavailable to every critic of my acquaintance until immediately before the public opening.

As a marketing tactic, Gibson's decision makes good sense. Enormous advance publicity and a wide release have given him the classic critic-proof opening, with crowds of the curious guaranteed for the first week. More important, he can sustain the box office he generates, having pre-sold *The Passion of the Christ* to a multitude of churchgoers who don't ordinarily hang out at the movies and certainly don't pay attention to reviews. (By now, quite a few members of this target audience will have seen a tract titled "Who Killed Jesus?" which is adorned on the cover with a photo of Gibson and on the inside with a strong recommendation for *The Passion of the Christ*. I picked up my copy on Broadway, from a Brooklyn-based evangelist.) Under these circumstances, Gibson correctly calculates that he should dismiss the reviewers, having nothing to gain from them.

But then, speaking as one who has been dismissed, I must complain of my unfortunate set of choices. Either I can catch Gibson's movie on opening day, February 25, and write about it then (in which case the article won't appear until mid-March); or else I can review *The Passion* now, unseen.

For the greater glory of cinema…

The Passion of the Christ is an intensely brutal movie, whose spiritual center is located firmly behind the camera. As director and co-screenwriter, Mel Gibson is all but ecstatic before the agonies he has so painstakingly staged, and with which he so completely identifies. His surges of emotion carry you through the picture—which puts the purported central character at a disadvantage.

James Caviezel, who plays Jesus, brings to the part an El Grecoish face and mournful demeanor that have served him well in somewhat similar roles: the saintly GI in *The Thin Red Line*, the buried and resurrected hero of *The Count of Monte Cristo*, the participant in a miraculous (if not altogether spooky) father-and-son relationship in *Frequency*. So lean that he looks tortured from the outset, as if his muscles couldn't quite stretch from one end of his long bones to the other, Caviezel takes naturally to the athletic round of sufferings imposed on him in *The Passion*; and yet his inherent otherworldliness, which you might have thought would infuse the creatural side of his Jesus with a suggestion of the divine, makes him opaque as an actor. Good film actors (such as Willem Dafoe in *The Last Temptation of Christ*, or for that matter Maia Morgenstern, who plays Mary in *The Passion*) have a knack for pulling in your attention and then directing it elsewhere, into the cinematic world around them. Caviezel, though, is always an object for the camera to study, never a consciousness that opens up its own viewpoint within the screen. (You might say the same for the beautiful yet perpetually blocklike Monica Bellucci, who is the film's Magdalene.) The casting of Caviezel is the telltale problem of *The Passion*; it betrays Gibson's desire as author, perpetrator, rapt witness and vicarious Christ to see for a Jesus he has himself made blind, to think for a Christ he's made thoughtless.

The decision to have the actors mouth Aramaic and Latin only worsens the problem. Although some viewers will be able to follow the dialogue unassisted (I know a handful of such people, all of whom teach at the Jewish Theological Seminary), the great majority of us will need to read the subtitles, so that our eyes must focus not on Caviezel's face but on the blocks of letters at the bottom of the screen. In this way, too, Gibson diminishes the performances while magnifying the importance of the text. Toward what end, I wonder?

In one sense, he is merely the latest in an odd but influential line of filmmakers who have aspired to make literal transcriptions of a text, or at least are said to have done so. The earliest was Erich von Stroheim, whose *Greed* (1924) became legendary as an exhaustive, paragraph-by-paragraph realization of Frank Norris's novel *McTeague*. The legend is nonsense, of course, as the critic Jonathan Rosenbaum has demonstrated; but it's persistent nonsense, which helped establish Stroheim's reputation as an artist implacably at odds with venal Hollywood.

Next in line comes a great Catholic filmmaker, Robert Bresson, whose version of Bernanos's novel *Journal d'un curé de campagne* is central to one of the most important polemics in film history: François Truffaut's 1954 essay "Une certaine tendance du cinéma français," the founding document of auteurism. In an astonishingly slippery maneuver, Truffaut used the alleged faithfulness of Bresson's film (faithfulness to the spirit, not the letter) in order to deride a competing adaptation by the screenwriters Aurenche and Bost. Truffaut sank these old-guard figures by exposing the liberties they had taken with the Bernanos text, and did so with such vehemence that you might have thought their unrealized project had actually been filmed. Talk about judging a movie by its screenplay!

The next text on the list, curiously enough, concerns the death of Jesus. In 1963, Manoel de Oliveira brought out his *Acto da Primavera*: a picture that faithfully and patiently records a passion play done in rural Portugal. The trick here is that Oliveira for the most part does not present *Acto da Primavera* as a documentary. Instead, after providing a brief frame, he lets the story take over, so that you soon feel you're watching a fiction film, performed by stiff but fascinatingly unselfconscious actors.

Then in 1978, in what was arguably his greatest achievement, this same Oliveira did for the classic Portuguese novel *Amor de Perdição* (Doomed Love) what Stroheim was only said to have done for *McTeague*. Over the course of a four-and-a-half-hour film, Oliveira has his performers act out the entire text—an exercise that sometimes requires them to pause in their tracks, while a voiceover narrator catches up with a lengthy patch of narration.

What do we learn from this brief history? That textual literalism in film has primarily been a matter of false claims, misdirection, illusionism and irony. Mel Gibson distinguishes himself in this tradition in two ways. First, he's dead serious, as if textual literalism could in fact be achieved. Second, he bases his work not on a novel or even a passion play but on a text that he takes to be inerrant—and by this move he doubles the stakes.

This doubling is what most troubles me. Yes, I'm also troubled by the encouragement that *The Passion of the Christ* may give to Jew-haters. A worry isn't necessarily baseless, just because the preposterous Abe Foxman voices it. (Nor is every reassurance to be swallowed, just because it comes from as smooth an actor as Mel Gibson. It's unthinkable that he would be an anti-Semite, Gibson explained on TV to Diane Sawyer; to be anti-Semitic would be un-Christian. To which I counterpose this statement by Godfrey de Bouillon, recorded after his Crusaders had slaughtered the entire population of Jerusalem's Jewish Quarter in July 1099: "And then, when we thought that the Savior had been sufficiently revenged by the death of the Jews and other infidels, we went with tears to worship at the Holy Sepulcher." The teachings that inspired de Bouillon were repudiated by the Vatican when I was just entering high school.) But, beyond my parochial squeamishness over this movie, I'm concerned at how Gibson forecloses any interpretation. "It is as it was." Disagree with the film in any way—even to point out how the Gospels are at variance with history—and you disagree with revealed truth.

However much you might play at seeing his work as just another movie, Gibson has gone outside the normal bounds of show business and into the territory of America's religious absolutists: John Ashcroft having himself anointed with oil, gay-hating lawmakers attempting to write Leviticus into the Constitution, antiabortionists shooting to kill, generals declaring holy war against the Muslim infidel. Our country has a great, great many such people who do not consider their convictions to be open to discussion. They maintain a significant hold on political power;

and since a lot of them have an antinomian streak, I doubt the rule of law would stand in their way, should we manage to loosen their grip. The ever-boyish and ingenuous Gibson, with his simple faith, has made *The Passion of the Christ* as a gift for these people.

Thumbs down.

The Nation, March 15, 2004

The Passion of the Christ (Part Two)

So Mel Gibson has been persecuted all the way to the bank. *The Passion of the Christ*—undertaken by him as a work of faith, and promoted to the faithful as if he, too, were about to be killed by unbelievers—is a box-office smash, to which I have contributed my own $10.25. Yes, I have now watched the movie (a day after deadline pressure and an absence of press screenings forced me to write about it unseen, for our March 15 issue), and I have found it to be worse than expected.

It's worse, first of all, as filmmaking. From the opening scene of Jesus's agony in the garden, with its silent-movie head-tossing and chest-heaving, its slithering snake (evil is afoot!) and $2.98 clump of trees backlit in a dry-ice fog, Gibson directs down to the audience, as if presuming us to be bumpkins used to a diet of corn.

When Gibson wants to impress us with the decadence of Herod's court, he whips up a scene that poor, saintly Jack Smith might have titled "Sodomite Fleshpots of the Orient" (only Smith would have done it better and wouldn't have been serious). When Gibson wants to illustrate maternal love, he shows Mary running in slo-mo through the bosky light of a flashback, hurrying to comfort a toddler Jesus who has scraped his knee. (This greeting-card image pops into her head when her adult son, flayed raw, tumbles beneath the massive beams of the cross—a conjunction of events that proves the flashback to be not just trivial but superfluous. Doesn't Mary have enough on her mind already?) And when Gibson wants you to understand that certain characters are evil, he makes sure they're double ugly. In fact everything has to be doubled before Gibson will trust you to get the message. By my count, Jesus falls not three times but six on the way to Calvary. At the moment of his death, it's not enough for the veil in the Temple to be rent, as in the Bible; an earthquake has to rip a chasm right up to the altar.

Gibson practices the aesthetic of the lapel-puller, who congratulates you, in an ear-splitting bawl, for entering the sideshow he won't let you pass by. Perhaps you'll excuse this directorial style as an artistic sin and therefore (in American eyes) venial. Perhaps you'll be willing to excuse Gibson's sins against language, too. (The Aramaic that his characters speak was clearly learned by the actors by rote, so that it comes out as gibble-gabble. The actors' Latin, by contrast, is pretty good, apart from its being utterly un-Roman. What you hear is the Church Latin of Gibson's youth.) The aspect of the film that you might not excuse is Gibson's interpretation of the Gospels, an interpretation he has sought to talk out of existence (as I argued in a previous column) by insisting that he's been true to the Bible.

True to which parts of the Bible, selected according to what principle? To begin formulating the inconvenient answer, I note that Gibson has taken as his principal source the Gospel of John—by common consent the most philosophically elevated of the four, but also (there's no delicate way to put this) the one that's explicitly anti-Jewish. Whereas Matthew, Mark and Luke write about a conspiracy of the "priests" and the "council," John writes about "the Jews," as if Jesus and the apostles had not belonged to this people. (Gibson reproduces the effect of John's rhetoric by a ready-to-hand visual device: He uses fine-featured actors, Mediterranean at most, as his good guys, while casting ostentatiously hook-nosed types as the heavies.) Gibson also makes the most of a statement in John that is not found in the synoptic Gospels, mitigating Pilate's guilt while emphasizing that of the High Priest: "He that delivered me unto thee," Jesus says to Pilate, "hath the greater sin."

No doubt Gibson would have made some people queasy simply by following this text; but he also would have been on relatively firm artistic ground. Let there be a cinematic *Passion According to St. John*. But Gibson went further. He introduced material from the synoptic Gospels into his main source—and these interpolations consistently exonerate Pilate and damn "the Jews." From Luke, Gibson takes the story of how Pilate hoped to let Jesus off with a flogging but then found this punishment would not satisfy the crowd. From Matthew comes a favorable mention of Pilate's wife, who calls Jesus a "just man" and urges her husband to avoid passing judgment. Gibson expands on both these elements, inventing for the first a concerned Roman soldier (who angrily orders an end to the flogging) and for the second providing a scene in which Pilate's wife befriends Mary and the Magdalene.

Of course, the most widely discussed of the passages that Gibson has stitched into his narrative also comes from Matthew; it's the one in which "all the people" say, "His blood be on us, and on our children." Although this line goes untranslated in the current release print, it is howled on the soundtrack and can be subtitled at any time into the modern languages of Gibson's choice.

Admitting, though, that the film's pattern of selection is suspect, why shouldn't we respect Gibson's beliefs and just shut up about it? He has told everyone that *The Passion of the Christ* is about God's love; and he has in fact incorporated several key scriptural passages about forgiveness of sin and love for one's enemy. It might be reasonable for viewers to believe Gibson—except that the film's action speaks louder than its words.

The most telling event, for me, comes just after Jesus on the cross has asked God to forgive the High Priest. "He's praying for you!" cries the amazed criminal at Jesus's left hand, who requests and receives absolution. Not so the criminal to Jesus's right. He mocks the act of grace he's just witnessed and is immediately set upon by a raven, which plucks out both his eyes. Instant, bloody retribution! It's not scriptural, but it's what Gibson wants, and what he expects the audience to want, too.

Gibson and his apologists will retort that the divine sacrifice of the crucifixion makes the issue of blame irrelevant. This rebuttal may be theologically sound, but it ignores the historical record and (when applied to this film) denies the evidence on screen. In structure, style and dramatic import, *The Passion of the Christ* is all about identifying and punishing unbelievers, a category that is defined, by today's absolutists, to include many, many people beyond "the Jews."

Now for the good news. Quite a few Christians have understood Gibson's project and are deeply troubled by it. They have not been silent; whereas I, having fulfilled my obligation to address the movie of the year, will say no more—except to thank the people of good will, of many denominations, who have recognized this picture for what it is: a blunt instrument in an angry hand.

The Nation, March 29, 2004

Kill Bill Vol. 2/The Saddest Music in the World

Antiquarian mishmash lathers the April screen. In *Kill Bill Vol. 2*, scenes recollected from thirty-year-old kung fu epics splash across images from spaghetti westerns and two-lane-blacktop shockers, as if projected one on top of the other in the haunted grind house of Quentin Tarantino's skull. Meanwhile, *The Saddest Music in the World* offers an unstable and tantalizing approximation of an older and more arty cinema: a moment that might almost be from *Metropolis*, which dissolves into something rather like *L'Inhumaine*, which melts into a passing semblance of *Love Me Tonight*, all of them realized in the cheap, foggy and fleeting style that makes Guy Maddin's mind resemble the Museum of Dry Ice.

How little it tells us, to say these films are composed of fragments of bygone pictures! How glad I am that the world has finally gotten beyond postmodernism, whose wearisome explainers used to claim such recyclings for their own! (As if Proust hadn't written his *Pastiches et mélanges*; as if there were no "Oxen of the Sun" chapter in *Ulysses*.) If we were to think about the contrast in spirit between Tarantino and Maddin, rather than the blunt fact of their both being hommagenizers, we might notice that the first wants to replicate the films and television shows of his youth, while the second moons over movies his parents might have watched when young. Tarantino glories aggressively in himself; since he's all right, then so are the pulp fictions that formed him. Maddin wonders uneasily at how he came to be; his heart being troubled, he seeks the trouble that must reside in those enigmatically beautiful old pictures.

As these directors' starting points differ, so do their rhythms. Think of how Tarantino saunters through a movie with a hipster's gait, now and then telling you how long you'll wait until the next big event. (Will two minutes pass before a drug takes effect? Then a character has two minutes of screen time to spin out a tale.) Maddin impatiently skitters from shot to shot, which he records with as many as eight cameras at once; he never has enough time to catch up with the past. Or consider the implications of the directors' manner of dress. Tarantino sometimes sports a Kangol cap. Maddin has been known to affect spats.

The contrast holds even on levels far more superficial than costume—plot, for example—although here description falters, there being far too much incident to summarize in *The Saddest Music in the World* and far too little in *Kill Bill Vol. 2*. Of the latter,

I need say only that the Bride (Uma Thurman) has three former partners left to murder, having previously dispatched two (plus a private army) in *Vol. 1*. This time she must exact revenge against trailer-dwelling cowboy Budd (Michael Madsen), one-eyed underhanded Elle (Daryl Hannah) and ultimately Bill himself—her lover, her boss, the father of her child (David Carradine, playing a noir version of his role on television's *Kung Fu*). Arithmetic would suggest a rate of 1.5 violent deaths per hour—a pace that Tarantino varies in an interesting way, to give himself leisure for extended sequences such as the Bride's return from the dead (for the second time in the picture) and her apprenticeship to the evil kung fu master Pai Mei (Gordon Liu).

What's the point of it all? Let me delay the answer long enough to note that *The Saddest Music in the World* has its own quota of violent deaths. Set on a snowy, nocturnal soundstage that represents 1933 Winnipeg, the world capital of sadness, Maddin's film concerns a radio contest sponsored by beer baroness Lady Port-Huntly (Isabella Rossellini), who means to capture the US market as soon as Prohibition is repealed. To promote her solace-giving brew, she offers a prize of $25,000 to the nation that boasts the saddest music. Teams race to Winnipeg to compete before an audience of suds-swilling, earflapped locals, with Siam pitted against Mexico in the first round, Canada against Cameroons. (The musicians play simultaneously, advancing menacingly on one another as a play-by-play team comments over loudspeakers.) Although the radio listeners understand these duels to be global in scope, they have a personal meaning for Lady Port-Huntly, since the Canadian representative, Fyodor (David Fox), is the retired physician and former suitor who drunkenly amputated her legs. The US contestant, a crypto-Canadian, is Fyodor's son, Chester Kent (Mark McKinney, who behaves like Gable in *It Happened One Night* and looks like Tom Hanks crossed with a porcini mushroom). A penniless Broadway producer, and the man Lady Port-Huntly really loved, Chester has an American's imperviousness to sadness, which he thinks is no more than a showbiz put-on, and which he therefore can deliver with more sass and pizazz than the other competitors combined. In this attitude, he is diametrically opposed by the Serbian representative, the veiled cellist Gavrilo, whose unbearably mournful performances are atonements for the deaths of 9 million people in the Great War. Nevertheless, Gavrilo is actually another crypto-Canadian: Chester's hypersensitive brother Roderick.

I could go on. (Maddin does, abetted by co-screenwriter George Toles, production designer Matthew Davies and especially composer Christopher Dedrick, whose score consists mostly of variations, demented and brilliant, on Jerome Kern's "The Song Is You.") The point is that *The Saddest Music in the World* is not only jammed with more shots, styles, musical excerpts and astonishing actions than *Kill Bill Vol. 2* but is more richly suggestive, too.

When *Vol. 1* came out last year, I remarked, tentatively, that Tarantino had introduced a theme that ought to be taken seriously: a woman's conflicting desire to wreak vengeance and save a child from violence. Whether this theme would play out seriously remained to be seen. Now that we have the second half of the picture, I'd say the answer is, "Not quite." To Tarantino's credit, he complicates the setup in a way that's just and moving. (It seems the most important child was corrupted before the Bride could rescue her. And who knows? Once the Bride is on the scene, maybe she'll do damage of her own.) In handling this idea, though, Tarantino is a forgetful screenwriter. He gets so caught up in his mazelike digressions that he's as surprised as you to turn a corner and find the film's emotional core standing there. What's he supposed to do with the main subject, now that it's on screen? He's not sure. He cracks a few jokes; he wraps up the plot.

So he leaves you this time with little more than momentary pleasures: locations in China and the California desert, Uma Thurman's miraculously versatile performance, some nifty tricks of framing. Not bad—but not equal to the best excesses of *Vol. 1*, which seem to have consumed most of Tarantino's inventive energy.

Guy Maddin's inventiveness does not flag. Whether he's fetishizing Isabella Rossellini's mouth, staging a funeral on ice skates, sliding a troupe of African drummers into a vat of beer or calling up the ghost of a dead child, he's unfailingly outlandish, hilarious, odd, wistful and genuinely, unappeasably disturbed. Maddin looks at a family musicale and envisions scenes of grotesque loss. He looks at national stereotypes and sees a broken family. And when he looks at old movies, he sees today's world, which is (you'll forgive the plot giveaway) set on fire at the end by an optimistic, can-do Yank.

Kazuo Ishiguro wrote the screenplay from which all this evolved. I'll bet he's as astonished as anyone.

The Nation, May 10, 2004

Cinderella Man

She was a saint, Renée Zellweger, with her brave chin all a-tremble, never saying a harsh word to her husband no matter how the little ones wheezed and shivered in the cruel, cruel cold, nor how many a morning, just to put something in their stomachs, she had to fill up the milk bottle at the tap the way they were watering drinks down at the saloon, not that her Russell Crowe would know anything about that, him being as good a man as ever let another bash in his brains for fifteen rounds and never touched a drop of anything stronger than beer, and only one of those in the whole of *Cinderella Man*, which ought to show you what a saint he was, never saying a harsh word to Renée Zellweger or so much as glancing sideways at another woman, what with the peripheral vision beaten out of his poor eyes, or threatening to shut one of hers, the way that no-good communist friend of his down at the docks used to frighten the wits out of his own wife, until he was trampled to death by the police in an incident they all very much regretted, it being the Depression and all, which as Russell Crowe explained was nothing more than a run of bad luck that could happen to anyone, so that he had to bury the blackguard atheist in the potter's field before he took up his boxing gloves again to a Celtic drone in the artful cinematographic twilight, and with his tooraloom, tooraloom he bled for us all, because it's better to cheer for one man getting his skull stove in than to pull together with the working stiffs for a Wagner Act that Ron Howard's audience never heard of, and when the last fight was over and Father O'Pratie had lifted his eyes to the God who loves us all, despite His excusable partiality toward the Irish, and the little ones were rosy-cheeked again, and even that Bolshevik's wife was eased in her heart's sorrow, Renée Zellweger knew she'd been right to pucker her brave little mouth and pipe up to Russell Crowe, "You are the champion of my heart, James J. Braddock," because a sentiment like that doesn't belong just in a screenplay, no, but was made to be cut out of the film and played on television to bring in the coppers from all decent men and their decent women, too. A grand story, *Cinderella Man*—but unlike *Seabiscuit*, it's got no good reason to make you wade through horseshit.

The Nation, July 4, 2005

Spider-Man 3

Does evil fall into the world like a rock from outer space? Does it spring from within us? Or is it merely the residue of our blunders—our trespasses, literally—which we commit while coping with circumstance? These are large questions for a comic-book movie to raise, especially when it's the sequel to a sequel. But whatever faults I can uncover in *Spider-Man 3* (just give me a minute), lack of ambition isn't one of them.

Not content to end this trilogy by having the superhero fight a bad guy, or even three, director and co-writer Sam Raimi has given Spider-Man the grandest possible send-off by making him struggle against evil itself. If you have not yet bought your ticket, please be advised that the outcome will not be conclusive. Don't even expect coherence. Like a CGI-crazed billionaire reshooting the funhouse scene in *The Lady From Shanghai*, Raimi has addressed his subject by multiplying and mirroring and fragmenting it, so that representative evils crash and splinter around a hero who never locates the definitive source of the threat. All that can be said for sure is that the proposed sources of evil, in aggregate, seem comprehensive, and that one of them may be discovered in the hero's own moral failings.

As we know from the earlier films, young, mutated Peter Parker was always apt to be self-involved and vengeful. Now, in *Spider-Man 3*, these faults begin to dominate his personality. Peter grows infatuated with celebrity, pursues a personal vendetta and ignores the feelings of his beloved Mary Jane. The result is further mutation, as he changes into jerk Peter, floppy-haired Peter, Peter with a ladies' man swagger and a sense of entitlement. You may judge the nature of the transformation by its critical site: a men's discount clothing store. But if personal emotion should seem too weak a cause for the existence of evil, *Spider-Man 3* offers a more elaborate explanation, in which Peter is a victim of malevolent goo from a meteorite. In this scheme—alternative to the first as an idea but simultaneous with it on the screen—Peter's worst traits would have been nothing more than weaknesses, had they not left him vulnerable to an alien intruder: some black, bloblike stuff, with a texture that's reminiscent of a fetishist's vinyl.

Despite its kinky sci-fi trappings, this is the metaphysical evil of old-time religion: an uncanny force beyond our power to comprehend, which may mimic its victim (as the space goo sometimes imitates a spider's scurrying) but comes from outside him.

The opportunistic blob has a will of its own, and like Satan goes to and fro in the earth, walking up and down in it. Here again, mutation occurs and reveals its nature by its critical site: a church steeple.

The third major site of mutation—yes, there's still another, the most impressive of all—looks like a huge concrete mixing bowl, overhung by a glowing electronic eggbeater. The sign posted on the fence outside claims this apparatus is an experimental physics station; but it's more like the place where bad luck, poverty and common ignorance get stirred into a threat to society. A poor brute named Flint Marko stumbles into this installation, wearing the most baffled expression that Thomas Haden Church can give him, and an outfit apparently copied from a 1930s French movie about the poetry of the lower depths. Marko enters the mixing bowl as an escaped convict, already presumed to be a danger to the public. He exits as a shape-shifting mass of sand: an invisible man, ground down by a world he doesn't understand, but newly capable of living outside the law.

I write these words and hear the groans and chortles of incredulity. Can a mere corporate product like *Spider-Man 3* be so layered with psychology, sociology and religious conviction? Of course it can—if you'll admit that the man charged with spending two years and a gazillion dollars on it might have thought about what he was doing. No one who watches without prejudice this extravaganza of doppelgängers, moral preaching and existential dread will complain that it's mindless. On the contrary: My complaint is that Raimi has loaded too many big ideas into *Spider-Man 3*. They drag this bag of kittens right down to the river's bottom.

The heaviness of the production is visible all too plainly at a vulnerable point, where Tobey Maguire's jawline is now softening into a jowl. I know, I don't look so great myself—but then, I'm not supposed to be a college student endowed with miraculous athletic gifts. With every close-up that Raimi takes of Maguire, especially those from a low angle, you're reminded that the *Spider-Man* series itself has aged, and like Peter can't pretend to have much ingenuousness to lose. Every once in a while, Raimi still manages a flash of the first movie's youthful charm: in a view of a parade reviewing stand, for example, where Cub Scouts seated in the front row blithely pass the time by kicking their legs. Just like Cub Scouts, you think. But quirky, naturalistic details like this one have now been almost abandoned, along with the first movie's bracing sense of New York's neighborhoods. A touristic view of Times

Square passes for local color. The film's "downtown jazz club" is a storefront restaurant with a dance floor and singing waitresses. Not even in Portland—though the worst part of this scene isn't the bogus setting but the tortured editing that's required to make Maguire look like he's dancing.

Forced humor, forced fun, a forced sense of reminiscence (the movie's so thick with long-established motifs, you'd think it was *Spider-Dämmerung*): These traits, combined with the grandiose theme, at last give you the impression not of ambition itself but of a desperate striving to be ambitious. It's the difference between creating an ingenious, delightful action sequence and telling the audience you've created one; between having Peter/Spider-Man race through well-defined streets so he can deliver a stack of pizzas (as in the beginning of *Spider-Man 2*) and having him whip through a random jumble of city views so he can stop and pose before a screen-filling American flag.

Note the operation of the First Law of Movie Dynamics: As self-importance rises, concern for common sense falls. Those unfamiliar with this principle might imagine that a writer-director's attention will be concentrated everywhere when greatness is the goal—that someone who so beautifully realizes the scene of Flint Marko's transformation into Sandman (a wonder of characterization and feeling, not just of special effects) will maintain the standard he's set. But see how the plot of *Spider-Man 3* jerks along over groundwork that was incompletely laid. Convenient butlers dodder forward to supply information the characters ought to have known years ago. Unlikely changes of heart seize Peter, and then are magically undone a reel later, just so a conflict can be advanced. These breaks in the storytelling are too severe to be excused as mere shortcuts, taken for the sake of economy; but they are also too careless to be enjoyed for their own sake, as you might luxuriate in the incongruities of a more dreamlike picture. Here, you just get bumped out of the movie, for no better reason than that Raimi couldn't be bothered to keep you in. He's got higher priorities: preparing a long, loud battle for the climax, and writing some lines of fortune-cookie wisdom—repent! forgive! brush after meals!—meant to justify the clanging.

If forgiveness is the main concern of *Spider-Man 3*, then Raimi certainly has mine. He's given me so much pleasure over the years (*For Love of the Game* notwithstanding) that I probably should be apologizing to him, for finding fault. But then, Raimi headed me off by working his own criticisms into the movie.

Through his affection for some of the supporting characters—a secondary love interest played by Bryce Dallas Howard, an evil twin to Peter (mostly comic) played by Topher Grace—Raimi implicitly disavows Peter and Mary Jane, who no longer seem to inspire him. You can feel his relief whenever he turns momentarily from Maguire and Kirsten Dunst (good as they are) to the new faces in the cast. As for the film's outstanding performance, it's surely given by that handsome mug James Franco, in the role of Peter's sometime friend and sometime enemy Harry. There's an airy freedom in the way Franco veers from obsessive rage to open-faced sweetness, from murderous scheming to heroic self-abnegation. Lucky him. He gets to play, while Maguire and Dunst are stuck discharging an obligation.

She never gets to relax in the movie, except in Franco's company. He never gets to enjoy being a bad guy—even in that jazz club scene—but acts out his evil under compulsion. These are two seriously clenched characters—and the strain you sense in them tells you something about the explicit self-criticism in *Spider-Man 3*. Raimi's story proposes that Spider-Man has now become too popular for his own good. The cheering crowds, the marching bands, the breathlessly impressed young beauties, the giant-screen video billboards: These ceaseless accolades weigh on Peter's soul, the film tells us, and sadden Mary Jane.

It takes little imagination to conclude that the success burdening the characters now drags on the series, too. Impute the problem to social injustice, individual moral frailty or an ambitious extraterrestrial blob, but *Spider-Man 3* is a come-down.

The Nation, May 28, 2007

Live Free Die Hard/Knocked Up

Continuing the tradition it established with *Independence Day*, Twentieth Century Fox celebrated this year's extended July 4 holiday by blowing up a major piece of Washington, DC. It was a nostalgia trip: The demolition of the US Capitol, along with portions of New Jersey, West Virginia and a stretch of Maryland interstate, was Fox's way of welcoming back Bruce Willis in his role as old-time working-stiff action hero John McClane, in *Live Free or Die Hard*. (Despite the title, no part of New Hampshire was harmed in making this motion picture.)

A dozen years have passed since Willis last raced around as McClane in *Die Hard With a Vengeance*—years in which the world saw what real devastation could be visited on an American city, and by men armed only with box cutters. The attack on the World Trade Center ought to have made a relic of McClane, the New York cop who goes *mano a mano* against terrorists, mother-fucker; and if the gravity of events didn't force this character into retirement, the weight of time on Willis's body might have finished him off.

But Willis runs his own production company and Fox needed a summer franchise movie, and so McClane, ever resilient, has been pressed back into service. Once more, he commandeers people's cars, tumbles from high places, fires bullets from an inexhaustible clip and absorbs an infinity of kicks and punches, if mostly from the neck up now, in star-saving close-up; while the still-popular spectacle of destruction has once again been offered to the American people for the pure joy of ka-blooey. Did you need more proof that September 11 did not, in fact, change everything? Then watch our hero of July 4, 2007, take out an Air Force fighter jet—yes, one of ours—using nothing more than his bare hands, an eighteen-wheel semi-trailer rig and a chunk of highway overpass. He's the box-cutter type himself.

His antagonists, though, continue to have the pretensions of sophisticates. *Live Free or Die Hard* is the tale of a strike against all the computer systems of the United States, as directed by a manicured white boy who could model for Zegna (Timothy Olyphant) and his equally unemotive girlfriend (Maggie Q), who is Eurasian by background and therefore comes accessorized with a cleavage-baring black jumpsuit and repertory of kung-fu kicks. "I'm in," these lovers keep murmuring to each other, though without anatomical reference, since the penetration occurs exclusively online. Exemplary creatures of today's high-priced thrillers, these villains know of no greater excitement than the sight of fingers typing, eyes staring at monitors and progress bars slowly filling. Download 15 percent complete. Download 18 percent complete. Download 17 percent complete. Please wait.

McClane, of course, begs to differ. He has no patience for digital flow, being a guy for whom "technology" is a handy fire extinguisher used for the impromptu incineration of opponents. Somebody halfway sympathetic to the audience needs to help this man. Enter the hacker, Matt Farrell: a surrogate character for all those 18- to 25-year-olds who watch movies for the sake of seeing computer effects. Played by Justin Long, an amiable performer best known for impersonating a Mac computer in TV commercials, Matt is both a plot convenience and a much-needed bridge between younger ticket buyers and Willis's 40-plus demographic.

As a member of the latter group (and then some), I enjoyed seeing an old guy battle the labor-saving software that now wastes so much of my time. I will also admit that the director (Len Wiseman) did a good job of stimulating my reptilian brain, a part of the body that creationists hold to be merely theoretical. The faithful want me to believe that God must love summer movies, since He designed my nervous system so the frontal lobes could be left idle while the core delights in bursts of pulsing orange fireballs set against an otherwise gun-metal palette. But we must evolve! Thoughts, prompted fitfully and feebly by Wiseman and the screenwriters of record, kept intruding on the sound-and-light show, mostly to comment on the ambiguity of McClane and his nerdy sidekick.

With McClane, the doubleness is familiar. He always mutters about being a tired, put-upon guy whom no one appreciates; but he's also the first to howl with delight, even before the audience can, when he drops someone down an elevator shaft. If McClane were as plain-spoken as we're supposed to think, his motto would be, "It's a dirty job, but somebody's got to love doing it." As for reedy, scraggly and bedraggled Matt, I suppose he should have a slogan, too: "When computers are outlawed, only outlaws will have computers." He enters the story as a cybercriminal, taken into custody by the cop who's almost a vigilante. By the end, Matt is almost a cop himself.

Live Free or Die Hard is the boot camp that whips this slacker into shape, for the nation's good and his own. The movie's terrorists, you see, are homegrown, and they operate by exploiting useful idiots ("as Lenin said") such as Matt. Witness the danger within: a lax and disaffected young American, self-righteously critical of public servants such as Fox News. ("Don't you know, it's all lies, put out there by corporate interests!") If Matt weren't carrying important information in his head, McClane might simply beat him to death, as he jocularly suggests doing at one point. Instead, he converts Matt, turning him into someone who respects authority and will take up arms against America's enemies. Or, to use the precise McClanean terms: Matt grows a bigger set of balls.

Which brings us to the not-so-secret theme.

Imagine today's inadequate man in a different mode. He still lazes about but in a cheerfully plump way; devotes himself to the computer but without striving for expertise; scoffs at the Man but does so in Los Angeles, where he's got plenty of company. Take Matt out of an action thriller and put him into a romantic comedy, and he might turn into Ben Stone, the guy with just enough balls to set off the plot of *Knocked Up*.

A box-office hit and critical success, *Knocked Up* has elicited commentary both for its sexual candor (in which it was outdone half a century ago by *The Miracle of Morgan's Creek*) and for its characters' decision not to resort to abortion. With all due respect for the political situation in which the film has emerged, I think this latter issue is beside the point. *Knocked Up* belongs to the genre that Stanley Cavell brilliantly defined as the American comedy of remarriage: films about a woman and man who have separated because their original union was false, and who now must work out a true way to live together. With allowances made for contemporary manners, this is pretty much the project of *Knocked Up*. There can be no abortion because the drunken one-night stand must lead to nine months of moral, social and emotional education.

But even though *Knocked Up* respects the conventions of the comedy of remarriage, it also departs from them by taking this deeply adult genre and regressing it toward childhood. Whereas the male lead used to be Clark Gable, Cary Grant or Henry Fonda, today he is Seth Rogen, an actor who is all baby fat and overgrown curls. The basic gag in *Knocked Up* is that Rogen's Ben is utterly outclassed by blond, buxom and camera-ready Alison (Katherine Heigl), to whom he can justly say, in drunken wonder, "You're prettier than me." The more elaborate gag is that Rogen seems perpetually surprised to have a growly voice and stubbled chin. He belongs in Pampers himself.

Whatever changes Gable and Grant had to undergo in their comedies of remarriage, they didn't need to learn to accept minimal adult responsibility. You may judge the distance between their era and ours by the fact that Rogen's education in *Knocked Up* barely rises to adult topics. He mostly learns to bathe, dress neatly, tidy his room, eat properly, engage people in conversation and read: training for a 6-year-old.

Meanwhile, what process of education does writer-director Judd Apatow propose for Heigl? On the most obvious level, none. She must learn to overlook the unappetizing exterior and love Rogen for the sweet, funny guy within—a task she's already proved she can accomplish, right at the start, given enough beer and tequila. This leaves her seeming unformed (embryonic, you might say) compared with predecessors such as Barbara Stanwyck and Irene Dunne—though more from Apatow's negligence than from any design. And yet Heigl, too, faces a subtler challenge (subtler, because it is relatively unexplored in the script): to break her dependence on an older sister with whom she lives as a semi-of-ficial boarder, sharing in her sister's family life while observing the unhappiness of her marriage.

If Cavell were to interpret *Knocked Up*, maybe he'd seize on Alison's deeper problem and identify the movie's essential question as one of community. What is the right relationship between a married couple and the people around them? The initial union of Alison and Ben is false because the characters won't budge from their existing groups. (His buddies keep him juvenile. Her sister and brother-in-law keep her mesmerized by domestic pain.) If Alison and Ben are to choose each other, rather than be joined by circumstance, they must therefore peel themselves away from these others, not so completely as to be disloyal but enough to form the beginning of a semi-autonomous community of their own—which is *Knocked Up*'s definition of a true marriage.

Fine with me—even though, for all the cinema I saw in *Knocked Up*, I could just as well have been watching television. I chuckled some; I smiled a lot. And this community business reassured me. "What if the peer-group standards in *Knocked Up* are plausible?" I thought. (And why wouldn't they be, with the gross now mounting above $100 million?) It would mean that while a large number of American men enjoy watching John McClane's rampages, they expect one another to be no more testosterone-charged than Matt the Hacker.

Very reasonable, I say—because in a decent community, men ought to nerve themselves up before getting into fights. On September 11, on United Flight 93, the men who really did go *mano a mano* against terrorists weren't professional heroes, ready to do violence at any time. They were a toy company manager, a public-relations flack, a couple of salesmen and a guy who worked for a software company. They might just as well have been Ben and Matt from *Knocked Up* and *Live Free or Die Hard*, each of whom spends an entire movie getting ready to assert himself.

Live Free or Die Hard is knowing enough to admit this reality, when in the end it proposes its own little comedy of misalliance, between Matt and McClane's daughter. Having survived the obligatory hostage ordeal, she has rediscovered her affection for the old paternal bully and is deeply grateful to him; but compared with Matt, she knows, Dad's a dinosaur.

The good news: If young Ms. McClane shares the apparent peer-group standards of women in today's movies, perhaps we may look forward to *Bringing Baby Up Hard*.

The Nation, July 12, 2007

Burn After Reading

When last heard from, in the closing scene of *No Country for Old Men*, Joel and Ethan Coen were revealing to Tommy Lee Jones that grace is freely given by the God they don't believe in. "Signs and wonders," Jones had murmured earlier in the film, using the Bible's words to stave off his dread of a meaningless world; but this struggle was his alone, to be observed by the Coens only at fitful intervals and generally from a distance. For their part, the wood-chipper boys seemed as comfortable as ever with the possibility that an abundance of greed and slaughter might be that and nothing more. Let the last word go to the sheriff with the tenuous faith. They'd already given the movie to the killer with implacable power.

Now, continuing with their carefree agnosticism where they'd left off, the Coens begin *Burn After Reading* with a view of earth that seems godlike, until they subject it to a pair of demystifications. In the first, which is immediate, you seem to descend through the turning clouds to a building identified as CIA headquarters. God's eye, evidently, is only a spy satellite. The second demystification, which lasts for the rest of the movie, proves that omniscience even on this mundane level is futile, since we live in an amoral world of petty betrayals and random mayhem. That's all right with the Coens. *Burn After Reading* is one of their comedies.

Full of clowns and foolery, signifying nothing, *Burn After Reading* is as deliberately self-canceling a story as you would expect from its title, or from its setting in an imaginary Washington where no one is the least bit interested in government. The sole character to come close to wonkishness is Osborne Cox (John Malkovich), the last living CIA analyst to wear three-piece suits and bow ties, who likes to hear himself rattle on about "mission" and "higher patriotism" but does so only because he's been fired for drinking. Now he whiles away the time by screaming obscenities, getting soused at the Princeton Club and composing his "memwah," which he believes will settle his scores. He's what Linda Litzke (Frances McDormand) would call a negative person.

She, by contrast, is very positively interested in her own appearance (which she wants to improve by means of four or five cosmetic procedures) and also in Internet dating, an endeavor that in her experience demands unswerving optimism. Cheerfully ignorant of the political currents around her, Linda understands nothing of Cox's memoir when a copy of it, stored on a computer disk, accidentally turns up in the franchise gym where she works.

Soon enough, though, at the prompting of her workmate Chad (Brad Pitt), she convinces herself that the disk might bring in money for her makeover.

Had the Coens chosen to add cartoon characters to their genre mix, an animated wiseguy of a rabbit might have popped up at this juncture, to point at the computer disk and hold up a sign marked MacGuffin. Or, rather, "MacGuffin." Forever keen to re-create film history and then undo the re-creation, the Coens this time have called up some of the trappings of a Hitchcock adventure—the backdrop of public monuments, the foreground of voyeurism, the blundering of an ordinary citizen into peril—but have frustrated Hitchcock's favorite device by introducing a mystery object that nobody wants to chase. Possession of the computer disk does set off all sorts of trouble for Linda, Chad and several other characters; and yet nobody, Ozzie Cox included, actually wants the thing. Hence the feeling of stasis that settles over *Burn After Reading*. The tone may be antic and frantic, but the incidents keep looping back on themselves, catching the characters in coils of repetition.

Maybe that's because the characters never learn. All of them are middle-aged, and all are determined to behave like adolescents. Ozzie sulks about the house like a kid who's doing nothing on his school break and just daring someone to criticize him for it. The flapping of his limbs might be due to mature alcoholism or to a teenage geekiness that never left him—which is only one of the ambiguities, and opportunities for misbehavior, in which Malkovich revels. Sadly, though, McDormand's miming of regression involves no such flights of invention: she merely pulls down her chin and pops her eyes in every close-up. If the character were written differently, you might think this was Linda's way of making herself look ingenuous. But since there's obviously no brain under that blond pageboy, nor any talent for duplicity, Linda's rancid girlishness must be real, leaving one of the film's main performances on the level of a mechanical trick.

This mugging seems all the more grim, given that the actors opposite McDormand perform with such rambunctiousness. The greatest joy of *Burn After Reading*—I'm tempted to say its only joy—is a runaway Brad Pitt in the role of Chad. Topped by a hairdo even more unfortunate than Linda's—a kind of sculpted butterscotch pudding shot through with a splash of cream—Pitt bounces through the film like a toddler in a 40-year-old's body, always sucking on a bottle of some sort, always rushing into situations and then having to wait there while his mind catches up.

Alone among the film's characters, Chad is indifferent to sex, or perhaps is presexual—a circumstance that Pitt seems to have welcomed as a liberation from his usual screen duties, releasing him into pure goofiness.

McDormand's other opposite number, who completes the motif of vain, middle-aged child's play, is George Clooney, here wearing the full salt-and-pepper beard of a dedicated home handyman. By profession, Clooney's character is a federal marshal. By avocation, he putters about in his basement workshop and also screws around on his wife. It's this latter hobby that links him to Linda and to the nerve-racked household of Osborne Cox—which means, I suppose, that Clooney is playing a human MacGuffin, shuttled back and forth to animate the plot. People do want him, and Clooney shows you why, patting his flat belly with animal self-satisfaction and grinning heartily at anyone who might like to see his teeth. It's fun to watch his looseness as this go-along guy, happily tossing away a line here, shuffling off a bit of physical business there.

But what does his character ultimately amount to? Just a rude sight gag in the basement workshop; just a mechanism for raising and lowering the middle finger (so to speak) in the audience's face.

As I stared at that visual message, in which the Coens told me what I could do with myself, I understood that my problem with *Burn After Reading* has little to do with style. It's fine that the Coens are obsessed with gleaming technique; if they weren't, they might turn out something like *Choke* (the movie that proves you can put Sam Rockwell into a twelve-step program for sex addicts and still generate no laughs). It would also be off the mark to complain of the obvious, that *Burn After Reading* is yet another Coen brothers gallery of grotesques. ("Do they like the people they create?" the brilliant film critic Kent Jones once asked. "I'd say yes, in the same way that a hunter likes his trophies.") Artists before them have given us tales told by or about idiots, many of which have even been funny.

So let the Coen brothers tell me that life is absurd, that the world is fallen, that God is illusory but Satan (or Javier Bardem) is emphatically real. I can take it. But when they call me an idiot for listening, I get a little impatient.

Though I suppose I could be positive, like Linda Litzke, and say that this time they haven't been hypocrites.

The Nation, October 6, 2008

Watchmen/Duplicity

April 1, 2009: They don't see me as I slip through this multiplex, down shadowy troughs of aisles that reek of the corruption of butter topping gone sour in perverse imitativeness and price inflation. Someday they will cleanse these aisles. Someday the bone-like crunch beneath my shoes, the viscosity like drying blood, will stop crying in my ears like the anguish choked back by an abused boy, the kind who's alone and smashes people and narrates highly regarded graphic novels. But not tonight. Tonight, in what we've made of America, even the dark rain that has been falling for hours in this theater won't wash away the sick popcorn of human depravity, because there are only three people left who are willing to buy tickets for *Watchmen*, and as I sink into a shame of lumpish upholstery the other two avert their eyes. One of them looks like Nixon.

So this is what we've become: a sparse and flaky excrescence on the surface of mass-market culture, like dandruff in the thin hair of an aging character actor. Soon the show will begin, and for 162 minutes I will witness the truth of *Watchmen*. Not the false truth of "a movie," which the others will see, but the true truth of a significant pattern in contemporary thought and social life, visible only to me and my dying kind. Freak, they call me. Psycho. Vigilante. Film critic.

For weeks, months, I've monitored this target. I've tracked the split between the authors of the graphic novel, the lawsuit between the owners of the movie rights, the argument among *Watchmen* observers over the plan to release this film with an R rating. (Yes, one of the superheroes has a big blue penis, and it's all over the trades that grasping moneymen want to expose this thing to teenage boys, but with their rancid, hypocritical R rating they've trapped themselves, because now teenage boys aren't allowed to walk down these mean aisles. They watch for free on the Internet.) I can already smell irony waft off the ideological forces, the economic imperatives, the currents of history thick with the past's nameless and forgotten plankton, all of them about to clash in this site of contention called *Watchmen*—and yet I know the others will see nothing of this, nothing except stop-time kung fu rumbles on the rain-slick nocturnal streets of a parallel-universe New York.

The movie starts. Immediately, I see the blue penis, and the special effects are staggering. It walks on its own. It speaks. I suddenly realize it is Clive Owen, clean-shaven for a change, striding up to inspect Julia Roberts's cleavage at a garden party. This is not *Watchmen*. It is *Duplicity*.

So once more I've underestimated them. In their hideous determination to maintain, at any cost, their monstrous order, they are even prepared to show me the wrong movie. "Wrong movie," I write in my critic's notebook; but I refuse to leave my bucket seat of refuge in this stadium-rowed arena of perpetual night. I will find the pattern, no matter what Rorschach blot they fling at me.

I wait, patient, concealed. And then the essence of the thing erupts, as I knew it would—the mindless violence of greedy apes clawing blindly at each other in a slow-motion rain. They're Paul Giamatti and Tom Wilkinson, pretending to be the heads of competing companies. I can see it's supposed to be a joke, this grimacing, flailing, kicking, spluttering, even though it grinds on, and on, like the molars of a syphilitic giant writhing in a fever dream. I shudder, gripped by a clammy fear that *Duplicity* has already shown me more than I was supposed to know.

April 1, 2009, half an hour later: The fight scene between Giamatti and Wilkinson is over. Now we're supposed to believe it was only an opening credit sequence. But was it? Julia Roberts and Clive Owen are back, pretending to be rival industrial spies for the Giamatti and Wilkinson companies, or cooperating spies who are faking a rivalry, or rival lovers who are faking cooperation. A distraction. I can perceive the real scheme of the movie emerging from all these postcard views and all this James Newton Howard music-by-the-yard. I see it in the way the spies tail one another in the street and then tail one another again, in the way Roberts and Owen speak lines in a New York scene and then speak the same lines in Rome, four years earlier. The mask falls away from the supposed creator of this movie, "Tony Gilroy," as I gasp at the brazen cunning that has titled this film *Duplicity*. This is the work of The Doubler.

Once again—no, twice again—The Doubler has struck at the heart of movie culture. In the guise of "Zack Snyder," visionary director of *Watchmen*, he has recycled pop artifacts into a story full of laborious flashbacks and repetitive sequences, all about people chasing after an illusion and learning that the power structure will never change. Then, in the guise of "Tony Gilroy," The Doubler has done just the same thing.

Now, too late, I stumble toward the exit, though I already know it leads nowhere. A chill wind blows trash through the deserted bunker of the multiplex, past rows and rows of empty theaters showing the same movie again and again. History has ended. The Doubler has won.

Somewhere, a forgotten child cries for her Lubitsch.

The Nation, April 20, 2009

Black Swan

How they would have enjoyed *Black Swan*, the Surrealists, back when they pretended the Paris movie theaters were public parks, to be used for picnicking and free-associative conversation! How they would have reveled in it, the camp followers of my '60s youth, delighting to see a movie claw its way up the gilded peaks of sublimity, only to display, for all eyes, the idiot underpants of bathos!

I laughed longer and louder than at any other movie this year; but before you try doing the same, be aware that you'll have to twitch and sigh through the first two-thirds, and then, when it gets good, face the wrath of people who are taking *Black Swan* seriously.

How they do it, I can't imagine. "We all know the story," cries master choreographer Vincent Cassel to his New York City ballet company as it begins rehearsals for *Swan Lake*; but just in case any members of his corps (or the movie audience) are slow, he summarizes the plot anyway, then promises that his new production will "make it visceral and real." A visceral and real *Swan Lake* makes as much sense to me as does Cassel's complaint to his dancers, a few scenes later, that "you're stiff like a dead corpse!" (It took three people to write this stuff.) But enough of Mr. Impresario. On to poor, childlike Natalie Portman as the little dancer he improbably chooses to play the lead, on the assumption that she can somehow discover her inner Black Swan.

This is the side of the movie that isn't so funny: its revival of the myth of the frigid girl, repressed and mother-dominated, who must be sexually awakened and also, unfortunately, has to go nuts. It's the same story as *Carrie*, told with a similar pretense of sympathy for the young woman the film is out to punish.

The difference is that after all the tiresome displays of pink wallpaper and stuffed toys to telegraph the heroine's infantilism, all the visits to the toilet to dramatize her abjection, all the studiously giddy camerawork and *Dancing With the Stars* choreography (which keeps Portman busy tossing about her arms and mugging, as she does her swoon fake), you get to the part of the movie where uncanny forces break loose—just as in *Carrie!*—and they're juicier than a bucket of pig's blood.

Black Swan is un film de Darren Aronofsky.

The Nation, December 20, 2010

Zero Dark Thirty

Over the course of a sometimes difficult career, Kathryn Bigelow has repeatedly proved that a woman can be a first-rate action director. Almost as often, she's also proved that a director can't become a first-rate filmmaker by choosing crummy scripts. *The Hurt Locker*, which she did with writer Mark Boal, was a welcome exception to her run of dubious projects. It was classically lean and direct, and had the added advantage of being released in 2008, when audiences were ready to see what the Iraq War could do to a soldier's spirit, and to understand what kind of spirit would be suited to the Iraq War.

Now, with *Zero Dark Thirty*, her movie about the CIA's search for Osama bin Laden, Bigelow has reunited with Boal but stuck herself again with a lifeless screenplay—and a lead actress to go with it.

The main problem with *Zero Dark Thirty* isn't that it revels in torture and endorses waterboarding as a surefire way to get information. Nor is the film's utter neglect of all political issues its principal fault. The worst I can say about *Zero Dark Thirty* is that it pretends the best reason for hunting bin Laden down was that it meant so much personally to one smart, determined woman, whose superiors at the CIA just wouldn't listen to her. Bin Laden might as well be one of the Tyrolean Alps, and the heroine Leni Riefenstahl.

Actually, she's Jessica Chastain, playing a CIA agent named Maya. No matter how many tricks Bigelow plays, shooting Chastain through glass and putting her in and out of chadors, headscarves, wigs and balaclavas, there is no disguising that Maya is a bystander for much of the film—never more so than in the most effective and extended sequence by far, a brilliantly executed re-creation of the raid on bin Laden's compound. The film keeps cutting away from the Navy SEALs to Maya sitting at her computer, as if she had something to do.

As it happens, though, looking on idly is what Chastain does best. She has posed her way prettily through an astonishing number of roles in the past two years and has managed to forget herself in none of them. In *Zero Dark Thirty*, she proves that it's not enough for a filmmaker to pretend that you're the lead character—even if you do have cheekbones out of a dream.

The Nation, December 24, 2012

The Wolf of Wall Street

Because Martin Scorsese has a mind full of movies, it's possible to guess what he was thinking about at the end of *The Wolf of Wall Street*: the last shot in King Vidor's 1928 *The Crowd*. Vidor, you may recall, finishes his portrait of a terrifyingly, heartbreakingly ordinary family by showing a face-on image of them in a theater, laughing at a vaudeville performance. Then Vidor pulls back the camera to reveal dozens, hundreds, seemingly thousands of their fellow theatergoers responding identically to the show. He leaves you staring vertiginously into a mirror image of the audience in which you sit, where you see yourself reduced to a dot. In a similar spirit, *The Wolf of Wall Street* also ends at a performance: a lecture that will supposedly reveal get-rich-quick techniques, given by Jordan Belfort (Leonardo DiCaprio), the brazenly amoral financial huckster who in real life is a convicted felon and in the movie is the main subject and narrator. As the scene concludes, Scorsese runs his camera over the rows and rows of Belfort's dull-eyed, blank-faced spectators, and at last you see the people who have been missing from the story for the preceding three hours: the suckers who gave their money to this crook. Look into the mirror, says Scorsese. They're you.

With this closing gesture, Scorsese finally, if tacitly, passes judgment on Belfort, who until this point has been allowed to run as wild as any picaro. At the same time, though, Scorsese implies a retrospective justification of Belfort's career, hinting that a man of such energy and talent could scarcely have restrained himself from fleecing these sheep. What strikes me about this finale is that it's the only moment of ambiguity to be found in *The Wolf of Wall Street*, and the only instance in which Scorsese alludes to a monument of film history. For the rest of the picture, it seems to me that he's thinking about the collected works of the Three Stooges.

It would be a dangerously brilliant insight, if in fact that's what Scorsese has done, to imagine the Stooges as a counterpart to Jordan Belfort's business enterprise: on the one hand, a highly profitable but frantically churning production unit that spat out two-reelers from Hollywood's Poverty Row without benefit of recognized authorship or taste; on the other, a lucrative, crass and deeply fraudulent penny-stock operation that emerged from the Poverty Row of Long Island boiler rooms without benefit of any credential other than a classy-sounding name, Stratton Oakmont. The faint simulacrum of Wall Street professionalism that Belfort put up at his headquarters, and the opulence of the toys (human, mechanical and pharmaceutical) that he bought with his loot, could never disguise the nature of Stratton Oakmont's business, which was valueless, in all senses of the word, even by the standards of the financial services industry. In much the same way, the dazzling high gloss of Scorsese's production, with its luxury of partying crowds and penthouse settings, does not cover up the essential Stoogeness of the movie's proceedings.

I don't think Scorsese wants to cover it up. DiCaprio, with bottle-brown hair sculpted just so and free-floating aggression telegraphed by his every gesture, clearly functions as the story's fast-talking, overbearing, plan-spinning Moe. (To quote the words of the immortal Homer, "Moe is their leader." *The Simpsons*, #9F01.) Jonah Hill, with horn-rimmed eyeglasses and an abundance of wavy hair, is the Larry equivalent, alternately currying favor and dithering into hysterics as Belfort's partner Donnie Azoff (an invented name). In place of Curly, we have the muscular, bullet-headed Jon Bernthal as Brad, a drug dealer and bagman who provokes slapstick and police activity. Margot Robbie provides the obligatory woo-woo-woo as Belfort's second wife—really, that's the extent of her job—and Jean Dujardin fulfills the duties of the upper-crust foil.

Conceptually, the scheme is a stroke of genius, made all the more daring by Scorsese's willingness to abandon all claims to respectability to carry it through. Unfortunately, though, Scorsese did not abandon the epic scale of his ambitions along with his auteurism. The result might have been predictable to anyone who has tried to sit through more than three Stooges shorts in a row. The characteristic traits build up, intolerably: the grinding pace, the deadening repetition, the pointless wordiness (Terence Winter's screenplay never shuts up), the self-congratulatory nyuk-nyuks. I suppose the wretchedness of the excess is to Scorsese's credit—though, really, by the time Jonah Hill effectively coughed a half-chewed hot dog into my face, I felt I'd laughed enough.

Socially conscious moviegoers who believe that artists should act as public scolds might not enjoy this slog themselves but will perhaps recommend it for others, on the grounds that somebody out there needs to see an exposé. Avant-gardish types might instead justify the experience by invoking the Bukowski fallacy—the belief that the most authentic artistic response to a nauseating reality is to vomit. Subscribing to neither view, and reluctant to think that Scorsese has gone so wrong, I have tried to talk myself into the enthusiasm that some of my trusted friends feel for *The Wolf of Wall Street*. Maybe, on the day I saw it, my responses were simply off. I have to admit, though, that all through the screening I kept muttering the same thing about this movie that I say about our current reign of financial despots: "I can't wait for it to be over."

The Nation, January 27, 2014

American Sniper

Ninja Arab is leaping across the sunbaked rooftops of Falluja, or Baghdad, or anyplace that honest, tender Chris Kyle must rid of savages. Slim and Satanic in his black pajamas, narrow-eyed and inscrutable under his black scarf and do-rag, Ninja Arab could presumably walk like a normal person toward his next lookout for wreaking heartless, inexplicable murder, but as the nemesis of Chris Kyle he must show some flair. Chris Kyle is known as the Legend. Though the movie he's in is based on a true story—of that we've been assured—decorum requires that he repeatedly confront an equally legendary Ninja Arab, so that the two may face off, and one die, in a climactic shoot-out on the dusty streets. Or over them, to be precise.

Chris Kyle takes a manly, Texas squint through his range finder. The shot is impossible, his buddies cry—but he will make it even so, because duty calls. Two duties. With the sniper rifle cradled in one hand, Chris Kyle picks up a satellite phone in the other and speaks with his beautiful wife back stateside. Does he tell her not to phone him at the office? Does he say he's a little tied up, dear, with a meeting, and a firefight, and a final showdown with the embodiment of pure evil? No. Chris Kyle, knowing what a man must do, takes time out of his busy day so his wife will understand that he loves her and will protect her, because he is a sheepdog, and she is a ewe. (That's what his daddy taught him, anyway, back at the beginning of the movie, without anticipating the overtones of cross-species husbandry.) "I'm comin' home," Chris Kyle drawls ecstatically into the phone. Then he squeezes the trigger, and a single bullet flies—far, far, far across the sky, as slowly as CGI can make it go, until Ninja Arab's damned head splatters all over godforsaken Iraq.

I'm sorry I had to write that. When *American Sniper* went into limited release in December, I devoted two sentences to it in my holiday wrap-up, thinking that was as much attention as the film warranted. Last month, I gave the picture six more words—within a parenthetical clause—while making a modest case for not despising *The Interview*. That should have been it. The film wasn't much good, I thought, and no one would be astonished to learn what *The Nation* thought of its politics. A journal of opinion, fine. A journal where opinions are barked on Pavlovian reflex, not so good.

Yet I see that something more has to be said, not because, as their patriotic duty, the usual suspects have lined up to praise the film, but because serious people—critics I admire, whose political sympathies are close to mine—keep insisting that Clint Eastwood worked profound moral ambivalence and heartfelt complexities of character into *American Sniper*.

I wish it were so. Eastwood's westerns certainly fit that description. So do his cop movies (the ones that aren't knockabout comedies) and his World War II diptych, *Flags of Our Fathers* and *Letters From Iwo Jima*. The most I can say for *American Sniper* is that it moderates the full-throated Yahoo roar of the memoir of the same title (written by and for Kyle) while remaining true to its spirit.

Why do people who would abhor the book respect the movie? Don't they notice its flimsiness? In the Eastwood version, Kyle gets his basic training on the cheap, in scenes cribbed from *An Officer and a Gentleman*. He acquires his wife (Sienna Miller) in a strenuously jocular meet-cute, which has her loitering, improbably alone, in a bar near a military base, groomed as if she'd walked in from a fashion shoot. Kyle's observational skills presumably come from reading Hardy Boys novels. ("Say, I bet that unctuous Arab is hiding something under this creaking floorboard!") The psychiatrist—wise, mature and readily accessible—who treats Kyle for post-traumatic stress disorder is a person more likely to be encountered in a promotional video for the VA system than in the average hospital.

All this is obvious—and it's also being overlooked, perhaps for two reasons. The first is Bradley Cooper, who as Kyle gives the movie its sole chunk of solidity. Bulked up in his face and torso until he looks like a 3-D special effect, slowed down in his speech to create an illusion of depth behind every utterance, Cooper imparts substance to a character type that movie audiences always adore: the principled, no-nonsense man of the West, who banters easily with his buddies, addresses women with wry gallantry and prevails in fights when he must. The performance is so strong, so credible, that you could ignore, if you wanted to, the absence of anything darker, such as the monomaniacal ambition and cruel self-righteousness that raged in John Wayne when he embodied this type in *Red River* and *The Searchers*, or the sense of guilt that nagged at Eastwood himself in *Unforgiven. American Sniper*'s hero kills over and over again with a clear conscience, except when a child is in his cross hairs; and, even then, he and the audience know the death is someone else's fault. I don't say this is an unrealistically simple portrayal of Kyle; if the book can be believed, it's fairly true to life. But life, as we ought to know, does not always get made into good drama.

Which brings me to the second reason why people might be reading more into the movie's Kyle than is actually there. In the past, Eastwood has given us good dramas, many of them, and his fans do not want to believe he's failed them now. I share the feeling. When Kyle takes his son hunting late in the film and remarks on what a serious matter it is to stop an animal's heart, I wanted to hear an echo of William Munny in *Unforgiven*: "It's a hell of a thing, killing a man. Take away all he's got and all he's ever gonna have." But there's nothing in *American Sniper* remotely comparable to Munny's follow-up line, upon being told that the man who was just murdered probably had it coming: "We all have it comin', kid." The whole point of the *American Sniper* narrative is that Chris Kyle does not have it coming. His wife and children may suffer because of his long, terrifying absences, but he has to go away. His closest buddy in Iraq may decide that the war isn't all it's cracked up to be, but for Kyle that doesn't call the mission into question. It just shows that even the best men can buckle under the strain.

People want *American Sniper* to come from the Clint Eastwood who directed *Unforgiven*, but it's made by the guy who talked to a chair at the 2012 Republican National Convention. Here, too, he's addressing a void: a character who has no crosscurrents inside himself and feels no conflicting ideas buffeting him from without.

You might object, in Eastwood's defense, that he's not out to judge Kyle but to present the man in his own terms, conveying his sense of himself and his world. But if that's the intention, how could we know? What's been abandoned in the transition from page to screen is precisely the "I" of the book, its worldview. All we can see here is the world itself—which Eastwood and screenwriter Jason Hall have furnished with Iraqis who are, at best, extortionate cowards, and at their almost universal worst are assassins in league with Ninja Arab.

I would rather have seen the book adapted for film as Manoel de Oliveira might have done in the 1970s. A voice-over performer, perhaps a woman, would have read the entire text of Kyle's autobiography on the soundtrack, while actors mimed the events on a beautiful stage set. The running time would have been five hours, and the movie would have lost every penny spent on it—but you would have had a real chance to think about Chris Kyle.

The Nation, March 2, 2015

Suicide Squad

It's time, in this summer of Trump and *Suicide Squad*, to think more closely about the uses of shock. Do outrageous provocations merely galvanize an otherwise inert body politic, as a brain-dead frog is made to twitch in the lab? Or can the tactical deployment of grotesquerie and offense fulfill a higher purpose, blowing the dust of habit off our eyes? Some aestheticians have argued that by making the ordinary seem strange, shock effects can renew the mind, refresh the will, and awaken the spirit to delight.

In which case, is the Trump campaign a work of art?

To the degree that ambiguity of purpose and unpredictability of effect are decisive in art, at least in the modern era, then yes, we have now become a captive audience to one of the weirdest road shows ever produced. I watch the performances and wonder: Where the hell is this going, and what does the man really want? Trump is nakedly avid beyond the political norm in his pursuit of material gain, whether from tax cuts, payouts to friends and family, or the sale of bottled water; but more tellingly, he exceeds other candidates in his urge for self-expression, a force so powerful in him that he'd rather sacrifice votes than abandon a one-liner. Not a principle, mind you—what few tenets he mouths go no deeper than the tan and the hair, and mean less to him than either. But by fending off the advisers who keep begging him to behave properly, Trump has proved to be paradoxically authentic in his need to unburden himself and unload on others. He's as emotively bold as van Gogh, with the difference that the severed ears he waves around belonged to other people.

Going beyond traditional ballyhoo to avant-garde outlandishness, Trump's campaign has turned American politics into a spectacle of the odd, the brutal, the uncanny, and the improbable. And it's not just politics-as-usual that his campaign has made to seem strange. Trump has slapped a surrealizing exclamation point on the full range of his own clichéd tastes and attitudes, as well as those of his supporters. Acres of gold and marble! Bosomy blondes! Red meat and red blood! White supremacy! Everyone has long recognized that such banalities are widely shared in America—but no one is used to seeing them paraded about in this way, except in the works of R. Crumb and Philip Guston.

Those are clearly the wrong points of reference, though, for the Trump *Gesamtkunstwerk*. If you want to know whether Trump, considered as an artist, will produce the promised spiritual benefits of his shock effects, you might do better to look elsewhere: at the wildly lucrative blockbuster *Suicide Squad.*

The closest analogue to the Trump campaign currently in theaters, *Suicide Squad* is linked directly to the candidate through one of its executive producers, Steven Mnuchin, who has gone on to head Trump's fund-raising efforts. But the money trail is the least of the reasons why this movie seems to emanate straight from Trump World. More to the point, *Suicide Squad* embodies, to the nth degree, our current standards of mainstream movie entertainment, which it then exposes as utterly bizarre.

The comparison with entertainments of an earlier period is unavoidable, since *Suicide Squad* harks back to *The Dirty Dozen*—Robert Aldrich's extraordinarily revisionist, antiheroic World War II movie, made at the height of the Vietnam War, which proposed that certain crucial Army missions were suited only to units of condemned criminals. The producers of *Suicide Squad* gave the job of updating this notion to writer-director David Ayer, a specialist in platoon movies (*The Fast and the Furious, Sabotage, Fury*) who must have seemed just the guy to dispatch a team of misfits through the old ultraviolence. But because Ayer is working almost 50 years after *The Dirty Dozen*, his misfits aren't soldiers but comic-book villains; the authority that has assembled them isn't the Army but a shadowy government agency outside any recognizable chain of command; and the mission for which they've been chosen is purely speculative—they only *might* be needed. But so long as they're waiting around, they may as well destroy an ancient extradimensional being from South America (I think I've got that right) who has the powers of a witch, talks like the voice-over for an old sci-fi movie trailer, and looks like a recently electrocuted Cara Delevingne.

This is as close to a perfect intellectual vacuum as you'll find outside the average Trump foreign-policy statement. Historical events and government structures are reduced to the status of rumor. Mortal threats are unspecifiable but omnipresent, coalescing out of black smoke and lightning flashes. A coldly arrogant, wine-sipping bureaucrat—"An African-American woman, by the way, have I told you that, folks?" as Trump might put it—wields power without regard for human life. From other corners of the DC Comics universe, occasional figures pop in and out like random headlines from the *National Enquirer.* And the world's hopes rest exclusively on the outlaws, who aren't bad people, you understand; they're just living affronts to political correctness—

like Harley Quinn (Margot Robbie), the fun-loving, Trump-ready, blond sex slave who is proud to live in a permanent state of juvenile regression.

Form, such as it is, matches content. Like so many other blockbusters that now pass for normal, *Suicide Squad* is a shuffled playlist of pop songs, a graphic display of trading-card stats (Deadshot, Killer Croc, Diablo—collect 'em all!), a ceaseless whack-a-mole game in which the splattering pests are human, a periodic shower of 3-D debris. Mishmash predominates. The members of the Suicide Squad are all "metahumans" with ungodly powers, except for the guy who's just good with firearms, or the crazy pigtailed girl who swings a baseball bat. The government wields absolute power over these characters and keeps them under constant surveillance, though it will allow them to contact arch-criminals on their iPhones. As for the supernatural South American, she can teleport and emit vaporizing energy bolts; but when confronted by the good bad guys, she prefers to engage in five minutes of fisticuffs. Does this make no sense? No problem! It will all be over in a couple of hours, not counting the trailers for similar mainstream productions, one of which will soon be the next to have "won the weekend."

As a lifelong enthusiast of cinematic delirium, I groan at the very thought of *Suicide Squad*. Loud, lurid, incoherent, and ostentatiously, meaninglessly rebellious, it doesn't lift you to the visionary bliss of a *L'Age d'or*, *Holy Motors*, or *Mad Max: Fury Road*. It drops you instead into a muddle of reflex reactions. And we must face facts: This is what the public wants—a large segment of the public, anyway—just as millions of voters want what they're getting through Trump's performances.

I'll leave it to *The Nation*'s political writers to assess the extent to which Trump's audiences have been shaken awake by his vulgar effrontery, flocking to him because no one else seems to address their grievances, versus the extent to which they're galvanized frogs. My role—a very modest one—is to consider the artistic merits of Trump's shock campaign, judging it according to the current standards of Warner Bros. and the major theater chains.

I say it stinks.

The Nation, August 26, 2016

Wonder Woman

I'm not sure why Gal Gadot, star of *Wonder Woman*, reminds me of an asparagus spear. Maybe it's because she's such a strikingly vertical figure. Maybe it's the sleek braid that often tops her stalk, or the air of healthful vigor she exudes, heavily redolent of thiamine and riboflavin. Or maybe I'm associating her too closely with the vegetative state of the movie in which she's been planted.

Yes, the "summer's most anticipated release" is a slog, a schlep, a bore, a brainless and unstoppable encroachment of kudzu across the world's screens. Anticipated by whom, by the way? By the people who chose to respond to a Fandango survey, the results of which have been cited by *The New York Times* with a bland credulity last accorded to polls favoring Hillary Clinton. Is there a connection? Not really—except for a misplaced faith in feminist exceptionalism. Many people, myself included, have deplored the American film industry's indifference toward stories about female characters of any description, its blindness toward actresses who have passed the age of 40, its malign neglect of women who stand ready to produce or direct films. That said, there is no reason to think that the world, or even the subset of it known as cinema, will improve solely because a comic-book-franchise blockbuster has a woman as its lead and another woman in the director's chair.

You can ask my teenage daughter. (She's better than any Fandango survey.) Did she benefit from the magical cliché of "empowerment" by watching *Wonder Woman*? "I can feel empowered," she told me, "without staring for two hours at Gal Gadot's butt."

Nevertheless: Had this spectacle given my daughter no thrill at all? "Ohmigod," she said, forgoing the "I am Diana, daughter of Hippolyta, queen of the Amazons, by Zeus" argle-bargle. "You walk out feeling stupider than when you went in."

Which, I think, is the point. The screenplay for *Wonder Woman*, written by Allan Heinberg from a yarn he concocted with Zack Snyder and Jason Fuchs, is an origin story about another, even dumber origin story, with a third origin story popped in toward the end. Flashback lurches into tedious flashback, while in the interim, blurs of jerky, chopped-up action and CGI explosions fill the spaces where you might have hoped for credibly choreographed battles. Left unemployed, your mind wanders after this or that odd detail: noting which historically oppressed groups the filmmakers have ticked off their diversity list (hey, a North

African *and* a Native American!), or puzzling over the film's curious version of narrative economy, which enables characters to surmount Olympian barriers and span thousands of miles merely by saying they've done it.

Mostly, though, you watch the protracted, single-entendre flirtation between Diana, daughter of Hippolyta, and a World War I—era Yankee soldier who has somehow barged into her island paradise. Because the soldier is played by Chris Pine, he not only looks great but is also nimble with banter, self-mocking humor, and the flummoxed reaction shot. Perhaps the best that can be said for *Wonder Woman* is that someone had the wit to cast Pine in the boyfriend role, and that the director, Patty Jenkins, knew how to use him as a foil for Gadot, improving the effect of the dumb-but-smart deadpan she's learned to perform. I admit she's a clever enough asparagus to get by with the act. Just don't expect her to threaten the memory of Carole Lombard.

What else has Patty Jenkins brought to the project? A film-maker who made an impression in 2003 with her very good first feature, *Monster*, starring an uglied-up Charlize Theron as the accused serial killer Aileen Wuornos, Jenkins certainly knows how to take command of a vehicle. But in the case of *Wonder Woman*, she seems rather to have been along for the ride. She was plugged in as the second-choice director for a property that was cast before she was hired, written by others to conform to the Warner Bros. franchise scheme, and bossed by a team of 13 producers (11 of whom are men).

In that light, it might be more appropriate to say that *Wonder Woman* teaches disempowerment—the lesson that special-effects blockbusters are now the driverless Ubers of cinema. The algorithm decides all, and the only destination it recognizes is a bank where you don't have an account. Once upon a time (goes the origin story), when the studio system was not yet defunct, a band of heroes called Auteurists championed those filmmakers who were capable of imposing their personalities on genre stories, affirming the individual in a society of mass production. In 2017, though, trying to detect a personal vision in *Wonder Woman* is as futile as searching for financial security by jumping into the gig economy, or resisting conformity by rushing to be the next to post on a social-media thread. I'm glad for Jenkins that she got the job. But has this crummy movie struck a blow for women? Tell it to the algorithm.

The Nation, July 3, 2017

Climax

On my way home from watching Gaspar Noé's latest film, *Climax*, I did a little reality-testing as self-defense. I had just seen Noé snatch away the ground from two dozen characters, and I wanted to know if he'd done it to me as well.

Jolting along with me in the subway were people of every faith and none, every gender and none, from many ethnic backgrounds and almost all ages and economic levels. During rush hour, as many as 258 of us will be packed into a car, united in discomfort, strain, and fatigue but otherwise not merely diverse but deeply divided. Multiply by 10 and you get the number of riders jammed onto the train, who by any reasonable expectation should be ready to lash out—and yet, over the course of 40 years of daily commuting, I can recall fewer than half a dozen fights or even shouting matches. Some theorists of animal behavior say we're hard-wired for aggression; some theorists of society think the corruptions of New York encourage every kind of selfishness and anger. Your own nerves, too, may tell you at times that conditions in the car favor a riot. Yet we ride on in the millions, getting along with one another so well that we hardly even notice we're doing it.

That's reality. To Noé, though, this sociability is a mediocrity and a sham, beneath which lurks the brutal, authentic truth. He means to plunge your face right into the guts of that terrible, beautiful Absolute. Never mind that it's more like the bowl of cold spaghetti proffered to blindfolded middle-school kids in a Halloween house of horrors. You'll plunge! And so will his characters—in this case, a recently assembled troupe of dancers, all young and fit but otherwise as disparate as subway riders, who are sequestered in an isolated building after a rehearsal and driven nuts by the LSD-laced sangria they unknowingly drink while partying.

It's possible, barely, that Noé had an idea when conceiving *Climax*. At the conclusion of the prologue—a series of video interviews with the members of the fictitious troupe—the company's manager babbles about how she's proud to take the group on a tour of America, where people don't see anything like the excellence of French dance. Cut to a dress rehearsal, conducted in front of a glittering tricolor backdrop, onto which Noé superimposes the title: "A French film and proud of it." Now you see, at considerable length, what the manager calls French artistry: a been-there-done-that mishmash of voguing, hand jive, street-dance contortionism, promenades on the diagonal, and writhing on the floor with a crotch-is-burning sneer. Pure mediocrity, endlessly repeated. Does Noé realize it stinks, and is he poking fun at French cultural pretensions? Is he also sticking a thumb in the eye of his French producers, including government funders? Maybe, briefly. But then it's time for the acid to kick in, and the characters to start reeling through some ultraviolence and the old in-out, in-out.

I admit there is virtuosity in *Climax*. It's extremely difficult to film long, hand-held takes in which the camera follows or encounters actors engaged in whatever the hell they've been told to do. It's even trickier if you meanwhile tilt the camera woozily, or turn it upside down, in sympathy with your tripped-out characters. But this is virtuosity without thought or purpose, other than to show that everyone's beastly. And though I can't say that any character in *Climax* is admirable, I note with added queasiness that Noé has chosen to make the ones with the darkest skin tones the most brutal and obscene.

There's a climax here, all right—the climax of a certain strain of European bad-boy cinema (it's always boys), in which fantastic visual skill is devoted solely to the lifting of a middle finger. Well, the same to you, Gaspar Noé. The New York rush hour is all the extremity I need—and it comes with a comity you evidently wouldn't believe.

The Nation, March 20, 2019

Clint and Marty in Boston

Mystic River

Clint Eastwood's *Mystic River* is perhaps the finest western ever to be set in South Boston. Huddled clapboard houses substitute for the raw-plank architecture of the frontier town; an industrial bridge provides background sublimity in the absence of mountains. As always in an Eastwood western, the action takes place in an enclosed community that prefers to operate by its own rules; and as always, terrible secrets haunt the characters. Terrible wrongs are avenged and redoubled.

Of course, some viewers prefer to classify *Mystic River* with Eastwood's police movies; and they're not entirely wrong. In the role of Sean Devine, a detective with the Massachusetts state troopers, lean and clean-featured Kevin Bacon closely approximates one of Eastwood's own tight-lipped cops, never raising his voice, continually struggling to hold himself in. But the Eastwood detective usually pursues some taunting, demonic version of himself. Devine must contend with a pair of contrasting alter egos, both of them figures from his childhood on these streets: Jimmy Markum (Sean Penn), the big man in his little neighborhood, and Dave Boyle (Tim Robbins), who shuffles meekly around the bars and back porches and sometimes thinks he's one of the Undead.

He is, at a minimum, unfinished. That much is obvious from a square of sidewalk into which Dave and his buddies scratched their names some thirty years ago: Jimmy, Sean, Da. Now the memory of the event that interrupted Dave's hand is literally set in concrete, right on the street: the visible sign of something lost in him, something irremediably broken in the neighborhood.

What might turn that lingering pain into a present danger? A saloon, a six-shooter, a code of manliness.

Based on a novel by Dennis Lehane, *Mystic River* tells about guilt and suspicion in a working-class neighborhood—about young people abused and murdered, about generation after generation raging for revenge. Clearly, this story moved Eastwood to a seriousness he hasn't practiced since *Unforgiven* and *A Perfect World*. In the less ambitious projects that have piled up in recent years, the unfussiness that is one of his chief virtues as a director has sometimes turned into his biggest flaw; you wondered, during certain scenes of *Space Cowboys* or *Blood Work*, whether you were seeing the movie or the dailies. In *Mystic River*, though, Eastwood's clarity and strength are apparent from the start, even in the casting of the briefest roles. It's enough, in the devastating prologue, to see three boys playing hockey in the street to know which will grow up to be Sean Penn and which is doomed to become Tim Robbins. When the grown-ups take the screen, their sureness matches the director's. The performances seem to enter their bodies straight up from the pavement.

Robbins is the one who deploys his technique most openly: pushing a Boston accent against his hard palate and up into the nose, inventing a complete body language of shrugs and hesitations. A slight studiousness hangs about the performance; and yet he's also the actor who becomes the most daring and spontaneous. Dave is falling apart; and Robbins really lets the pieces crash. You see the effect not so much when he gets to scream—anyone can flail about—as in the quieter scenes, as when he tells his son a bedtime story that runs out of control. Dave's words, which are disturbing in themselves, become all the spookier for Robbins's way of listening to himself, as if he, too, were puzzled by what's coming out. Eastwood completes the mystery for him, shooting him against a background of infinite darkness, with only the left half of his face visible in a window's pale light.

Eastwood subjects Sean Penn to no such murk. As Jimmy, a convenience store owner with a dead daughter and a surprisingly complicated agenda, Penn has all the forcefulness that's been drained from Dave plus a few gallons more, despite his coming before you with a furrowed brow and gray at his temples. You sense this man is too old to be acting like the neighborhood tough; but like Dave, he's been tugged back into the past, reverting to a role he gave up years ago. Jimmy can still carry it off, but it weighs on him, as Penn shows you. He wears his muscles like a suit of armor; he rarely hauls his voice out of the lower dungeon of his throat.

Of the three leads, Bacon must remain the most controlled, not just because the character demands it but also because he's filling in for an icon. Sean Devine is the part a younger Eastwood would have played. Bacon, of course, is not an icon—he's famously versatile, which precludes such status—and yet he succeeds in making the role his own, despite having to deal with the distraction of a wretchedly underdeveloped subplot. In addition to its other elements, *Mystic River* is a story of three marriages: Jimmy's with the equally tough Annabeth (Laura Linney), Dave's with the equally tremulous Celeste (Marcia Gay Harden) and Sean's with a woman who is absent for almost the whole movie. Why is she absent? What must Sean do to get her back? How does his implied failure intersect with the other characters' problems? The answers drop into the story very late, as if by magic; while Bacon, a consummate pro, pretends that all is normal.

This is merely to say that the film suffers from the false moments—some improbable, others annunciatory—that usually come with a Brian Helgeland screenplay. I also might complain that the rhythms are sometimes choppy (there being none of the long, fluid sequences that you found even in *The Bridges of Madison County*) and that the music, by the composer Clint Eastwood, ought to have been cranked down a few decibels by his director.

Minor shortcomings, in the context of everything the film gets right. *Mystic River* may be a western at heart, but it knows its old-style city neighborhood as few other American films do. How accurate, how just, that practically the only bright color in this movie should burst out at the very end, when two shattered families pass before the cold eyes of a cop who knows everything and can do nothing. It's autumn, and a little parade is going down the street; people are doing their best to celebrate. Soon, you can tell, the first snow will fall; at which point the wounds will be buried still deeper, under a uniform, wan, grayish blue that hides but can never numb.

The Nation, October 27, 2003

Correction: The Mystic River does not run through South Boston, nor is *Mystic River* set in that neighborhood. It takes place in Somerville, as readers pointed out to my shame.

The Departed

Great artists do more than express emotion; they also invent it. The difference comes through most clearly when there's no subject matter to distract you—when you listen to Beethoven and Chopin, for example, or Armstrong and Coltrane, and hear how they called up ranges of feeling that were new to the world. But you can just as well experience this opening of emotional territory when you look at a Velázquez painting, or read *Dubliners*, or watch a sequence of classic filmmaking.

Here's something of the mood that Martin Scorsese invented: The Rolling Stones churn and rumble and keen on the soundtrack as the camera cruises like a vintage Chevy into a low-ceilinged urban storefront. You take in all at once an atmosphere of shadows, tribalism and menace; you sense the directorial momentum, as if the engine that drove you inside had been left running.

Scorsese introduced this feeling many years ago, in *Mean Streets*; but since then he has ventured far from the Little Italy that served as a platform for the emotion. He went to Las Vegas and Tibet, 1930s Hollywood and ancient Judea, testing and stretching himself as great artists do. In so doing, he left behind the mood that was initially so striking, and so peculiarly his. I thought it was missing even in *GoodFellas*. I hadn't expected to encounter it again.

Yet here it is once more, revived for two and a half hours nonstop in *The Departed*. You might be surprised that Irish Catholic South Boston should have provided the opportunity for this stunning return, but I tell you the range of emotions would be characteristically, authentically Scorsese's even if *The Departed* were set in Kowloon.

Which, in a sense, it is.

Sources close to the production inform me that Scorsese was initially reluctant to direct *The Departed*, since this producer-initiated project is a remake of the Hong Kong thriller *Infernal Affairs* (2002, directed by Andrew Lau and Alan Mak). Fans of *Infernal Affairs* (who are many, like the sequels) know it to be a clever, stylish, fast-moving and superficial action movie focused on the game-playing of two men who lead double lives. One, known to everyone as a police detective, works secretly for a mob boss. The other, known to everyone as a gangster, works undercover for the police. How these two deceivers chase each other through *Infernal Affairs* is far more important than anything they might feel during the pursuit. The characters' one or two moments of obligatory heartsickness do nothing to disrupt the picture's conventional sentiments of loyalty toward elders, chivalry toward women, fraternal respect toward a worthy adversary.

To Americanize this story, the producers of *The Departed* (who are also many) handed a translation of the script to screenwriter William Monahan. With considerable energy and a great trust in the power of foul-mouthed insult humor, Monahan went about transposing the events and characters to South Boston, a milieu he evidently knows something about. (I take it on faith that his grandfather was not originally a Manischewitz.) This package then went to Scorsese, who might have turned it into a mannerist exercise, like *Cape Fear*, but instead directed the movie as if every moment meant life or death, not just for the characters but for himself.

Start with the voice: a low, rattling sound, at once angry and mocking, that introduces the story of *The Departed* with a patch of seemingly omniscient narration. Later, when this frightening noise issues from an identifiable character, someone will guess that the speaker suffers from throat cancer. But nothing is truly eating this man, except the acid of his own amoral power. The voice belongs to mob boss Frank Costello (Jack Nicholson), who very soon will be a player in the drama but who for the first crucial moments of *The Departed* figures more as the *genius loci* of South Boston.

Images as ragged as the voice—shaky, fuzzy, archival—accompany his opening words, showing you the street fights that broke out in this neighborhood during the school-integration struggle of 1974. Then Costello himself steps onto the screen in devilish silhouette, a lean and stooping Spirit of South Boston, with long hair sweeping back from the forehead and a scraggly beard pointing down from the chin. Costello will prove to be an artist of sorts, a social philosopher, even a mentor; but he is first of all a man who rules by torture and murder, which leaves him looking none too clean. Like the people who attacked the school buses, he prefers his neighborhood to remain as it is: his own private hell, where "I beg your pardon?" is registered by smashing a beer stein against somebody's skull.

I must immediately deny that this representation is faithful to the lives of South Boston's good citizens. Nor do I think that Scorsese means it to be perceived as factual. Like Clint Eastwood, who turned Somerville into a surrogate Wild West town in *Mystic River*, Scorsese is working within a genre—though in this case the conventions are loose, since the director himself established them. The genre of the Scorsese picture can be open in form, as it was in *Mean Streets* (which an Italian-American friend once described to me, with fervor, as "the greatest documentary ever"); or, by contrast, it can be a closed system, as it is in *The Departed*, where the emotions and themes play out entirely within Scorseseland. You may, as a result, rate the present movie lower than *Mean Streets*; but then, understanding the nature of the game, you may also want to allow Scorsese his conceit, and Frank Costello his Mephistophelian allure.

He's the only character who's free to enjoy himself, you see, and so he stands apart from the two main protagonists. These are Costello's mole within the State Police and the State Police mole within Costello's mob—men who must never show their true feelings, and so are played, respectively, by Matt Damon and Leonardo DiCaprio. While Nicholson, the great cat-tearer, is busy tattering his every scene, Damon and DiCaprio keep their energy contained, suggesting far more than they show. Damon's chief asset here is that wide, ingenuous grin, which proves, on closer inspection, to be a cold apparatus for sifting and swallowing. Rising emotions bump against it and sink back down; lies filter through; and all the while nothing moves on Damon's face, except for a passing shadow. DiCaprio, by contrast, relies for effect on his level, hot-eyed gaze and a chronic tightness at the top of his throat. Though he, too, conceals and controls everything, he must at times appear to act on impulse (as when, like any credible Southie gangster, he beats the crap out of someone). Prescription drugs help him maintain the imposture; but the simultaneous expression of adrenaline and suppression of self sometimes leave this man in a state of quivering immobility.

When DiCaprio shows up, unannounced, at the door of his love interest, neither entering nor leaving, neither volunteering anything of himself nor asking openly for anything from her, she gapes at the glowering, hard-breathing figure and says, "Your vulnerability is freaking me out right now. Is it real?"

He takes a moment to consider the question, then replies, "I think so."

What makes *The Departed* so wrenching—far more than the tension of the plot or the abundant violence that provides its release—is the terrible honesty of this answer. The man might actually want to be vulnerable, just for a moment—he might even approach an admission of vulnerability. But by this point he's entangled so completely in lies that he doesn't know for sure, and neither do you. Few of us face situations as extreme as this character's, yet few will fail to recognize the confusion. On that level, it doesn't matter that *The Departed* is a closed system. Scorseseland is true to people's minds and hearts as we know them.

On the sociological level, though, *The Departed* does suffer from its self-enclosure. The woman to whom DiCaprio has come in his hour of need is a police psychiatrist, played with resourcefulness, valor and a vested gray suit by Vera Farmiga. Whether she deserves an Oscar nomination or the Bronze Star I can't say, but Farmiga makes what can be made of the character, who through wild coincidence (and a shocking inability to say no) winds up in bed alternately with Damon and DiCaprio. The women in *Infernal Affairs* were no stronger as characters, but at least there were two or three of them. Can there be, in all of Boston, only one woman to soak up all this suffering? The contrivance may not bring down *The Departed*, but it does expose the movie's walls as being shakier than they should be.

Matt Damon and Mark Wahlberg (as a detective sergeant) may bring genuine Boston accents to the movie; Martin Sheen (as DiCaprio's true boss) may add the weight of his Irish Catholic gravity; but this is ultimately just ornamentation, like the inconsequential subplot that worsens Costello's already unforgivable corruption. It doesn't matter that this latter complication is based on events that actually happened in Boston. *The Departed* was filmed in Massachusetts, but it is set wherever boys trade their lives for an armful of groceries, and men suffer their bones to be broken rather than risk being called fags or pussies. This is not a specific location—not anyplace capable of being documented—but it's real enough.

It's also a place that's essentially cinematic. You see that especially when the mannerist in Scorsese takes over, and he begins paying homage to *Infernal Affairs*. In one sequence, he copies (and outdoes) Lau and Mak's fast, nervous pans and multiple setups; in another, he sets the action as close as he can to Hong Kong, in Boston's Chinatown. You might even read one key event in the story as a filmmaker's allegory: A police operation fails because the technicians didn't install enough hidden cameras, leaving the director (that is to say, the officer in charge) to rage about not getting his coverage. In recent years, when Scorsese has inserted such knowing little touches into his movies, they have seemed to interest him more than the story itself. In *The Departed*, they're always absorbed into the relentless, compelling flow.

It's not just DiCaprio's character who is put into a state of trembling immobility. For the entire running time of *The Departed*, I felt adrenaline pumping through me and yet could neither fight nor flee. I could only watch, in amazement and admiration. And when the movie ended and the credits rolled, I remained stuck to my seat. I wanted a little time, before I tried walking, for my heart rate to go back down.

The Nation, October 5, 2006

Satirical Rogues

American Splendor

Here's our man, starring in a movie about himself. Notice the clumping, simian gait; the aggrieved set of the lower jaw; the habit of rubbing the back of the skull, either to quiet a nagging idea or else, more likely, nudge it into more aggressive life. Alone, eyes downcast, our man strides in medium shot and long shot through the cold Cleveland streets. He no longer needs to look at these surroundings; he knows them so well that he can watch them anytime on his eyelids' screen. Rarely, though, is the screen of American cinema touched by anything like these rows of brown brick apartment buildings, all breathing their perpetual cabbage steam; the plots of frozen weeds, carefully secured behind chain link; the factory yards, empty in the afternoon light of winter, or maybe just empty nowadays; the long prospect, around the corner of a one-story commercial block, up the level street toward Canada. Similar views of the real Detroit figured in Curtis Hanson's *8 Mile*; the authentic Omaha has been a player in Alexander Payne's movies. Few similar examples come to mind from recent cinema, though, and none where the city and its son are fused so thoroughly to the hard bop tenor of Joe Maneri's "Paniots Nine."

Anyone with ears can understand how Maneri's music fits the scene. His sound is biting, asymmetrical, lyrical, propulsive and right. But you have to be like our man himself—a scholar of the bypassed, an arguer out of the obscure, for the obscure—to know that Maneri recorded this cut in 1963 and then waited thirty-five years for its release. In fact it was our man, Harvey Pekar, who in his role as a jazz critic helped bring this music out of absolute darkness, into the penumbral repute it now enjoys.

Speaking of penumbral repute: From off the streets of Cleveland comes the movie about Harvey Pekar—the man who has shown how great it is, and how frustrating, to remain on the streets of Cleveland. From off the streets of Cleveland (as he says in his comic books) comes *American Splendor*.

In equal measures a biopic, a drama and an elaboration of Pekaresque themes, the *American Splendor* movie will first of all satisfy those who (like me) have avidly followed the comic since it began appearing during the Ford Administration. Like the best of the Conceptual artists who flourished in those years (no doubt to our man's disgust), Pekar created something brilliantly new by using the old, Modernist trick of putting an object into an alien context. Duchamp, early in the century, had collaged a bicycle wheel onto a wooden stool, implicitly substituting these mundane things for a sculpture on a pedestal. On the same principle, Cindy Sherman in the mid-1970s began to collage her own image, in various get-ups, into film-still settings; and Pekar inserted his T-shirted, clumping, skull-rubbing self into that environment of superheroes, the comic book. (The gesture was all the more Conceptualist for requiring no traditional artistic skill. Pekar wrote the *American Splendor* stories and left the drawing to others, beginning with his old friend Robert Crumb.) Granted, earlier writers had created autobiographical comics—I think, for example, of Justin Green, with his *Binky Brown Meets the Holy Virgin Mary*—but they hadn't achieved Pekar's wonderfully bracing results. In *American Splendor*, reality looked more real than ever—grimier, odder, funnier, more melancholy—for having erupted inside a comic book.

In that sense, we fans don't even need to see the *American Splendor* movie to love it. Conceptually, it's enough for us to scan the cast list and see that the magnificent character of Mr. Boats has come to the screen—Mr. Boats, the righteous and gnomic head of file clerks at the VA hospital in Cleveland, where Pekar worked for virtually all his adult life (he retired in 2001). We're at last going to see that chubby, bow-tied figure in the flesh (here embodied by Earl Billings); we're going to listen to him hold forth against today's music—"Trash!"—while pounding his fist into his palm and ignoring all other lines of dialogue. A Möbius twist: In place of the real human figure we had intuited through the cartoon, we now have a fictional (though human) equivalent to the drawing.

But there's more, and better. Pekar's file-clerk buddy at the VA hospital, Toby Radloff, the drawling, bachelor prince of Cleveland's nerds, appears in the *American Splendor* movie in dual form, as both an actor (Judah Friedlander) and himself—sometimes within the same frame. And more: Pekar and his long-suffering, long-simmering wife, Joyce Brabner, come onto the screen in at least three incarnations, as actors (Paul Giamatti and Hope Davis), cartoon images and the real Joyce and Harvey.

The writer-director pair who have realized the movie, Shari Springer Berman and Robert Pulcini, understand that this multiplicity is part of both the appeal and the unstated meaning of *American Splendor* comics. Different artists draw Pekar, so his looks keep changing, even while his character remains true to its disgruntled, stuck-in-Cleveland self. Thematically, these variations help to convey Pekar's message that "Ordinary life is pretty complex stuff." Dramatically, they provide the movie's Joyce with an opportunity to comment nervously on Pekar's apparent mutability when she is about to meet him for the first time, having spent the previous months as his pen pal. At his invitation, Joyce has come to visit from Wilmington, Delaware, and is looking around the Amtrak station for her host. What to expect? Some artists, she thinks, make Harvey look like a young Brando (and there's an example of such a drawing, collaged into a shot of the waiting room). Others depict him as a hairy ape (another collage effect); and Crumb has these wavy lines coming off him, like a bad smell. "Those are motion lines," Harvey explains in voiceover. "I'm a fast-moving guy." Then he appears to Joyce in the flesh—that is, in Paul Giamatti's flesh—to hold out his hand and offer the world's all-time champion blind-date opener: "I want to make one thing clear up front. I've had a vasectomy."

Berman and Pulcini have found the heart of their movie in this first, impossibly funny meeting of Joyce and Harvey, and also in the later episode (which Joyce and Harvey turned into a comic book) of *Our Cancer Year*, when he was undergoing chemotherapy and she was keeping him going. You don't ordinarily think of delicacy and emotional nuance in scenes involving people who collapse before toilets (as they do in both these sections of the movie); but the interplay here between Joyce and Harvey is as touching as it is hilarious, thanks to the acute honesty of the movie's source material, the filmmakers' deadpan direction and (above all) the virtuosity of Giamatti and Davis. Both actors perform precise imitations of their real-life models (as you can see easily enough through on-screen comparisons), and both go far beyond mimicry, to suggest that beneath the surface of each lives a world of experience, much of it either disappointing or infuriating. As soon as Davis-Joyce and Giamatti-Harvey meet, you can see they were made for each other, God help them. They're so quick to read one another's minds, and often so bad at it, that the simple exercise of choosing a restaurant not only leads them to someplace they both loathe but compels them to stay there. Neither of them can laugh off the mistake and offer to leave; so you do the laughing for them. Later that same evening, when it turns out that Harvey had read something correctly in Joyce and cared enough about her to act on it, you're also moved for them.

These are the scenes I most admire, where Berman and Pulcini have been true to Pekar's comic and their own movie alike. Sometimes, though, they've made a choice, retaining their movieness at the expense of Pekar's peculiar achievement.

He did not just collage himself into comic books; he also collaged in the ordinary passage of time. The *locus classicus* of this effect: the uproarious one-page "story" titled "Standing Behind Old Jewish Ladies in Supermarket Lines." The point of this page (drawn by Crumb) was the very pointlessness of the time that Harvey was wasting, since he could do nothing, nothing at all, to speed the picayune transaction holding him up, or to alter the centuries-old culture of the co-religionist he wanted to strangle. Like so much of *American Splendor*, this page is a triumph of observation, which is achieved as if for its own sake, leading nowhere.

Berman and Pulcini recreated this scene in their movie—and against the spirit of the original, they turned it into a plot point. Harvey becomes exasperated, as the old Jewish lady kills his time; Harvey realizes his life is slipping away; Harvey goes home and writes the first stories of *American Splendor*. I hasten to say this moment plays just as well as the filmmakers intended; so do all the moments that have been added up into a narrative, with learning and growth and a big hug at the end. But playing well isn't necessarily Pekar's intent. As an artist, he resists the satisfying wrap-up, in a way that's closer to the filmmaking of Jim Jarmusch or Aki Kaurismaki, or for that matter the music of Joe Maneri, who is, tellingly, the only hard bopper on the soundtrack.

This isn't to say that Berman and Pulcini have betrayed Pekar, or made the kind of movie he would deride as Hollywood bullshit. But they've been more accommodating to convention than he would be, a bit more commercial—which is intriguing, since they also understand the hipster ethos to which Pekar is loyal.

They know it's not a cult of failure, though nonhipsters often misunderstand it as such; they show us that Pekar has in fact burned for success all his life. But he has demanded that it come to him; he will not change his clothes, floss his teeth and go out to meet success at a bar where chardonnay costs twelve bucks a glass. Give in to phoniness even that much, and the next thing you know you're making excuses for big corporations and feeling superior to guys like Toby Radloff. Of course, most people, including Toby himself, don't worry about such compromises; they would gladly take success on the world's terms. But Pekar is one of those hotheaded, old-fashioned people who won't give up their politics, their vinyl or their faded plaid shirts. They want to keep everything real—even in their comic books.

We've met some of these people in earlier movies: notably Terry Zwigoff's *Crumb* and *Ghost World*. Now, in the wretched summer of *The Hulk*, a new comic-book movie reintroduces us to them, just when we need it most.

Splendid.

The Nation, September 1, 2003

Borat/Flags of Our Fathers

To start by oversimplifying—and why not, in an election year?—movie culture has forever been split between Charlie Chaplin and D.W. Griffith. From Griffith we get the aspiration to grand scale and elevated tone, massed armies and multiple story lines, with the director's visual power integrating personal narratives into historical simulation. The Chaplin tradition also has its artistic ambitions, despite being raffish and outwardly improvisational; but it focuses less on the creation of a cinematic world than on the realization of a star performance that never fully abandons the joy of a swift kick in the pants. For the moment, Clint Eastwood's *Flags of Our Fathers* is the most notable descendant of the Griffith line. The Chaplin line—as carried on by another English comedian sporting curly hair and a funny mustache—is currently represented by *Borat: Cultural Learnings of America for Make Benefit Glorious Nation of Kazakhstan.*

The public has now chosen between these traditions, as it does from time to time; and for this round it has decided the question by an epoch-defining majority. In one weekend, *Borat* grossed a reported $26.4 million: as much as *Flags of Our Fathers* took in during its first seventeen days in release. I am not such a fool as to think that immediate ticket sales determine a film's worth; nor would I judge a movie's social impact by its usefulness to op-ed commentators (who for the moment cannot live without *Borat*). That said, I can recognize a cultural turning point when it smacks me in the kisser. Griffith has been trounced. Chaplin rules.

And *Borat* is the movie of the year, the picture that makes all other films irrelevant. Do I like it? In my office as cinematic guinea pig of the American left, do I approve? Yes, but so what? I look upon *Borat* in awe, as I would gape at the sublimity of a tidal wave sweeping everything before it. Public solemnity? Obliterated. Displays of craftsmanship? Drowned. Respect for any authority, any institution, any individual (other than an impecunious Alabama call girl)? You've got to be joking.

Mere anarchy is loosed, and its name (bless him!) is Borat.

For those readers who have been studiously ignoring the world around them, I should explain that the title character, Borat Sagdiyev, is not so much a persona as an imposture, foisted on unsuspecting people by his creator, Sacha Baron Cohen. Supposedly, Borat is a broadcast journalist from Kazakhstan, which is here depicted in prologue as a life-affirming rural shantytown, vibrant with rape, incest, arms-dealing, neighborly ill will and festivals of Jew-hatred. (Is the depraved, mostly toothless populace meant to be Muslim, by any chance? "No," says Borat. "We follow the Hawk.") This nation, though glorious, knows that it might yet have room to make benefit; and so Kazakhstan's Ministry of Culture, or something, has sent Borat to the United States to shoot an informative documentary about life in a different part of the world.

The gag—unstated, but unmissable—is that the film you are watching really is a documentary of sorts, shot by director Larry Charles, about an America that mirrors the imaginary Kazakhstan. Our nation, too, proves to be a place of race hatred, arms-dealing, seething hostility and unrestrained horniness, where the populace seeks to justify itself by appealing to a very Hawk-like religio-jingoism. The major difference between the two countries (other than the indoor plumbing) is that America is an actual site of these grotesqueries, as revealed through the unscripted interactions that Cohen, in the guise of Borat, enters into with real people, from subway riders in New York City to an alarmed team of security guards in Orange County, California.

Because Cohen has a daredevil's nerve (he never stops being Borat, no matter how much trouble he gets into), and because some of his adventures were shot covertly, *Borat* might be likened to a combination of *Jackass* and *Candid Camera*. But to say this is merely to acknowledge that Cohen remains true to his roots in television comedy (as Chaplin did to the music hall) and appreciates the disruptive potential of a live chicken, when it's released in the wrong place at exactly the right time. The more important point about the performance is that Cohen's Borat is a guileless man (almost)—naïve, certainly; stupid, without question; but enthusiastic, ingenuous and eager to please—so that the audience instinctively warms to him and even wants to protect him, the most obscenely offensive movie character of our time.

The effect is not just double- but quadruple-edged. Double, because Borat's apparent harmlessness highlights a corresponding goodwill, or even innocence, in many of the racist, chauvinist fools he meets and makes fun of. Maybe, if you are strenuously correct in your attitudes, you assume there must be something monstrous about drunken white frat boys who believe that "minorities" are keeping them down; or self-styled Southern gentry living a fantasy of antebellum elegance; or right-wing politicians working the crowd at a Pentecostal church. In their own eyes, though, these people are kind, decent, generous and patient—qualities that Borat in fact elicits from them, even as he slips in the knife.

The third and fourth edges come flashing from Cohen's aggression, which Borat's sweetness does not conceal. Consider the scene in which he visits an antiques shop in Dallas, where items of Confederate memorabilia are on display—"to celebrate our heritage," the proprietor explains. Borat, being a clumsy fellow, soon trips over his own feet and smashes some pieces, then falls backward while trying to right himself and smashes some more, then fails to steady himself with an awkwardly outstretched arm and so forth, until he's reduced an entire aisle to shards. On one level this is classic slapstick. On another it's punishment, meted out (with breathtaking peremptoriness) for the crime of complacency about slavery. You or I might dream of exacting such payback. Cohen actually gets it.

By being shameful and shameless in a single gesture, which is carried out with almost unprecedented exuberance, *Borat* sets loose raging torrents of laughter—reason enough for its popularity. But if you want to account for people's excitement about this movie— their sense that *Borat* is doing something in the world—you might look instead to the directness of Cohen's attack, and the deceptive simplicity of his method. These are Chaplin qualities. Everyone knows they're abundant in *Borat*; but they cannot be found in *Flags of Our Fathers*.

This is no fault of Eastwood's film. *Flags of Our Fathers* happens to be very good: intelligent, compelling, lovingly made and strikingly appropriate to our present moment in history. As you will have heard by now, the movie dramatizes the experiences of three of the men who were photographed raising the American flag over Iwo Jima. It follows their brief public careers as heroes (sent on a cross-country tour to sell war bonds) and contrasts them with the agony of the battle they had just survived. So this is a war picture about the power of pictures in wartime: about the conversion of bloody chaos into meaning, and the transformation of fallible, suffering men into figures of virtue. For Eastwood, who has long brooded over the folklore and the reality of violence, this theme feels entirely natural. (So, too, does his empathy with one of the protagonists, a Pima Indian named Ira Hayes. Having mourned over racism in many previous films, Eastwood makes it a central topic of this picture.) If the screenplay is short on dramatic tension—with writers William Broyles Jr. and Paul Haggis following dutifully in the footsteps of established fact—there is more than enough physical conflict to keep the picture moving. Maybe the narrative doesn't crackle quite enough; but how would prospective audiences know?

People do understand, though, just by looking at the newspaper ads, that *Flags of Our Fathers* will be weighty, impressive, instructive, magisterial. These are the strengths of Griffith's tradition—and they are fatally ill-timed, now that Cohen's hit-and-run vehicle is careening into theaters. Moviegoers have clearly elected to go with the swift, the mobile, the riotously vulgar; and it doesn't surprise me that they made this choice just days before the general population voted (far less decisively) for change.

Borat is a triumph for truly pissed-off Americans: younger ones especially, who feel the time has passed for polite exposition and patient analysis. They just want to laugh their heads off, as the whole existing order is mowed down. How many such citizens are there? I have no idea. But I know that cultural change doesn't require a majority, only an invigorated critical mass; and that's what *Borat* is creating.

Not since Dylan went electric…

The Nation, December 4, 2006

Notes on an
Undead Industry

Assault on Precinct 13

Half a century has passed since Manny Farber wrote in these pages about underground films, by which he meant the urban crime movies watched by male loiterers near the Greyhound station, in theaters whose dank gumminess rivaled that of the bus terminal's restrooms. The close fit among setting, audience and cinematic expression particularly recommended such movies to Farber, who recognized meaning and purpose where others saw only inadequacy. He noted, for example, that these so-called action pictures often showed little more than views of men standing around on a sidewalk, waiting for something to happen. The something, when it came, was often an inventive way to torture human flesh.

Very little changed in the world of movie-watching between the publication of that great essay and 1976, when *Assault on Precinct 13* first unspooled near America's bus terminals. All right, a lot had changed. The studio system was gone, a generation of film-school graduates was breaking into the big time, and a surprisingly large audience could now name the makers of Farber's underground movies and believed that these directors deserved the name of *auteur*. Still: Time in 1976 could be wasted as cheaply as in 1950 at a city-center moviehouse, if you weren't squeamish about the people sitting behind you, the stuff sucking at your shoes or the spasmodic shadows passing across the screen, made up half of existential dread and half of anomie. You paid a buck or so to get indoors, and *Assault on Precinct 13* showered you with an hour and a half of unreasoning, unstoppable blood lust, loosed from those imaginary ganglands of Los Angeles where the only stable, responsible types were those whose criminality had risen to the level of a career. As the story of a siege at a police station, the movie provided long stretches of dead time. As an updated and citified version of Howard Hawks's *Rio Bravo*, it also gave you glimpses of character, though without Hawks's warmth and breadth of vision. The approach was more like that of the Cossack narrator of one of Isaac Babel's *Red Cavalry* stories, who goes back to his village to confront the landowner: "I stomped him for an hour or more, and during that time I got to know something about him and his life."

This isn't to say that *Assault on Precinct 13* qualified as a classic. ("Archaizing" would have been a better word for its effect.) The picture was just something you could discover on your own, in a public place. Its maker, John Carpenter, had not yet achieved fame and riches through *Halloween*. The theaters where it showed had not yet split into multiplexes, with ticket prices in the double digits. The event-movie era, with its thrilling box-office reports, had barely begun; and "home video" still meant whatever the TV was broadcasting.

So the release of an all-star, Franco-American remake of *Assault on Precinct 13* is worth noting, as another milestone on our journey away from old-fashioned film culture.

Rather than being cast like the original, whose performers you will not be able to identify unless your name is Tarantino, the new *Assault on Precinct 13* may legitimately be said to star the actors Ethan Hawke and Laurence Fishburne, with John Leguizamo, Drea de Matteo, Maria Bello, Brian Dennehy, Gabriel Byrne and Jeffrey "Ja Rule" Atkins in supporting roles. Note the whiff of prestige. Observe as well the pairing of a strong, menacing, above-the-law Black killer with a younger, weaker, vacillating white cop—a combination that inescapably brings to mind Hawke's previous outing in such a role, in the Oscar-winning *Training Day*. Despite being sent out into the wasteland of January, despite having roots in grind houses, this *Assault on Precinct 13* expects to be taken seriously by at least some portion of the audience. You might even say it aspires to partake in an American "tradition of quality."

That latter, poisoned phrase was of course the boast of the French studio filmmakers of the 1950s, who provided such a useful enemy to the rising critics and directors of the New Wave. The ironies of history: Once upon a time, younger French cinephiles made room for themselves by tearing down their elders, which they did by promoting American action pictures over the supposed best work of their own country. The taste and ideas of these auteurists, when subsequently imported to America, taught people here to respect Sam Fuller, Nicholas Ray and (eventually) John Carpenter. And now a French producer (Pascal Caucheteux) and a French director (Jean-François Richet) have paid homage to Carpenter's earliest hit, imparting to the project the very artiness that the New Wave wanted to escape.

They have brought a decorative sensibility to *Assault on Precinct 13*. You see it in the pretty latticework that the bad guys create, when they poke their red laser beams into the darkened police station. You see it in clever-cute tracking shots, such as the one of cops and criminals pairing off to defend the entrances of the precinct house. And then there are the snowflakes, each as big as a horsefeather, which float through the backlit, piney woods of Detroit as *Assault on Precinct 13* climaxes in the killing of its ninth identifiable figure. Maybe tenth.

I lost count, because of all the people associated with this movie—Jean-François Richet, screenwriter James DeMonaco and no fewer than six producers—none thought it important to track the fates of all characters who have names and dialogue. I know, this movie is a shoot-'em-up, and convention decrees that the bad guys (who in this case are faceless behind armored masks) may drop as the autumn leaves. But did a cop die in that overturned van, or was he just soaked in blood? Did the bad guys really let Brian Dennehy go, or did they take him off-screen and shoot him (which is what I'd do, every time)? Convention decrees that these matters should not remain a mystery; and yet they go unresolved here, even though DeMonaco made time for Laurence Fishburne to articulate his views on the inevitability of death and the absence of God.

In the tradition-of-quality action picture, the dialogue groans with philosophical weight, while the plot twists grind with improbability. (Exactly how did Brian Dennehy find apparent release in the bad guys' hands? Really, don't ask.) The women characters are no longer just blond-mopped expanses of thigh and cleavage; now they are strong and independent, so they can also *talk* about sex. As for the film's horse-feathery notion of Detroit: When a picture is expected to play for two or three weeks in nondescript multiplexes and then spend the rest of its life on DVD shelves, it may as well leave undefined all relationships of physical and social space.

I am making *Assault on Precinct 13* sound like a terrible movie. It's not. Ethan Hawke is good in his opening scene, as an undercover narcotics cop (and utterly unbelievable throughout the rest of the movie, when he's a tousle-headed desk sergeant); Laurence Fishburne delivers another of his carved-from-a-block-of-ebony performances, which is OK with me; and John Leguizamo stands out in the role of a junkie who has the bad luck to be in the precinct's lockup when the siege begins. (According to the press hand-outs, Leguizamo took the trouble to invent a back story for his character—something the writer and director hadn't thought to do—which explains why the movie seems three-dimensional when he's around.) Some of the action sequences are fun, too, particularly when the rag-tag defenders are first fighting off their robotic assailants; but Richet's invention soon flags. By the third time a gun-wielding heavy was brought low with an improvisatory thrust of a sharp object, the carnage had lost its gaiety for me.

Here, then, is today's overground action thriller: a picture whose raffishness, far from being inherent, amounts to a marketing tool, just like its choice of cast members (all of them known for better roles), its semaphoric appeals to be taken seriously, its French and auteurist pedigree. You could, if you chose, waste some time with it, especially in this empty month. But if you want to recapture just a little of the spirit of 1976, you'll have to buy a ticket to something else you want to see at the multiplex—*Million Dollar Baby*, *House of Flying Daggers*, *Hotel Rwanda*—and then afterward, for your double feature, sneak into *Assault on Precinct 13*.

The Nation, February 7, 2005

Pirates of the Caribbean: Dead Man's Chest

It was a dark and slimy film—and yet, as it wound its way slowly into the third hour, it undeniably lit people up. Looking around the movie house, you could see instant-message screens glowing everywhere, as a bored preview audience distracted itself from *Pirates of the Caribbean: Dead Man's Chest.*

To be rained on incessantly; to be chained and flogged; to be slapped in the face with tentacles, spewed with mucous, drowned in murk, subjected to an endless booming racket and repeatedly tortured, gerbil-like, upon different versions of the medieval wheel: These are only some of the imaginative pleasures for which the Walt Disney Company now expects you to pay. And because the sadistic merchant wields corporate power at its most omnipresent, submissive millions are even now presenting themselves to be "entertained," with nothing but cellphone flashes to signal a feeble and belated resistance.

Two and a half hours of cinematic slog, lightened for only a second or two by Johnny Depp's mugging or Keira Knightley's kisser; and at the end, poor sucker, you learn there is no end, but only a come-on for *Pirates of the Caribbean 3*! Had this insult to the nervous system been inflicted in darkest February, when studios clear their shelves, you might have understood the affront, if not excused it. But *Pirates of the Caribbean: Dead Man's Chest* is a summer blockbuster, and so it gives frightening evidence that its studio felt no need to do better.

The Nation, July 31, 2006

Inglourious Basterds

It came as no surprise that every response to *Inglourious Basterds* came as no surprise. When word goes out that a film will be about the Holocaust but not really, because it's actually about old movies; when it's expected to be a slam-bang adrenaline-powered summer thrill ride but not really, because a major American film-maker has conceived it, then positions about the picture become so many pre-dug holes, waiting for occupants to tumble in. Merely by calling the film *Inglourious Basterds*—as if its contribution to the vast body of World War II cinema might amount to a couple of misspellings plopped into a title copied from an earlier, cheaper film—Quentin Tarantino promised indelicate pleasures to those who wanted them and pre-emptively shrugged off criticism from those who might want more. It was, in a way, a self-protective move—perhaps even a timid one, coming from a filmmaker who makes his living by a show of boldness; and many more were evident in the trailer, the print ads and the prerelease puff pieces, all calculated to ensure that nothing could be said about *Inglourious Basterds* that *Inglourious Basterds* had not first said about itself.

So I choose to have no opinion about this film. Indifference is the only unforced response left to me.

This isn't to say I'm indifferent to evidence of widespread credulity among those viewers of *Inglourious Basterds*, fans and detractors alike, who accepted the improbable claim that a film can refer to nothing but other films. Nor am I indifferent to a situation in which the entire reception of a film can be produced along with the movie. We have gone beyond cinema's long-familiar modes of culture and commerce: DeMille marketing his epics as a redemption for their own sins, Minnelli both exposing and reveling in the dream factory's artifice, Hitchcock instructing audiences in how to think about a Hitchcock movie, Herschell Gordon Lewis outraging every decent feeling (and so, predictably, attracting a cluck of admirers). With *Inglourious Basterds*, we reach one of those moments that tell us we're in new territory, where unforeseen, uncontrolled reactions are being foreclosed as never before.

This complaint, as I said, is not about the film as such; nor is it meant exclusively about Tarantino. Despite the colossal assertions commonly made about him, he's only one of a great many people who have brought us to this spot. I'm concerned with the aggregate. With some of them coming in from the industry side and others from the side of vulgar Kaelism, they have executed a kind of pincer movement over the past decades, and in so doing have swept us all toward those holes in the ground.

Start with the industry. For the past quarter-century, it has largely devoted itself to expanding the field of in-home entertainment while reducing the role of theatrical exhibition—a development that has required companies to scramble for appropriately scaled economies of production and distribution. The solution has been the institution of a multi-tiered system: big-budget films released onto thousands of screens at once, under the names of major studios; more modestly budgeted pictures given platform release by the studios' specialty divisions and by a surviving handful of midsize distributors; microreleases sent out by small companies for a round of one- or two-week runs at a few theaters dotting the country; and an unquantifiable mass of dumped-on-to-digital material.

One consequence of this recently evolved system has been the cretinization of most pictures released by major studios during the first ten months of the year, followed by the release of ostentatiously brow-furrowing pictures for the final two (which are dedicated to awards-qualifying runs). Another consequence has been the invention of a prestigious "independent film" made up of those midbudget pictures that have been chosen for platform release and a publicity push. Because these Mercury Sables of American cinema don't need to make $60 million over the opening weekend, as the Ford Expeditions do, they can afford on average to be less crude and lumbering, and so to some degree represent an alternative. The fact that these movies have been picked out for promotion, rather than being left to clamor for a slot at Anthology Film Archives, suggests that the marketers of "independent film" sense a limit to the public's appetite for alternatives.

Of course, to listen to the industry's shills—entertainment reporters, dutifully crying out the box-office figures—you'd think those carefully respected limits did not exist. In standard accounts, the so-called independents have mounted a critical challenge to the major studios, which are said to resent the lack of respect accorded really lucrative pictures. Yet look at how in mid-November these same shills can announce which pictures will contend for Academy Awards, almost before the screenings have started. The industry is strangely quick to reach consensus. And notice how the same movie titles then show up week after week through February, some representing Fox and some Fox Searchlight. Despite the expansion of choice supposedly fostered by the independents, for four months of the year no more than ten movies are talked about.

If *Inglourious Basterds* should turn out to be one of them, nobody will even know to which tier of the system it belongs. Tarantino and his producers, the Weinstein brothers, are closely identified with the official version of independent film, and the reported budget of $70 million is not huge for an action picture starring Brad Pitt. But then, Universal Pictures shares production credit with the Weinstein Company, and the film opened on more than 4,000 screens, making it a tossup whether *Inglourious Basterds* is also a big-studio release. Judge from this how little friction the top tiers can cause each other and how smoothly Tarantino fits into their economy. He knows how to work at just the scale the industry needs—and his aesthetic is just right for the notion of film art that has coalesced in America since the 1970s.

I have called this notion vulgar Kaelism, knowing that Pauline Kael would have derided one of its principal tenets: that the movie theater ought to be a refuge from artistic norms and imperatives, where we're all free to revel in trash. "Yes, but," Kael would have said—in fact, did say—and the "but" was the bigger part of her argument. To the vulgar Kaelist, though, movie trash now comes with an imprimatur. Pump into this mindset a few more ideas that have become denatured by constant recirculation—a concept of Hollywood history that grossly overvalues genre filmmaking; a version of auteurism that's little more than hero worship; a definition of "cinematic" that's always about speed and movement, never framing and duration—and you've got the cloudy condensate that now sloshes through the heads of fan boys and pop film critics alike. It might seem at first glance that these people are engaged in the long-established practice of discovering meanings and artistic merits in products that look like mere entertainments—but that's no longer the game. They're fetishizing the authorial look of entertainments that are careful not to be too meaningful.

It's obvious why this attitude toward film would be wonderfully encouraging to a system in which second-tier products must be different but not that different. And the tier system, in turn, has warmly nurtured the vulgar Kaelist attitude, whether it's found in fans, filmmakers or (in Tarantino's case) both.

Let me say again: Tarantino is one participant among a great many in developments that have proceeded haphazardly, often catching up other filmmakers in similar ways, if not always with similar success. (Look at the career of Tom Tykwer, from *Run Lola*

Run to this year's dismal *The International*.) But if the route that has taken us here is meandering and muddy, its outcome is plain enough. The number of films in mainstream discussion has shrunk (even while the sum total of films and film chatterers has swollen); and of these few, a significant number will be considered artistically valid precisely because they don't give you much to discuss, other than the skill of a genius director at delivering recognizably movielike sensations.

The Nation, September 16, 2009

Superhero Movies: Threat, or Menace?

Avengers: Infinity War

I'd be tempted to call them numberless, all the cameo appearances that Stan Lee has made in movies based on his Marvel comics, except that IMDb has counted 32, the most recent being his turn as a school-bus driver in *Avengers: Infinity War*. My favorite of the Marvelmeister's walk-ons, though, is not in any film but in Michael Chabon's novel *The Amazing Adventures of Kavalier & Clay*, where Lee kibitzes over breakfast with other historical funny-book men in the Excelsior Cafeteria on Second Avenue.

The year is 1954 (God alone knows the year of *Avengers: Infinity War*), and Lee is as worried as any of his compatriots about an impending congressional investigation into their corrupting influence on America's youth. Here as elsewhere in the novel, Chabon reminds you that people thought of comic books as the disreputable trade of men with arrested talents and crude taste, who profited off childish minds at a dime a throw. To the MBA mentality that nowadays passes as mature, Lee's genius appears in hindsight as the entrepreneurial feat of having converted such dross into an empire worth billions. To Chabon, though, it was precisely the cheapness of comic books that made them glorious and even magical, with their muck capable of soaking up blatant wish fulfillments, unembarrassed desires, visions that were literally fugitive.

Which is to say, I don't care whether *Avengers: Infinity War* disappoints or surpasses the forecasts of industry analysts. Nor am I going to write off the movie solely because it's the latest in a series of products financed, shaped, and marketed by a powerful corporation. (It's a little late in the day—almost 100 years late—to doubt whether works born of a big company can really be art.) My only question is whether enough old-fashioned, unadulterated crap survives in this picture to make it worth a few hours of your time.

Avengers: Infinity War certainly can't compare with other recent fantasies like *Mad Max: Fury Road* and *The Shape of Water*. It lacks the directorial flair of those pictures, their committed performances (nobody here plays for her life like Charlize Theron and Sally Hawkins), their full-throated themes. (All that *Avengers: Infinity War* has to say about the world is that Malthusian genocide would be wrong. Noted.) The film's one true distinction is that it cannot stand on its own. Not only is it incomplete despite a running time of 149 minutes (there will be a second part), but its action would be meaningless to anyone who hasn't seen a good many previous Marvel pictures. This isn't a question of a plot's being spun out over three, four, or five films, as is now common. It's the exceptional matter of disparate plots being sucked together, for the purpose of giving fans more than 20 popular characters at one sitting.

By "characters," of course, I mean the fusions of actor and role that audiences greet with cheers when Chris Evans shows up as Captain America, or Chadwick Boseman as Black Panther. Despite the film's near-perpetual flow of mayhem, from New York City streets to spaceship interiors to the blasted surfaces of derelict planets, much of *Avengers: Infinity War* plays like late Howard Hawks, in that there's little more to contemplate than characters teasing each other. Audiences know the quirks of these screen personalities so well, and have grown so fond of them, that the directors of *Avengers: Infinity War*, Anthony and Joe Russo, can get their biggest laugh just by having the usually flippant Robert Downey Jr./Iron Man stand still for five seconds in speechless exasperation.

That said, screenwriters Christopher Markus and Stephen McFeely have supplied a story, which appropriately (given the goal of bringing together as many characters as possible) is a tale about achieving a prophesied outcome by collecting things. This organizational pattern runs so deep in our imaginations that you'd have to call it preliterary. It's the basis of every scavenger hunt, and of fictions that include *Harry Potter and the Deathly Hallows*; Steven Spielberg's recent, not uninteresting *Ready Player One*; and even *Macbeth* (a play about a man who step-by-step amasses promised titles and ordained catastrophes). In *Avengers: Infinity War*, the objects that must be sought are magical gemstones. Their pursuer, zooming through the galaxy in a giant spokeless Ferris wheel, is Josh Brolin, who has been animated to look very large and purple, with a chin like a locomotive's cowcatcher, as the idealistic mass murderer Thanos.

Thanos has his moments of pain and dread—but none, needless to say, as deep as those of his fellow serial killer Macbeth, or as rich as the thematic ambiguities and poetic extravagances that enmesh the Scottish tyrant. The Russo brothers are working for the simpler satisfaction of sheer agglomeration, and they go about their task without a trace of the cinematic sensibility that would be a rough equivalent to Shakespeare's poetry. You needn't think *The Shape of Water* is a masterpiece to understand what Guillermo del Toro meant when he spoke of wanting to create a monster movie in the style of Douglas Sirk. It was the idea of a born filmmaker, someone who feels how an effect of light, an angle of view, and a camera movement can combine to make meaning. Whether the Russo brothers can do that sort of thing, I don't know, but it's apparent they didn't even think to try. Having risen in the business by working on quirky television sitcoms, they're all about pace: Just keep the dialogue bouncing and the actors in frame.

And there you have the redeeming unadulterated crap. Though the Russos' expensively produced "film" is currently playing in theaters, where exhibitors score extra cash by providing 3-D, *Avengers: Infinity War* already looks like it belongs on hand-held screens, computer monitors, and household panels. For all its commercial mass, it floats along without the gravity of self-importance, as if it were any other item that might be called up or dismissed from the day's menu of diversions. It's not, of course. The so-called Marvel Universe is so large that *Avengers: Infinity War* can be almost entirely self-referential, holding itself aloof from the rest of pop culture. At one point, in fact, Iron Man in effect orders Tom Holland/Spider-Man to stop mentioning movies from outside the Marvel bubble—but that only adds to the sense of weightlessness.

Having grown up in movie culture, I feel a pang at this sign of its demise. But I also honor the humble wish that this new product fulfills. It offers audiences more than thrills, fantasies of power, or visions of riches. It gives them a temporary community; it stages a reunion. Hail, *Avengers: Infinity War*! The gang's all here.

The Nation, May 4, 2018

Captain Marvel

They had Bayreuth. We have the Marvel Universe.

Or so I've thought, as we pass the weeks between the release of *Captain Marvel*, which introduces Brie Larson as the Universe's latest superhero, and the opening of *Avengers: Endgame*, which, as all sentient beings know, will require Larson to swoop in and undo the galactic holocaust wreaked last year in *Avengers: Infinity War*. Notice the urge in the Marvel Universe to unite all things in heaven and on earth into a single grand scheme. Notice the intuition that this immense structure is teetering, with the one-eyed father of plots (not Wotan, but Samuel L. Jackson as Nick Fury) perhaps unable to hold out against Marveldämmerung. Except, of course, he will. All sentient beings already know that, too, much as they believe (though now I'm just guessing) that Larson, as the Brünnhilde of today's all-encompassing artwork, very likely has flown in not to perish in the flames but to blow them out.

I say all this not to mock the Marvel Universe but to praise it.

Think of what Bayreuth meant to the bourgeoisie of 19th-century Europe. After their struggle against hereditary power left them victorious, but also vaguely ashamed, as they compared the coarse, money-driven world they were building to the glories and charms they saw in the past; after they watched an oceanic mob rise to engulf them in 1848, then subside again, temporarily, behind a seawall they knew was leaky; after their homes had been crammed with a miscellany of riches grabbed from the world beyond Europe, and their churches emptied of certainty, these new lords of the planet went on pilgrimage to Bayreuth, where their triumphalism, avidity, guilt, and self-loathing were resolved into the transcendence of a new art. They took their seats in a cavernous theater that seemed like the interior of the skull of Richard Wagner, the genius who, by himself, had transformed the chaos outside into an art of the future within. The sounds and visions of a single great mind surrounded them: unitary, complete, immense, and wholly unsullied by contemporary affairs. At Bayreuth, you thrilled to the ultimate reality of Northern myth and medieval Christendom.

The Marvel Universe, too, is a world unto itself, as you'll know if you've ever been talked at by a true fan. But no pilgrimage is required. If you want to experience it within a group enclosure, the map is conveniently dotted with them, many providing frequent, overlapping start times for the sounds and visions. If you don't want a group enclosure, the latest fractal of the ensemble will soon come to you, to be enjoyed on your home TV or that little computer you carry in your pocket. There are multiple, perhaps infinite points of entry, as the purveyors of this cosmos recently explained in *Spider-Man: Into the Spider-Verse*.

And who are the purveyors? Not a lone genius (however jocularly that idea was suggested, and simultaneously mocked, by the many cameo appearances of Stan Lee, may his memory be a blessing). The Marvel Universe is created and operated by a global corporation. This is art for an era in which not only God, but also the individual, is dead. Old-fashioned filmoids like me may cling to the personalism of the *politique des auteurs*, but even we understand that's become a reactionary cause. Witness how easily the Marvel Universe absorbs indie authors, such as Ryan Coogler (two blinks after *Fruitvale Station*), or the directors of *Captain Marvel*, Anna Boden and Ryan Fleck, who only a few years ago were making the social-realist *Half Nelson* on the cheap in Brooklyn. The truly progressive art of our time—progressive in the Wagnerian sense of anticipating where our culture may go—issues from a business organization and is marketed to everyone: not the self-appointed enlighteners of bourgeois imperial Europe, but all of us droplets sploshing about in the sea that had the Bayreuthers so worried.

What totalizing experience do we droplets purchase with our tickets? What anxieties and contradictions does the Universe scheme resolve and transcend in 120-minute increments? Surveying the content of these movies and the point in comic-book history from which they spring, I note that they have a moment of crisis at their origin, as the *Ring* cycle had in 1848. In the background of them all is the Cuban Missile Crisis, the assassination of John F. Kennedy, and the Vietnam War. (The movements for Black and female liberation, not so much—although of late the enterprise has caught up retroactively with *Black Panther* and *Captain Marvel*.) These movies tell us over and over about covert government operations gone wrong, technological advances and medical experiments turned monstrous, fantastically wealthy heads of corporations arrogating to themselves the rights of sovereign powers. And that's the hopeful stuff. Far from sheltering the audience from contemporary affairs, the Marvel films obsessively remind us of the actually existing systems that swirl above our heads, beyond the control not only of a democratic populace but often of the elites who purport to direct these powers.

To take the present example, *Captain Marvel* is the dual origin story of an extraterrestrial warrior come to Earth and of Nick Fury, the former soldier turned high-level spymaster of the *Avengers* series, who receives quite an education by tagging along behind the eponymous superhero. The year is 1995; the place at first is Los Angeles, where Vers (pronounced "veers," as in changing her direction or mind at high speed) has crash-landed on a mission and drawn the baffled attention of Fury. In addition to discovering that advanced civilizations flourish beyond the solar system and occasionally treat Earth as a pit stop (emphasis on "pit"), Fury eventually learns that the difference between a ruthless terrorist and a desperate freedom-fighter is sometimes one of perspective. Given his years in the CIA, he might have known that already—but he receives fresh instruction from Vers, who grows considerably in strength and self-knowledge through her adventure on a backward planet. Among her biggest lessons: humans are resilient, sisterhood is powerful, and new technologies may be used for peaceful purposes but often aren't. She also learns that authorities are sometimes less than honest, soldiers may be sent to die in ignorance, and her true purpose is to end war, which she can best do by kicking ass on an interstellar scale. As I said, contradictions.

I enjoyed all this thoroughly and didn't mind that the main contradiction was heightened, not transcended, by Vers's coming into the full awesomeness of her abilities. Larson makes something more than formulaic out of Vers's grit and impetuousness, Jackson takes the trouble this time to play the nuances of his character (since the filmmakers, for a change, have given him some), and Boden and Fleck do an admirable job of touching on humble details and common interactions amid the CGI fight-or-flight extravaganza. (This is a superhero movie in which somebody has to wash the dishes after dinner, and somebody has to dry them.) I look forward to *Brünnhilde II*.

That said, I can't pretend that my era's total work of art is everything I want. Wagner, the rotten asshole, wrote staggeringly novel scores that opened a century's worth of possibilities for musical composition. The Marvel Universe movies are for the most part amusing, well-made, not without their thoughtful side, and have contributed nothing new to cinematic art.

And yet the field is not moribund. Look at *Roma*. Look at Bi Gan's *Long Day's Journey Into Night*, which is now flooding a few scattered US theaters with its daredevil spirit (after provoking near-riots in China among audiences who thought they were going to see a normal movie). Wonders are still being performed, but these are the one-offs of stubborn *auteurs*. The Marvel Universe series, though worthy of being called the defining artwork of our epoch, nevertheless shrinks from innovation, and so reveals something disheartening about the limits within which we live.

Why we accept them, I don't really know. But I can tell you that when Wagner's audiences showed up at Bayreuth, they got a breakthrough artistic experience of historic proportions, despite all the bad faith involved. We get a Gesamtkunstwerk that always stops short—and it's not as if our own faith is all that good.

The Nation, March 28, 2019

The Dark Knight Rises

Less than forty-eight hours after the massacre in Aurora, Colorado, I found myself eavesdropping on an enthusiastic discussion in a college-town sandwich shop about *The Dark Knight Rises*, the movie that had provided the occasion for the shootings. "Is it as good as the last one?" asked a young woman who had not yet seen the film. "How was Anne Hathaway?" To which I would have replied, had I been the one asked: no, terrific and what difference does it make?

Let me be clear: neither *The Dark Knight Rises* nor the previous episodes of Christopher Nolan's Batman trilogy can be blamed for the slaughter in Aurora. To say otherwise would be to diminish the culpability of the killer on the one side, and on the other of his enablers: all the well-organized forces that keep weapons in such ample circulation. To refuse simplistic notions of cause and effect is the necessary, responsible way to look at this catastrophe, but it's also a daylight answer to a nighttime horror. In Aurora, at the midnight show of an action movie about indiscriminate, irrational violence, a man masked and armored like an action movie character wreaked indiscriminate, irrational violence. Some survivors recalled that when the killer burst through the door, they thought at first he was part of the show.

This is not the sort of thing that people in the industry want to think about, and they sure didn't. "The mass shooting at a Colorado movie theater on Friday dented ticket sales for 'The Dark Knight Rises,' but not by much," Brooks Barnes reported in the *New York Times* on July 22, adding that the $162 million brought in over the weekend, although "huge," fell below prerelease expectations. (Mulling over the possible causes of this disappointment for Warner Brothers, Barnes speculated that "some moviegoers were either not in the mood to watch a violent comic book caper or worried about theater safety after the carnage" — an acute analysis, which cannily dismissed other possibilities such as a plague of locusts.) The online publication *The Wrap*, edited by the former *New York Times* Hollywood reporter Sharon Waxman, showed even more exquisite sensitivity: "Will Oscar Voters Look Past the 'Dark Knight Rises' Tragedy?" it asked, six months before the announcement of the Oscar nominations for 2012 and several days before the last of the funerals.

If the art of violent, horrific films involves allaying our worst fears by playing them out, then there was something artless in this rush to normalize the release of *The Dark Knight Rises* without any lingering over the aspect of Aurora that ought to terrify the industry: the perfect fit between film and massacre. The valiant Roger Ebert was virtually alone among the commentators I read in acknowledging the likelihood that the killer wanted, in some way, to insert himself into the movie world, or at least into its aura of celebrity—but even Ebert did not contemplate what the audience had been expecting to receive from this particular movie, and how this time they really got what they paid for.

A daylight rebuttal of such thoughts might insist, correctly, that the Aurora killings were a terrible anomaly. This response pushes the discussion away from lived experience and into the realm of statistical analysis. It asks us to calculate the odds of being gunned down in a movie theater and perhaps compare them favorably to the risks of driving to the supermarket. Take comfort if you can; or else, if you can bear to, think about Veronica Moser-Sullivan, the 6-year-old who was murdered. It is none of my business why she was at the midnight show. Maybe she'd been hearing about Batman and had begged to go. Maybe her parents could not get a babysitter and so had brought Veronica, figuring she would soon fall asleep. All I know is that if the child stayed awake, the last images she saw before she died were of bound, hooded men being shot through the head and thrown out of an airplane.

Because terror came at that little girl not only from the auditorium but from the screen—indeed, in her last moments, she could hardly have distinguished between the two—I have come to feel that it does matter whether people call *The Dark Knight Rises* a "good" movie. If we can show no other respect to the victims and their families, let us at least avoid debasing the concept of goodness. I have already earned my own little share of culpability by having praised *Batman Begins* and *The Dark Knight* without enough reservations. What I seek to do now—without pretending to elevate myself to the status of a policy-maker, and I hope without descending to the level of journalistic scold—is simply to make a proposal about critical evaluations. I think that all judgments of *The Dark Knight Rises* made after July 20, 2012, ought to consider the Aurora massacre as intrinsic to the movie.

This is not a difficult standard to meet. Even before Aurora, *The Dark Knight Rises* was characterized by an opportunistic (I might almost say parasitic) relationship to public events. We now need to add one more to the mix, which notably includes the protests mounted over the past few years against the managers and manipulators of great pools of capital. In the movie's comic book world, these protests become eruptions of populist chaos.

Occupy Wall Street could not have been a primary model for this aspect of *The Dark Knight Rises*, given the time it takes to prepare a film—although the production schedule did allow Nolan to direct some scenes of disorder in and around Wall Street in late 2011, in the wake of Occupy. But there were plenty of earlier precedents for him to draw from, such as the protests at the London G-20 summit in 2009, and it's worth noting that Nolan's previous Batman film, *The Dark Knight*, opened on July 14, 2008. Maybe that date—Bastille Day—and the subsequent full onset of the financial crisis stuck in his mind. *The Dark Knight Rises* not only dwells on the have-nots' outrage over economic inequality, but it also incorporates several direct references to *A Tale of Two Cities* and features, as one of its set pieces, a street mob's successful assault on a prison, freeing more than a thousand violent professional criminals.

The Bastille, by contrast, held only seven helpless wretches, but Nolan is not one to let mere facts get in his way. Throughout the trilogy, he has told us that when a man puts on a superhero outfit, he stops being a person and becomes a symbol instead (though of what, exactly, it's impossible to say). Just so, in *The Dark Knight Rises*, the principled and overwhelmingly nonviolent protests of past years stop being themselves and are turned into content-free, mindless outbursts of fury, with the people of the lower depths (who are they, exactly?) improbably rushing to the side of the master terrorist who blew up half their city and, what's worse, interrupted a football game.

This is the cinema of social hallucination, and there's nothing new about it. Fritz Lang was already practicing it in the 1920s, when he poured the many anxieties of his day into the all-purpose container of Dr. Mabuse. Nor is there anything new in thinking that a villain who arises where "the structures break down" can be defeated only by an outsider like Batman, a sorrowful vigilante who is willing to bear the guilt. John Ford gave us what may as well have been the last word on that subject fifty years ago, in *The Man Who Shot Liberty Valance*.

The modes and themes of *The Dark Knight Rises* are venerable, but that doesn't mean the way they're used is praiseworthy. What the writer-director of *Inception* has now given us is a picture so crammed with worn-out ideas and big, empty gestures that it might as well be called *Recapitulation*. Here are predictable plot twists, familiar from a hundred other movies; long recollections of the earlier Batman films, played with brooding self-importance; solemn platitudes inserted where the dialogue ought to go; and far too many passages that are meant to be overpowering but bludgeon instead.

Of the latter, the most telling example might be the battle between the Gotham police and the guerrilla army led by Bane (Tom Hardy), a villain who seems to have been assembled out of hand-me-down World Wrestling Entertainment paraphernalia and the outtakes of a Hannibal Lecter movie. When the cops advance on Bane and his troops, they march down the narrow canyon of a city street, so they are unable to maneuver either left or right but must walk straight into the sights of an enemy with greater firepower and a superior position. Nolan might not know much about tactics, but as a filmmaker he ought to be familiar with at least one version of *The Charge of the Light Brigade*. He should have cared that his deployment of forces made no sense—but, again, the grand statement is everything, the material details nothing. To the thunderous plodding of yet another damned Hans Zimmer score, the police rush forward in suicidal glory and win the day because, well, that's what they do.

To this episode we must now add one more senseless scene of bloodshed, perpetrated by a man who almost certainly thought that he, too, was "making a statement." They always do. We have seen this movie before, as Roger Ebert wrote, and in the case of *The Dark Knight Rises*, I don't think we needed to. Despite the presence of Anne Hathaway, who by herself can do no wrong, what we have here is clearly not good.

The Nation, August 27, 2012

ScarJo,
Beyond Good and Evil

Under the Skin

Dressed in a faux-fur jacket, tousled brunette wig and lipstick the color of fresh blood, Scarlett Johansson drives a white van through Glasgow and its outskirts in the genuinely creepy *Under the Skin*, scanning for men who are on their own and offering them rides. Something about this behavior is seriously wrong, as you may guess from its round-the-clock nature, the nerve-twisting violin motif that accompanies it, and the way the shotgun-side passengers keep disappearing.

You would expect that a young woman who picks up strange men is putting herself in danger—and by the end of the film, you will learn that Johansson is indeed vulnerable. For most of *Under the Skin*, though, some conspiracy is gaming the ordinary pattern of sexual attraction and male-female predation for purposes that director Jonathan Glazer leaves mostly to your imagination. If you're looking for languorous, sensuous menace, he'll give you all you'd like, with the help of his co-writer, Walter Campbell, and the source novel by Michel Faber. If you want information, though, Glazer will gradually, almost grudgingly, supply little more than some views of an uncanny ritual, which suggests that whatever Johansson might be, she (or it) isn't human.

I suppose the word "alien" has to come up at some point. If so, we're talking about extraterrestrial beings that have traveled here on rings of light (the only method of transport Johansson seems to use, other than the van and an occasional bus) and that inexplicably need a supply of human flesh, though not necessarily for food. Although an experimental nibble of chocolate cake turns out badly for Johansson, that doesn't mean her victims are being flushed into a vat of nutrients. Maybe they're used as fuel, medicine, perfume or recreational drugs.

All we know for sure is that past a certain point, Johansson relents in her collecting. She has begun to stare curiously at her own reflection. Perhaps she has developed some fellow feeling for her prey. If so, I can say that *Under the Skin* also puts the viewer in touch with what it means to be human, and in startling ways. There are images in this film unlike any I've seen before: veils of light made from the movements of thousands of people, lacquered traps that can engulf men mesmerized by desire, the human form emptied into a twisted, drifting husk. These were all new to me; and so, too, were Glazer's evocations of our fear, brutality, frailty and kindness.

The Nation, May 26, 2014

Lucy

Within the past twelve months, Scarlett Johansson has been an alluring and rapidly expanding artificial intelligence in *Her*; a seductively murderous extraterrestrial in *Under the Skin*; and now, in *Lucy*, a superintelligent, post-sexual, sometimes deadly freak of evolution. For a woman who is two inches shorter than Woody Allen, this is some résumé. It's obvious that the game but vulnerable waif of 2003's *Lost in Translation* did not just grow up but has gone on to transcend the merely human, and in record time. Why this should have happened isn't so clear.

Given the disparities in financing and distribution among the films I've just mentioned—which vary from the artisanal to the mega-industrial—as well as the differences among them in style and tone, it would be a mug's game to rush into defining Johansson's new screen persona, let alone to speculate about the wishes and anxieties floating about in the culture that might have coalesced to create it. As a mug, though, I will observe that the change began in 2010, when Johansson first played the comic-book character Natasha Romanoff, also known as the Black Widow, in the *Iron Man* and *Avengers* cycles.

Although Johansson has served as little more than an incidental attraction in these movies—much as the Black Widow herself has been mostly a supporting player in the Marvel Comics universe—these interlocked series enabled her to do something that *Vicky Cristina Barcelona* could not: reach a large enough percentage of the world's population to register sociologically.

Thanks to the Black Widow role, the public for the first time entertained the possibilities of a Johansson who could not be measured precisely, there being, almost by definition, no such thing as a five-foot-three superhero. Her manner was now almost flippantly imperturbable, as befits someone who knows she can take time out for a cell-phone call while being interrogated and threatened with torture—this actually happened in *The Avengers*—and then, as if tired of the game, single-handedly squash her half-dozen captors. Perhaps most important of all, Johansson's attitude toward her body changed. As the Black Widow, she treated her catalog of sexpot features as if they were so many pieces of the superhero costume: items that identified her but were something to have and use, rather than be. To the millions of fans versed in Marvel mythology, this aloofness from her own seductiveness was explicable not as the trait of a traditional *femme fatale* but as a consequence of bioengineering. The Black Widow's strength, speed, endurance and longevity had been injected into her in a Soviet laboratory.

Once this image of Johansson was established—$1.5 billion in worldwide theater revenues for *The Avengers* did a lot of establishing—it was not improbable for other filmmakers to extend and complicate the fantasy she had come to incarnate. In *Her*, Johansson was unimaginably superior to the man with whom she'd been paired and ultimately felt a little bad about it; in *Under the Skin*, she preyed at will on the male humans around her and came to feel troubled by the practice; but in both films, she maintained the sound and appearance of an attractive woman only because that's what men were looking for.

As the title character in *Lucy*, Johansson at least starts out as a female human being—one who enjoys her sexuality, too, to judge from the presence at the beginning of a boyfriend who is cute in a hulking way, though morally dubious and blatantly casual. What Johansson becomes, though, in her first starring role in a blockbuster, is the Black Widow in metamorphosis. She struggles through a violent new episode of bioengineering to attain perfect knowledge, or godhead, or maybe the ultimate hands-off romance, but at least a really nifty revenge.

An auteurist would ascribe this most extreme elaboration of her new image not only to Johansson (or her manager) but also in large measure to the writer-director of *Lucy*, Luc Besson. The auteurist would not be entirely unjustified. An unabashed entertainer, Besson figured out long ago that Godard was right: all you need to make a movie is a girl and a gun. But whereas Godard took that to mean that he could supply the minimum requirement and then stuff in as many ideas as he liked, Besson mostly wants to throw in more guns, some chases, a lot of bright colors and comic moments, and then just one Big Idea, which usually has something to do with love. To his credit, the girl (or woman) never blends into the elaborately ornamental furnishings of his cinematic contraptions but is their uncannily powerful motor, whether she's the high-fashion assassin of *La Femme Nikita*, the Supreme Being of *The Fifth Element* (born into our world as Milla Jovovich dressed in an Ace bandage) or, for traditionalists, *The Messenger*'s Joan of Arc.

In *Lucy*, Besson has dropped Johansson into Taipei (for reasons that perhaps only the production's accountants fully understand) and ensnared her initially none-too-bright character with a stereotypical East Asian mob: bulky men with close-cropped hair, goatees and dark suits, who dwell in glass high-rises and wash the blood from their hands with bottled Evian. These people brutalize the terrified Lucy but then, by inadvertently overdosing her on a new designer drug, make her very, very smart, as well as fearless, enormously strong, preternaturally calm and no longer quite human. Her ensuing quest for full self-realization, serious payback and a lot more drugs—it's all the same—takes her to Paris, where she calls on the awestruck assistance of a visionary neuroscientist (Morgan Freeman, playing the wisest-man-in-the-world role that used to go to Sam Jaffe) and a roughly handsome police detective (Amr Waked), on whom Lucy plants a single kiss, just as a reminder to herself, on her rise beyond the corporeal.

These events, like the dialogue, are cheerfully preposterous ("I'm colonizing my own brain," Lucy informs the scientist) and guiltlessly violent ("We never really die," she explains) and go down as refreshingly as a chilled summer cocktail. (I might have said "as easily as the drug merchants' purple crystals," but those make Lucy slam into the ceiling and emit blasts of light from her mouth. They also elevate her cerebral activity, which would not be optimal for watching this movie.) Employing an Osterizer style, Besson mixes in a bit of exorcism movie here, a funny stock-footage montage there, a dollop of vintage Friedkin, a dash of decade-old Tarantino, pulses the concoction with the sci-fi effects button and pours for your pleasure—which might be considerable, if you feel any affinity for Johansson.

Some critics in the past have found her more winning than impressive, more pleasant than adept; but in *Lucy* she makes the most of every moment of her character's transformation. During a farewell phone call to her mother, she effortlessly holds the camera throughout a very long close-up, meanwhile touching on emotions that are both flooding into Lucy as never before and quickly receding from her self-colonized brain. When saying goodbye to her roommate in Taipei—a young woman as witless as Lucy herself used to be—she solemnly offers expert medical advice (this is the sort of thing she suddenly knows) and then, more to herself than to her friend, flashes the ghost of a kindly smile. To the degree that Lucy's adventure is even temporarily plausible, let alone engaging, it's because Johansson makes it so.

But again, what is the import of this new screen persona that Johansson has taken on? To get some perspective on her evolving image, let me take a quick detour into an even more lucrative summer blockbuster, *Dawn of the Planet of the Apes*.

It's a thoroughly mediocre movie—I'm sorry to say that, considering that its predecessor in this new cycle, *Rise of the Planet of the Apes*, was so unexpectedly good—but instructive for the way it has altered a durable, and adaptable, pop-culture myth. The *Apes* series began in 1963 with a satirical novel by Pierre Boulle—in effect, a late voyage of Lemuel Gulliver—that addressed anxieties about complacency and conformity in a society fascinated by its own affluence. In Boulle's story, the apes evolved to fill a niche abandoned by humans, who had devolved through sheer passivity. By the time the first *Apes* movie was released in 1968, with a screenplay by the formerly blacklisted Michael Wilson and *The Twilight Zone*'s Rod Serling, the reason for humanity's downfall had changed. The focus of the anxiety was now aggression and militarism; we humans were bomb-wielding "maniacs" who had willfully blown up our own world.

In the new *Apes* cycle, the anxiety has shifted again. Although the latest film still dwells on an irrational propensity toward warfare—among humans and apes alike—the immediate cause of all the trouble is genetic engineering. The satire now tells us that we are too clever and powerful for our own good when we meddle with our cells, and not nearly humble enough toward other creatures.

Perhaps this fear about the unforeseeable consequences, internal and external, of medical science tells us something about the need that Scarlett Johansson has begun to fulfill. She has become the sex kitten who repeatedly goes beyond sex—all the way to digital self-propagation in *Lucy*—provoking thoughts about physical urges even while escaping the body's limits. She is the product of advanced artifice (by Soviet spymasters, American computer scientists, creepy aliens or Asian drug lords) who nevertheless feels a twinge of benevolence, or at least pity, for those of us still mired in nature. A public worried that their own bodies might be spinning out of control—from toxins, viruses, electronic self-alienation, Frankensteinian self-modification—might want to feel excited, threatened and reassured all at once about the biological future. If so, the figure of Johansson in her Black Widow iterations is answering that desire, and doing so, more often than not, with a light touch and a wink.

But if Johansson represents something new, she also represents something tried and true at the end of *Lucy*. As so often happens, especially with a writer-director like Besson, the movie ultimately refers only to other movies—and so it's possible to see Johansson's evolution in this picture as an ascent through the film-production hierarchy. When she is approaching full mental strength, for example, she finds she can relax in a chair and make time and space scroll back and forth with a flick of her hand. In effect, she's become a film editor, sitting in front of a digital console. But when she hits 100 percent, the need for such technical tricks falls away because she is now all-pervasive, like the air that everyone breathes.

In other words, she's attained the omnipresence of a true movie star. If you can say nothing more about Johansson in *Lucy*, that much is beyond dispute.

The Nation, September 1, 2014

Who's "We"?
Bujalski and Solondz on Community

Storytelling

What Minotaurs lurk in the polite American mind, hungering within the contortions of liberal conscience? Even the most not-for-profit filmmaker—a documentarian, a socially responsible type—may turn a corner in his soul and discover a beast in the path, gnawing on the bones of an interview subject. The tender lover bumps blindly into a creature that howls for dirty sex; the tolerant democrat gets screwed, or worse, by the bogeyman she pretends she doesn't believe in. These monsters, and more, inhabit the labyrinth—or rather, the clean and well-lit suburbs—of *Storytelling*, an educational new film by Todd Solondz.

When I say "educational," I mean that both of the tales that *Storytelling* comprises are concerned with schools. The first, much briefer section of the movie takes place at a university in New Jersey, where Vi (Selma Blair) studies in the writing workshop of a gravely superior author, Mr. Scott (Robert Wisdom). The movie's second part is set mostly in the home of a well-to-do Jewish family, whose eldest son, Scooby (Mark Webber), is about to wash out of high school on a lukewarm tide of inertia. One way to sum up *Storytelling* might be to say that Vi wants to learn and does, though (like most of us) she finds the lesson she gets isn't the one she'd expected. Scooby does not want to learn. Like most of us, he's taught a good lesson anyway.

But before I elaborate on either of these moral tales, I'd better attempt another definition. Who's "us"?

The question presents itself early in *Storytelling*, because Solondz constructs the movie as a brilliantly calculated series of provocations. The appropriate series of responses—the ones that will make the provocations seem worthwhile—are likely to come only from a certain audience. In honor of the fictional New Jersey family in the second part of *Storytelling*, I will call this audience the Livingstons, who used to be the Levinsteins. Not that Solondz needs a Jewish audience to get the desired effect. What matters is that his viewers recognize themselves in characters who enjoy material comfort, believe firmly in their own good intentions and feel a part of mainstream American life. Would Mr. Scott, from the first part of *Storytelling*, respond to the movie as required? I think he'd be grimly amused, and maybe even impressed; but as a Black man of a certain age, he also might feel that this party's been thrown for someone else.

The true audience (or is it target?) would more likely be Vi, who is mild, beneficent and white. Although she escapes the lash in the first writing workshop we see—a session made excruciatingly funny because the participants lie transparently or not at all—Vi later invites a much riskier form of pedagogy, after she runs into Mr. Scott at a bar. She comes to the table where he's drinking alone; she babbles something about admiring him. Mr. Scott drags on his cigarette, taking the time that belongs only to those who are in control, then replies by laying his hand over hers. To this much younger, much weaker, much less articulate person, he says only, "You have beautiful skin."

What happens next, in Mr. Scott's rooms, cannot be shown on an American screen. An orange rectangle drops down over the characters, as if we needed to be protected from a sight that Americans have long been eager to imagine. The scandal this time has nothing to do with the action we might witness; it's all about the attitude that the movie leads us to adopt. Mr. Scott is playing out a heartless drama of power and powerlessness; and Vi, the character with whom we're asked to identify, deserves everything she gets.

I dwell on this event in the first part of *Storytelling* because it seems to be the nerve center of the film. From here, you can shoot to almost any point in part two. You could link this chamber scene to the climactic moment when Consuelo (Lupe Ontiveros), a Salvadoran housemaid, commandeers the destiny of the whole Livingston family. You could think of Mr. Scott when Scooby Livingston grants a cold sexual favor to the boy who loves him. You might compare Vi to the wonderfully inept Toby Oxman (Paul Giamatti), the would-be filmmaker whose documentary about Scooby provides the framework for part two. There's something Vi-like in the way that Toby, for all his apparent innocence, agrees to serve professionally as a conduit for contempt. Or does that contempt make Toby the white schlemiel twin of Mr. Scott?

As these examples suggest, *Storytelling* is a meticulously balanced movie, despite its asymmetry. You can see both of these qualities full-blown if you imagine Vi and Mr. Scott next to another pair in the film: Mr. and Mrs. Livingston. For the latter roles, Solondz has cast the spherical John Goodman as husband to linear Julie Hagerty, creating a classic sight gag. What interests me, though, isn't just the contrast of physical types; it's the way that the contrast is hilarious with the Livingstons but not funny at all with Vi and Mr. Scott. I attribute the difference in effect to social attitudes—it's the difference, in film history terms, between *The*

Birth of a Nation and a Laurel and Hardy comedy—but also to the varying weights of the roles. Vi and Mr. Scott are central to part one; Mr. and Mrs. Livingston are peripheral to part two. Yet here's the subtlety of Solondz's filmmaking: He makes the camera gaze blandly at both pairs of characters, as if visual incongruity were not the doorway to a labyrinth but a simple fact of nature.

There's something similarly simple, and perhaps deceptive, in the cruel justice that Solondz visits on his characters. The punishments, though horrible, are a little too neat. To some of the film's detractors, this criticism also applies to the author's self-inflicted wounds. In this view, Solondz's implied self-portrait as Toby Oxman is a mere dodge, tossed into the picture to excuse the general mockery.

I can produce no evidence to counter this criticism, except for my own emotions. I felt, at the end of their stories, that Vi and Scooby were in a condition beyond either mockery or pity. They were, in a word, stuck. And it seemed to me that Solondz, who had done the sticking, had performed it with the effortless precision of a Zen archer.

Here's how Solondz shoots in *Storytelling*: Hand, arrow and bull's-eye are one. The aim does not falter, because the archer is the target—and so, I suspect, are you.

The Nation, February 18, 2002

Palindromes

We have all bumped up against people (close relatives, maybe) whose beliefs do not yield to respectful prodding but only become more rocklike. We have all, at one time or another, turned stony ourselves. This is a hard fact that needs confronting, which Todd Solondz sets out to do in *Palindromes*.

Like Solondz's other features (*Welcome to the Dollhouse*, *Happiness*, *Storytelling*), *Palindromes* is an uncanny balancing act, poised at all times between grotesquerie and realism, humor and agony, scorn and sympathy. It rarely allows you a single response. It often holds you back from responding at all, so cool is its manner and so outrageous its subject matter, which in this case exceeds Solondz's past repertory of adolescent misery, sexual anxiety and suburban social aggression. This time, venturing out of his usual New Jersey settings, he risks emotional engagement with the Christian right, as experienced by a runaway Jewish girl who sympathizes with its antiabortion agenda even at its most violent.

The girl, Aviva, is played by a succession of performers. There's nothing inherently odd about this; filmmakers often cast different actors to portray a character at different ages. But Solondz does more. His multiplying Avivas include a boy (Will Denton), a much older woman (Jennifer Jason Leigh) and, in a key sequence, an abundantly fleshy young Black woman (Sharon Wilkins). This latter choice is particularly nervy, since Wilkins has the look of the stereotypical gospel shouter, and Aviva at this stage has been taken in by rural evangelists, who tour their variously damaged foster children as a song-and-dance act for Jesus.

By putting Wilkins into this sequence, Solondz tacitly overcomes the incongruity between Aviva and her new family; he gets you closer to these people than you might have gone otherwise. At the same time, the casting serves as a distancing device. I thought of Hitchcock's explanation for having shot *Psycho* in black and white: Had it been in color, nobody could have stomached the blood. Had one actress embodied Aviva in *Palindromes*, maybe nobody could have stomached the intensity of her suffering.

There is also a third reason for Solondz's trick: It tests the disillusionment of a character, Mark Wiener (Matthew Faber), who serves almost as a mouthpiece for the filmmaker. People don't change, Mark says toward the end of *Palindromes*. They like to think they do, but they don't. This certainly would be true of Aviva, who from earliest childhood has been single-mindedly bent

on having children. And yet, having heard Mark out, she walks off and morphs from Jennifer Jason Leigh into Shayna Levine.
Written in a style of scrupulous meanness and directed so as to confound every automatic reaction, *Palindromes* is as far as you can get from activism. But it is, even so, a remarkable act of political filmmaking, one that acknowledges the stubborn impenetrability of ourselves and our society and yet manages to wedge open in them a little space for thought.

The Nation, May 16, 2005

Life in Wartime

Moviegoers who are familiar with Todd Solondz's 1998 *Happiness* will immediately recognize the characters and situations in this new film, *Life During Wartime*—though I rush to say that prior knowledge is not necessary, and will serve (for those who have it) mostly to confirm that Solondz, grown middle-aged, is no longer tempted to disfigure his work with a too gleeful cruelty. His three incompatible sisters from *Happiness*—one housewifely, one timidly artistic, one consumed by her worldly success—have now left New Jersey for sites of forgetting, in Florida's Jewish belt and the hills above Los Angeles: places where you don't see much that looks like it has a past, and the light and color (in Ed Lachman's cinematography) have the suspect sweetness of a gumdrop. The past lurks anyway, returning in the form of schoolyard rumors, wheedling phantoms and a man who was said to be dead and acts like it.

This latter figure is Bill (Ciáran Hinds): once a practicing psychiatrist and paterfamilias and now a slablike ex-convict, whose crime was to have raped a young boy. As he lumbers from the penitentiary toward Florida, unannounced and heavily quiet (he seldom speaks, and the scenes around him are filled with silence), his sister-in-law Joy (Shirley Henderson) is making the same journey south, to take temporary refuge with the remnants of Bill's family. Young Timmy (the freckled and prodigious-eared Dylan Riley Snyder) is preparing for his bar mitzvah, where he will speak of the example set for him by his father. (He's been told that Dad died in combat, defending us from the terrorists.) Bill's former wife, Trish (Allison Janney)—designated as the normal member of Joy's family, and well medicated to maintain that status—is aflutter with the surprise of new love. She has met a divorced man of mature years (Michael Lerner), himself recently arrived in Florida; and though he's thick-bodied, Punchinello-faced and half a head shorter than her, he seems to her a decent man and a real man, whose slightest touch gets her babbling like a brook. As for Joy— piping, frizzy, high-strung and hopelessly misnamed—she would like to start a new life (having fled from her own version of the impossible husband) but is constantly being accosted by the ghosts of the old.

It's the third sister in the family (Ally Sheedy), self-advertised conqueror of LA, who supplies the title for the film, asking if the little people around her (like Joy) don't know there's a war going on. But it's Joy, with her wan but persistent desire to make the world better somehow, who aligns the film's themes, as a magnetized needle will align iron filings. What if a stricken conscience isn't enough to make someone stop doing terrible things? What if people simply can't change what they are—even after they've turned into Joy's ghosts? Yes, there's a war going on, unseen by these characters (though often worried about), and it colors everything; but the real struggles of *Life During Wartime* are happening within, and they're lost, over and over.

Which isn't to say that *Life During Wartime* is a grim movie. It's by Solondz; he knows how to make you laugh, if only by reflex, as when you're goosed in the solar plexus. But beneath the deadpan outrageousness there's outrage, and beneath that there's a profound sorrow, which is now more empathic than in any of his past films. You feel it running through all the performances, but most of all in the fierce ones: by Hinds and the remarkable young Snyder and (in a brief but stunning turn that has to be mentioned) Charlotte Rampling. Here, I think, is where a comparison to Christopher Nolan's *Inception* isn't misguided. Nolan is the kind of filmmaker who figures out his framing and editing and then lets the actors use what time and space he's allotted them; but Solondz starts from the pace and tone he sets with the actors and builds the framing and editing around that.

This used to be called humanistic filmmaking—though given Solondz's views on what humans are, that might not sound very appealing. So let's name this method the Chase: the real chase, not the one that the Nolans cut to. Let's hear it for that damned pursuit of *Happiness*.

The Nation, August 30, 2010

Computer Chess

Made with far more droll wit than money, Andrew Bujalski's *Computer Chess* returns you to around 1980 for a competition among programmers, who have gathered to test their machines in a round-robin chess tournament. Although world-historical worries surface now and then—speculations about the impact on humans of artificial intelligence, and rumors of the usefulness of computer chess research to the Department of Defense—the characters generally focus on more immediate concerns: team rivalries, software glitches, the use of recreational substances and the presence this year of a woman (welcome!). The programmers, many of whom are played by nonprofessionals, are made to seem as endearingly ungainly as the era's big-box computers with their cursors blinking on phosphorescent screens, or as the black-and-white videotape cameras that seem to have recorded the movie.

One of the pleasures of *Computer Chess*, as Kent Jones remarked in *Film Comment*, is its relaxed and faithful depiction of the manners of a brainy little society. Another pleasure, maybe, is its rewiring of film history. Much of *Computer Chess* seems to be a reversal of *2001: A Space Odyssey*, complete with machine-human rivalry, the manifestation of a mystical fetus, and an iris shot (from the computer's point of view) of two men wondering how to make the program behave. The period is the past rather than Kubrick's future, the image quality is crummy rather than spectacular, the technology is laughable rather than awe-inspiring, and this time (spoiler alert) the machines win. For good measure, Bujalski also puts some spin on another film by Kubrick (a onetime chess hustler), *The Shining*, setting *Computer Chess* not in a grand old Colorado hotel but in a cheap new motel in Austin, Texas, where the spooky presences are cats who multiply in the rooms, and the innocent who wanders the halls is a fresh-faced programmer from MIT.

By ignoring a great many details that do not fit into these connections, I might be falling prey to a confirmation bias. (Another reason to like *Computer Chess*: it's the kind of movie in which characters warn one another against such fallacies.) But if Bujalski did not want me to think about film history, why did he cast a movie critic, Gerald Peary, as the grandmaster who presides over the tournament? If we must endlessly gaze on global catastrophe in the movies, greeting it not with a whimper but a satisfied yawn, I'd rather do it in the company that Bujalski has devilishly assembled.

The Nation, September 16, 2013

Results

Cobie Smulders never walks in *Results* if she can jog, never jogs if she can run, and when forced to sit prefers to settle her sweatpants on an exercise ball. Guy Pearce, who is older and better socialized but equally committed to personal improvement, conducts most of his conversations on the balls of his feet, as if wanting to illustrate his words with a little shadowboxing. At moments of high emotion, he will grab a ceiling bar in mid-sentence and perform intricate airborne torture on his abs.

He is Trevor, the sincerely uplifting owner of a fitness club in Austin, Texas, and she is Kat, his star trainer (if she says so herself) and the self-appointed disciplinarian of all humankind. Neither can stay still for longer than it takes to enjoy a cool, tall glass of mashed chlorophyll; and yet you can't imagine an unpleasant odor rising from these beautiful people, even at their most glistening. The scent of overpowered deodorant and long frustration that occasionally wafts from *Results* emanates exclusively from Danny (Kevin Corrigan), the gym's strangest, saddest, flabbiest, and most troublesome client, and ultimately its most enlivening.

Not that Danny seems likely to redeem anybody, himself least of all, when he first shuffles into the gym's office, to slouch next to a life-size plastic model of the human spine and pelvis and blink at Trevor's yellow T-shirt and positive attitude. What will be Danny's goal in beginning a fitness program? Trevor asks brightly, bouncing the helpful jargon of managerial science off his perfect teeth. Danny stares, then mumbles, "I wanna be able to take a punch," in the tone of someone who's already absorbed a few. His gaze is as unembarrassed as the uncombed tufts of his thinning hair; his speech pattern as unrushed and off-kilter as his gait. As if to make sure he's been understood, Danny mimes smacking himself in the jaw a few times.

Just as you and Trevor are beginning to wonder if you're dealing with a mentally deficient bum, Danny volunteers, "I got money," and contracts for private lessons. When Kat shows up for the first—having bullied the entire gym into letting her claim the new client—she finds Danny's cavernous McMansion empty except for a scattering of furniture still covered in plastic, a freshly wall-mounted TV, and a complete set of exercise equipment. Asking if he can pay in advance, he writes a check for two years.

A kindhearted comedy about people who work fiercely toward physical perfection and business success, and about the blessings brought to them by a man who pursues neither, *Results* is writer-director Andrew Bujalski's latest foray into the byways of American subculture. In his previous film, *Computer Chess*, he brilliantly recreated the milieu of the grad-school coding nerds of a generation ago. In *Results*, he gets his fun from a social niche that is more widely shared and contemporary but no less idiosyncratic.

Could any country besides ours have inspired a UK immigrant like Trevor to create the Power 4 Life gym? (The "4," he eagerly explains, signifies physical, mental, emotional, and spiritual strength.) In case you don't know the answer, you find out when Trevor drives halfway across Texas to visit his hero, a Russian exercise master (Anthony Michael Hall), only to hear this more skeptical immigrant laugh at America's faith in limitless individual achievement. ("Choose your misery" sums up the Russian's worldview. "You can cry, or you can work.") Even within our endlessly optimistic nation, among that relatively small slice of the population with money, time, and energy to spend on exercise classes, membership in the onward-and-upward club is not universal. Look at the lapsed client whom Kat chases down on the street, catching her with a cupcake in her SUV. Look at the man who tells Kat he's quitting the program—quitting!—because "you can't do this your whole life." Look at Danny.

A fundamentally un-American character (which is to say, a native New Yorker) who affirms the triumphant randomness of life's rewards and productively seduces Kat and Trevor from their purity, Danny would be a classic lord of misrule, if not for the depths of awkwardness and pain that are written into the role, and Corrigan's faultless candor in playing them. Corrigan has dwelled in the bottom half of cast lists throughout most of his prolific career, credited as a variety of thugs, addicts, comic villains, and (to cite the title of one of his few starring vehicles) *Some Guy Who Kills People*. By dignifying Corrigan in his full scruffiness, even to the point of having him assert a climactic "I'm not a douche bag," Bujalski has elevated this excellent actor to long-overdue prominence, meanwhile embedding an analogue of Danny's redemption into the making of *Results*. More important, Bujalski has also ensured through Corrigan that *Results* is thornier and more satisfying than it might otherwise have been.

Unlike *Computer Chess*, which was exceptional in every way—quasi-academic subject matter, largely nonprofessional cast, disjunctive narrative, and self-conscious form—*Results* does not declare itself to be a cleverly devised artifact. It is content, almost, to be a conventional narrative, satirizing one of the easier targets in American life while proceeding along the well-known track of romantic comedy. But whereas *Computer Chess* was all about the processes in people's heads, *Results* is a movie about bodies, which justifies itself through the enormous pleasure it takes in the athleticism of Smulders and Pearce.

Viewers who know her principally from television's *How I Met Your Mother* expect Smulders to be a gifted physical comedian, but they might be surprised by the speed and strength in which she revels here, and by the conviction she brings to Kat's underlying rage. (As Danny notes, it's one of Kat's more attractive qualities: "Her whole anger thing just turned me on. It was hot.") As for Pearce, it seems unfair that an actor pushing 50 should still be able to do oblique crunches like that, or persuade you, even while demonstrating such prowess, that Trevor is essentially a pushover. Nice guys finish last, says the famous sports adage; but fortunately for Trevor and Danny, they have Kat to make them winners.

I reveal nothing you haven't already surmised when I say that Trevor, Kat, and Danny are all happy at the end. *Results* would be untrue to its American ethos if they weren't. If we just work hard enough, we're all going to be healthy and beautiful and live forever in mutually supportive love, achieving goal after goal. Bujalski doesn't believe a word of it; but just the same, he's made *Results* as a kind of experimental comedy to test the proposition and has discovered he likes it. I bet you will, too.

The Nation, June 8, 2015

Support the Girls

A light-fingered, warmhearted comedy about coping with the intolerable, Andrew Bujalski's *Support the Girls* takes place in and around a brews-and-boobs restaurant—I mean, a family-friendly entertainment business—called Double Whammies, located on a frontage road of Interstate 10 in south-central Texas. You've probably traveled along similar stretches of highway, though directors rarely bother to capture them as intensively as Bujalski does, filling the opening of the movie with views of looping ramps and overpasses, sunless arcades of sooty concrete, sextuple straightaways vibrating with a perpetual whoosh and rumble. You'll probably recognize the strip-mall architecture, too, even if you've never turned into a one-story, faux-ranch establishment such as Double Whammies for a signature Big-Ass Beer and a precisely clocked three minutes of flirtation. Bujalski's setting is the American ubiquitous; and his central character, bar manager Lisa (Regina Hall), might be termed the American overlooked, as one of countless working women who keep themselves and everyone around them going, and do so with a smile.

The only thing uncommon here is the plot—not in its incidents (which are as ordinary as a PBR) but its structure. *Support the Girls* is a rare house-of-cards movie. Watch the first inadvertent nudge. See the whole thing tumble.

Hints of instability begin with the film's first human sound, which is Lisa's sniffling as she sits in the Double Whammies parking lot, crying behind the wheel. Only after starting at a sudden rap on the car window—it's a good-morning from Maci (Haley Lu Richardson), the waitress who will later be described as an angel sent to teach everyone about good attitude—does Lisa put on her professional grin and hop out, ready to march into a day's work.

She has a platoon of new job applicants to stuff into pink belly shirts and try out (Double Whammies evidently being a business with a high turnover); the young son of an employee to shelter until a waitress from another shift can be recruited for child care; and a kitchen to inspect (discreetly, glancingly) for evidence of rats. There's also an impromptu, not to say surreptitious, car wash to organize to raise funds for a waitress who was jailed the previous night, having decided to deal with an abusive boyfriend by aiming her car's front fender at him. And then there's that strange noise in the restaurant's ceiling.

Upon investigation, the banging overhead turns out to be a would-be burglar trapped in an HVAC duct. He's handled easily enough, the local cops being Double Whammies regulars. But the man's extraction proves to be the push that destabilizes everything for Lisa, until she eventually breaks down in the women's room in front of her closest workmate, Danyelle (Shayna McHayle)—breaks down laughing, that is. The alternative of screaming is still premature.

Bujalski, a stealthy filmmaker, develops these incidents in a style that's easygoing on the surface, as suits his mundane though odd choice of milieu. (In previous films, he's passed time in motel- and mall-based subcultures like computer-chess tournaments and fitness clubs.) Bujalski saves his punchiest image-making for the end—and even then, his strongest effects are not just understated but silent. Right before the climax, a series of wordless shots from Danyelle's point of view tells you everything she won't even bother to say about the men in Double Whammies and their notion of what's not just permitted, but cool. At the stunning finale, you know instinctively that Lisa, Maci, and Danyelle are sensing their mortality, and their freedom, simply from the way they look up to the sky. Until reaching those high points, though, Bujalski tips you off to his art only when he cuts to the next shot a little before you anticipated it, or unexpectedly spikes a scene's emotional pressure. He keeps knocking you off balance, gently, seemingly with no dire threat; but in the cumulative effect, you feel what it's like to be a card slipping down in Lisa's painstakingly constructed life.

Bujalski can make that collapse matter to you because Hall, as Lisa, is so solid. She's used to being the anchor of ensemble casts—in *Girls Trip*, for example—and here again she plays straight woman to bouncy Richardson, fierce and forthright McHayle, and others like Lea DeLaria as the bar's loyal, proudly butch customer, Bobo. All Hall has to do among these flightier characters is remain grounded (she's dug into the Texas soil so well that when she requests help from a friend, she asks for a "fiver"); broadcast decency with the strength of a clear-channel station; and show, from the gut, how Lisa pulls herself back together after each new catastrophe. Which is to say, Hall does everything.

Have I mentioned, by the way, that I smiled almost nonstop through *Support the Girls*? I did that not because Bujalski was trying to be funny, or because it's amusing to see homely, boozy, out-of-shape men judge the looks and character of young women, but out of pleasure at the warmth and mutual responsibility that

Lisa shares with her workmates. Maybe some of them are no better than they ought to be—and yet together, in an unacknowledged combat zone off the roar of I-10, they have some real laughs behind those professional smiles. They make a life.

The Nation, October 22, 2018

Late Kiarostami

A few years ago, when moviegoers in this country were just beginning to learn about Abbas Kiarostami, I heard a crowd of New Yorkers berate him for having put a snatch of Vivaldi onto a soundtrack. These audience members had paid for an Iranian experience, and they damn well wanted the music to go with with it. Kiarostami, puzzled by their complaint, blinked impatiently behind his tinted glasses. "But Vivaldi's music," he finally said, "is like the sun. It belongs to everybody."

In the conviction that Kiarostami, too, belongs to everyone, I will introduce his most recent film, *10*, by recalling a bit of New York City lore.

One night in 1950, the story goes, a hanger-on came into the Cedar Tavern and sat down at the bar beside Franz Kline. "I have just seen the worst show ever," the man announced happily. "Barnett Newman, at Betty Parsons. Nothing's there—nothing at all!"

"The gallery's empty?" Kline asked.

"There's one painting, and it's nothing."

"How about that?" Kline mused. "Barney's showing just one painting."

"I mean, there's a bunch of paintings, but they're all the same. Just one color."

"All the paintings are the same color?"

"No, this one is red, that one is blue, the other—"

"Ah," Kline said. "Solid colors."

"Yes, except for this ridiculous stripe."

"A stripe, too? What kind of stripe?"

"Just the same damn stripe everywhere. In the middle, over to one side, over to the other."

"So it moves, this stripe. Just one to a painting."

"One, two. Who cares? All Newman did was make stripes, straight up and down."

"Same height every time, I guess."

"Well, no. They run top to bottom, and the paintings are different sizes."

Kline sipped his beer. "Different sizes, different colors, different places where the stripes run? I dunno," he said. "Sounds pretty complicated to me."

Which is to say that Kiarostami's *10* is nothing—absolutely nothing, except for scenes of an unnamed woman (played by

Mania Akbari) driving around Teheran in a car. She makes ten trips in the course of the film, each time conversing with a single passenger. Sometimes the camera is fixed on her, sometimes on the passenger; and sometimes Kiarostami cuts back and forth between the two. The episodes vary in length; the routes take the car speeding along highways or nosing through congested streets; the time shifts between day and night. Some of the passengers ride only once; others show up in multiple episodes. Costumes change. Lines of dialogue echo between one segment and another. It's pretty complicated.

And like a Barnett Newman canvas, it's also supersaturated with meaning. Consider the first episode, which introduces the driver's son: a round-faced, jug-eared boy on the verge of puberty, with bowl-cut hair, a Western logo T-shirt and the last traces of a childhood lisp. No sooner has he pitched himself into the passenger seat than he and his mother are yelling. He hates her for having divorced and remarried; he hates his stepfather; he hates the lie his mother told, when she said his father was a drug addict.

But she had to lie, the mother screams back. It was the only way to get a divorce. "A woman has no rights in this society! I was like a zombie!"

And so, using the most rudimentary of techniques to record a seemingly unscripted exchange, Kiarostami announces the theme of *10*, at the highest decibel level. This woman demands her freedom and will go on demanding it, even if the effort makes her sound harsh, even if (as often happens in unscripted exchanges) the effect is not entirely happy.

The boy keeps covering his ears, twisting in his seat and nearly whimpering as he cries, "Don't shout!" And because he's just a boy, because he still lisps, because the camera for the first dozen minutes shows only him, his plea temporarily outweighs her self-justification. We begin to feel sympathy for the driver—and get a fresh charge of meaning—only at the end of this first episode, when Kiarostami at last cuts to her. That voice on the soundtrack, so self-righteous and insistent, turns out not to have come from a harpy. It belongs to a strikingly elegant young woman, done up in lipstick, chic sunglasses and the loosest white headscarf the law will allow.

Over the course of the next episodes, Kiarostami will contrast this woman with her sister (a more drab and nervous type), a sobbing friend who has been dumped by her husband, a young acquaintance who is uncertain of her boyfriend and is now seeking religious faith. Though wonderfully dense in their particularities, these characters are also mirrors of the driver, who might have become like any of them. At the mysterious emotional core of *10*, though, are back-to-back encounters with two passengers who are more remote as possible selves, since they differ markedly from the driver in age and social station. These central characters, who remain all but unseen, are an elderly woman who talks of prayers and pilgrimages and overflowingly fecund families, and a prostitute.

About the elderly woman, I need say only that the driver listens to her with a mixture of curiosity and irony. A chic young modern woman cannot adopt such untutored piety, but neither does she dismiss it (as becomes evident during later rides).

The prostitute makes a far trickier passenger. It's not just that she gives voice to attitudes that are meant to shock. (She laughingly dismisses the difference between streetwalkers and married women, saying, "We're the wholesalers, you're the retailers.") What makes the prostitute so compelling is that she *only* gives voice. It's nighttime when the driver picks her up; the scene outside the car window is dark except for the passing streetlamps and shop windows, and the driver's face flashes in and out of view. The prostitute cannot be seen at all—which makes her mocking, drawling speech seem as intimate as if it came from inside the driver's head. What was the driver thinking, anyway, when she picked up this woman? Why won't she stop now and let her out, as the prostitute keeps requesting?

Here, in what is literally the murkiest passage of *10*, Kiarostami opens up desires that are far more unruly than the demand for equal rights before the law. "Pretend I'm a man," the driver says at one point, ostensibly to encourage conversation—to which the prostitute raucously shoots back, "I've never worked that field!" The reverberations of that line ring through later episodes—and so, too, do some of the prostitute's phrases, which the driver will repeat, though without the corrosive cynicism.

As even this incomplete sketch might hint, Kiarostami builds up a pattern in *10*—a mosaic, you might say, in which the relationships between the parts seem to change each time you blink. It's a mosaic on the subject of freedom—and the most astonishing thing about it, perhaps, is that Kiarostami achieved it by giving up control of the movie.

In an exceptional feat of look-Ma-no-hands filmmaking, Kiarostami fixed digital video cameras to the dashboard of the car, turned them on and then stood at the curb as his set and actors drove away. He was absent during the shooting of every scene in *10*; he probably didn't even know exactly where Akbari would drive. Of course, he must have prepared the performers, and he chose which takes to use afterward; but whatever you see on the screen truly happened before the camera, as it used to happen in the old actualities footage that was cinema at its most basic.

You might even say that *10* is so basic, so radical, that it brings you back to the biomechanics of cinema. Because Kiarostami's camera is stationary within a traveling car, the image remains still and yet moves. This is, of course, the nature of film: A succession of photographs blurs into apparent motion. The blur is subjective, illusory, directionless—and in *10*, it pulses with the longings of women in a real time and place.

What emerges from this minimalist, form-obsessed movie, as if from the body of cinema itself? At its climax, the film contrives to show you what cannot be shown in today's Iran: the image of a bareheaded woman. That a ruse is involved—a ruse that needn't be explained in this review—should come as no surprise to anyone who has followed Kiarostami's career. Once again, the director (and nondirector) has lied with beguiling simplicity, and so called up the complicated truth.

The Nation, March 24, 2003

10 on Ten

An extended paean to the digital video camera—"a lightweight, discreet companion on my real and imaginary travels"—serves as one of the "lessons on cinema" in *10 on Ten*, a documentary monologue by Abbas Kiarostami that just had its New York theatrical debut at Anthology Film Archives. It's as direct and straightforward a little film as you could imagine, and since it's by Kiarostami, it's as tricky as hell.

The film was prompted, he says early on, by the comments of people who saw *Ten* and were evidently disappointed by its urban setting. Some said they were used to seeing landscapes in Kiarostami's films; *Ten* was shot inside a car, which drove through the streets of Tehran. So *10 on Ten* begins as a compromise. It is shot entirely inside a car, driven by Kiarostami; but the route lies outside Tehran, in the green hills that were the setting for *Taste of Cherry*. He has returned to this spot, Kiarostami says, "to express my sympathy with viewers." But he also lets drop another purpose for coming back: "In the future, I may no longer find a reason to bring my camera here." That sounds ominously final, when you recall that *Taste of Cherry* was about a suicide—but Kiarostami says no more, passing on at once to his lessons.

They address his preference for camera, subject (everyday life), script (as little as possible), location (the automobile, since it makes people feel secure and yet confines them, pushing them to express their feelings), music (as little as possible), actors (nonprofessionals, of course, though someone trained may do in a pinch), costumes and makeup (whatever the people like to wear) and director (nonprofessional actors need a nonprofessional director). He talks to the camera. The landscape unfolds behind him, at several different times of day. And questions arise. If the confinement of a car encourages self-expression, then what feelings does Kiarostami need to get out? If clothing is a basic expression of identity, then what is he showing us about himself, with his informal, open shirt but off-putting, tinted eyeglasses?

And why does he doubt he'll be coming back here? *Ten*, he says, was about the objective, social problems of women; but *Taste of Cherry* was about the inner life of a man. What has Kiarostami just revealed about his own inner life, driving around the landscape of *Taste of Cherry*?

10 on Ten is a structuralist, documentary mystery story.

The Nation, March 21, 2005

Certified Copy

When Abbas Kiarostami made his first appearance at the New York Film Festival, in 1992, I had the privilege of sitting next to him as moderator for his press conference; and so I can testify that the assembled film intelligentsia wanted him to be a wog. They meant it in the nicest way, of course.

"Mr. Kiarostami," went the first question after the screening of *And Life Goes On*, "why did you use Western music at the end?"

The music, Kiarostami explained, conveyed the mood he had wanted. Next question?

"But this is an Iranian film," a second journalist protested. "Why did you use Western music?"

Kiarostami repeated his answer, after which a third journalist asked why he had used Western music.

With a glint of impatience now flashing behind his tinted eyeglasses, Kiarostami said, "I think of Vivaldi the way I think of the sun. He belongs to everybody."

That ought to settle the matter, I told myself. And yet, when the next journalist raised his hand, we heard, "Mr. Kiarostami, when the man was listening to the radio in his car, why did you use Western music? It sounded like Tangerine Dream."

"It was the theme music for the radio news," Kiarostami replied. "In Tehran, we hear it all day long."

A reasonable answer; you might even call it a neorealistic one. But even so, a vocal faction of the audience clearly was not satisfied. Kiarostami had shirked his responsibility to be Iranian and nothing but.

The irony of this consumerist demand for authenticity—or rather for a supposed son of the third world to enact authenticity—was surely not lost on the director of *Close-Up*. Today, as Kiarostami's new film *Certified Copy* enters US theaters, bringing with it an endless mirror play of originality and replication, a deeply insoluble puzzle about felt experience and play-acting, I think of the reception it got at the 2010 Cannes and New York festivals—ecstatic in some cases, but lukewarm or dismissive in many others—and wonder if Kiarostami's problem once again might be insufficient wogitude.

The insufficiency arises from the film's being his first feature made in Europe (we may discount a contribution to an anthology a few years ago): a French-Italian co-production shot in Tuscany, starring Juliette Binoche and the opera singer William Shimell. Not a speck of Farsi; not an Iranian in sight. Judging *Certified Copy* solely on this basis, a cynic might suspect that the film represented nothing more than a plush paid vacation for Kiarostami. But then, think of where you might have seen something like this before: an all-but-plotless travelogue set in Italy, tracking the interactions between a beautiful, vibrantly dissatisfied woman of ripe middle years (who speaks a fluent but accented English) and a sleek, silver-haired British gentleman given to smug pronouncements (addressed to her) and outbursts of disparagement (directed at the locals). True to its title, *Certified Copy* is an imitation—of Rossellini's *Viaggio in Italia*.

This is hardly the first time that Rossellini's film has been mimicked. Godard did it in *Contempt*. Why should Kiarostami have any less right to do it now? Is one imitation more authentic than another? We're getting into the topic announced in the first scene of *Certified Copy*, where a British author with dubious credentials (Shimell) appears before a small audience in Arezzo to lecture about his latest book. It is an art historical essay in praise of replicas, which have a long and noble tradition of their own, as he points out, and which deserve (in his view) to be accepted as equal to the original works. Joining the audience for this talk—tardily, raptly, distractedly, briefly—is a local antiques dealer (Binoche), who brings along her own replica: a teenage son.

She seems to be raising him on her own; but maybe the boy is also a replica of the author. This possibility suggests itself the following day, when Binoche and Shimell get together for the awkward, outwardly purposeless appointment that takes up the rest of the film. Meeting for what seems to be the first time, with no apparent knowledge of each other's lives, they get into her car, drive aimlessly for a while and then (at her suggestion) visit the town of Lucignano, a spot the Tuscans consider propitious for weddings. Here, amid an overabundance of white dresses, cut flowers and broadly grinning hopes, Binoche and Shimell gradually start bickering, about the fifteen years of grievances that have piled up in what seems to be their marriage.

Are they strangers who just now came together, or a wife and husband who fell apart long ago? Which is the reality, and which the illusion? Kiarostami, as skillful a tease as ever, makes it irresistible to guess at an answer, even as he ensures that it's futile to decide on one—because *Certified Copy* deliberately if subtly contradicts itself. Any reading of the situation turns out to be wrong. All you really know about these two people is that their little irritations with each other, and their big complaints, are similar to those of hundreds of millions of other couples, as if married life itself were a genuine imposture—as if Binoche and Shimell (who are, after all, a couple of actors) were performing from an nth-generation copy of an anonymous antique script, which nevertheless demands real emotion.

Reduced to this proposition, *Certified Copy* would be banal. But as an experience, it is nothing other than an escape from banality, as Binoche and Shimell convert the familiar into the spontaneous, moment by moment—and at strikingly different tempos. In any given pair of close-ups, Binoche will be making her pupils dart about like dark fireflies and sending half-suppressed thoughts racing across her features like the shadows of clouds; while Shimell, exuding the vanity of an opera star, sits there and breathes. You might describe the actors as engaged in a counterpoint of male phlegmatism and female hypersensitivity—until the end, when he becomes the jumpy one, and she (half-dressed and smiling knowingly) lolls across a bed in the dusk of a hotel room.

That last image is something Kiarostami will never get to shoot in Iran—which may help to explain why he would leave behind the land of Tangerine Dream radio music and make a film in Tuscany. But then, there's a sense in which every other image of *Certified Copy* has appeared in earlier Kiarostami films. Once again, you see the narrow, twisting lanes, the darkened basement, the road cutting through a rolling countryside, the shaggy-haired boy, the loquacious cafe owner, even the cat who makes her way into every shot of a sequence. If the Iranian settings and figures have now been translated into Italian, I doubt it's because Kiarostami was short on ideas. My sense is that he has recovered what was authentically his by imitating what belonged to somebody else.

It sounds tricky, this game of self and other, and it is. But as always with Kiarostami, it's also as direct as can be. The signature images of *Certified Copy* are probably the pair of frontal close-ups in which first Binoche and then Shimell peer straight into the camera. They are studying themselves in the mirror—and we, evidently, are their reflection.

The Nation, March 21, 2011

Like Someone in Love

Abbas Kiarostami, who twenty years ago introduced a great wave of new Iranian cinema to the festival, is now working outside Iran. For most directors, the result would be deracination. For this wily old master, it's been an opportunity to discover new depths and quirks of human feeling in refreshing new settings. He directed *Like Someone in Love* in and around Tokyo, working with an all-Japanese cast and crew, and somehow came out with a Kiarostami film. Or maybe it also has a little bit of Renoir. Everyone in the film has his or her reasons: the college girl from the provinces who is trying to stop working as an escort, the rough-hewn auto mechanic who has decided that he's her fiancé (without exactly having consulted her), and the kindly old sociology professor (or is he a john?) who winds up pretending to be her grandfather. Very tricky; very engaging.

The Nation, November 12, 2012

24 Frames

Quiet, non-narrative films like Abbas Kiarostami's posthumous *24 Frames* are often tagged as "poetic," the default term for anything that has neglected to squeeze itself into a commercially viable genre. Good enough. Let's start with a few lines from a poem, Wallace Stevens's "The Snow Man":

> One must have a mind of winter
> To regard the frost and the boughs
> Of the pine-trees crusted with snow
> And have been cold a long time
> To behold the junipers shagged with ice…
> …and not to think
> Of any misery in the sound of the wind…

And here is the first of the 24 framed images that compose Kiarostami's film: a full-screen reproduction of Pieter Bruegel the Elder's painting *The Hunters in the Snow*. Three men returning from their labors, their backs turned to you, trudge toward a vast, frigid valley, dogs following their sunken tracks, ravens perched in the bare branches above, the peaked, snow-thatched roofs of little houses dropping away below. You contemplate the utter stillness. You feel time has stopped.

Then a plume of smoke begins to rise from a chimney in the painting. A fresh flurry of snow drifts down, accompanied by the whistle of wind. Crackling and cawing break onto the soundtrack — from the fire being tended near the inn at the picture's left, from a bird swooping across the center of a mottled, overcast sky — and a real dog (I mean, the filmed image of one) wanders in, just to nose around. Then the dog trots out of the painting, the snow lets up, the wind dies down. Having given you a few moments of "life," Kiarostami returns you to the painting and to silence — to a time that's frozen. Like the "listener" in "The Snow Man," who has learned to become "nothing himself," you now behold "Nothing that is not there and the nothing that is." Fade to black.

It's not hard to imagine Kiarostami himself fading to black, very slowly, during his time making *24 Frames*. He puttered over the film in his basement in Tehran for three years, assisted by the digital animator Ali Kamali, who used a video program to layer movement and sound onto *The Hunters in the Snow* and dozens of scans of Kiarostami's nature photographs. It must have been an absorbing process, which continued even after Kiarostami was hospitalized with cancer. By the time of his death, he had created more than enough computer-animated photographs to make up the 24 he wanted for a film—24 being the number of frames that ordinarily translate into one second of movie time. Each of his "frames," though, lasts four and a half minutes. Kiarostami had figured out a new way to stretch time, but he couldn't defeat it. After he died in July 2016, his son Ahmad completed the work.

Given this history, skeptics might wonder if *24 Frames* conforms to Kiarostami's final intentions, or if he'd even had time to formulate them. Some naysayers might also think the primary materials for *24 Frames*—Kiarostami's still photographs—are too slight to support 114 minutes of cinematic meditation. For the moment, let's just say there's an overwhelming consistency of imagery, process, and mood in *24 Frames*, which makes the film feel very much like the considered work of a single artist—and not just any work, but the last testament.

Bruegel's painting makes all the difference, establishing motifs that run through the next 23 animations of Kiarostami's photographs. It's winter in these images more often than not, with snow deep on the ground and trees shaking under gray skies. Dogs and birds show up frequently. (Crows might be the stars of the movie, given how often they hop and croak through the scenes.) Hunters make themselves felt in Kiarostami's frames, too, though only off-screen, through the sound of their guns. The difference from Bruegel's painting is that, with a few notable exceptions, a human presence is implied but unseen. Fences run across the unpopulated landscapes in some of the frames; in others, the landscape is glimpsed, or obscured, through the windows of uninhabited rooms.

There's also transient, invisible evidence of humanity in the music that's matched to some of the frames: an old tango by Francisco Canaro, Maria Callas performing "Un Bel di Vedremo," Janet Baker singing the Schubert "Ave Maria," or an instrumental number by the Naqsh Duo, two young Iranian women whose compositions sound like traditional Persian music crossed with *Quartet for the End of Time*.

Do these occasional patches of music violate the principle of Stevens's "The Snow Man," introducing the something of human desire into the fundamental nothing of the natural world? I'd rather say they set up a push-and-pull. Sometimes you feel dissolved into the scenes that Kiarostami has created, as if snow and wind were one with the birds and animals—as much inside them as outside—and one with you, too. (The land, Stevens writes, is full of the "same wind" that blows "in the same bare place / For the listener.") At other times, you sit back and wonder at how much emotion you're pouring into a scene with which you have only the most tenuous connection. This generally happens in the episodes in which you're separated from the landscape, seeing it from inside a house (or, in one case, a car) while hearing the recorded music that someone has chosen to play. But who? Nobody's in the room. The listener, too, has dissolved.

Whether the episodes are underscored by music or only by "natural" sound effects, they can be pitiless in their simplicity, as when two horses spar in a blizzard, or a prowling cat snatches a bird out of a burrow in the snow, which is immediately filled by another bird. The frames can be quizzical as well, or droll. A herd of cattle strolls in threes and fours across a deserted beach, with the cows looking for all the world as if they belong there. (Later, the same computer-animated herd walks through a clearing in a forest, just as improbably, and just as convincingly.) Or: A puppy on the beach runs up yapping to a seagull and scares it away. A moment later, the puppy re-enters to yap at the empty space where the seagull used to stand.

Whether you chuckle or brood, you think all the while of how the apparent motion in these photographs is an illusion—like the fictitious evidence that Kiarostami invented of an ongoing world outside the frame; like the impression of time unspooling naturally in scenes whose duration was arbitrarily decided and artificially fixed. In other words, you keep thinking about the essence of film-making. In his great fictions—and, even more, in the quasi-documentary fictions—Kiarostami pulled off the magical trick of keeping you aware of the movieness of the movie without ever distancing you from his characters. He was, in that sense, an anti-Brecht, who refused to alienate anybody. *24 Frames*, though, has almost no characters except for the birds and animals—and they don't do the two things that most interested Kiarostami about human beings, which are that we care for one another and we lie. So I wouldn't argue with a moviegoer who finds *24 Frames* too contemplative an experience. And yet there's the departure of the final frame, inhabited by Kiarostami himself—or rather, this being a grand lie, by someone who implicitly represents him.

The setting is a room at night. A figure, seen from behind, lies face-down on a desk, dozing. Next to the figure, a computer monitor displays a freeze-frame of an old English-language movie. Maybe we're looking at the film this person had been watching before falling asleep. Or maybe we're seeing the person's dream, projected onto the little screen nearby. Either way, the picture gradually jerks into motion. The movie's scene continues; the actress and actor slowly kiss.

As a filmmaker subject to the laws of the Islamic Republic of Iran, Kiarostami was never permitted to show people kissing. But at the close of his life, using *24 Frames*, he finally got to do just that. The music he chose to accompany this great moment is lushly sentimental. The image on the monitor is grainy and pixelated, and the person who would presumably be most interested in watching it is left fast asleep. No matter. As a warm filmmaker with a mind of winter, Kiarostami had learned that absurdities and impediments are as much a part of the world, and himself, as snow and wind. Everything was frozen, and the body was dying of cancer—and yet the kiss could happen.

The figure sleeps. The screen on the desk says: "The End."

The Nation, March 5, 2018

Haneke Shmaneke

The Piano Teacher

The Piano Teacher is a pan-European remake of *Whatever Happened to Baby Jane?*, with French stars Isabelle Huppert and Annie Girardot playing the sacred-monster roles and Austrian director Michael Haneke fastidiously avoiding the camp humor that alone could have saved the movie. Set in Vienna and cast (except for the leads) with German-speaking actors, whose lips flop like dying fish around their dubbed French syllables, *The Piano Teacher* is a combination of immaculately composed shots and solemnly absurd dialogue, much of it about the music of Franz Schubert. "That note is the sound of conscience, hammering at the complacency of the bourgeoisie." Sure it is. Add a sequence in which Huppert humps Girardot (her own mother!) in the bed they share, throw in an extended sex scene where the characters grandly ignore any risk of interruption (though they're grappling in a public toilet), and you've got a movie that ought to have made classical music dirty again.

But to judge from critics' reactions, Schubert remains the touchstone of respectability, and *The Piano Teacher* is somehow to be taken seriously.

The aura of high-mindedness that cloaks the action (at least for some viewers) emanates mostly from Huppert. No matter what her character stoops to—doggie posture, for the most part—Huppert seems never to lower herself. She maintains her dignity because she is being brave. She is acting. She is allowing herself to be shown as sexually abject before an athletic younger man, Benoît Magimel, who has a cleft chin and peekaboo blond hair. Huppert has been similarly abject in recent years, in Benoît Jacquot's *The School of Flesh*, for example. I wonder what hope other women may nurture for themselves after 40, when this wealthy, celebrated, greatly accomplished and famously beautiful woman has no better prospects. I know we're expected to give prizes to Huppert for such ostentatious self-abnegation. (Last year, at Cannes, she collected a big award.) But what pleasure are we supposed to get from seeing the character humiliated?

A dishonest pleasure, I'd say; the same kind that's proposed in *The Piano Teacher*'s now-notorious scene of genital mutilation. The meaning of the scene, for those who are pleased to give it one, is of course transgressive, subversive and otherwise big word-like. See how (women) (the Viennese) (the middle class) (fill in the blank) are repressed, how they turn against themselves, how they make themselves and everyone around them suffer. Then again, if you subtract all that guff about the complacent bourgeoisie, maybe the scene means nothing more than "Ew, gross!"

I have admired Haneke's films in the past, beginning with the antiseptically grim *The Seventh Continent* and going on to the tough, much-maligned *Benny's Video*. When Haneke has proposed that clean, affluent, educated people may do horrible things, I have agreed, as of course I must, accepting what would have been a mere platitude for the sake of the films' clear vision and genuine sense of dread. But as I watched Huppert's preposterous impersonation of a music teacher, I began to wonder if Haneke knows that characters can be something other than horrid.

The dynamics of Schubert's music represent emotional "anarchy," says Huppert at one point, in a pronouncement that would get a pedagogue sacked from any self-respecting conservatory. Listen to Rudolf Serkin play the great B-flat piano sonata, varying his touch with every breath, and you will hear not anarchy but imagination. It's the quality most lacking in *The Piano Teacher*—followed closely by warmth, humor, realism and purpose.

The Nation, April 29, 2002

Caché

I begin with the straight razor, the razor blade, the keen metal stud, the hacksaw—all the tools that have sliced into human flesh in Michael Haneke's films, advancing his plots while they mirror his style. His images are cold, gleaming and precise; his view of characters, dispassionately cutting. Think of Haneke as a clinician, dedicated to treating society's ills, and his movies will seem like scalpels. Think of him as a less benevolent type, and the films become Austrian chain saws.

It seems that most viewers have seen the scalpel in his widely admired new picture, which for the American market has been helpfully subtitled right in its name, as *Caché (Hidden)*. Like virtually all of Haneke's films, this one scrapes away at the surface of polite European affluence to lay bare the moral rot beneath. Daniel Auteuil stars as Georges, the host of a popular French television show about recently published books; Juliette Binoche plays Anne, his appropriately elegant wife; Lester Makedonsky is their teenage son, Pierrot, whose ways are (of course) impenetrable; and Maurice Bénichou appears in the crucial role of Majid, the figure from a dark past.

The slightly melodramatic note in my summary is intended, as it is in *Caché* itself. Beginning with the first image—a stationary long shot of a residential street in Paris, held and held until the ordinary, day-lit scene fills with dread—Haneke practices his version of Hitchcockian suspense, and even offers the ploy of a thriller plot. As you soon learn, that opening view of the street is part of a surveillance video of Georges and Anne's home. What snoop made the cassette and then dropped it at their door? Why are they being watched? As the couple, already bickering in their first scene, start to imagine threats and cast about for clues, you are drawn into their sleuthing, even as you realize you're somehow searching for yourself. Georges and Anne are unnerved because they've been seen—and there you sit, hypocrite voyeur, observing them and wondering who has exposed their discord.

A sophisticated gambit, expertly played. Even if you dislike *Caché*—and I do—it's impossible to deny the formidable intelligence at work in the film. There's a reason Haneke was named best director at Cannes, why *Caché* got a prominent slot in the most recent New York Film Festival, why at the end of 2005 various critics' groups and the European Film Awards cited *Caché* as the year's best picture. There's also a reason to resist *Caché*—but to propose it, I'll need to conduct a quick review of Haneke's career.

He began his work in feature films in 1989 with *Der Siebente Kontinent* (*The Seventh Continent*), an exquisitely, immaculately depressing examination of a middle-class Austrian family that no longer found life worth living. Was the movie a case study, an allegory, a diatribe, a warning? The power of *The Seventh Continent* lay in its being all of these and none—an effect that Haneke achieved by avoiding any explanations, whether psychological or sociological. He just (just!) showed the surface of things.

His next film, *Benny's Video* (1992), was even stronger. Once more, the milieu was the Austrian bourgeoisie; once more, the plot hinged on a horrifying, senseless act of violence. Some viewers, rushing to provide an explanation for the crime, decided that *Benny's Video* was made to decry television's baleful influence over the young. But Haneke's presentation of the story was again so objective, with each detail given such precise and independent weight, that no single reading of the story would do. Did Benny kill because he had too much money, too little love and guidance, too loose a connection to the three-dimensional world, too close a connection to the Nazi past, too conflicted a libido, too evil a soul? Yes.

From these early works, it was clear that Haneke's approach could be compelling; but it also could prove facile, as it did in his third film about the eruption of violence, *71 Fragmente einer Chronologie des Zufalls* (*71 Fragments of a Chronology of Chance*) (1994). The alternative title, *Amok*, tells all you need to know about the story. A young man goes about his banal life and then goes postal; and this time the audience doesn't wonder why he kills. He slaughters people because Michael Haneke can't figure out what else a fictional character might do.

This incapacity of Haneke's imagination reached a crisis point in *Funny Games* (1997), which consisted of almost nothing but acts of torture and murder, as visited upon a middle-class family. Most people have found the movie unwatchable; but it's worth noting anyway, as the first film in which Haneke posed the question of the audience's complicity in the acts shown onscreen. As if taking up the simplistic, blame-the-media reading of *Benny's Video*, Haneke had his bad guys in *Funny Games* provide one of the staples of movie entertainment—the thrill of bloodshed—and then keep providing it relentlessly, until viewers could be entertained no more.

Of course, Haneke is too smart a man, and too alert a moralist, to have been content for long with this crude method of gagging people on their own appetite for violence. Taking his first major foray out of Austria, into the world of French co-production, he went on to make the thoughtful and challenging *Code Unknown* (2000): a deliberately disjointed, discontinuous puzzle-picture about an actress (Juliette Binoche) and her photojournalist boyfriend (Thierry Neuvic). By profession, in their separate ways, this couple sold the public an opportunity to sympathize with suffering humanity, as glimpsed in exotic images of war and terror; but when a horror was taking place right where they lived, the actress and photojournalist shut their eyes and ears.

By now the political and social implications of Haneke's film-making could no longer be elided, as they had been in his earlier work, since his fictional world had grown more expansive. *Code Unknown* encompassed a polyglot, multiracial, border-crossing cast of characters, some of them affluent, some poor, some working hard and just getting by; and nobody was the clear moral superior of anyone else. Even a righteously indignant young man of African background, who seemed at first to be a voice of conscience, could prove at another moment to be careless and self-indulgent; even the actress, however encased in the privileges of her career, could abruptly become the sympathetic victim of an ugly, biased assault.

Most important of all, *Code Unknown* explicitly questioned the responsibility of the actress and the journalist for the images they presented to the public. In so doing, the film also implicitly questioned Haneke's moral position. Was he bent solely on exposing unpleasant realities? Or was he, like the audience, hoping to gratify his own appetite for thrills?

These were precisely the questions that Haneke did not ask in making his next picture, *La Pianiste* (*The Piano Teacher*) (2001), which turned out to be his first international hit. Well, you can't argue with success. But since you can object to it sometimes, I will say that this picture, to me, seemed to be little more than an exercise in humiliating Isabelle Huppert. That she cooperated enthusiastically in the abuse excused nothing. Why would Haneke have wanted to make Huppert crawl, grovel, cover herself in filth and pretend to mutilate her flesh? And why should he take this famously beautiful and talented woman and make a spectacle of her character's being too old and undesirable for a young man? Was it because this teacher at a Viennese conservatory represented the dead weight of bourgeois culture? (But she didn't. The scenes of her pedagogy were so absurd, she might have been Professor McGonagall at the Hogwarts School of Ivory-Tickling.) Or was Haneke, as some viewers supposed, casting a searing gaze into one woman's tortured soul? Sheer melodrama, if so—and again, he was the primary torturer.

But he was a torturer who had succeeded in amusing himself while giving the people what they wanted. Now he has managed the trick again, with *Caché*.

What is it, exactly, that's hidden in this story? Moviegoers who don't want to be tipped off should stop reading now. For everyone else, I will explain that two underlying mysteries come to light in the film. One is an actual state crime of the early 1960s—the murderous suppression of Algerians living in France—which the French would prefer to forget. The other is a private, fictional wrongdoing from the same era, which Georges at age 6 committed against an Algerian boy. *Caché* links the two into a single chain of social and personal guilt, while suggesting (in the manner of *Code Unknown*) that people who are concerned about distant crimes should also pay some attention to what's happening at home.

Yet *Caché*, unfortunately, is not *Code Unknown*. Despite Haneke's inclusion of significant Algerian characters, he has contracted his social world again, so that you're locked into Georges and Anne's pricey milieu. And they're bad people. Never mind that Georges sinned decisively when he was only 6. We are meant to understand that he was a rotten, greedy little racist then, and he's a rotten, greedy big racist now. The film's Algerians, by contrast, are good people—so good that Majid (stop reading now, if you don't want to know) will actually slit his own throat for Georges. Obliging Arabs! They kill themselves to save white men the trouble.

Haneke the Slasher wields his knife again. The writer-director of *Code Unknown* would have examined his own impulse to make Majid die. But the current Haneke never posits his complicity in the scene. Only the audience is complicit—and not in any violence against Arabs. We voyeurs, sitting in the safety of our movie theater, participate imaginatively in the torture of Georges and Anne only. No wonder that this exposé disturbs the conscience so little; no wonder that the film's most ardent admirers have turned out to be people of Georges and Anne's own station. Far from being an expression of liberal guilt (the charge against which some commentators have defended the movie), *Caché* is an appeal to liberal self-regard.

And a fancy one at that. With Auteuil and Binoche as his stars, with the best Parisian living spaces as his settings, Haneke strips away only the most chic trappings of bourgeois respectability. The performances: superb. The cinematography: glistening. The directorial skills: worthy of golden palms.

They should have called it *Cachet*.

The Nation, January 30, 2006

The White Ribbon

Three times a day for the past two months, alerts from a web magazine have pried open my e-mail box with sharp little exclamation points. The reason for this vandalism: I must be told that *Avatar* has now pulled ahead of *The Hurt Locker*, or vice versa, in the Oscars competition.

If these were the only reasonable choices for Best Picture, then I suppose I would hope for the victory of the one that dares to talk politics. (That would be *Avatar*.) But really, only a mug looks to the Oscars for relevance; and how much fun can you expect from them, when Marvin Hamlisch's brilliantly unhinged score for *The Informant!* didn't even get nominated?

I'd rather ignore the whole thing. But because the nominees in the perennially slapdash foreign-language category include Michael Haneke's *The White Ribbon*—Audiard's *A Prophet* is another—this might be the moment at last to bring up an awkward subject.

To his admirers, Haneke is a figure of probity, whose immaculate and unnerving formal sense is matched by moral rigor and unsparing social conscience. He shows us the nasty truth about our world, and ourselves, and does so with such uncompromising clarity that we can't look away. For those who feel this way, *The White Ribbon* is a great achievement. Shot to resemble August Sander's classic photographs of peasant life, it is the story of ghastly assaults, some explained, many unsolved, in a German village on the eve of World War I. What do they mean? As one of the film's characters says in retrospect, this story may shed some light on "events that happened later in our country." But the use of the conditional is a dodge. Haneke leaves no room for doubt: you are witnessing the origins of Nazism.

Except that you're not. Haneke's historicism, too, is a dodge (even if he's empty-headed enough to believe in it), given that the punitive tendencies and sexual misery of *The White Ribbon*'s characters are a free-floating condition throughout his films, belonging to every era and therefore to none, explaining everything and therefore nothing. Had *The White Ribbon* presented itself as just another Haneke horror show—see the monsters! feel glad you're not them!—I would have to accept it. But it makes a larger claim, which is so bogus that I finally have to protest: if you want a faithful depiction of Nazism, you'd do better to revel in *Black Book*.

The Nation, March 22, 2010

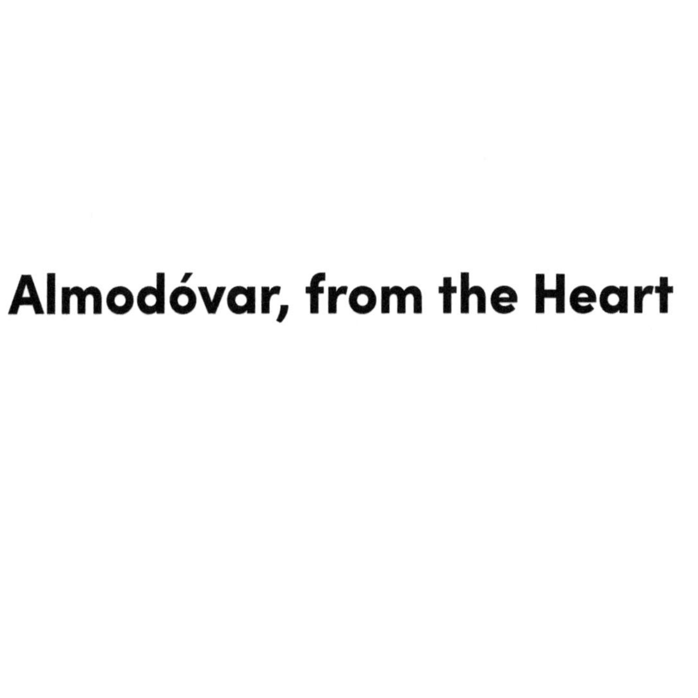

Almodóvar, from the Heart

Talk to Her

November has been melodrama month at the movies. First Todd Haynes brought us *Far From Heaven*, which he ought to have called *Imitation of Imitation*. Now comes Pedro Almodóvar with *Talk to Her*, so we can see the real thing.

When a film is as touching and true as *Talk to Her*, it deserves to be praised on its own. Nevertheless: I note that only one of these melodramas makes itself bigger than life through generosity, by giving its characters the boldness and color we'd all like to have. The other achieves grandeur by making life small: judging every character in advance, reducing every situation to a slogan—the sort of unexceptionably liberal slogan on which your average Democrat could run, and lose.

Of course, I'd be lying if I said that Haynes alone condescends to his characters. There's a woman in Almodóvar's new movie—a television talk-show host—whom the filmmaker demeans three times over. After being treated as a functionary, who exists solely to bring together the *real* characters, she's made to splutter and thrash, like a frog who's missed the lily pad. And for the third insult, she's given nothing better to croak than this platitude: "Talking about problems is the first step toward overcoming them."

This is serious, in a movie titled *Talk to Her*. The professional interviewer has cheapened conversation.

That said, all the other characters in *Talk to Her* are amateurs in their speech—lovers, I mean—and receive the deepest consideration from Almodóvar. That's true even for the chatterbox concierge who charms the screen for thirty seconds; even for the prison warden who feels the full gravity of the words he says, however few. As for the major characters:

Marco (Darío Grandinetti) is a wandering writer by trade: an author of travel guides, who walks and talks as if he were himself a slim and stubble-chinned suitcase, somewhat battered by life and holding the bare necessities within. Seen from his point of view, *Talk to Her* would be about the loss of three loves. The first is a softly beautiful young woman, blond and needy, who made Marco wretched when they were together and makes him wretched now that she's gone. The second love is Lydia (Rosario Flores)—fierce, lean-muscled, strong-featured, Andalusian, a woman who has sliced her way into the ranks of professional bullfighters. When she, too, begins to slip away from Marco, the third love enters: chubby young Benigno (Javier Cámara).

A voyager who binds himself to three such different types must be polymorphous in his affections—which makes Marco a good match for Benigno, the sexually amorphous stay-at-home. What would *Talk to Her* look like from his viewpoint? Instead of being about loss, it might be concerned with the presence of three beloved people: his late mother, for whom he cared throughout his adolescence and who still hovers in his thoughts; a young dancer named Alicia (Leonor Watling), whom he nurses in a clinic where she's been lying in a coma; and Marco, who ventures into Benigno's place of employment when he visits the comatose Lydia. "Talk to her," Benigno advises Marco. He says it with an openness, a lack of affectation, that makes speech itself seem a daily miracle.

Benigno's voice sounds light and lyrical; his gestures are rounded and smooth. "What is your sexual orientation?" Alicia's father wants to know (a question he asks while Benigno is firmly kneading his daughter's left thigh). The answer is the one he wants to hear: "I like men," Benigno tells him, his face meanwhile betraying the slightest hauteur. Does this man understand nothing of life? Benigno's feelings can't be frozen into categories. They take shape as if they were blobs in a lava lamp—a lava lamp, say, like the one that sits at the head of Alicia's bed. Its amniotic colors will eventually fill the screen in close-up, at the moment when candid, loving, endearing Benigno commits his unforgivable crime.

To pause and take stock: So far we've got a female bullfighter, a ballerina, a hunky globetrotter and the harmless friend down the hall, all caught up in a situation out of a medical soap opera. Sexual barriers don't exist, legal bounds are broken—and none of this seems the least bit outrageous. The Almodóvar who once invited you to laugh at lurid improbabilities now has you rapt before them, as you marvel that a world full of pain is also so various and surprising.

How does Almodóvar pull off the trick? With infinite care. The meticulous symmetry of his plan should be obvious by now: Marco and Benigno, diametrically opposite types, each love two women, one who has vanished into the past and one who lies unconscious in the present. At no point in *Talk to Her*, though, does this scheme feel diagrammatic, because Almodóvar keeps your eye on the movement of time, not on the structure that time flows through. He's always skipping ahead or flashing back, shifting effortlessly among memories and fantasies and present-tense events, zigzagging between Benigno and Marco. His touch is so sure that he can even spring a newly invented "silent film" on you—something goofy and erotic—and do it without spoiling a moment of high tension.

But then, Almodóvar does not pull off the trick alone. He's got his brilliant actors, who are so right in their roles that you might imagine *Talk to Her* had been cast first and written later. Within a perfectly balanced ensemble, Cámara stands out as Benigno—in part because he's been given the most contradictory of the characters to play, and in part because he's found a way to signal the furtiveness within the well-padded body, the guile beneath the comforting flesh. It's an extraordinarily fine performance; but then, Grandinetti is just as good in the leading-man role of Marco (who might have been the sorrowful gunslinger, had this been a western), and Flores is indelible in her every defiant gesture as Lydia, from knocking back a drink to staring down Marco to kissing her medals as she dresses for the fight.

These players, and Almodóvar, justify melodrama in the best way possible. They use its simplifications to increase the complexity of emotions. Hiss the villain and cheer the hero: That's the camp version of melodrama, which you may still encounter (in its academic form) in Haynes's *Far From Heaven*. But Almodóvar gives us melodrama with right and wrong but without heroes and villains. He uses its artifice to bring the characters closer to us—by which I mean, quite literally, those of us who are sitting in the dark.

You can look at *Talk to Her* from the viewpoint of Marco or Benigno, or you can watch it as someone in a theater seat. Make the latter choice, and you see that the movie is about performances: some of them given by people who live outside the story (the dances by Pina Bausch that frame the movie, the concert by Caetano Veloso that occurs as an interlude), some of them given by characters within the narrative (Lydia with her bullfights, Benigno with his imposture). The film begins in a theater, where it brings you face to face with audience members like yourself; and the film ends in a theater, where two people seem to be sensing each other, happily, wordlessly, across the void of an empty seat.

But is the seat empty? It belongs, by implication, to a missing character; yet it also makes room for you—right in the center of the screen.

The Nation, December 9, 2002

Bad Education

As times change, so do the questions that a movie prompts. Had I seen Pedro Almodóvar's *Bad Education* in another season, I might have begun this review by asking about the new possibilities the movie finds in the old devices of film noir: the heartsick voiceover, the dark and secretive settings, the love object in the blond wig. Or, dazzled by the narrative structure, I might first have looked into Almodóvar's use of frames within frames: for example, the flashback envisioned by a man who is a character in another character's screenplay. The film's emphasis on reading deserves investigation—for the first half of *Bad Education*, people do almost nothing, on a literal level, except pore over texts—and so does the personality of the lead actor, Gael García Bernal, who is much more convincing here than as Che Guevara in *The Motorcycle Diaries*. (Why so? Because, unlike Che, his present character is *supposed* to put you in mind of Julia Roberts.)

I'd like to ponder all these matters. But I saw *Bad Education* in the last weeks of the election campaign, when the United States plunged further into the condition of a church-based autocracy; and so two questions about *Bad Education* obsess me above all others. Can Almodóvar be considered a political filmmaker? If so, what difference does it make?

Certainly his career has benefited from, and reflected, a great political change. Almodóvar made his first, short films in 1974-79, as Franco's church-based autocracy crumbled and fresh air came rushing into Spain. His first features, made in the early 1980s, breathed a druggie, anticlerical, polysexual atmosphere, which seemed designed (as J. Hoberman wrote) to give a heart attack to any senior Phalangist who strayed into the movie house. But if you think this information pins down Almodóvar's politics, you have temporarily forgotten the possible coincidence of queer fun and political reaction. (Witness *Interview* magazine in that same period, with its celebration of the world's most fabulous fascists.) Also, you might recall that Almodóvar's characters almost never discuss public events or try to influence them. Except for a single scene, involving a street demonstration—an action carried out by frustrated medical workers—politics as such have scarcely entered his films. So why do I keep wondering if *Bad Education* has a political nature?

No definite answer springs from the plot, or the fraction of it that I can reveal in good conscience. Enrique, a young filmmaker (Fele Martínez), is working in his deeply shadowed office one day in 1980, casting about for a story to tell, when an unexpected visitor drops by and announces himself as Ignacio, an old friend from boarding school (García Bernal). "My first love," says the wonderstruck filmmaker. The reunion falters slightly at first, then becomes more deeply awkward once the visitor explains that he is now a professional actor, who is available for work and also happens to have with him an original screenplay. Unable to beg off, Enrique agrees to read the script and soon discovers that it evokes his youth, when the two boys fell in love at a provincial Catholic school and were harshly separated by Father Manolo (Daniel Giménez-Cacho), a literature teacher with a tormented, hands-on infatuation with Ignacio.

That's a lot of domination for one movie—and we're still in the setup. Father Manolo, in the "true story" flashback, wields unjust authority over the boys; Ignacio, in the screenplay, returns to the school years later (as a blond drag artiste) to exert a dubious power of his own, by blackmailing the priest; and Enrique, in the present-day story, makes full use of his right to film the script or reject it, to hire the would-be actor or dismiss him. I suppose these contests could be called political, especially given the role in them of a large and forceful institution. (As Lenny Bruce used to say, it's the only *the* Church.) But as the film unfolds, its power relationships turn out to be unstable and are played out within an invariably intimate domain. The struggles enter the public arena only to the extent that they supply material for a film—and then it's an intensely personal movie, since Enrique not only puts his own story on screen but also serves as the unmistakable double of Pedro Almodóvar.

Once again, possible political meanings slip away; and yet, because of the film's chronology, they never disappear completely. The elaborate narrative scrambling in *Bad Education* forces you to notice that it's 1964 when the boys fall in love and are torn apart, in the depths of the dictatorship. When Ignacio returns as a blackmailing drag queen, it's 1977, when so much that had been repressed in Spain came bursting forth. Enrique decides to shoot Ignacio's script in 1980, when Almodóvar released his first feature. As I reflect on this time scheme, and on the facts that ultimately do not come out in Enrique's production, I am reminded of an eloquent passage in a recent article by Colm Tóibín, about the mood in Spain immediately after the dictatorship:

> History resided then in locked memories, half-told stories, unread archives. In some families the silence was complete; the children, as they grew up in the bright new democracy, simply did not know what their parents had done in the war. Many people born in the 1950s and 1960s have unfond memories of their father growing grumpier and more silent as the war was mentioned, or having one story, which seemed to mask other more dangerous stories, told over and over, until it came to resemble a bad alibi.

A bad alibi: When Almodóvar's early features came out, they too contained a silence beneath their insistent, hectic transgressions—a silence about the nature of the society that had given birth to the filmmaker, back in the 1950s, and had nurtured him to adulthood. To Almodóvar's fans, there was nothing significant about this omission. The mere existence of his movies was said to be revelatory enough; and faced with Almodóvar's extravagant talent, many of us who sensed something hollow in the fun were willing to put aside our doubts.

To Almodóvar's immense credit, though, he did not stop doubting. Starting about ten years ago (around the same time that he began to write *Bad Education*), he transformed his work, shifting its mode from travesty to melodrama and imbuing it with a new emotional maturity. Now, in *Bad Education*, he retraces his career to its beginning and, through the figure of Enrique, imputes to himself a guilty secret—not the worst secret that the characters bear, but creepy enough. Within the confessional setting of this film noir (so appropriate to the story's ecclesiastical background), Almodóvar owns up to having founded his work on dishonesty, manipulation and misdirection.

Perhaps you will interpret these sins as entirely personal. Maybe, going further, you will also see them as the source of artistic failings. (At the end of *Bad Education*, Enrique sets out to create films with "PASSION"—the word fills the screen—leaving us to wonder what truths might be obscured by those giant capital letters.) Or, thinking of the silences in post-Franco Spain, you might sense that the confession has wider implications. Surely it's significant, in a movie that's so concerned with reading, that when

Enrique scans the newspapers for story ideas, he never bothers with the front page but prefers to sift through the disasters and oddities in the column-fillers. Like all but the most scandalous and doomed of the characters, he's engaged in a strategy of avoidance—until the story of *Bad Education* breaks in on him.

So yes, Almodóvar may now be considered a political filmmaker. He is concerned here with the aftermath of the Franco period, rather than the religious dictatorship itself, and he focuses his attention narrowly, not on civic life but on the troubled personal responses of individuals. But, that said, he has now touched on the political context as never before, and in so doing has retrospectively deepened his entire body of work.

Does it make a difference?

As the shadows fall over my half of the population—the half that is taunted as "elite" while being utterly disempowered—I think that *Bad Education* may have something to tell us about living through the next years. Not that Almodóvar offers any advice. What he tells us becomes intelligible only on the actors' faces: the look of fear as two boys try to hide in a darkened bathroom; the visible anguish of a culpable priest praying for mercy; the contortions of self-righteousness and self-disgust that play across Enrique's features; and most fascinating of all, most unreliable, the multiple faces worn by García Bernal as victim, villain, ingénue and opportunist.

This is Almodóvar's version of political expression. Look: These are now our moral possibilities.

The Nation, November 29, 2004

Volver

The first time I watched Penélope Cruz lip-sync "Volver," the old song that lends its sentiments and title to Pedro Almodóvar's new film, I wept—though why, I couldn't have said. The voice was dubbed; the musical idiom had been shifted, with Spanish imperiousness, from tango to flamenco; and the character's deepest motivations could only be guessed at, since Almodóvar was waiting for the final reel to reveal them. As perfect moments go, this one was odd and incomplete; and yet, when a plump droplet spilled across Cruz's eyelashes, tears came to me, too.

The next time, of course, I was prepared. Now every implication of the scene was known; every seam of Almodóvar's narrative stitchery had been exposed. I wept even more, as the title might have foretold. *Volver*: to return. All the emotions came back.

What else returns in this beautifully improbable movie? The list might begin with an actress, Carmen Maura, who is closely identified with Almodóvar but had long been absent from his films. Next comes the character Maura plays: a ghostly mother who reinserts herself into her family's affairs, while giving off (despite death) the flatulent scent of life.

Then there's a repeated wrong. Years ago, Maura's character unwittingly harmed her daughter (Cruz), who now has done much the same to her own teenage child (the indelible Yohana Cobo). Like the wind-powered turbines you periodically see in this movie—the characters having come from a town of incessant gales, which are said to drive people crazy—the story keeps spinning back to these recurring elements, and more: a scuffed suitcase, a native landscape, a good deed, a corpse.

Memories of older films return as well, as they often do in Almodóvar's work. They are for him what biblical texts used to be for English poets: basic materials of thought. And so in *Volver* he imitates a bit of *Psycho* here, some *Mildred Pierce* there, to articulate his ideas. If I had to explain the themes in general terms, I'd say they concern the sin of not seeing what's before your eyes. *Volver* is about invisibility as a just punishment for this sin; about the false visibility, or self-exposure, promoted by a degraded form of show business; and about the revelations made possible, by contrast, through a true performance, which can be public and personal at the same time. Most of all, though, *Volver* is an exciting crime story, comedy and tear-jerker about the ways these themes may loop back through generations of women.

Which just goes to show you: To explain *Volver* in general is to explain nothing at all. That's why Almodóvar needs his scriptures, including (most significantly) a clip from Visconti's *Bellissima*. A segment of that film, appearing late in *Volver*, encapsulates the events as no synopsis could. It also transforms Cruz retrospectively into another example of something that returns. Implicitly, the excerpt makes her a double of *Bellissima*'s star, Anna Magnani.

As types, the two are not much alike, except for their swarming heaps of dark hair. Cruz pokes skyward instead of pulling toward the earth; she lingers over her emotions, nestling them within, rather than hurling them out impatiently. Whereas Magnani instinctively, famously, shouted for help, Cruz is capable of suffering in silence. But as Almodóvar knows, his star can stride through a working-class district with all the authority of her predecessor. She, too, can seem to carry in her limbs the weight of a long day's labor. And if her body is too finely drawn to be entirely convincing in her present role—"These characters are always big-assed women," Almodóvar has written, "and Penélope is too slim"—a loving director knows how to show off what flesh there is. In an early shot that summarizes much in *Volver* and foreshadows more, Almodóvar photographs Cruz from directly above, so that the perspective lines run down the inner surface of her breasts into the profound shadows of a cleavage that the costumer keeps perpetually exposed. The character is standing at a kitchen sink, stoically washing the evening's dishes, while you gaze over this site of troubled, uncontainable sexuality, looking down toward the object at the vanishing point: a very large, very sharp knife, which will only temporarily remain clean.

Of course, any dramatist can bring out a knife in act one. But once the knife has been used, it takes an Almodóvar to blend realism instantaneously into melodrama, and melodrama into a moment of comic relief that's cutting in its own right. First Cruz's character feels the full moral gravity of her situation; then, though worn out by a day on the job, she has to set to work again with mop and rubber gloves. When interrupted at her grim task by a knock on the door, she next must hold off a friendly but inquisitive neighbor. "Did you hurt yourself?" he asks solicitously, having noticed a splash of blood on her neck. Fortunately, Cruz knows what makes men look away. With a dismissive wave of her hand, she explains, "Female trouble."

I give away this joke—and only this one, I promise—because it so neatly demonstrates the superiority of *Volver*'s women to its men. For a long while, in fact, you might imagine there aren't any men, but only one man here, another there. Taken singly, they're pretty bad, or weakly good. Viewed in a cluster—as they're seen, I think, only once—they can literally make a character gasp.

The women, by contrast, are almost always shown in a group: organizing meals, doing one another's hair, exchanging stories, giving or receiving aid. Much of the buoyancy and humor of *Volver* comes from this female conviviality—as when, for example, Cruz abruptly goes into the restaurant business and elicits impromptu help from half her neighborhood. Even the ghostly mother wants to be sociable—which is why she gets rid of her veil of loose white hair, so she will no longer look like one of Mizoguchi's spirits dressed in a cheap housecoat. Some of *Volver*'s biggest laughs come from Maura's down-to-earth manner, as she overcomes the indignities involved in rejoining human company. (When put in a tight spot, she can't just vanish, as a normal ghost would. She needs to duck under the bed, with the smile of a kid playing hide-and-seek.) At the end, though, when she once more returns to her solitude—or almost goes back to it—the sweetness of Maura's resignation gives the film its deepest pathos.

For that final return, Maura steps back into a region of time-lessness—someplace that's separate from her daughter's world of bustle and worry ("I'm busy," Cruz continually complains) but is different as well from the conventional image of eternity. The film starts in a small-town cemetery, where women are busy cleaning the tombs. It concludes within the shadows of an old provincial house, where Maura will tend not a slab of marble but another woman's body and spirit. Sociability and hope win out in *Volver* over solitude and despair—tentatively, just a little—if only because "ghosts aren't supposed to cry."

The living may weep, though—which brings me back to that core scene in which Cruz performs the title song. I think "perform" is the right word, even though you hear someone else's voice, because Cruz makes her whole face sing: "Though time's passing, which wipes away the whole world/ By now has killed off my oldest, dearest dreams/Still I hold within me, hidden like a treasure/Just the simple hope to come back home."

Why is she crying out these lines, and crying over them? On the public level, she is thanking the patrons of her restaurant, and maybe showing off a little for them. More privately, she sings because her mother, who's been lost, taught her "Volver" many years ago, and now she wants to give this song to her own daughter, who came close to being lost.

Cruz sings in two directions at once, to the past and the future, weeping for both. And if on first viewing you don't fully understand why she feels as she does, you weep for her anyway, just because she's there, in the present, alive. You, as her audience, help to make her so.

The Nation, November 20, 2006

Hard Facts

Domestic Violence

Frederick Wiseman has spent a lifetime piecing together sounds and images captured from the daily flow. These patchwork projections of our common life play across the screen without voice-overs, written texts or talking heads—with no explanation at all, except for the baldest statement of subject matter. *High School, Hospital, Public Housing*: Weigh these brief titles against the ensuing events—three or four hours' worth of them, usually—and you understand that Wiseman's concerns are both social and philosophical. How much experience must we accumulate to gain a little knowledge? How much, or how little, does our knowledge inform the evidence of our senses?

In his latest documentary, *Domestic Violence*, Wiseman reveals that this philosophy can be a matter of life and death.

Imagine a cramped house somewhere in Tampa, Florida, late at night. In rooms where the lights are turned low or turned off, the camera's lamp casts a glare over bare walls, sparse and rumpled furniture, and the thin, shirtless torso of a man. He has the hair and mustache of George Armstrong Custer and a low-voiced drawl to match, deployed with pride in his vocabulary and a drunkard's pretense of self-possession. He is the one who called the police, and who greets them with a long-neck beer in his hand. He says he wants no trouble to arise from his dispute with the woman in the bedroom.

On the face of it, the man's complaint might seem plausible: He wants the woman to leave his property, and she won't. But since, by his own admission, she has lived there for nine months— long enough to establish legal residence—the two cops must take General Custer into the next room, to consult with the other party about her wishes. They find her holding on to the bed as if it were a lifeboat, from which she might be tossed at any moment. She says she has a bad bladder infection; she says she's exhausted; she says she'll be willing to leave in the morning, but for now she has to sleep. Most of these pleas emerge through tears, the hands raised in exasperation, the face averted. You see little more of the woman than a blond ponytail and a baggy T-shirt, even when the key words pop out: The man recently shot at her with a rifle.

At this assertion, the male cop glances toward the female, who nods. Yes, Custer had been arrested and released not long ago. "I'm really scared of him," the woman says, weeping. So why did she come back to his house? "I have nowhere else to go," she wails, as if she's both desperate and fed up with the question. Will she now let the cops take her someplace safe? "I'll sleep on the couch," she insists, and on her way through the doorway she brushes past Custer. He has just promised the cops that if she stays, it won't be a peaceful night.

This scene is the conclusion of *Domestic Violence*. I give a lengthy account of it not to convey its impact—how could I even approach the horror?—but to testify that the surface details mean much more than they would have, had you witnessed them earlier in the film. On a philosophical level, the scene's placement at the end of the film amounts to an empirical proof: What you've learned changes your understanding of what you see and hear. On the human level, what you see and hear amounts to utter catastrophe. Because this woman has not learned certain lessons that other women in the film have absorbed, she understands her situation in a way that's likely to get her killed.

Wiseman brings us to this terrible knowledge by giving *Domestic Violence* a double structure. On one level, the film plays as a linear progression, taking place over the course of weeks or months. We follow a number of women and their children as they move out of abusive situations and into a shelter, where they begin to take control of their lives. On another level, the film plays as a cycle, which seems (through clever editing) to take place over the course of one day. We start by visiting scenes of abuse in the hours after dawn; we end at night, with one more devastating episode of violence.

These two kinds of time do more than overlap in *Domestic Violence*; they yield an intolerable tension. When night falls and we find ourselves back in hell, sliding down one more turn of the spiral, we don't despair—we revolt, because we've seen that there's a way out of the cycle.

This double movement begins with images of blue skies and white clouds over downtown Tampa. Office towers gleam in the early light; the world looks peaceful and clean. It takes only a few shots of highway traffic, though, to lead to another Tampa: a city of squat bungalows, housing projects with boarded-up windows and dirt yards, strip malls with flashing signs for pawnbrokers and "Full Liquor Topless." "It's a real bad neighborhood," a helpful citizen comments, as a bloodied woman is wheeled away from her home on a gurney. "Drugs, prostitution... Myself, I'd be scared to raise kids around here."

You're privileged to hear these words because Wiseman and his cinematographer, John Davey, rode along with the Tampa police as they responded to complaints of domestic violence. Apart from being astonished at the filmmakers' skill—how did they catch these scenes without spooking anybody?—you're also likely to be impressed by the grimness of the settings and the patience of the cops. For the moment, *Domestic Violence* plays out on a terrain of material need and armed legal force. The trickier ground is still to come.

It's the ground of the victims' emotions. Wiseman begins to enter this territory through scenes shot at a crisis center, where counselors take phone calls from women hoping to flee their homes. "Listen, Karen," one of the counselors says in close-up, "no one is going to judge you. You have been wronged. We do have a shelter that you can come to. No, you can't bring your bird. What kind of a bird do you have? We have a counselor here who knows a lot about birds."

Next come scenes in which women enter a shelter called The Spring. ("Has he ever threatened to kill you or himself?" asks one of the counselors, going down her list of screening questions. The newcomer thinks it over. "Me," she says.) Although a staff member of The Spring later points out, emphatically, that men may also be battered, everyone we see at this point is female: both the new clients of the shelter and the workers who provide their point of entry. Male counselors will pop up later; but for now it's the trustworthy female staffers who take down the inventory of abuse: verbal, financial, social, physical. They get the newcomers settled into their rooms, rustle up clothes as needed, talk about goals. They are so empathetic, they can turn a check for head lice into an occasion for encouragement.

Now, the initiation done, we get to the film's heart: group discussions among the adult women and classroom sessions with their children. As the mothers know, these two things are one. The women tell one another about childhoods steeped in fear, shame and deprivation. They recall how they learned to expect battering, and even to accept it. They ask how to save their kids from replicating their lives of violence.

You've heard all this before: Abuse begets more abuse. You can mouth the sentence as you would the brief, bland syllables of Wiseman's title. But here, underlying the words, is experience. You see women with scars on their faces, scabs across the nose, bruises on the arms. You learn about a terror that was so intense, its victim was willing to live with half her face reduced to a pulp rather than leave the man who took a crowbar to her. The language of psychological uplift isn't stale to these women, who bear in their flesh the marks of low self-esteem. The words they learn at The Spring are a revelation to them, and a potential lifeline to their children.

That's why the final, nighttime episode of *Domestic Violence* fills you with such outrage. You now know, in your gut, why the victim doesn't leave—even with the man threatening her to her face, even with the cops offering a way out. Faced with this awful realization, you might feel it inadequate to say she's been beaten into cooperating with General Custer. Such a statement comes close to blaming the woman for her suffering; it amounts to mere words.

But here's what's even more awful: For lack of those words, she might suffer till she dies.

The Nation, March 4, 2002

Our Brand Is Crisis

When a political consultant plans to smear someone "in a way that cannot be connected to us," he probably should not explain this scheme to his client while a documentarian stands nearby with a video camera. The dumb violation of this rule, by someone who is paid to be smart, turns out to be among the smaller ironies in Rachel Boynton's *Our Brand Is Crisis,* a feature-length account of the work done by the US firm of Greenberg Carville Shrum during the 2002 election in Bolivia.

The biggest irony: After maneuvering its candidate into the presidency, by a margin so slight it could have been attributed to humidity, the GCS team saw him chased from the country only a few months later, amid clouds of tear gas and the cries of the wounded. "What went wrong?" asks Boynton, off camera, to GCS pollster Jeremy Rosner.

"There are conditions," he replies, "that democracy ultimately can't deal with."

Rosner is a likable man—soft-spoken, smiling, blatantly thoughtful, like a Reform rabbi who talks football at dinner parties—and so you hesitate to blame him personally for this world-historical shrug. The problem explored in *Our Brand Is Crisis*—vividly, though far from completely—does not lie in individuals but in the accepted definition of "democracy," whether peddled in Bolivia by GCS, in Iraq by Paul Bremer and the Lincoln Group or in (you supply the name) by the World Bank and the International Monetary Fund.

But enough of the general problem. Let's follow Rachel Boynton's example and get down to cases.

In 2002 the wealthy businessman Gonzalo Sanchez de Lozada (known as Goni) hired GCS to advise him on his run for the presidency. At the time, he was dead in the polls. Most voters thought his name was synonymous with "unemployment," since the policies he had pursued during an earlier term as president, from 1993 to 1997, had invited foreign corporations to buy large chunks of previously state-owned companies and then permitted them to cut their workforce. Goni claimed that as a result of his "capitalization" program, 500,000 people now held new jobs; but few Bolivians, apparently, had seen one of these recent hires in the mirror. To a very large segment of the public, Goni was a failure: remote, arrogant, representative of the past (he was in his 70s) and suspiciously North American. Having grown up in the United States, he spoke Spanish with a broad Chicago accent.

But to the consultants from GCS, these were faults of image, not substance. They liked Goni's version of free trade and privatization. ("This guy had the best formula for getting his country out of poverty," Rosner insists.) They probably liked his Chicago English, too, and his Bill Clinton hair. Goni is the sort of man with whom North American elites can feel comfortable. GCS just needed to figure out how to sell him to an electorate that is overwhelmingly poor and Indian. Boynton shows how it was done, through a process the GCS operatives surprisingly allowed her to document, perhaps through an arrogance of their own, or perhaps through a conviction that their beliefs are self-evidently correct. As Rosner explained to Boynton, the GCS brand is "progressive politics for a profit."

For Goni, though, the brand was crisis.

GCS told him to repeat, at every rally and in every interview, that Bolivia had reached a point of no return. He would save the country from this crisis. His GCS slogan, emblazoned on every banner, poster and TV commercial, declared "¡Sí se puede!" ("Yes we can!") To insure that Goni stayed on message, GCS limited him to one daily appearance: the "photo of the day." Focus groups, convened and studied by Rosner, allowed GCS to check the response of ordinary Bolivians to each particular of the campaign, with the richly comic result that Goni's poll numbers went into immediate decline.

The candidate in the lead was Manfred Reyes Villa, mayor of Cochabamba. *Our Brand Is Crisis* takes note of Reyes Villa's success more or less as the GCS team did, as a strategic challenge for the Goni campaign to overcome rather than as a substantive matter to investigate—an understandable choice (since Boynton couldn't include everything) but one that left an opportunity unexplored. Boynton might have helped viewers understand why Goni was so unpopular, and why Reyes Villa's city had something to do with it, if she had only acknowledged the so-called water revolt, which had convulsed Cochabamba two years earlier.

In 1999 the Bolivian government had leased Cochabamba's water supply to a private company, founded and controlled by the Bechtel corporation. Almost at once, people were hit with rate increases as high as 200 percent. According to eyewitness reports by Jim Shultz (who won a Project Censored award for his stories), a family living on the minimum wage of $60 a month suddenly had to pay a quarter of its income to keep the tap open. By mid-April 2000, after general strikes and bloody riots, Cochabamba's citizens succeeded in driving Bechtel from town, forcing the government to cancel the water contract.

Although the Bechtel contract was not signed during Goni's presidency, jockeying for the water rights had begun while he was in office, and the spirit of the enterprise was not unfamiliar to him. Voters everywhere in Bolivia knew this; but the GCS consultants clearly did not care, and Boynton, behaving a bit too much like her subjects, does not even mention the revolt. Relying on a direct cinema approach, for both good and ill, she sticks with the events she could capture firsthand.

These include the launch of a negative TV commercial against Cochabamba's mayor. I have already mentioned Boynton's stunning success in recording the planning session. Now I should note the success of GCS's negative campaign. A few sneering questions about Reyes Villa's income, a single old photograph of him in military uniform, and the frontrunner's poll numbers dropped. In yet another irony—hilarious or not, you decide—GCS got further, unexpected help from the US ambassador, who stepped into the campaign with a denunciation of another candidate, Evo Morales. On the strength of this recommendation, Morales surged in the polls, probably drawing voters away from Reyes Villa, and Goni moved into a dead heat with the frontrunner.

Now Bolivia was ready for James Carville. Few voters would have unbent themselves from their daily burdens to rise and stare at his advent; but every viewer of Boynton's film will thrill to the glittering eyes, the wolfish grin, the surplus of patter above matter that make him a star. Carville rightfully became a leading man in 1993, with Chris Hegedus and D.A. Pennebaker's documentary *The War Room*, and he has now played himself (or someone just like him) in perhaps a dozen movies and TV shows, including the unfairly maligned *K Street* (which he helped produce). He is now more than a consultant and more than a media personality. He has become, in himself, a moving-image genre, which assimilates real-world events into the category of "a James Carville picture." He did it with *Our Brand Is Crisis*, too, without even giving Boynton much of his screen time.

I don't mean this as a criticism of Boynton. She has put together an absurdly funny, sometimes horrifying, frequently revelatory documentary that clearly begins from the model of *The War Room* (or the earlier *Primary*) but then ventures into important new territory. Let everyone watch *Our Brand Is Crisis*. When you see it, though, maybe you'll sigh, as I did, at the disastrous story arc that is now integral to the James Carville genre.

Are Carville's clients more enlightened than Karl Rove's, his business practices more ethical, his political beliefs more humane? Sure. And Goni, for all I know, might indeed have had the best program of any candidate in 2002. (There were a lot of candidates—and Goni, despite his faults, had made some real advances during his first presidency.) But as *Our Brand Is Crisis* makes clear, with its scenes of chaos following Goni's squeak to victory, elections ought to be about something more than steaming up people's emotions, venting the pressure and then hoping the populace will simmer down again, so the work of capital markets may go on undisturbed. "There are conditions," as Rosner said, "that democracy ultimately can't deal with." But this is "democracy" as Ben Sonnenberg has mordantly defined it: "the Christianity of capitalism."

At the end of *Our Brand Is Crisis*, you see Jeremy Rosner, the true believer, speak with revulsion of the rise of Evo Morales—an ascension that Rosner and GCS did their unwitting bit to assist. Morales, in Rosner's view, is an "irresponsible populist." Maybe.

But what of the irresponsible democracy peddlers?

The Nation, March 13, 2006

Into Great Silence

Carthusian monks do not ordinarily allow visitors into their charterhouses, let alone visitors with cameras; but when German filmmaker Philip Gröning asked if he might document the order's founding monastery, La Grande Chartreuse, the fathers kindly said they'd think about it. Sixteen years later, having thought enough, they wrote back to him with permission to make *Into Great Silence.*

These are people who do not like to be hurried, or disturbed. They share just one meal a week, on Sunday, and speak freely to one another only on their weekly walk. Otherwise, for the great majority of the day and night, each monk studies and prays alone in his cell, or does chores at the greatest feasible remove from his fellows. You can picture the bafflement of these men in 1984, when Gröning proposed that his film would help publicize them. You can imagine how much Gröning must have changed by 2000, to be ready to devote six months to living and working in La Grande Chartreuse, handling all the equipment by himself and shooting without lights, so as not to distract the monks.

Because Gröning worked within these limits, you see in his film only the Vermeer light of sunshine as it rakes through a garden window and burnishes a cell's wooden floor; the veiled light of a gray sky thick with snowflakes; the contained red fury of candlelight magnified through glass in an extreme close-up; the isolated, floating pools of light, separated by sheer blackness, in which the monks sit in the midnight chapel, chanting their prayers. Very often, too, light varies within a single shot, as when Gröning shows you a time-lapse view of an Alpine valley, with dawn fog drifting away in the brightening sun to reveal the distant cloister. By the end of *Into Great Silence,* after you've spent 162 minutes of contemplating the monks and their experience, you may wonder whether the better part of our lives is spent just registering the changing light. But then, if we were to stop chattering, we also might register the infinite gradations of sound you hear in the film: creaking floorboards, rustling broadcloth, a shovel's rasp in winter, birdsong in spring and the ringing of bells every day, all day and night long.

By practicing a simplicity like that of the monks themselves, *Into Great Silence* sharpens your senses and, even more, your awareness of time. You receive no theology from the film, apart from a scene at the weekly communal meal where a monk reads aloud from the works of St. Bruno of Cologne; but gradually, you do get the impression that something immaterial has become present before you, in a kind of time that does not fly or drag or even pass but stays with each monk like a companion.

When time behaves like this there's no story to give away, so you won't object to knowing that the film begins and ends in winter, with identical shots of prayer, falling snow and candlelight. In the middle, as you'd expect, there's a thaw, and summer comes. Toward the beginning of the film, you see two young novices being admitted to the monastery. (The more conspicuous of them is an African named Benjamin.) Toward the end, you see a very old and infirm monk lying in bed, preparing to take his leave. In the life of La Grande Chartreuse, these are big events, which you come to understand aren't events at all. They're more like threads in the fabric that a stooped, long-bearded monk measures out in his attic workshop so he can sew a robe for Benjamin—fabric that another tailor will someday use for patches when Benjamin no longer needs it.

You will notice, by the way, that when Benjamin is formally accepted into the monastery, he passes down a row of seated monks, each of whom rises in turn to embrace the novice and then silently raises his cowl, as if resuming his isolation even in the midst of ceremony. Part of the challenge that Gröning faced was to convey solitude as the essential experience of La Grande Chartreuse while allowing viewers the periodic relief of scenes of human contact. Of these, the most unexpected and exhilarating comes near the end, when the monks go for their walk. Fresh snow has fallen, and so the men, seen in a static long shot, trudge up a hillside and then slide down on improvised skis, or just their bottoms, with their whoops and laughter echoing across the valley. Almost as surprising is a scene of barbering, where the monks groom one another with electric clippers that dangle from an overhead cord. (What's startling isn't so much the technology as the noise.) The most moving of these quasi-sociable scenes, though, is the one in which one monk nurses another by spreading ointment on his limbs. The emotional warmth is palpable; the sight of hands on bare flesh, almost shocking.

I come to the aspect of *Into Great Silence* that may be called experimental, or even underground. In the days of the Warhol Factory, Parker Tyler wrote that the essence of underground cinema is to show things you're not supposed to see. In the 1960s, this material was mostly sexual. Today, when perversion has been superseded by niche marketing, Gröning has found in the hermit's cell one of the few remaining zones that the camera is forbidden to penetrate.

So I don't think I'm merely free-associating when I say that a recurring feature of *Into Great Silence*—a series of protracted shots in which the monks sit one by one for their portraits—is a deliberate imitation of Warhol's *Screen Tests*. For the unsurpassably worldly New Yorkers of Warhol's little films, Gröning has substituted the least worldly of people; but his portraits of the monks still offer a suggestion of underground thrills, and even sex. "You have seduced me, Lord," reads a text before each series of these shots, "and I let myself be seduced."

This hint of the taboo may explain my feelings about a stunning moment that comes late in the film, during another of those leisurely views of a monk praying in his cell. After kneeling for quite a while at his bench, the man rises, then unexpectedly approaches the camera, looks directly at Gröning and smiles. In his expression I saw pleasant fatigue, and calm acceptance of Gröning. But there was something more, perhaps: a trace of cockiness, such as you might see in someone who was glad to have been filmed making love.

Love-making in the mundane sense, of course, goes unseen in *Into Great Silence*, though you might wonder about its chances of happening. Liqueur-making certainly takes place, but you don't see any of that, either. I suppose the process is proprietary. But nothing other than that trade secret seems to have been hidden from Gröning, who was allowed to study the monastery in such detail that when he photographed the chapel font in close-up, he captured the surface tension on the water. Thanks to Gröning's care, every tick of the anteroom's wall clock, every passage of footsteps down the vaulted corridor, every fold in a monk's robe or wrinkle beside his eyes or brush of his fingertip against a book's yellowed pages fixes you with the force of an intimate revelation.

Here is a lifetime's worth of spiritual exertion and physical labor, which has been compressed into the six months of Gröning's stay in the monastery and then further distilled into a little more than two and a half hours of film. Rarely is time so intensified, or so pure. If you want the experience, you need just a little patience.

The Nation, March 12, 2007

12th & Delaware

The most suspenseful movie I have seen in a long time, with the most unsettling characters and the most devastating conclusion, recently enjoyed its New York theatrical premiere and then closed on the same evening. Ordinarily, I would call this an injustice; but there is really nothing unfair about the reception given so far to Heidi Ewing and Rachel Grady's *12th & Delaware*, unless it's the assumption that a documentary selection of the annual Human Rights Watch Film Festival (where this picture was the opening-night feature) must be the cinematic equivalent of boiled leafy vegetables. Yes, *12th & Delaware* might be good for you. But given the film's effect on the heart rate, I'd say the kind of good it delivers is closer to what you'd get from an aerobic workout—an effect you will be able to experience when HBO broadcasts the movie on August 2, as part of its new season of documentaries.

The topic is the campaign against abortion, as played out at the title intersection in Fort Pierce, Florida, on a street corner where tangles of low-slung electrical cables droop over shed-like ranch houses and their strips of sidewalk, a little more than 100 miles up from Miami along Interstate 95. Here, in a building that's been painted orange so clients can spot it easily, a married couple, Candace and Arnold, have run an abortion clinic for many years; while more recently, across the street, a Catholic group has converted the facing property into something it calls a pregnancy care center. Listen to the members of the antiabortion group, and you hear that the center speaks on behalf of unborn children and persuades mothers not to commit a grievous sin. Watch what the center does, and you see that it mostly waylays the confused (who were looking for the clinic); offers free ultrasounds captioned "Hi Mommy" (along with medically inaccurate brochures and blood-curdling video screenings); and provides a base for the day-long demonstrations and one-sided shouting matches that the group mounts across the street.

Granted, the characterization I've just given is based entirely on the evidence that Ewing and Grady chose to present in *12th & Delaware*. But that's just the point. Ewing and Grady won extraordinary, prolonged, close access to both the clients and the personnel of the pregnancy care center—notably its director, a petite, pinch-featured, middle-aged woman named Anne Lotierzo, who opened her consulting rooms to the filmmakers, walked around wearing their radio microphone (so her words could be picked up at a distance) and seems never to have bothered to watch what she said or did. Pretty much the whole first half of *12th & Delaware* is shot among Lotierzo's circle, and mostly within her pseudo clinic. In the course of this immersion into one local instance of the anti-abortion movement, you see Lotierzo rig evidence, peddle falsehoods, browbeat and condescend. Anything goes, apparently, for reasons best articulated by Lotierzo's spiritual adviser, Father Tom Euteneuer, when he explains (in a sermon delivered in church) that the fight is against "the powers of darkness." The abortion industry, he preaches, is "looking more and more like a diabolical religion"—a ritualized blood sacrifice offered on the perverse altar of an operating table. "There's got to be demons involved in that."

From this detail and many others in the first half of *12th & Delaware*, you may derive the unhappy lesson that the conflict over abortion probably will not be resolved by reasoned compromise. ("I know it will end," Lotierzo says. "I just don't think it's going to be...pretty.") From the second half of the film, shot in large measure within the abortion clinic, you may learn what it means to seek medical treatment, and give it, under siege.

A door that you had seen only from the outside now closes as you watch from within; and with this elegant transition, the film moves to the other side of Twelfth Street, where there's a lot of peering through the slats of Venetian blinds, scanning the screens of surveillance monitors and leafing through a scrapbook of news reports about the violent deaths of abortion doctors. (The film was made in the wake of the 2009 murder of Dr. George Tiller.) With the picketers pressing within a millimeter of the legal limit whenever Arnold drives in or out of the clinic, and with some of the angrier protesters walking up to the windows to bellow at the women inside, the possibility of violence is part of the atmosphere, like the Florida humidity. You see how it weighs on Candace—though she bears up well with her gentle, solicitous manner and comfortably plump physique. A whim of the God of documentaries: the abortion provider turns out to be the most maternal figure in *12th & Delaware*.

So tense and compelling is the film in its matched claustrophobias—moral on one side of the street, physical on the other—that one scene even made me wonder whether Ewing and Grady had needed to intervene. An ethical borderline was clearly crossed when the most threatening of the antiabortion protesters, a hulking man with a shaved head and a propensity for rage, managed to identify one of the abortion doctors. It was standard practice, you see, for Arnold to pick up the doctors at remote locations (in this case the parking lot of a Wal-Mart) and throw a sheet over them, which the doctors would not remove until the clinic's garage door had safely closed. This system broke down on a day when the filmmakers took a ride with Hulk and witnessed him locate an abortion doctor's car and write down its license plate number. With great satisfaction, he remarked (on camera) that he was going to pass this information to some people who would "know what to do with it."

I asked Ewing, via e-mail, whether she and Grady had warned the doctor. "We first immediately investigated whether an illegal act had taken place in our presence and if we were required to contact the authorities," she replied. "It turned out the pro-life subject had not broken the law but we felt compelled to contact the appropriate party who would inform the doctor and the driver to change their meeting point."

That making *12th & Delaware* could put Ewing and Grady into this situation—and that watching the result can in effect do the same to you—is a sign of the film's strength and daring. The sign of its terrible sorrow is that the filmmakers could not step in for the people who most needed intervention: women pregnant at 15, or pregnant by men they feared, or pregnant with their sixth child when they had no resources for the existing five. These were, these are, the women caught between Lotierzo's version of help on one side of Twelfth Street and a line of angry demonstrators on the other. For them, the best Ewing and Grady could do was bear witness.

You should, too.

The Nation, July 12, 2010

Nostalgia for the Light

From the great documentarian Patricio Guzmán (*The Battle of Chile*) comes a stunningly beautiful essay film, *Nostalgia for the Light*, set at once in Chile's utterly barren Atacama desert, in troubled human memory and in the vastness of intergalactic space. As Guzmán notes in voiceover, the Atacama has almost no humidity (it is the only brown spot on our planet, as seen from space), and so it's ideal for studying both the stars and prehistory. You see perfectly preserved petroglyphs of ancient Indian peoples; and you see clusters of astronomical observatories—white-domed scientific mosques under a uniformly blue sky—which record gorgeous tracks of light from a million years ago. You also see corpses. The Atacama is where miners labored and died in the nineteenth century (the little forests of their grave markers are the only vegetation in sight), and where the Pinochet regime dumped many of its victims in the twentieth. There are women who still go into the desert, day after day, looking for fragments of bones of their loved ones. Now grown old in their work but determined to continue, the film's Victoria and Violeta are two more researchers into the past, just like the archaeologists and astronomers.

Nostalgia for the Light is dealing, then, with time at three different scales; with a varied and compelling set of witnesses and explainers; with the harsh mysteries of one of the most extraordinary places on earth; and above all with responsibility—to ourselves, our society, our species. I don't know how you can put more into a film, or make one that's more deeply moving.

The Nation, March 21, 2011

Pina

For a lively movie about death—one that will easily make it onto my twenty-best list for 2011, or even some versions of my ten-best list—let me recommend *Pina*, a documentary by Wim Wenders about the work of the late Pina Bausch and her company, the Tanztheater Wuppertal in Germany.

I mention the company especially because Wenders has filled the movie with individual testimonies from Bausch's dancers and longtime collaborators, often preceding or following the spoken account with a scene of that particular artist in action. The little speeches, recorded after Bausch's death, are in essence eulogies, which sometimes give an unnerving impression of abasement before the Great Leader. (Her eyes were always on me; she saw into my thoughts and spoke just one word; I struggled to discover what she wanted me to give her.) But they also offer great insight into the singular physiques and personalities that Bausch brought together in the dances you see generously excerpted in the film: *Le Sacre du Printemps*, *Café Müller*, *Vollmond* and *Kontakthof*.

Wenders shot these productions, performed at the Wuppertal theater, in 3-D, and his use of the technique is nothing less than revelatory. Sometimes you float among the dancers; sometimes you soar back from them and see them arrayed like living pop-up figures. You experience the space of the stage as Bausch and her company do, or, as a magical alternative, see it through the eyes of the production designers, who examine their proposed sets in little boxes that suddenly become populated by the tiny, animated figures of the company. Perhaps most stunning, some of the pieces burst out of the theater and into the real, 3-D world, as the dancers perform in street traffic, on a traveling monorail, up the side of a mountain.

What's most moving about *Pina*, though, is not the sense of space but of time: the sections of old black-and-white, 2-D images of Bausch that show how the years passed, and the amazingly jaunty *danse macabre* by Bausch that Wenders weaves repeatedly through the film. Her entire company, arrayed in a line, struts slowly through different scenes to an old-time jazz tune, smiling as they perform a simple repertoire of hand gestures to show the cycle of the seasons, again and again. Hello, life. Goodbye, life. Just passing through. Swell to be here while it lasts.

The Nation, January 23, 2012

How to Survive a Plague

This might sound like stereotyping, but I was around back then and I know: many of the people featured in David France's moving and invigorating history of AIDS activism took an interest in old films. Thinking about the cinephiles among them, living and dead, and the commitment to human dignity that they continue to inspire, I began to wonder halfway through the movie if France should have borrowed a title from the 1940s and called his documentary *Why We Fight*.

The name certainly would have fit this record of relentless struggle, but on further reflection, I realized that any implied comparison between this film and Frank Capra's wartime propaganda series would have been unjust. France's work is more honest in its mode of addressing the audience than Capra's, more heartfelt and nuanced. Besides, the title that France actually chose, *How to Survive a Plague*, does more to capture the sense of immediate risk that was common among the collective heroes of his documentary, the members of ACT UP (AIDS Coalition to Unleash Power). The words also hint at the ultimate success of these people in the face of terrible odds, the uproarious do-it-yourself spirit they often displayed and, above all, their talent for developing the guidebooks they desperately needed—and that nobody else was going to write.

For those who have forgotten or didn't know, *How to Survive a Plague* recalls that ACT UP produced more in the way of paper goods than posters, signboards and manifestoes. Its members also researched and wrote their own medical glossary on AIDS, the first national treatment-research agenda and eventually a reorganization plan for the National Institutes of Health, which under Senator Ted Kennedy's auspices was incorporated into law. This was the self-help, policy-wonk aspect of ACT UP, which set a standard of effectiveness among recent activist movements that probably remains unsurpassed.

In its other main aspect, without which the treatment researchers arguably would have been left silent and invisible, ACT UP produced furiously inventive street theater and miles and miles of videotape. From the very start, in 1987, the fans of old movies in the group—as well as the publicists, artists and media industry professionals—showed up at every meeting and demonstration with camcorders in hand.

As a print journalist at the time, reporting on the epidemic from within, France had only a pen and a notepad. But he remembered all those camcorders—and to make this documentary (which is, remarkably, his first film), he set about locating and studying the scattered tapes. By his reckoning, he eventually assembled 700 hours of material, recorded by thirty different individuals and groups, in order to choose what to show, helped by the editors T. Woody Richman and Tyler Walk.

Thanks to their selection, you suddenly find yourself in a columned meeting hall at the Lesbian and Gay Community Center in Greenwich Village, under an old stamped-tin ceiling bristling with fans and exposed pipes. You scan the faces of the men and women crowded together—so many of them looking so young, and all the more heartbreaking for the ghostly contrasts in the images—and listen to an excited announcement that in just twelve hours, this group is going to Take! Over! City! Hall!

Anger dominates the ensuing montage of early demonstrations: on Wall Street, where the group protested the impossibly high cost of AZT, the only drug then approved for managing HIV infection; at St. Vincent's Hospital, where a kiss-in (more aggressive than it sounds) jammed the rooms where people with AIDS were often denied treatment—and sometimes roughed up in the process; and at City Hall, where some 5,000 people railed against Mayor Ed Koch and his administration for practicing the silence that ACT UP famously equated with death. Outbursts were only to be expected. (If you don't know or have since forgotten, France provides vintage examples of the public discourse of Senator Jesse Helms and Cardinal John O'Connor.) It's striking, though, to see that even as the group's emotive tactics channeled rage outward on the street, within the walls of its home base—at least in the early stage of ACT UP's history—the keynote was not anger but a contagious exuberance.

Maybe it was the way high spirits spread throughout the group that enabled them to be generated at all—a possibility that comes to mind as France jumps from the meetings and street actions to introduce his key figures and the burdens they individually bore. Peter Staley, one of the people in the film who more or less represent ACT UP's treatment and research side, recalls how he watched the early Wall Street demonstration from the sidelines as a deeply closeted bond trader—someone whose workplace mentor casually remarked that the marchers deserved to die for taking it up the ass. Bob Rafsky, prominent among the figures in the film who more or less represent the street-action side, had worked in public relations until he fell ill. He was the heckler to whom candidate Bill Clinton said, in 1992, "I feel your pain." Videos of Rafsky's family birthday parties become a poignant motif throughout the film, as his beautiful young daughter gets older and Rafsky himself grows weaker.

Larry Kramer, chief instigator of ACT UP, also makes a few appearances, notably in a scene where he erupts during the group's later period of infighting. France has no hagiographic delusions and so documents the self-doubt that settled in once the AZT that the group fought so hard to secure didn't pan out as the magic bullet many had first hoped; the mutual suspicion and hostility that took hold as tactics diverged and class divisions seemed to open; the anger that turned inward as the death rate accelerated with no hope in sight. Kramer could scold a fractious meeting into order with his Jewish mother act: "We are in a plague, and this is how you behave?" But high spirits did not return until a new class of drugs that ACT UP members had pushed for and helped shepherd through clinical trials—protease inhibitors—came into use and suddenly tamped down the virus.

One of the lessons that might be drawn is that when you think you're already doomed, there's no point in giving up. In a *60 Minutes* interview from 1992 that France cuts into the film, Ed Bradley asked Peter Staley and others, "Do you expect to live to see a cure?" One after another, the answer is no. But at the end of the film, in one of France's most stirring sequences, you see the middle-aged faces of Staley and a half-dozen fellow activists as they appear today, having made good on the title.

Like the very best documentaries about political movements, *How to Survive a Plague* makes you feel humble and, at the same time, extraordinarily proud.

The Nation, October 1, 2012

The Act of Killing

The silence has recently begun to lift on the state-organized, American-backed massacre of civilians in Indonesia in 1965—66, a slaughter so widespread that some have called it genocide. In 2010, for example, Indonesia's Constitutional Court made it legal (within limits) to publish the testimony of survivors, and in the past several years hundreds of witnesses have had the courage to speak. Still, the pall of the massacre hangs so heavily over the country that a number of the Indonesians who helped Joshua Oppenheimer make his documentary *The Act of Killing* prefer to be listed in the credits as "Anonymous." On the film's evidence, which varies in strength from hair-raising to mind-boggling, the regime that consolidated its power half a century ago remains proudly in control, and the killers, at every level of society, are not only unrepentant but boastful about their crimes.

Imagine seeing Indonesia's vice president address a large para-military organization, Pancasila Youth, to thank it for its support, to praise gangsters and vigilantes for having made the country free, and to encourage these quasi-official thugs to continue to threaten violence. That's the sort of outrageous moral inversion that *The Act of Killing* documents at base level, when the filmmaking method is plain point-and-shoot. For the real kick, look to the more ambitious scenes documented within the mind of Anwar Congo, one of the men in North Sumatra who did the hands-on killing.

A so-called movie gangster, who made a living in the early 1960s by scalping tickets at Medan's theaters, the slim, halo-haired, grandfatherly Congo seems to have been more than willing to speak on camera about the murders he was recruited to commit. (He is often accompanied in these scenes by a sidekick, Herman Koto, who seems too young to have joined in the slaughter of 1965—66, but who cheerfully associates himself with it anyway.) Congo was not content merely to reminisce for Oppenheimer, or even to demonstrate his favorite method—garroting—at the actual site of the crimes. According to an essay by Oppenheimer that appears on the film's website and in its production notes, Congo and Koto were eager to re-create the murders as scenes from the types of films they love—crime thrillers, war movies, westerns—with themselves as the stars.

I can't say to what degree they volunteered this idea and to what extent Oppenheimer elicited it from them. (The film, as distinguished from Oppenheimer's written account of it, is full of deliberately unresolved puzzles and oddities.) All I know is that *The Act of Killing* begins inside a couple of these cinematic deliriums, which Oppenheimer realized according to Congo's instructions, and never fully emerges after that from a tone of bizarre fantasy.

In between the passages of real-world reportage, you see heads sawed off (from stage-prop dummies), faces beaten raw (or rather covered in horror-movie makeup), cowboys saddling up to kill the Commies (urged on by Koto in a dance hall madam's gown), and 1940s cops (or are they gangsters?) giving the third degree to a sobbing, sniveling bit player. The fact that this volunteer actor is the stepson of someone killed in the massacres gives his brief film noir scene a jolt of realism, but does nothing to awaken you from the nightmare.

Oppenheimer has said that he hopes the genre movie scenes he created for Congo and Koto will give audiences an insight into the killers' imaginations, so we can understand why these men were willing to murder and how they can look back today with an apparently easy conscience. That sounds reasonable—and yet it seems to me that the power of these micro-movies is less explanatory than evocative. What's evoked, moreover, is often unsurprising, although vividly grotesque. As you'd expect, the killers exude a creepy brio in their savagery, while performing for the camera with an equally predictable but disturbing amateurishness that comes close to seeming ingenuous.

But maybe these little movies reveal as much about you, the viewer, as they do about Anwar Congo. They attract and repel, continually pulling you into *The Act of Killing* as if into a freak show, and pushing you back whenever you think of the underlying horror. In the end, the little movies also speak to your need to see somebody answer for the murders—a need that's gratified when Congo begins to unravel. Although he may still enjoy legal impunity, the process of reliving his crimes through film acting finally inflicts on him an emotional retribution. Again, it's no surprise—but only a saintly viewer, or a dishonest one, will deny that the outcome satisfies.

Maybe Oppenheimer had loftier goals; but at minimum he has, like the wise Mikado, made the punishment fit the crime. That the resulting merriment, if you can call it that, does not feel at all innocent makes *The Act of Killing* one of the few films now in theaters that demands to be seen.

The Nation, July 22, 2013

The Black Panthers: Vanguard of the Revolution

Television images of the 1965 Watts riots jolt across the screen toward the beginning of Stanley Nelson's magnificent documentary *The Black Panthers: Vanguard of the Revolution*, as a baritone newscaster declaims the obvious: "Relations between police and Negroes throughout the country are getting worse." Well, yes, assuming that "relations" meant the rise and fall of billy clubs in white hands onto Black skulls, the forward swing of rifle butts from white shoulders into Black chests. The archival montage goes on for only a few seconds—this time, at least—but it's so awful that it feels like a year. Or 50, if you've been following the reports from Ferguson, Baltimore, Staten Island.

So you walk into a different theater to catch F. Gary Gray's *Straight Outta Compton*—a sometimes buoyant, sometimes soggy fictional account of the fortunes of the gangsta-rap group NWA— and what do you see? White cops shoving young Black men over the hoods of cars, jerking arms behind Black torsos, rubbing Black faces onto cement. Are relations getting worse, or staying at the same damned level? Given the temporal continuity of the two films—Nelson's ends for all practical purposes in the mid-1970s, while Gray's effectively takes up the story 10 years later—the least you can say is that history repeats itself: the first time as tragedy, the second as show business.

Which is not to deny the canny fashion sense that the Panthers bring to American political life in Nelson's film, or the outrage that comes booming from NWA in *Straight Outta Compton*. Gray revels in the righteous indignation of Ice Cube, NWA's best-known lyricist (and one of the movie's producers), especially when the character rebuffs the ignorance of white scolds. NWA is neither exploiting gang violence nor glorifying it, Ice Cube insists again and again (*Straight Outta Compton* is nothing if not repetitive); the group is reflecting the reality outside its front door. As for the Panthers' style, "That look...became a hit," Kathleen Cleaver proudly recalls in Nelson's documentary, smiling at the memory of how young Black people across America, whether in or out of the party, suddenly had to have a natural, a beret, and a black leather jacket.

Of course, it's useful—maybe even necessary—in movement politics to have both depth of purpose and theatrical appeal. But to portray the Panthers, Nelson has to encompass all this and much more: the quasi-delusional recklessness and disciplined community work, the ego-driven squabbling at the top and hopeful courage in the rank and file. It's a near-impossible task—and yet he succeeds in creating a coherent picture of the messiest, most contentious radical group of a chaotic era, and arguably its most consequential. "We know the party we were in," cautions onetime Panther leader Ericka Huggins at the start of the film, suggesting that Nelson is facing the proverbial problem of getting six blind men to describe an elephant. By the end of the film, he has very coolly put that elephant back into the room.

Call it a trick of montage. Nelson and editor Aljernon Tunsil have a magician's touch for giving life to period music and archival images, as well as a scholar's resourcefulness in digging them up. When the voice-over explains the Panthers' earliest exploits— trailing police patrols around Oakland with weapons in hand (perfectly legal at the time, under California's open-carry statute) to discourage the use of excessive force—you see part of the scene in footage shot from inside a Panther cruiser. When interview subjects recount the incident that first brought the Panthers to national attention—striding with their rifles onto the floor of the State Assembly in Sacramento (sheer inadvertence: They were looking for the gallery)—you watch the episode unfold through perhaps half a dozen visual sources, both homemade and commercial, which take you from the moment of arrival in the parking lot to the politicians' denunciations.

To such materials, Nelson adds a wealth of present-day interviews with former Panthers (some of them practiced in their recollections, others touchingly candid), along with newspaper and magazine clippings, excerpts from government documents, writings by anonymous young party members, and testimonies from historians, movement lawyers, journalists, police, even a retired FBI agent. I can't call the research comprehensive; party cofounder Bobby Seale seems to have been unavailable for interview, and there is deafening silence about the known murders committed by Panthers, with or without direct orders. Still, Nelson has compiled more than enough information to present an account that is admiring when it comes to the idealism and self-sacrifice of many party members, and notably unflinching when it comes to the details.

In the words of various witnesses, the party's growth was too rapid and undirected. ("Nobody asked these people, 'Why are you here? What do you want to accomplish?'") The most prominent spokesperson, Eldridge Cleaver, was uncontrollable (or flat-out "crazy," in the laughing opinion of former Young Lord Felipe

Luciano), and a cult of personality was fostered around jailed cofounder Huey P. Newton ("a fucking maniac," in the words of another party veteran). The rank and file, concludes one of the historians, did not have the leaders they deserved.

To the seething despair that settled into the Panthers' hearts after the assassination of Martin Luther King Jr., add the desperation instilled by police raids, relentless spying, spurious prosecutions, manipulated suspicions and outright murder, all orchestrated from Washington, DC, by J. Edgar Hoover. No doubt the darkest episode in Nelson's film, and perhaps its core, is the tale of Fred Hampton, chairman of the Illinois chapter of the Panthers, who died as the direct result of Hoover's COINTELPRO operations. The rare leader who was worthy of his followers, the 21-year-old Hampton—inspired in his oratory and gifted at building coalitions—was betrayed by his bodyguard (an FBI informer) and executed in bed in 1969 by officers of the Cook County State's Attorney's Office.

Maybe this is as good a moment as any to jump ahead to NWA and its chart-busting hit, "Fuck tha Police."

NWA didn't sell music so much as authenticity—its audience was buying the thrill of hearing brutal truths about Black America shouted in the language of the street, by people who knew—and authenticity is a promise as well of *Straight Outta Compton*, made manifest in everything from its scenes of police mayhem (including multiple showings of the Rodney King video) to the casting of O'Shea Jackson Jr. in the role of his father, Ice Cube. You're meant to feel that the bass on NWA's tracks sounds like a police battering ram breaking down the door of a drug house (one of the first things to happen in the movie), or to hear Dr. Dre's percussive turntable-scratching as another kind of rat-a-tat.

Yet despite its striving for the reality effect, *Straight Outta Compton* begins much like a summer blockbuster from the Marvel universe, introducing its quickly characterized superheroes one after another: pugnacious, fast-talking drug-runner Eazy-E (Jason Mitchell), dutiful son and sonic dreamer Dr. Dre (Corey Hawkins), and smoldering, watchful scribbler Ice Cube. Once these legendary figures team up and unite their uncanny powers, it's only a matter of time before something becomes airborne: the camera, in this case, which at the literal and figurative high point of *Straight Outta Compton* dives over the heads of the crowd at a Detroit arena, swoops around the stage where NWA is performing "Fuck tha Police," and soars back out again.

This is F. Gary Gray's directorial ecstasy, which comes rather too early in the proceedings for the movie's good. Liberated by NWA's full-throated denunciation of police racism, and especially by the group's defiance of police orders never to perform that number, Gray leaves the Earth behind and brings you along with him. After that, you've got about a two-hour slog left, through contract disputes, management problems, professional rivalries, and a lot of standard-issue showbiz parties.

But the memory of the flight over the Detroit arena remains; and if you see *The Black Panthers: Vanguard of the Revolution*, it might connect with another moment of defiance and liberation. In December 1966, just four days after the execution of Fred Hampton, Los Angeles police deployed their recently organized SWAT team in its first major raid, targeting a Panther headquarters. This time the Panthers were awake and prepared. Objectively, the best that can be said for their resistance is that the ensuing four-hour standoff ended with all of them alive, though in police custody. No newly flourishing headquarters sprang up in the ruins that the SWAT team left behind. Nationally, in fact, the Panthers were heading toward schism, disarray, and effective demise, on what turned out to be a three-year schedule. But for at least one of the party members in that siege, Wayne Pharr, the shoot-out was a peak moment never before experienced. "I felt free," he says.

Watching these films today, in the wake of the killings in Ferguson, Baltimore, Staten Island, I'm struck by the distances that we have and have not traveled, and by the urgency and inadequacy of expressing outrage. I'm willing to accept the authenticity of *Straight Outta Compton*, even in Marvel-universe form, and readily acknowledge that NWA's music has felt liberating for millions of people; but I also think it's significant that the movie devolves so thoroughly from superhero exploits to a story about business. As the closing montage makes clear with its testimonials to NWA, the movie's subject ultimately isn't freedom, or even free expression, but success.

The Black Panthers: Vanguard of the Revolution is a deeper and better-made film, and consequently more challenging. While acknowledging that the Panthers tapped a vein of anger with very mixed results, sometimes failing to channel either the rage or themselves, Nelson shows you what a mass-based radical politics can feel like, and reminds you that you haven't seen its like for a while. Judging from the evidence, I'd say our era is post-NWA more than post-Panther, and that Black Lives Matter is still not so much a movement as a social-media campaign.

Straight Outta Compton has been playing in theaters "everywhere," which is also the general location where you can hear NWA's music. *The Black Panthers: Vanguard of the Revolution* goes into theatrical release in September, beginning with a run at Film Forum in New York.

The Nation, September 14, 2015

13th/I Am Not Your Negro

The imaginary locus of the New York Film Festival shifts across the globe year by year, depending on where the heftier selections cluster. Some past editions have made me feel as though I'd spent a lot of time in Taiwan, Iran, or Romania, though the primary dream site has most often glittered about 3,600 miles to the northeast of the festival's home. I've sometimes left Lincoln Center after a full day of Francophilia and fantasized that I'd stumbled into Paris's previously undiscovered 21st arrondissement, when I was really just blinking at Broadway.

Imagination came to rest differently at this year's festival, the 54th, settling not on one locus but on every place where African Americans have struggled, suffered, and invented themselves. In a decision that broke with the past, since no previous opening-night selection had been a documentary, the festival began with Ava DuVernay's burningly urgent *13th*, a historical survey of white America's hands-on methods of keeping Black America down, from the years of post-Reconstruction terror through our present era of stop-and-frisk and "stand your ground." Then came the films that bulked out the impression of a festival where Black lives mattered: Raoul Peck's knotty essay about race in America, *I Am Not Your Negro*, proudly bearing the credit "Written by James Baldwin" because it is based entirely on his texts; Barry Jenkins's moody, impressionistic *Moonlight*, a drama about a gay youth's coming of age in the Liberty City section of Miami; and *I Called Him Morgan*, Kasper Collin's archival reconstruction of the loving, fatal convergence of the lives of jazz trumpeter Lee Morgan and his wife Helen, a proudly independent woman who first rescued him from the streets and then murdered him.

Four overlapping aspects of one vast subject; four distinct methods of bringing that subject to the screen. (For a fifth, I might look beyond the festival to Nate Parker's *The Birth of a Nation*.) Maybe the best way to begin mapping this cinematic territory is to refer to one of the passages that Samuel L. Jackson recites on the soundtrack of *I Am Not Your Negro*—a fragment, I believe, from *Remember This House*, Baldwin's unfinished meditation on what he'd known firsthand of the life and death of Medgar Evers, Malcolm X, and Martin Luther King Jr.

Starting from a recollection of the time Evers asked for his company on a murder investigation, Baldwin took flight into an aria about the Deep South towns he'd just passed through, the civil-rights campaigns he'd observed without sweating out the calculation of how many people might be injured or killed, the groups he'd known well (from the NAACP to the Nation of Islam) but had not joined. As Peck's complex, often allusive montage of archival images plays across the screen—film footage of Evers in the driveway of his home and Freedom Riders on a bus, still photographs of civil-rights workers in coffins and an old-time NAACP chapter posing on risers—Jackson's soundtrack recitation rises to Baldwin's moral climax. He had chosen to be a witness, Baldwin wrote, rather than a participant; and as a witness, his responsibility was to move as freely as possible.

In *13th*, Ava DuVernay comes down on the participants' side of this divide. With the aid of co-screenwriter Spencer Averick, she marshals witnesses and facts, constructs arguments and charts, buttonholes you in your seat and then tries to yank you upright, not to applaud but to act. Because she bears down so forcefully on her material, and on you, DuVernay also constrains herself. Her use of archival images, for example, is never allusive or evocative, like Peck's, but strictly illustrative, nailing exactly the point she intends to make. But then, DuVernay is not aiming for freedom of movement in *13th*. Her goal is inexorability.

Essentially the film version of Michelle Alexander's *The New Jim Crow: Mass Incarceration in the Age of Colorblindness*, *13th* lays out a history of the successive means by which Black Americans have been clawed back into the economic and social servitude from which the 13th Amendment was meant to free them. No citizen, according to the amendment, can be held captive and compelled to labor except as "punishment for crime"—a reasonable stipulation, perhaps, but one that quickly became an escape clause for those who find it convenient to remove Black people (men especially) from the free workforce. In the years since the Civil War, African Americans have been variously defined as vagrants, loiterers, disturbers of the peace, rapists, insurrectionists, and (in more recent decades) murderous drug dealers. Who benefited as the prisons filled and a Black man's odds of being incarcerated at some point in his life rose to one in three? White politicians, from Richard Nixon through Bill Clinton and Donald Trump; a multitude of corporations, whether they're outsourcing jobs to penitentiaries or operating prisons of their own; and a large cadre of lobbyists, consultants, broadcasters, moviemakers, editorialists, and think-tank blowhards who have profited by converting mass incarceration from a brutal method into (God help us) a culture.

As an artist, DuVernay naturally pays close attention to the promulgation of that culture. Her film is full of depictions of the Black criminal, from D.W. Griffith's *The Birth of a Nation* through newscast videos of the Central Park Five. As she presents testimony from interview subjects who include Michelle Alexander, Van Jones, Henry Louis Gates Jr., and (for a surprise) Newt Gingrich, posing them in workaday loft or office spaces (or, in the case of Angela Davis, a magnificent ruin), DuVernay repeatedly loops back to the old images, reinforcing the argument that African Americans have been subjected to wave after wave of criminalization. Meanwhile, her hip-hop soundtrack (with lyrics flashed across the screen) and dreadful montage of recent police killings drive home the message that every part of our history is still fully present, and still cries out to be addressed.

I cannot tell you how it might feel to watch *13th* as an African American. My response is that of a supposedly white person (as Baldwin might have called me) who had many of the facts already at his command when he entered the theater but was not prepared for the cumulative force that DuVernay gives them. She piles up information until it becomes emotional knowledge—and it's awful.

o   o   o

With Raoul Peck's documentary *I Am Not Your Negro*, it's not necessary for me to speculate about how an African American might feel about the matters under discussion. One particular Black man told us, with an eloquence almost unmatched in American letters.

His words ring through the film in three different voices. One, as I've mentioned, belongs to Samuel L. Jackson, who recites various passages by James Baldwin, inhabiting the words without imitating the author's podium manner. Since so many of these texts are recollections, let's call this the autobiographical voice. The second voice is public: It belongs to a Baldwin seen in archival footage as he lectures, debates, and holds forth with various talk-show hosts. From this voice, you get entire paragraphs unfurling like defiant banners in a high wind. The third voice also comes from the archives—a television interview conducted by Kenneth Clark in 1963—but this Baldwin speaks haltingly, testing his phrases before uttering them, even seeming to weigh the words before he'll let them off his tongue. This is the writer's voice, which you're privileged to hear composing authentic James Baldwin sentences in real time.

Memoir, analytical polemic, and behind them both the restless movement of an intellect fearlessly probing both itself and its situation in the world: Raoul Peck combines all three in *I Am Not Your Negro*. The images, as you might expect, are not always straightforward. While the texts that Peck has chosen address many of the issues covered in Ava DuVernay's documentary *13th*—for example, the violence inflicted on people of color by self-designated whites, in the streets and on the movie screen—the accompanying pictures might show anything from the shadows cast by elevated railroad tracks on a ghetto street to a view of Mars from a science-fiction movie. You can't predict their rhythm, either: A shot of the New York City subway begins during one of Jackson's monologues, and only after half a minute does the text arrive at Baldwin's recollection of a clandestine meeting on a platform. This isn't just a matter of expert, often associative, editing, but of keeping time according to a moral clock. A mention of Baldwin's return to New York from Paris in the 1950s summons up a view of Times Square today. A talk-show discussion about the perilous state of America, recorded in the late 1960s, merges without comment into still photographs of the riots in Ferguson, Missouri.

This is what I call freedom of movement. As much as I admire what DuVernay has done, and as much as I respect her choice of the participants' side, I think that if the New York Film Festival had chosen its opening-night selection on artistic merit alone, the slot would have gone to the moral witness of *I Am Not Your Negro*.

The Nation, November 7, 2016

Let It Fall

During the spare hours when he wasn't writing and producing *Guerrilla* and *American Crime* for television, working on a yet-to-be-titled Marvel superheroes project, or crafting the screenplay for *12 Years a Slave*, the furiously industrious John Ridley somehow made time to direct *Let It Fall*, a lengthy documentary about 10 years of mounting African-American outrage in Los Angeles, 1982 to 1992, and its culmination in the Rodney King riots.

Despite Ridley's ambition, he is not the first to have worked this territory. Ezra Edelman expanded *O.J.: Made in America* to epic proportions, and won an Oscar, by situating the trials of O.J. Simpson within an ample narrative about the ingrained white supremacy of the Los Angeles Police Department in that same period and everything that flowed from it, from smashed houses to broken families to trails of corpses on the streets. If you saw *O.J.: Made in America* last year, some of the dreadful events it revisited will still be fresh in your mind, so that you recognize even the archival footage when you re-encounter it in Ridley's film.

But for all the sociological sweep that Edelman brought to the subject, he was essentially making a true-crime picture, with one person in the foreground and a murder trial at its climax. Ridley's game is different. He wants to understand this decade through the experiences of more than a dozen people who were intimately caught up in these events, and (just as important) to understand the people themselves. He pieces his narrative together from the accounts of retired police officers of varying rank, African-American residents of the South Central neighborhood, a family of shopkeepers from Koreatown, a Japanese-American family from suburban Alhambra. In drawing these people out, he has fully respected Jean Renoir's insight in *Rules of the Game*: "What's terrible is that everyone has his reasons." As for the climax of his story, it isn't anything so ritualized and contained as a jury verdict. It's a fire, which rages across Los Angeles for days.

You know, from the start, that the fire is coming, and you may even recall some of the fatalities that led to it. First a 20-year-old Black man, James Mincey Jr., died at the hands of white cops, who applied a chokehold to him after a routine traffic stop. (The woman who was his girlfriend at the time tells the story.) Then a young suburban woman, Karen Toshima, was caught in the crossfire of gangs that had spilled out of South Central and into Westwood (her brother Kevin tells the story): a death that alarmed

LA's more privileged citizens and brought the full paramilitary force of the LAPD to bear on Black neighborhoods in Operation Hammer. A 15-year-old African-American girl, Latasha Harlins, died when a Korean-American shopkeeper, Soon Ja Du, abruptly decided to shoot her in the head, a crime that was clearly recorded by a surveillance camera, and for which Du received a sentence of five years' probation without jail time. (The story is told by a woman who was in the shop, waiting while her little brother played Pac-Man.) Then came the verdict in the case of Rodney King, an unarmed man bludgeoned into a pulp by police officers wielding metal batons (because, to their disgust, they were no longer allowed to use chokeholds). Although this incident, too, was recorded on videotape, the trial ended with no punishment whatsoever being meted out to the perpetrators. (The accused cops declined to be interviewed for the film, but Ridley gets the story from another policeman who was present, and who testifies, without shame or irony, that "What I witnessed at the scene was 100 percent LAPD policy.") After that, Los Angeles exploded, and still another victim became famous: Reginald Denny, a white truck driver who was dragged from his vehicle by Black rioters and stomped nearly to death.

As the movie unfolds, you know very well that the looting and burning are on the way, and also the stomping; and yet Ridley manages to build suspense by introducing his witnesses gradually, without always tipping you off about who they are and what part of the history they saw. You often have to guess at why you're listening to someone, and what might lie behind his or her words. In one key instance, you don't even get to see the speaker, though his testimony frames the narrative from the beginning. Only at the conclusion of *Let It Fall* do you understand the roles of half a dozen of the people on-screen or see their emotions at full force, as teased out by Ridley during the interviews. It turns out that some attacked Reginald Denny, one videotaped the beating, and one left the safety of his home to try to bring Denny to a hospital, guided (as he tells it) by the voice of God.

The name of that rescuer is Bobby Green. There are other surprising heroes in *Let It Fall,* as well as characters who confess with pain to their failings, and people who suffered devastating loss and yet speak with forgiveness and understanding. There are also villains—but not many of them. The truly awful, such as former police chief Daryl Gates, appear only in smirking, self-justifying archival footage. The interview subjects who come close to being villains—people who to this day are bitter and enraged, and have blood on their hands—turn out to have their reasons, just like everyone. Gary Williams, who was charged with beating and robbing Denny, assures Ridley that he can have compassion for anybody. But on April 29, 1992, he says firmly, "The compassion line was closed."

Let It Fall is a single comprehensive history of how Los Angeles tore itself apart from 1982 to 1992, and also of a dozen or more personal tragedies. It's like looking into the heart of all those single flames that made the conflagration.

The Nation, April 26, 2017

In the Last Days of the City

Beautiful, brooding, and astonishingly two-faced, Tamer El Said's *In the Last Days of the City* is a quasi-documentary fiction with both multiple precedents and none at all. You could locate it within world cinema's heritage of city symphonies (the place, in this instance, being Cairo); the line of intensely imagistic, narratively unsettled Arab-language pictures best represented by the Syrian avant-garde (whose filmmakers, I fear, might now be worse than embattled); or the Western European tradition, perfected by Michelangelo Antonioni, of movies about sad, lonely people walking around and staring at things. All these triangulating references are apt—and yet they don't give you a fix on Said's picture, because it simply won't sit still.

Said shot *In the Last Days of the City* from 2008 through at least the early part of 2010 (or so I'm estimating, based on the scenes of street celebrations after an Egyptian victory in the Africa Cup of Nations), working from a script he wrote with Rasha Salti. He then assembled the film from the footage he'd amassed—about 250 hours' worth, according to one account—continuing the editing into 2016. Hence the Janus faces: The film looks forward through the eyes of Khalid (Khalid Abdalla), who is too preoccupied to realize he's witnessing the beginnings of the 2011 Tahrir Square uprising; it also looks backward through the eyes of Said, who knows that the stirrings of democratic rebellion he captured back then have culminated (for now) in authoritarian stasis. These two gazes coexist within one set of images.

If that makes *In the Last Days of the City* sound challenging to watch, you should know that it is above all a richly sensuous film, which strives to accommodate the thick, shifting layers of sight and sound that overwhelm verbal descriptions of Cairo. But, yes, magical achievements such as the Janus vision are difficult not only to create but also to receive. Do not expect the conventional comforts of heart-pounding suspense.

If time is like a river—not a bad image for a movie that has the Nile flowing through it—then most filmmakers struggle against the current. They devote themselves to the art of getting people to care about what might come next, whereas Said knows that film, by the laws of physics, can only record images of what the river has just borne away. If you care about the subject before the camera as Said cares about Cairo—very deeply—then narrative drive counts for very little next to the fact that you're experiencing love and loss 24 times a second.

That's what seems to matter most to Khalid as he wanders through downtown with his camera. A slim, quiet, thirtyish man born into an artistic family, Khalid has the inclination and the resources to spend his time working on a documentary about... what? The project, which seems as interminable as psychoanalysis, mostly involves collecting and editing interviews with women who are on their way out of his life—his mother (Zeinab Mostafa), who is dying; his former lover (Laila Samy), who is about to leave the country—or who say they have nothing to tell him, like the theater director (Hanan Youssef) who is fed up with his asking about the old days in Alexandria. "No more nostalgia!" she shouts at him, adding that when he gets back to his stuffy apartment, he ought to open the windows for a change.

But Khalid, in the tradition of Chekhovian characters at a triple impasse—personal, artistic, world-historical—has no problem with his apartment, other than needing to leave it. Buildings are being demolished all around, and it seems that he too will have to move within a couple of months, though his real-estate agent can't seem to find him a place without chickens roosting in it.

So Khalid drifts with the current: not exactly in the moment (because he's always mulling over the past, and shooting scenes that vanish before his eyes), but swimming in the perceptual flood. The irony, of course, is that he doesn't see what time is carrying him toward, even when he inadvertently catches it on film.

Sometimes, he passes a little crowd chanting that the Quran must rule. At other times, he walks by a few rows of demonstrators calling for the ouster of Egyptian President Hosni Mubarak. Always there are soldiers and plainclothes cops—the former staring ahead blank-faced, the latter looking around with vulpine appetite. As a title card announces, these images begin in December 2009. At that point, two years before the uprising, they're just threads in the fabric of the city to Khalid—neither more nor less important than a stooped beggar woman, a bright little girl selling cigarettes in the midst of traffic, a veteran of the 1967 war retelling his stories for the thousandth time in a cafe, or the views through taxicab windows that turn Cairo into an unfolding shallow-focus band of shimmering light and color.

Khalid can try to grasp these elusive sights and sounds, but he has no one to share them with—no one to think with him about what the effort of filming means—except for three friends his own age who are also about to slip away. All three are visiting filmmakers who have come to Cairo for a panel discussion; one resides in Beirut, another in Baghdad, and the third—having fled Iraq's bloodshed—in Berlin. (They are played, respectively, by Bassem Fayad, Hayder Helo, and Basim Hajar.) *In the Last Days of the City* is at its most energetic and convivial, and also its most argumentative, when the four buddies are together, talking through the night and then driving through the streets at dawn with video cameras in their hands. Each visitor faces his own artistic and political dilemma; each promises to send Khalid some images so he can finally finish his damned movie. Then the friends scatter, to become hovering absences like all the others.

Now that *In the Last Days of the City* has reached the United States, beginning with limited runs in New York and Los Angeles, it is irresistible, if facile, to compare it with the Brad Anderson—Tony Gilroy thriller *Beirut* (which is, by the way, not a terrible movie). The obvious difference is viewpoint: One is internal to the place and culture, the other external. But the more important distinction is open versus closed form. Said is willing to give you something that is all the more affecting for being discontinuous and inconclusive—a deliberately paced leap toward the impossible. No film about incipient failure could be more brilliant about looking back while falling short.

The Nation, April 23, 2018

Wars and Rumors of War

Jung/Kandahar

When you look at certain films side by side, you begin to see reality shape the imagination. Here's *Jung (War) in the Land of the Mujaheddin*, a blood-and-guts documentary about life in Afghanistan two decades into the present slaughter. Right next to it is *Kandahar*, which addresses the same subject in the mode of poetry. The first, made by the Italian team of Alberto Vendemmiati, Fabrizio Lazzaretti and Giuseppe Petitto, comes at you with the urgency of war-front journalism. The second, written and directed by Iran's brilliant Mohsen Makhmalbaf, operates under an entirely different kind of pressure. It's driven by a need to describe things clearly and, in the same gesture, to transform them.

Do you need to choose between these two approaches? I'd say no. In the first place, circumstances have given must-see status to both pictures. In the second place, the films keep overlapping.

Both *Jung* and *Kandahar* begin with the arrival of would-be rescuers, whose helicopters bob like mechanical gnats over the deep-cleft mountains. First we see the terrain, which is vast, daunting, magnificent; then come the people, who are starving and shattered. Many figures are incomplete, with limbs ending abruptly in a stump; and too often the bodies have vanished altogether, to be replaced by ambulatory drapes. What's it like to be an Afghan woman, buried within the burqa's folds? In both films, the camera tries to show you, taking an outward peep through the face-covering mesh.

The filmmakers who ventured into this country in 1999 and 2000—outsiders who came not just to rescue but to report and polemicize—seem to have built their statements from the few available terms: hunger, pain, displacement, vastness, obscurity. Think of these elements as representing a base condition, and tremble—because what you're seeing was the irreducible experience of yesterday's Afghanistan, before the United States started bombing.

Jung doesn't pretend to build its limited vocabulary into anything shapely. The movie wants you to see that it's been jerry-rigged, in much the same way as its protagonists improvise a hospital with whatever comes to hand. The rescuers in this case are two medical professionals from the aid group Emergency—surgeon Gino Strada and nurse Kate Rowlands—who enter Afghanistan with the veteran journalist Ettore Mo. Thanks to his longstanding relationship with the Northern Alliance, Mo is able to introduce the medical team to Burhanuddin Rabbani, the ousted president of Afghanistan, and to the (now late) military commander Ahmed Shah Massoud, who grant permission to build a hospital within their territory. The hospital, Strada explains, is intended for civilian casualties of landmines. In the next breath—perhaps insuring his hosts' cooperation, perhaps bowing to reality—Strada adds that he'll treat combatants as well.

But what does it mean to be a noncombatant in Afghanistan? The filmmakers bring us to the marketplace of Charikar, the town selected for the hospital, to meet the civilians: war widows reduced to beggary, young children employed as metalworkers. A scrawny boy rattles off his workshop's list of products, and then, as if having reached the end of his possibilities, rattles them off again. A woman, bent and desiccated, tells us her life is unbearable, yet cannot be escaped: "Not even Death wants the people of Afghanistan."

As for the fighters: The camera takes us into the hovel that was serving as Charikar's dispensary, so we can see how Strada pulls shrapnel from the hole that used to be a man's eye, or how he removes the bloody pulp dangling from a teenager's thigh. Strada works with no X-rays and precious little anesthesia, in an operating room heated by a dung-burning stove. When he learns that he can't change his scrubs between operations or use a fresh amputation saw—where's the autoclave, by the way?—he temporarily stalks out, leaving the teenager strapped to a cruciform table.

Can things get any worse? Sure. The Emergency medics fly back to Italy to arrange for a shipment of supplies; by the time they return, the Taliban have taken Charikar. Strada and Rowlands have to set up in another area, amid the tents of refugees. Medical care? "There are 100,000 people out there with nothing," Rowlands snaps.

Things can also get better. In August 1999, seven truckloads of supplies and equipment get through from Italy, and Strada and Rowlands set up a real hospital in Anbar. They hire a staff, 80 percent of whom are Kurds; they banish weapons and burqas from the wards and even persuade the Northern Alliance to park its tanks elsewhere. Considering what you've witnessed till now, you will perhaps excuse *Jung* for treating these achievements as a climax, and for turning Strada and Rowlands into heroes. There, too, reality seems to have shaped the storytellers' imaginations.

Besides, in its final effect *Jung* is anything but celebratory. The film ends with scenes of Afghans in the midst of mourning and burial, and of the Emergency team making plans to open another hospital—this one, for the sake of political neutrality, to be built in the Taliban zone. You don't need the perspective of recent events to see the irony. All of the Emergency facilities may have been blown up by now, and all the patients with them; yet as Strada, Rowlands and the filmmakers seem to have understood, the likelihood of futility was in this case no excuse for inaction. *Jung* is rough, visceral and harsh—but it's also undespairing, and indispensable.

Kandahar, too, is an indispensable film, though in an utterly different mode. Shot in Iran, in and around a village of Afghan refugees, it's more fantasy than reportage, like Makhmalbaf's earlier *Gabbeh*. The director found dunes and wretched sojourners and shaped them into a country of his own; he looked into the face of Nelofer Pazira, listened to her hopes and fears, and dreamed a story. Upon seeing Makhmalbaf's vision of Afghanistan, some have been shocked at its lighter-than-air beauty. Yes, the film is marvelous to look at, for all its horror, chaos and absurdity. Rotting plants sometimes give off a wonderful phosphorescence.

It's useful to know that Pazira, a Kabul native who now resides in Canada, came to Makhmalbaf in the late 1990s and asked for his help. She wanted to enter Afghanistan to search for an old friend, whose most recent letter, about life under the Taliban, amounted to a suicide note. Would Makhmalbaf accompany Pazira and film her journey? No, he said. But then he sneaked into Afghanistan on his own, threw himself into research and started writing a screenplay, with the lead role crafted for Pazira.

So we have *Kandahar*: a story about an Afghan-born journalist with the suggestive name of Nafas, or breath, who comes back from Canada hoping to rescue her sister. Having been left behind years ago when the family fled, this sister has now sent a letter announcing her intention to commit suicide during the last eclipse of the twentieth century. By the time Nafas reaches a camp on the Iranian side of the border, the eclipse is only two days away. Nafas must now cross the desert to Kandahar as a lone woman, outfitted only with a tape recorder, a wad of dollars and the unaccustomed weight of a sage-green burqa.

It's easy enough to locate *Kandahar* within a tradition of symbolically charged, quasi-documentary road movies. (Think of *Viaggio in Italia*, *Apocalypse Now*, *Lamerica*.) The challenge, once the categorization is done, is to watch Makhmalbaf's uncanny images and characters without becoming giddy. The astonishment starts with the revelation of Nafas's face, with its gently elongated features and clear hazel eyes. She lifts her burqa to say her name, and the veil's mesh casts a sharp grid across her forehead: a stamp of prison darkness, you might say, on a face briefly turned to the light. Soon this woman will be courted with a ring torn from the finger of a skeleton. A scoundrel by the roadside will offer to sell her a set of prosthetic legs—his mother's, he claims—saying it's good to keep a pair handy. A doctor will examine her through a tiny peephole in a curtain, which reduces Nafas to scattered parts: an eye, an ear, a mouth. Then, in English, he will warn her of the danger she faces, just before he removes his false beard.

It seems that everyone in *Kandahar* is disguised in some way. There's Nafas, who crosses the border pretending to be someone's fourth wife; the doctor (Hassan Tantaï), who lacks a medical degree but knows enough to prescribe bread, three times a day; the young ring-bearer, Khak (Sadou Teymouri), expelled from a Koranic school for faking his way through the chanting; the roadside scoundrel, who winds up hiding under a burqa. He's the comic relief. The real import of the burqa becomes clear when Nafas at last sees the eclipse: not an astronomical event, but the masking of sunlight through the veil.

The Nation, December 10, 2001

Divine Intervention

If Elia Suleiman's face were a cartoon, then the single short, white brush stroke dabbed into his black hair would perhaps be the beginning of a thought balloon, perpetually forming above the left eyebrow. One after another, ideas pop loose from that creased forehead and float through his new movie, *Divine Intervention*.

His image of his hometown, Nazareth: the place where Santa Claus got chased down and killed. His picture of his father, late in life: a man who sits at the kitchen table, endlessly sorting a pile of mail. His notion of Palestinian romance under Israeli rule: a rendezvous at a highway checkpoint, where lovers separated by the Green Line meet in a car for an orgy of handholding. His metaphor for freedom: a balloon decorated with a life-size drawing of Yasir Arafat's head, released from the West Bank to drift over Jerusalem.

Like a silent comedy—like Suleiman's 1996 debut feature, *Chronicle of a Disappearance*—*Divine Intervention* is made up of an expertly timed series of such wordless, deadpan scenes. They make you recall that a gag is something that either incites laughter or else stifles speech. Not that the characters in *Divine Intervention* are entirely mute. The father (Nayef Fahoum Daher) can let loose an obscene, ear-scorching tirade against his neighbors in Nazareth, all the while waving a friendly good morning to each; an Israeli soldier at the checkpoint can decide to act like the emcee of an insane game show, in which Palestinian contestants must follow whatever instructions he shouts through a bullhorn. Language usually hurts in *Divine Intervention*. For laughter, and imagination, and maybe even hope, Suleiman needs to keep quiet, even though his silence is heavy with longing.

You will notice that his face seems older than its 42 years—older than the face of an American look-alike and contemporary, such as Robert Downey Jr.—with the jowls softening below the unmoving soft lips, the liquid eyes starting to droop beneath that hyperactive expanse of forehead. It must weigh on the flesh, to be a real Palestinian but have only a potential Palestine. Certainly a weight of some kind has brought down his father, who's come to lie in a hospital ward. (Of course, in a Palestinian hospital, everybody smokes, doctors included. This, at least, you can't blame on the Israelis.) And yet the smooth-faced love of E.S.'s life—the wonderworking woman (Manal Khader), the handholder—looks so fine that soldiers stand dumbfounded at the roadblock, helpless to stop her legs from scissoring past in a white Paris dress.

That's how E.S. imagines her, anyway. As he did before, in *Chronicle of a Disappearance*, Suleiman has claimed the movie's sadness and slapstick for himself, while making a woman responsible for all its beauty, vitality, worldly wisdom and effective political resistance. I assume he knows this choice is old-fashioned and romantic, in a Chaplinesque way. Out of love for Chaplin, who knew something about dispossessed people and what movies might do for them, I'm willing to play along—especially since the coolly self-assured Khader actually carries off the role.

The scene in which I hesitate to play along is the one where Khader turns into a levitating ninja, who strikes down a squad of Israeli soldiers with a magical barrage of stones. Yes, it's another of E.S.'s fantasies; yes, he's entitled to it; and yes, it brings to a new height the contrast between Khader's buoyancy and the men's heaviness. But when I think of how many Palestinian kids have been killed or maimed while throwing stones, when I think of how little the Palestinians have won through such flailings, I feel that this scene, alone among the fantasies of *Divine Intervention*, descends to the polemical and, worse, to intellectual dandyism.

But that's one scene. As for the rest: *Divine Intervention* is a brilliant merger of poignancy and absurdity, humor and outrage, made by one of the most extraordinary writer-actor-directors in contemporary film. It's the work of someone whose pained thoughts have burst loose from his forehead, only to be pinned down again as the yellow cards of a scenario writer; someone who nevertheless has learned he can shuffle those cards at will, or even tear them up, and so bring forth surprises. Maybe a lost father can come back; maybe love can end in something better than craziness. Such artistic reworkings of the yellow cards may not be truly godlike; but for anyone who watches *Divine Intervention*, they offer a release that's like the first buoyant possibility of freedom.

The Nation, February 10, 2003

Rana's Wedding/Ford Transit

The extraordinary Palestinian filmmaker Hany Abu-Assad has received the Nestor Almendros Prize of the Human Rights Watch International Film Festival and is represented in this year's selection by two of his films.

Rana's Wedding is a fiction that tracks its title character through a busy twelve hours as she hurries back and forth between Jerusalem and Ramallah. Her complex agenda: to defy her father, marry her bohemian boyfriend (who has at least one other woman hanging around—but what the hell?) and remain in Palestine rather than be carried back to Egypt. As Rana, Clara Khoury starts out in a fog, works up to a fury and ends up out of breath but exultant—which is the kind of thing that any actress likes to do, and which she carries off with a winning combination of sharp intelligence and ugly-duckling grace. You feel how right Rana is to want to stay in this place. She fits perfectly into a setting that Abu-Assad has caught brilliantly, and of necessity on the fly—a Jerusalem that's torn up, sinuous, maddening to negotiate and beautiful.

The Jerusalem-to-Ramallah route that Rana takes fictionally is itself the subject of the second of Abu-Assad's works in the festival: the documentary *Ford Transit*. In part, the film is a portrait of an outgoing, wised-up, slightly edgy young man named Rajai, who drives one of the West Bank's innumerable jitney vans. (They're the only reliable transportation for Palestinians, who ride them in stages from one roadblock to the next.) The film is also a travelogue, a study in sociology (since Palestinians from all walks of life ride the jitneys), a deeply responsible meditation on suicide bombing and an anthology of political essays. Providing the latter are some well-known figures, including Palestinian leader Hanan Ashrawi and Israeli-American filmmaker B.Z. Goldberg, whom Abu-Assad invited into the van for interviews.

Sorrowful, uproarious, clever, alarming and argumentative by turns, *Ford Transit* is a first-rate movie—one of those rare documentaries that seem to grasp a situation effortlessly, and as a whole. You could hold a Human Rights Watch Film Festival and show no other picture.

Fortunately, though, there are twenty-seven more.

The Nation, June 23, 2003

Fahrenheit 9/11

Not the judgment of film critics but the passage of time will decide whether Michael Moore's *Fahrenheit 9/11* can change the world. Change, of course, is the whole purpose. Whatever satisfaction Moore derives from his ever-mounting income and awards, he clearly will consider this picture a success only if it helps drive George W. Bush from office. Voters will write the real review. I can merely fill time until November, with the thought that *Fahrenheit 9/11* might be interesting as a movie after it has done its work as politics.

As with any good polemic—and this is an excellent one—you sit in the theater thinking of how someone else would respond, some imaginary "undecided" in a swing state, or perhaps your Uncle Max the Republican. You don't much monitor your own reactions. But then, as you leave the movie house, you might notice that the sidewalk chatter sounds oddly muffled, the traffic looks a little blurred, as you begin to realize that your attention has not come outside with you; it's still in the dark, struggling with the feelings that *Fahrenheit 9/11* called up and didn't resolve. Are you outraged, heartbroken, vengeful, morose, gloating, thoughtful, electrified? Moore has elicited all of these emotions and then had the nerve—the filmmaker's nerve—to leave you to sort them out.

I think there are two bundles of messages in *Fahrenheit 9/11*, one political and one emotional—and while the first is about as ambiguous as a call to take up pitchforks and torches and storm the castle, the second is too complex to unsettle those in power. It works to unsettle *you*. It's what makes *Fahrenheit 9/11* a real movie.

For clarity's sake, then, let's start with the politics: the film's bill of particulars against Bush, and also against the Democratic leadership, which in Moore's view has colluded most shamefully in the misrule the world now suffers. The prologue to *Fahrenheit 9/11* revisits Bush's rise to power in late 2000, paying particular attention to the hunched posture of the Democrats who let him step on their backs. Here are Dick Gephardt and Tom Daschle, counseling "acceptance" of the non-election; and here is Al Gore, mildly officiating over the Senate session that legitimized the theft of his presidency. For the first time in *Fahrenheit 9/11*, but certainly not the last, Moore tells his story through borrowed but decidedly nonstock footage, which you most likely have not seen before—in this case, a scene of members of the House, all of them

African-American, coming forward to contest the election, while Gore calmly rules their objections inadmissible because no senator, not one, would satisfy Congressional rules by signing on to them.

Moore's antagonists, being Republican, won't go so easy on him. Their attacks will no doubt include the charge that his film is Democratic Party propaganda. You should understand from the preceding the flimsiness of this accusation—although it's true that Moore spares us the sight of one notable Democrat, John Kerry, voting to authorize Bush to start a war on his own say-so, at any time that suited him.

But enough of Democratic malfeasance. Who is this Sage of Crawford, that he may choose for us between life and death? Moore answers, in part, with more footage you probably haven't seen until now: a substantial portion of videotape from the morning of September 11, 2001, when Bush and his handlers staged a photo opportunity at an elementary school in Florida. After an aide whispered to him that a second airplane had struck the World Trade Center, Bush sat in place for seven minutes, pretending to read a book titled *My Pet Goat*. Have you ever before had a chance to study his face on that morning? Has anything other than this movie made you feel the unendurable length of his inaction? What do you suppose he was thinking for all that time, as he stared into space? Moore himself asks that last question on the soundtrack, as a way of opening a biographical digression about Bush, his family and their business interests. This section of the film will particularly incense Moore's attackers, who will pronounce on him the dependable slur of "conspiracy theorist."

So, to digress on my own:

Moore alleges no conspiracies. He merely says that Bush has motives beyond those he's willing to state. To make this case, Moore begins by showing that the Bush family in general, and George W. in particular, have received lavish support over the years from the Saudi elite, including the bin Ladens, and have offered valuable help in turn. Unlike the actualities footage that Moore uses in the film, these facts are by now widely known—although it was news to me that Prince Bandar, the Saudi ambassador, dined with Bush at the White House on September 13, 2001. In speculating about this dinner, and about the subsequent airlifting out of the United States of more than a hundred Saudis when everyone else was grounded, Moore goes only so far as to say that the overwhelmingly Saudi makeup of the September 11 attack teams could have proved embarrassing to Bush. He would not have wanted journalists just then to begin looking into his personal ties to Saudi interests, or to ask whether any useful information had emerged from the two dozen bin Ladens who had been in the country, and whom he soon spirited away without the indignity of questioning.

Nothing conspiratorial about that. The worst you can reasonably say of this section of the film is that it gives Moore the opportunity for one of his man-on-the-street pranks. He films himself and Craig Unger (author of the book *House of Bush, House of Saud*) in front of the Watergate complex in Washington, directly across the street from the Saudi Embassy: a choice of location that insures interruption. Sure enough, onto the scene drive carloads of Secret Service agents, who just want to ask, politely, why a film crew is working on this spot. The agents move off readily enough when given the answer, although one of them seems abashed when Moore blandly delivers his punch line: "I didn't realize the Secret Service guards foreign embassies."

In fact, reasonable people may find this to be the best part of the section.

You may have heard, by the way, that Moore is less of a presence in *Fahrenheit 9/11* than he was in his previous pictures. Actually, he's always with you, in voiceover; but he does perform for the camera less than usual. At times, his stunts serve to drive home a point, as when he accosts members of Congress on the street and offers them recruiting brochures, in case they want to enlist their children in the military. At other times, his antics are pure comic relief. (After complaining that the House passed the USA Patriot Act sight unseen, Moore corrects the situation by reading the bill aloud to Congress, circling the Capitol in an ice-cream truck and reciting the provisions over a loudspeaker.) Either way, though, Moore makes sparing use of this sort of material in advancing his main charges against Bush.

The first principal accusation is that Bush had gotten along just fine with the Taliban before September 11 (which is demonstrable) and didn't much care about fighting them afterward (which is unproved but plausible). Bush invaded Afghanistan, Moore claims, because he had to be seen to do something, because the war helpfully diverted attention from the Saudis and because those closest to him would gain lucrative contracts for a natural-gas pipeline. Moore's second accusation is that Bush undertook the war in Iraq for even shadier purposes. As *Nation* readers knew, and as others have since caught on, Bush attacked without even the excuse he'd had in Afghanistan of pursuing bin Laden. There were no terrorists in Iraq to destroy, no military threats to counter—and unless you define "democracy" as the creation of profit-making opportunities for Halliburton, no process of democratization to pursue.

There is also a third principal point, most devastating of all. But before I go into that, let me digress once more, to sum up the impressively varied materials that Moore assembles to make these arguments.

The film contains, as I've said, a few of Moore's little skits, along with a lot of borrowed actualities footage, which is usually surprising and sometimes shocking. (How many shots have you seen of daily life in Baghdad immediately before the war? How many dead and wounded Iraqi civilians have you looked at close up?) In addition, you find pop-culture images, which Moore takes over for purposes of sarcasm or parody (as when he remakes the TV western *Bonanza* as the Bush adventure *Afghanistan*); talking-head interviews with expert commentators (such as former counterterrorism chief Richard Clarke, former FBI agent Jack Cloogan and Senator Byron Dorgan); a range of texts and graphics; patches of direct cinema (for example, an excursion to a shopping mall in Flint, Michigan, with a couple of Marine recruiters); and, most critical of all, filmed encounters with ordinary citizens, who pretty much have the frame to themselves while Moore stays quietly out of the way.

The most important of these citizens, the one who takes over the final portion of the movie, is Lila Lipscomb of Flint, mother of Sgt. Michael Pedersen, who served in a helicopter unit in Iraq and was killed in action sometime after "the completion of major combat operations." Lipscomb is a pleasantly robust woman of modest means, patriotic and Christian in convictions, guileless in manner, whose role in the polemic is simple: She is meant to embody disillusionment. Having once despised all protesters against war, feeling that they were slapping our soldiers in the face, she now grieves over a dead son, whose final letter home said of Bush, "He got us out here for nothing." In a succession of artfully spaced scenes, which constitute the film's third damning charge against Bush, Lipscomb speaks of the meager possibilities open to most young people in Flint; she recalls having encouraged her own children to enter the military, believing it to be a good thing to do and a good opportunity; and at the end, bereft, with Moore trailing behind, she visits the White House (or as close to it as you can get these days) and says she is glad to be there, since it gives her a place to put her anger.

Lipscomb makes a very efficient witness—but she is an intractably complex movie character. She just doesn't fit Moore's scheme. He generally relies on economics to explain the behavior of the elite and psychology to account for the rest of us. (As you may recall from *Bowling for Columbine*, he is very interested in the way politicians and the communications media use fear to grab attention and elicit compliance.) But when it comes to Lipscomb, Moore (to his great credit) forgets about his standard categories. For perhaps the first time in his career, he shows someone as a fully rounded personality, animated by beliefs and loyalties that he does not necessarily share but must respect; and so he allows her emotions to overwhelm his cleverness.

This is the point at which *Fahrenheit 9/11* may overwhelm you, too. Perhaps it will seem trivial to a pollster, counting and recounting those swing votes, that this campaign tool should also qualify as a work of art; but I can't believe the effect will be lost on moviegoers.

Fahrenheit 9/11 is Michael Moore's most urgent diatribe and also his best, most moving film.

The Nation, July 12, 2004

Gunner Palace

What might it mean to call a film indispensable? Perhaps not much. At base level, we'd merely be asserting that other films (maybe the vast majority) are candidates for the garbage heap. Since experience so powerfully ratifies this definition, we might say, in plain words, that an indispensable film is a keeper. But what would we keep it for?

The pleasure of its parts, to begin with: a personality, a setting, a moment that is worth revisiting. Beyond that, we might mean that the film as a whole is an experience we can no longer imagine being without. It has changed us and so has become a part of us. This is a more forceful definition, though one that still covers a great many cases. I have known people who considered the masterpieces of Yasujiro Ozu to be transformative in this sense, but also George Cukor's *Les Girls*.

But then there's the strongest and most restrictive meaning. An indispensable film is one that we keep because we have no other choice. An urgent circumstance thrusts it upon us, as the battered shield is pressed on the hero of a quest romance. Were we to let it drop, we would fail a situation much larger than ourselves. I think the documentary *Gunner Palace*, by Michael Tucker and Petra Epperlein, is indispensable in this highest sense. Every adult citizen ought to see it. So should every kid over the age of 13.

The circumstance that forces *Gunner Palace* upon us is the Iraq War. The United States government has declared victory in this conflict more than once; a semblance of Iraqi self-government has been established; and still 150,000 American troops patrol the country, to the incurious approbation of their countrymen. What exactly do these troops do? How do they feel about it? Despite all the yellow ribbons, no one (except for immediate family and friends) seems to want to know. I offer this judgment not as my own opinion but as the angry, disdainful verdict of several of the soldiers in the 2/3 Field Artillery—the Gunners—who opened themselves to Tucker.

For a month in the autumn of 2003 and another month early in 2004, Tucker lived in Baghdad with soldiers in the 2/3, who apparently accepted him as their own. It's not improbable that they should have done so. Americans are an astonishingly candid people (so noted an Iraqi interpreter, interviewed in *Gunner Palace*) who will pour out their life stories after knowing you for all of ten minutes. They are also a media-saturated people, who willingly play to a camera because they already imagine themselves in show business. (The film is full of soldiers who doubled as rap artists, rock stars and stand-up comedians.) Mostly, though, Tucker's subjects seem to have been grateful for the attention, however short-lived. Did they think that anyone back home understood what they were going through? The answer—the eternal soldier's answer, adapted for an era of cable TV—was no. We're "just entertainment," said one, "better than any action movie." Said another, "You'll forget me by the end of this movie. You'll forget all of us." As the unit's leading poet, Specialist Richmond Shaw, declared, "For y'all this is just a show, but we live in this movie."

It had a hell of a set, too. The 2/3 was stationed in a bombed-out palace formerly occupied by Uday Hussein, giving the unit a billet with three strata of architecture: the self-aggrandizing gaudiness of the old regime, covered with a thick layer of rubble and then topped with the quasi-suburban functionalism of today's Army (which supplied inner tubes for recreation in Uday's swimming pool, and even materials for a putting green). "The staircase is still pretty safe to use," a soldier explained to Tucker on an introductory tour, pointing amid the wreckage to a buddy mounting a grandiose, spiraling heap of marble. A note of triumph. ("Now we own this place.") A note of fatalism. ("But it might collapse under our feet.")

The reason for the fatalism became clear whenever Tucker rode out of the palace with the 2/3. The unit had been equipped and trained to hold back a Red Army advance across Germany, not to police the streets of Baghdad. Now they were bumping along in their Humvees through the Adhamiya district—a place where Uday used to feel comfortable—keeping order among people who dabbed the walls with pro-Saddam graffiti, staged anti-occupation demonstrations at the mosque and planted the occasional roadside bomb. Early in the course of production, Tucker was with the Gunners when they thought they'd discovered one such improvised explosive device lying on a major street. The soldiers stopped traffic in both directions; they hung back and conferred among themselves. After fifteen minutes, while Tucker somehow kept the video camera steady in his hands, one of them walked up to the suspect object and gave it a kick.

The daily round. Tucker's video diary gives you the sense of a cycle, at once repetitive and nerve-racking, of daytime patrols and nocturnal raids, interrupted by periods of blowing off steam in the palace. (One notable poolside party had the title of

"Gunnerpalooza.") Thanks to the immediacy of Tucker's video-diary format, the effect in *Gunner Palace* is alternately gripping and surrealistic, although somewhat murky as well. He recorded exactly one woman dancing with the guys at Gunnerpalooza but was unable, or unwilling, to apply his eyewitness method to the obvious question: So what do these people do for sex?

Unanswered questions of a more troubling kind are suggested by Tucker's footage of the nighttime house raids. In one instance, he videotaped the troops as they arrested two brothers on charges of building bombs. Who had accused the men? Neither the footage nor Tucker's voiceover will tell. All we learn is that the soldiers found no evidence—but forwarded the detainees to Abu Ghraib.

Of course, the merit of Tucker's approach is that it treats you as a grown-up. You are free to ask your own unsettling questions, and also to acknowledge that much of what Tucker saw the Gunners do was useful, even admirable. He videotaped them as they picked up a ragged, glue-sniffing kid off the street and deposited him, with extraordinary gentleness, in a safe place. He followed the soldiers into an orphanage, where they spent their Saturday morning feeding lollipops to the children and cradling newborns. He watched as the unit's patient, thoughtful, thoroughly decent commander, Lieut. Col. Bill Rabena, brought calm to a shouting match at a meeting of the District Advisory Council; and Tucker was there for the follow-up, when Rabena provided a handgun and small-weapons training to a female council member whose life had been threatened.

For those of us who have opposed the war, it is important—indispensable—to witness the care and self-restraint of these soldiers. Maybe they were on their best behavior with a video camera around—maybe Tucker had harsher footage, which he chose not to show—but there is still plenty in *Gunner Palace* to put to shame the standard Brechtian caricatures.

As for those who endorse the war: It ought to be indispensable—required, in fact—to listen to the soldiers' voices in *Gunner Palace*. You hear the cold, suppressed rage when they come to the scene of a bombing, expecting to help the wounded, only to be stoned by the crowd. You hear professionalism strained to the snapping point when they arrest one of their former interpreters, who has been accused of aiding the insurgency. Disillusionment freights the words of one soldier, who loves being in the Army but feels like "I'm not defending my country anymore." Weariness and disgust hang in the throat of another, who has been assigned to shape up the Iraqi forces: "I can't train someone who doesn't give a shit. These people are just here to pick up a paycheck. The minute we're gone, you know what'll happen." And from the unexpected source of the unit's premier flake, Specialist Stuart Wilf, comes the voice of pained conscience at the end of the movie, when Tucker asks whether he can rationalize the violence. "I don't think it's worth the death of someone's family member," Wilf replies. "I don't think you can rationalize a child dying."

The Nation, March 21, 2005

Occupation: Dreamland

Although *Occupation: Dreamland* was filmed entirely in Falluja, only two of its three main settings are Iraqi. Those places are the shadowless streets, their bleached yellow walls huddling together on a dusty plain, seen in long shot during daylight hours; and the murky interiors of houses, shot after sundown with a nightscope to yield shaky, close-up, glowing-green views. The third principal setting, by contrast, might as well be a lamp-lit American dormitory, cluttered with rumpled beds and wallpapered with pinup photos. This is the barracks of the 82nd Airborne's Alpha Company, 1/505.

Here the soldiers feel sufficiently at home to talk about their discomfort—their contempt, despair and rage—at stepping into foreign spaces. "I was never out of the country before, except for booze runs to fuckin' Mexico," marvels Pfc. Thomas Turner, expressing a commonly held sense of disbelief. Like many of his buddies, he says he never imagined that enlistment in the Army would result in his being sent to someplace strange and dangerous. You have no cause to doubt that his frayed ingenuousness is real, or that Sgt. Eric Forbes is voicing an equally common response to this posting when he says of Falluja, "I hate these people."

Forbes makes that comment soon after a fellow soldier has died in a roadside bombing, so you may take the remark as no more than situational. Forbes seems to have no existential loathing for Iraqis—in fact, he describes them as caught haplessly in the way, as the United States lunges for oil—but whatever hostility he's sparked in Falluja, he will return it, and with twice the firepower. At their most gung-ho, soldiers like Forbes think of combat as a release from the tension of policing the Iraqis. "I like bein' shot at. It makes it interesting," claims Staff Sgt. Ryan Mish, who says that sometimes "I just want to light everybody up." On the more mature end of the scale, the soldiers regard the occupation as an end in itself, self-perpetuating and self-enclosed. "What are we securing here?" asks Capt. Terence Caliguire at a staff briefing. "We're securing essentially ourselves. So what are we protecting? I don't know."

Shot in January and February 2004 by Garrett Scott and Ian Olds, this admirably direct and spare documentary is the second feature released this year to record the lives of American soldiers in Iraq. It follows Petra Epperlein and Michael Tucker's *Gunner Palace*, which was shot in Baghdad at almost the same time (autumn

2003-winter 2004), and which focused on soldiers in the 2/3 Field Artillery. At the risk of sounding heartless, I will describe *Gunner Palace* as the more entertaining of the films. It dwells on the surrealism of the Field Artillery's having billeted itself in a bombed-out pleasure palace, and it makes the most of the soldiers' desire to play to the camera. Freestyle rappers, poets and platoon flakes are much in evidence. Also, while it presents a thoroughly unsentimental view of the war, *Gunner Palace* gives a varied account of the occupiers. You sometimes see them trying hard to help Iraqis; you witness moments of generosity and even tenderness.

Occupation: Dreamland is a drier experience, and a more somber one. Its lightest scene records how one GI tries good-heartedly to converse in phrase-book Arabic, despite getting stuck at "*Salaam aleikum.*" In a more touching sequence, Spc. Patrick Napoli uses an Army manual to drill his squad in sign language. The soldiers work hard at it, and Napoli expresses pride in momentarily being a leader. But he adds, "I'm in Iraq. It's a little late for a sign language class."

That's as hopeful as it gets in *Occupation: Dreamland*, a picture in which most of the soldiers admit to having enlisted for lack of anything better to do, and now find they have nothing to look forward to other than self-preservation. Why the sense of futility? The reason becomes clear whenever Arabs take over the scene (as they never do in *Gunner Palace*), to deliver extended, impromptu street tirades against the occupation. They shout at the soldiers through an overburdened interpreter, and they shout at the filmmakers, too. You're not in Baghdad any longer, the men warn. "This is Falluja. Be careful of Falluja."

And why should the foreigners be careful of this particular place? On this subject, *Occupation: Dreamland* is silent, Scott and Olds having chosen to present only what they recorded themselves, during one slice of time. So, if you rely solely on the words spoken in the film, you might conclude that Falluja is populated by principled anticolonialists, or perhaps tradition-bound paternalists. (There was much outrage on the streets, when Scott and Olds were in town, about the Americans having taken a woman into custody.) On the other hand, if you've absorbed some of the news media's standard phrases about Falluja—Sunni Triangle, Baath loyalists—you might write off much of the anger as the rage of a corrupt minority at losing power.

Or perhaps you know more. Maybe you've read of how Saddam Hussein wasn't all that fond of Falluja, whose clerics had been annoyingly independent. Maybe you can even remember how Falluja, though correspondingly cool toward Saddam, became a center of insurgency. In April 2003, just three weeks after US tanks entered Baghdad, American troops opened fire on a protest march in Falluja, killing a reported fifteen people and wounding seventy-five. After that, the citizens were dead set against Americans—a piece of information that was highly relevant to Alpha Company, and might be relevant to your understanding of its soldiers, but cannot be gleaned from *Occupation: Dreamland*.

In short, you have to bring your own context to the picture, which is that much poorer for its own stinginess. I would not stress this complaint, except that every record we can get of the occupation is crucial. Fighting is no longer beamed into everyone's living room as it was during the Vietnam War. The pictures are now available mostly to the funny people who visit art houses and rent obscure DVDs, or who might tune in to a premium cable channel that's showing *Gunner Palace* or *Occupation: Dreamland*. Precisely because this core audience is limited, the information in the documentaries shouldn't be. Every new viewer who stumbles across these films is statistically significant.

That said, Scott and Olds can claim the integrity of having given you just what they saw and heard themselves during six weeks in residence with Alpha Company. The material may be fragmentary and ambiguous by nature, but it was hard won, and it has an undeniable force. This is what it's like to be bored, itchy, angry, isolated, underprepared and far outnumbered among a foreign people who hate you. This is what many of us art-house types will never know firsthand.

The Nation, October 10, 2005

Paradise Now

Khaled is the skeletal hothead with the Richard Widmark sneer. Saïd is more the Clive Owen type: a brooding hunk with soft lips and bottomless eyes. At the young men's place of employment, an auto repair shop, Saïd is the one who tries to talk his way around an abusive customer. "Your bumper was put on straight," he says soothingly. "It only looks crooked because the ground slopes." When this explanation doesn't go over, it's Khaled who steps up with a crowbar to level the bumper by smashing it.

This scene, establishing the characters and social world of two young buddies, might have come from any film in the neorealist tradition, made anywhere in the world over the past half-century. If you've seen more than three such pictures, you can guess what will come next: The friendship will be tested, in circumstances that will include a tentative romance and a run-in with the law. *Paradise Now* fulfills these expectations; but it does more, because the setting is present-day Nablus, the love interest is the daughter of a slain Palestinian militant and the crime is a suicide bombing—or, as Saïd and Khaled think of it, a martyrdom operation.

Directed by Hany Abu-Assad (*Rana's Wedding*, *Ford Transit*) from a script he wrote with producer Bero Beyer, *Paradise Now* is as well researched and responsible a movie as we're likely to get about the who, how and why of Palestinian suicide attacks. Some viewers have faulted the film for assuming the miseries and humiliations of life under Israeli occupation, rather than demonstrating them; others have complained that the film sticks too closely to the experience of Saïd (Kais Nashef) and Khaled (Ali Suliman) and so may excuse their dreadful methods. But most people, I think, will see *Paradise Now* as a great balancing act in which Abu-Assad poses a set of moral and political weights atop his teetering, fallible characters.

As Abu-Assad is quick to state, *Paradise Now* is a movie, not a report or a polemic. In his interviews, including one conducted at *The Nation*, he has explained that the subject of suicide bombing allowed him to combine two of his favorite types of film, the action thriller and "the boring genre" (that is, observational works about daily affairs). Life in the occupied territories is so uncertain, he says, that if you just show people drinking a cup of tea, you've already got a suspense scene. Add a ticking bomb, and the requirements of a thriller are formally met.

By taking this cinephilic approach to his material, Abu-Assad in no way cleared himself of addressing the reality, which is why he prepared for the film by doing extensive research. But he was so determined to work within movie conventions that he insisted on shooting *Paradise Now* on location, in besieged Nablus, using 35mm film—a decision that risked his own neck and the many necks of his crew and ultimately proved unworkable, due to missile attacks and mine explosions and the kidnapping of his location manager. He had to complete the film in his native Nazareth—but by then, Abu-Assad had written *Paradise Now* into the history of impossibly difficult productions, from *Intolerance* through *Fitzcarraldo*.

More important, he had gotten an exceptionally good picture.

The momentum is continuous from very early in the film, when Jamal (Amer Hlehel), a fellow with a professor's corduroy jacket and lecturing manner, draws Saïd down a deserted passageway to tell him that his mission with Khaled is set for tomorrow. To lend support to the volunteer in this joyful moment (and to keep him locked in), Jamal honors Saïd's family by inviting himself to dinner and sleeping over in Saïd's room. You feel as if Saïd has just turned into a bullet in the cylinder. And as you follow the stages of preparation the next day—the transfer to a safe house, the videotaping of a martyrdom speech, the fastening of the explosive belt and dressing of the bombers in inconspicuous suits (so they look like freshly shaved toughs from *Reservoir Dogs*)—everything contributes to the sense of a quick, claustrophobic one-way passage.

Yet neither chance nor choice will go away. By the time Saïd gets to the safe house, he is silently carrying along a second consciousness: his awareness of Suha (Lubna Azabal), who is beautiful and welcoming and has given him something to live for. As the daughter of a famed militant, she has impeccable nationalist credentials; and yet she is a disturbance, too, having recently come to the West Bank from the diaspora, bringing with her a culture and a politics more capacious than anything Saïd has known. Her wide smile and easy talk already make him wobble in the chamber. Then, when mishaps crop up in the mission—from a comically bungled videotaping to a dangerously mistimed rendezvous—Saïd finds himself literally on the loose, traveling through the landscape as an unguided human projectile.

And Khaled? He, too, is under unexpected pressure. Despite a temperament that's ill suited to the task, he has to mollify the furious mission commanders, find his way to Saïd and save his friend's life — temporarily.

So, in its form, *Paradise Now* is about a race against the clock, but also something more. It's about the contrast between confinement and freedom of movement, a contrast that plays out simultaneously as physical, political and moral. Physical, because the action of the movie takes you from cramped streets and piled-up buildings into a space that's so shockingly open it might as well have zero gravity. Political, because Khaled and Saïd say that the Israeli occupation is a "lifelong imprisonment" from which their mission is the only possible jailbreak. Moral, because however much they feel that they have no alternative, decisions always lie before them.

Some of these points emerge in the dialogue. But the remarkable achievement of *Paradise Now* is that the debates and speeches, though urgent, always function as part of a cinematic texture. It's an action thriller; it's a neorealist buddy picture. It's something new in the movies, and extraordinary.

The Nation, November 7, 2005

The Road to Guantánamo

A prisoner squats in the darkness of his cell, cowering under an assault of strobe lights and screeching music. You sit in the darkness of a theater, your imagination ripped open by flickering lights and a soundtrack mix. An interrogator makes up a cover identity for himself, tosses out misleading information, rattles his suspect with evidentiary photos that may not prove anything. A feature filmmaker invents characters, stretches truth to fit the plot, patches in news footage without regard to the original context (or shoots fictional scenes and makes them seem documentary).

Maybe I'm comparing apples to oranges here—or grenades to pineapples. But on the formal level at least, Michael Winterbottom and Mat Whitecross's *The Road to Guantánamo* mimics the actions of its most shadowy characters: the American officials who held captive and brutalized three young British men, all of Pakistani background, on the grounds that they were (as George W. Bush says) "bad people."

Since I greatly admire *The Road to Guantánamo* and hope millions of people will see it, I'd better be able to justify its use of the always dubious techniques of docudrama. So, to establish a base level of reality, I begin with a question: In what did the alleged badness of Asif Iqbal, Rhuhel Ahmed and Shafiq Rasul consist? Here are the facts of the case of the Tipton Three, as you may learn from sources such as the Center for Constitutional Rights.

In September 2001, shortly after the attacks on the World Trade Center and the Pentagon, 19-year-old Asif left his home in Tipton, outside Birmingham, and flew to Pakistan to prepare for his impending wedding. His friends Rhuhel and Shafiq soon joined him on vacation, along with a fourth buddy named Monir (later lost on the road and presumed dead). Though not unusually devout, the young men were religious enough to visit a mosque while knocking about Karachi; and there they heard, and responded to, an imam's call to support their fellow Muslims in Afghanistan, which was then facing American invasion.

It is not clear to me, either from my reading or from the film, what exactly Asif, Rhuhel and Shafiq thought they might do in Afghanistan: fight against the Americans, provide humanitarian aid or just look around. Considering their youth and history of recklessness (we'll get to that), they may not have had any clear idea themselves. What we do know, with reasonable certainty, is that they crossed the border, quickly realized they'd ventured into a scene of diarrhea-inducing chaos and then (once the bombs started to drop) discovered they had no sure way to leave. After a week or so, the swirl of events carried them from Kabul to the Taliban outpost of Kunduz. There, amid a horde of men surrendering to Northern Alliance forces, they were put onto a hellish transport to Shebargan Prison.

After that, things turned ugly. In late December 2001 US forces took possession of Asif, Rhuhel and Shafiq, who by mid-February 2002 were living in chain-link cages in Guantánamo, at Camp X-Ray. At its core, *The Road to Guantánamo* is a dramatization of the treatment the men claim to have received there, and subsequently at Camp Delta, from which they were at last released into British custody in March 2004. For more than two years, they had been kept imprisoned without any legal process, to be endlessly interrogated and (by any meaningful definition of the word) tortured—first on the possibility that they might know something about Al Qaeda, and then on the assumption that they were themselves Al Qaeda members. We may gauge the baselessness of these suspicions from the fact that the three are not still shut up in Camp Delta.

And what of the possibility that they'd wanted to take up weapons with the Taliban? We may judge the seriousness of that scenario by the fact that British authorities held Asif, Rhuhel and Shafiq for just one day of questioning in London before releasing them, without charges, back into the general population of Tipton.

So much for the facts. Now for the movie.

The Road to Guantánamo entwines three kinds of narration. The first consists of testimonies given straight into the camera by Asif, Rhuhel and Shafiq. They are in their mid-20s now, robust and bearded (the latter two in the flowing style of the pious). All three speak with quiet self-assurance, laughing incredulously more often than voicing anger—though you'll notice that Asif's eyes no longer work together well.

The film's second narrative strand is a dramatization of these testimonies, shot in Pakistan, Afghanistan and Iran and featuring previously untried young performers (Rizwan Ahmed, Farhad Harun, Waqar Siddiqui and Arfan Usman) playing the principal roles. These boyish actors, though thoroughly convincing, look nothing like the men you see in the interviews; and so the film subtly marks their scenes as re-creations, despite the immediacy and intensity of these episodes—the jostling market crowds and jouncing buses, the swarms of flies, the shiny new six-foot-square cages.

In style, these parts of the movie recall Winterbottom's remarkable 2002 film *In This World*, which re-created the journey of an Afghan boy, Jamal Udin Torabi, from a refugee camp in Pakistan to the streets of London. The probings and dartings of the hand-held camera, the unsettling rhythms of the editing, keep you caught up physically in the scenes, which tend to emphasize corporeal experience: how the characters washed, what they ate, where they went to the toilet. But for all that, you may remark during the episodes at Camp X-Ray and Camp Delta that you're not witnessing events but watching a reconstruction of them, based on the inmates' memories. You may wonder: Did the guards force prisoners to kneel in just this way, eating gravel while presenting their buttocks? When a five-man team in riot gear came to seize someone, did they quick-step as you see here, single-file, so they looked like a giant black caterpillar? We'll probably never know; the Guantánamo manual of procedure is not likely to be published. These visceral realizations may therefore be the closest we'll come to the truth, even though they are, admittedly, just realizations.

So *The Road to Guantánamo* establishes an implied distance between its fictionalizations and the facts—a distance that meanwhile keeps collapsing, due to the film's third type of narration: clips of news footage, and studio-produced voiceovers made to sound like a reporter's off-camera commentary. This material is the glue of the movie, sticking scenes together with a layer of information or a gloss of authenticity. The reportage, both fake and real, thickens the emotion (as does the film's other glue, the soundtrack music, which is the usual Winterbottom minimalism— like "Adagio for Strings" boiled down to syrup). It also adds a weight of objectivity to whatever you're seeing, no matter how subjective the underlying source.

Now, I don't have any problem with this approach—but then, neither am I the sort of person who denies that something awful has been going on at Guantánamo. Those who prefer to believe (despite all evidence to the contrary) that the abuses are minor and necessary—that Guantánamo holds only terrorists and their allies, who are treated no more roughly than they must be—may seize on Winterbottom and Whitecross's double game as an excuse to dismiss the whole movie. These critics (I'm sure they're out there) will insist this docudrama is culpable on both the formal and ethical levels.

Do the ends justify the means? That depends, I suppose, not only on the nature of the ends but on whether the means have a chance of achieving them. From documented facts, rather than docudrama, we know that the means used at Guantánamo, besides being repugnant in themselves, are wildly unlikely to deter the world's terrorists. By contrast, the means used in *The Road to Guantánamo* are both artful and effective.

Besides, if *The Road to Guantánamo* may be compared to an interrogator because of the tricks it practices—playing on the audience's suggestibility, for example, by compiling battle scenes out of a handful of night-scope images and a whole lot of sound effects—so too might it be likened in shadiness to the Tipton Three themselves. The young men's salvation, it turned out, was their history of run-ins with the law. "The police were our alibi," one of the men says with satisfaction, noting that he'd been reporting to his probation officer during the whole period when supposedly— so the interrogators said—he'd been off training in an Al Qaeda camp. It's possible for a well-timed misdemeanor to clear you of a hanging offense; and a bit of directorial fudging sometimes can make a film more rather than less ethical.

Winterbottom and Whitecross went to extraordinary lengths to tell the story of the Tipton Three, hauling their crew on a long, risky, dusty journey. That's the adventurous part, which made this production a road movie for the subjects and filmmakers alike. The defiant part has to do with a sense of quiet outrage that runs through the picture. Some of this tone comes from Asif, Rhuhel and Shafiq themselves, but some also comes from the filmmakers' clear determination to do justice to their story.

It's a story that goes far beyond the immediate characters. As Winterbottom and Whitecross show, the Tipton Three were kept at Guantánamo long after it had become obvious that they had no connection to terrorists. How many others, then, are still imprisoned, even though the jailers know they're guiltless? How many remain caged, or shut up in solitary confinement cells, only because the authorities don't want to admit they shouldn't have been kept at all?

Until we get an accounting, let's be grateful we've got the docudrama.

The Nation, July 3, 2006

9 Star Hotel

To savor the full irony of the Israeli documentary *9 Star Hotel*, you need to know something more than director-cinematographer Ido Haar tells you. He's a practitioner of direct cinema, committed to whatever evidence his lens and microphone might capture; and so he plunges straight into the horrid absurdity of his story, assuming that his primary audience needs no instruction about its setting. Everyone in Israel is familiar with the new city of Modi'in, a vast project being constructed midway between Tel Aviv and Jerusalem according to a master plan by architect Moshe Safdie. But for those who could use the information, I quote from the city's promotional brochure: "Ever since the establishment of Israel, the country's leaders have dreamed of reviving the ancient Jewish town of Modi'in, a symbol of Hasmonean heroism and of the conservation of the Jewish and national identity of the people of Israel. The establishment of the city of Modi'in in the 1990's was the ancient Jewish dream coming true."

9 Star Hotel records a few details about some of the laborers who pour concrete, hammer lath and lay stone for this dream. They are young Palestinian men who have no jobs in the occupied territories but no permits to work in Israel. So they live in shanties hidden in the hills and dodge three distinct security forces every day, going back and forth from building Modi'in.

You see them from a distance as the film begins, two or three at first, then as many as a dozen pouring down a grassy hillside at dawn. From afar, they seem a part of the landscape. But then the camera is suddenly in their midst as they hurry through a pine forest, each lugging a knapsack or duffle bag, and then dash across a highway. You hear their heavy breathing, and the lookout's warning about police patrols. Not for the last time in *9 Star Hotel*, the image becomes a jerky assemblage of pavement, sky, somebody's back, then the temporary respite of tall grass. At this stage, early in the film, all you know of the characters is this collective blur. But after some shots of the construction site, the scene changes again to the men's encampment. They cook tomato stew in the communal pot. They retire to their shelters: a hive of wooden crates, covered variously in plastic tarps and salvaged draperies. They chat deep into the night about the homes they've left, their families, their memories; and so these official non-persons take on names, characters, individuality.

As you come to know these people, you may wonder: How invisible are they? Surely drivers on the busy highway must see them; Haar shows you scenes of the men running across traffic. Sometimes Israeli children see them, too—as when the men come across three Jewish kids in a field outside Modi'in, who cadge some construction materials for play. And even though Haar recorded no interactions between the laborers and their foremen, somebody on the building site must have looked at these people long enough to hire them. Everybody sees—but nobody chooses to notice, except for the cops who are charged with running the men down.

Thanks to Haar, though, you also notice. You find out where these men bathe, which songs they sing, how much they earn, what happens to them when they're sick or injured, what they think about the Israelis. (A hint: They're not big fans.) You stay with them through the long nights of watching headlights pass on the distant highway, and through days on end when it's raining and there's no work to be had, so they just hole up, useless, in their boxes.

Why did these frustrated, hunted men trust an Israeli to camp out with them and bring along his camera? Maybe it was a way to keep their spirits up. You see throughout the film how they sustain themselves through joshing, bull sessions, scavenging, reminiscence. Perhaps they found one more outlet in Haar, who gave them a way to show themselves. It's the least they could want—but more than the promoters of Modi'in are willing to allow.

The Nation, June 11, 2007

No End in Sight

Like a dictator's statue in a grandiose plaza, the Iraq War can be seen and hated from various angles. Some filmmakers have loathed it through the eyes of US soldiers (in *Gunner Palace* and *Occupation: Dreamland*), others from the viewpoint of Iraqi civilians (*My Country, My Country* and *Iraq in Fragments*). These documentarians observe the war from ground level. Charles Ferguson, who wrote, produced and directed the invaluable *No End in Sight*, hates the war from a novel perspective. He looks at it from the top, or as close to it as he can get.

At telling moments in *No End in Sight*, an inserted title will dryly explain that Ferguson failed to secure an interview with this or that subject: Dick Cheney, Donald Rumsfeld, Paul Wolfowitz, Paul Bremer. But here are some of the people who did talk to him: Gen. Jay Garner, who ostensibly ran Iraq for a few weeks in 2003 as director of the short-lived Office of Reconstruction and Humanitarian Assistance (ORHA); Ambassador Barbara Bodine, in charge of Baghdad for ORHA; Col. Paul Hughes, director of strategic policy for the occupation (2003); Col. Lawrence Wilkerson, former chief of staff to Colin Powell; and Robert Hutchings, chairman of the National Intelligence Council (2003-05).

Ferguson relies on other sorts of witnesses as well (journalists, academics, soldiers, Iraqi officials) and a dense compilation of archival footage that ranges in effect from absurdity (Rumsfeld's news conferences) to horror. But it's the well-credentialed informants who establish the character of *No End in Sight*, by means of their privileged knowledge of the war and their shared experience of having been overruled by the Cheney-Rumsfeld inner circle. These are the people who weren't listened to. By adopting their perspective, Ferguson unquestionably gives a slanted, partial view of the war—but one that is indispensable and peculiarly damning.

The peculiarity is evident in the way Ferguson allots his screen time. Although *No End in Sight* recounts more than twenty years of history, from the Iran-Iraq war to the present, by far the longest section of the film covers a period of just four months, from January 20 to May 23, 2003. On the first of those dates, while preparing to invade, Bush assigned responsibility for postwar Iraq to the Pentagon, which would act through the newly created ORHA. On the latter date, Paul Bremer of the even newer Coalition Provisional Authority (CPA) finished undoing everything that ORHA had been trying to achieve.

ORHA had begun assembling an interim Iraqi government. CPA dismissed the attempt. ORHA had sought to work with whatever Iraqi managerial class it could locate. CPA effectively got rid of all trained personnel by banning Baath Party members from public employment. ORHA had been registering members of the Iraqi army with the aim of organizing a police force and national guard. On May 23, the CPA disbanded the army, plunging into desperation the families of some 400,000 now-jobless men with guns. In Ferguson's eyes, the history of the Iraq War is essentially a story about these early, rotten decisions, which by the end of May 2003, he argues, had already consigned the country to chaos and civil war.

How does Ferguson go about making this case? A typical sequence (reconstructed here in approximation) might begin with archival footage of the looted National Museum and the immolated National Archive, with a voiceover narration (spoken by Campbell Scott) setting forth the bare facts of the event. Iraqis in the ruins cry out the heartbroken commentary. From this setup, Ferguson cuts to interviews with Hughes, who testifies that US troops were made to stand by ("There was no order to establish martial law"), and with Barbara Bodine, who makes it clear that this idleness was deliberate policy. ("The word came from Washington not to interfere with the looting. There was to be no police work.") You see further images of buildings being ripped apart, machinery being carted away in the streets, fires raging, people sifting through rubble. A journalist, in this case Nir Rosen, sums up the situation: "Guys with guns took over—and they were the Iraqi guys with guns." Then comes a clip of Rumsfeld cutting up at a news conference: "Stuff happens."

The method is almost rhythmic in its regularity: sobriety from the voiceover, aptness and force from the archival images, quiet anger from the informants and then a punch line of utter obliviousness from Rumsfeld. Applying this formula to the period that most concerns him, Ferguson reviews each major decision made by the White House—to toss aside the State Department's postwar planning, to occupy Iraq with scarcely enough troops to secure Peoria, to allow Baghdad to be stripped to the walls—and establishes two critical points: The outcome was catastrophic, and the catastrophe was predicted.

But perhaps I should say Ferguson conducts this review for almost every decision. The six months preceding January 2003, when the "intelligence and facts were being fixed around the policy" (as the Downing Street memo put it), get only a blink of screen time compared with the four months that followed. Granted, the film acknowledges Bush's haste to make war against Saddam Hussein; but acknowledgment is not prosecution. *No End in Sight* provides scant information about the Bush Administration's knowing lies and none at all about critical matters like the UN weapons-inspection program or the international movement that warned against invasion. (Some correct predictions, evidently, are less respectable than others.) Saddam's crimes, by contrast, take the screen in vivid detail. In this way, the film treats as plausible the first and most disastrous decision.

This approach isn't entirely unexpected. A first-time filmmaker who in his other life was a senior fellow at the Brookings Institution and a member of the Council on Foreign Relations, Ferguson is most interested in studying how a clique of top officials, lacking in military experience and self-isolated from dissenting opinion, made mistake after mistake in implementing policy. He is not interested in thinking about a much wider range of people—including Council on Foreign Relations types, prominent journalists and current frontrunners for the Democratic presidential nomination—who acquiesced to the bunglers as they prepared for war.

Not that I'm taking names. I just want to point out that the emphasis conforms to the analysis. If you believe, as Ferguson does, that ORHA personnel were "trying to save a country" (so the voiceover states), then it makes sense to blame the insurgency largely on the CPA's blunders and to date its effective start as the bombing of UN headquarters in Baghdad on August 19, 2003. But if you believe that the very existence of ORHA was part of the problem, then you might say the insurgency started much earlier, on April 28 and 30, before Bremer even landed in Iraq. On those dates, US soldiers fired into crowds of demonstrators in Falluja, killing at least thirteen people and wounding many more. *No End in Sight* discusses the later, better-known upheavals in that city, but it does not mention these April protests and deaths, which perhaps had some small influence on anti-American sentiment. To speak of them, even in passing, might suggest that the occupation was doomed from the start—or at the latest from within three weeks of the US conquest of Baghdad.

All of which is merely to say of Ferguson: an interesting slant makes for interesting blind spots. I would judge his film not by its peculiarity but by its power to condemn, which it exercises with stunning authority. *No End in Sight* convicts the Bush Administration more clearly, specifically and forcefully than any previous documentary has done, and more wrenchingly than any book could do. No matter how deeply you read in the growing literature, you will not receive what this film offers: the frustration and sorrow on Barbara Bodine's face, the ragged edge in Paul Hughes's voice, the bafflement in Jay Garner's eyes as he thinks back on his betrayal. Ferguson brings you face to face with the actors in this terrible history, as they recount how Bush, Cheney, Rumsfeld and Rice went about slaughtering their own soldiers and devastating the people of Iraq.

Shall we say that mistakes were made? *No End in Sight* records so many of them, which were all so obvious, that suspicious minds might wonder if they weren't committed deliberately. Put yourself into Cheney's head, if you dare, and imagine the advantages. A permanently chaotic Iraq might require a permanent US military presence, justifying unbounded wartime powers for the President and providing an inexhaustible supply of Jenkins's ears to wave at Iran. Maybe the ruling clique was so cold-blooded as to want this civil war. Or maybe, as Ferguson suggests, the problem was just that America's political class ceded power to the arrogantly stupid.

The Nation, August 13, 2007

Standard Operating Procedure

Who is Pfc. Lynndie England? Anyone can tell you: she's the woman in the Abu Ghraib pictures. The world recognizes her as a slight female figure standing on the left side of the frame, holding a leash connected to a naked, manacled male figure sprawled on the right. Most people could place Spc. Sabrina Harman, too, if shown her most notorious snapshot. She's the grinning young woman who leans into the picture from the top, flashing the thumbs-up over an iced corpse. We know about England and Harman because of photographs; and from there, it's a short step to imagining that we know them through photographs.

No doubt the Lynndie England and Sabrina Harman who speak to the camera in Errol Morris's documentary *Standard Operating Procedure* are also creatures of photography. Colored shadows with a synchronized soundtrack, they live within the confines of Morris's film much as their younger selves are contained in the Abu Ghraib pictures. And yet when the silent, frozen figures of your memory give way to these images that move and talk, you are likely to feel a shock—not of recognition but of alienation. No longer the criminal gamin with boyish hair, England is suddenly a dour, resolute, puffy-faced woman dressed in a denim jacket. "When we first got there, the example [for treating inmates] was already set," she says defiantly. "It was OK." And Harman, with her thick curls grown out and her lips made up with color, now appears not at all like the sadistic, T-shirted imp of the still photographs. Sober but also a little ingenuous, she seems half gawker and half witness of conscience: "The first thing that I noticed [in Abu Ghraib] was this guy with underwear on his head, handcuffed backward to the window." Another "looked like Jesus Christ... I had to laugh."

Once you gather your impressions of a dozen such interview subjects, weigh their testimonies, wince again at the display of photographs (far more of them than you've probably seen before) and mull over Morris's ghostly evocations of the setting, you may begin to understand *Standard Operating Procedure* less as a reconstruction of facts than as a study in estrangement. Morris wants you to sense the otherworldliness of Abu Ghraib, a place he represents as an airless, windowless, round-the-clock delirium of shouts and banging, filth and raw concrete, huddled bodies and incoming shells and bizarre, ritualized ordeals. He wants you to experience the absurd gap between what happened in that other world and how US officials characterize what happened. (The film takes its title from the categories of the Army's Criminal Investigations Division. As former CID Special Agent Brent Pack explains to the camera, no one from Abu Ghraib was indicted for placing a hood over a man's head, standing him on a box with wires attached to his arms and telling him he'd be electrocuted if he fell off, because that isn't a crime—it's standard operating procedure.) And Morris wants to estrange you from one more element of this nightmare: the pictures that were the primary evidence of its existence and the government's primary means for placing blame on a handful of guards. We know about the torture in Abu Ghraib because of photographs; but what we know through these photographs, as Morris demonstrates, is far from complete.

For example, the photographs seem to show Harman gloating over her victims. Was that why she took the pictures? In speaking to Morris, Harman claims an entirely different motive: she, too, was a documentarian. She didn't think anyone would believe what she'd found in Abu Ghraib, and so she took photographs as proof. In support of this story, Morris puts on the screen some of the letters Harman sent home, in which she expressed her unease at the events around her. But if that was how she felt, how does she account for her beaming face and approving gesture in the ugliest of the photographs? "It's just something that automatically happens," Harman explains. "When you're in a photo, you want to smile."

Lynndie England: "[Cpl. Charles] Graner never would have had me standing next to [the man on the leash] if the camera hadn't been there."

Spc. Jeremy Sivits, sentenced to one year in prison for photographing naked prisoners stacked in a pyramid: "I was asked to take [the picture]. I'm a nice guy. I took it."

Even in hell, it seems, people conform to the etiquette of photography: pose, say cheese, help someone record the scene. *Standard Operating Procedure* never suggests that these behaviors excuse what you see in the photographs; it merely points out, again and again, that you don't see everything. States of mind, stage directions, the presence of people just outside the frame—all these may have been significant at the time, but they're invisible now.

And so, too, is the prison's code of conduct. This is the biggest piece of unseen evidence, Morris argues: the set of military norms established in Abu Ghraib. Some of the soldiers who were caught in the photographs, and punished for being caught, adopted those norms with culpable gusto. Others simply soaked them up. ("We didn't kill 'em," a self-justifying England says of the prisoners. "We didn't cut their heads off.") But no matter which individual a snapshot memorialized, at whatever place and time, the camera could not record the governing etiquette, which held that you did indeed have to stop short of decapitation, though not by much.

Unable to bring this code into sight, Morris brings it into mind by interviewing Janis Karpinski, former brigadier general of the 800th Military Police Brigade in Iraq—the highest-ranked officer to have been punished for the events at Abu Ghraib. Buttoned up in a suit, Karpinski sits straightbacked before Morris's camera, her hair pulled tight, her chin jutting out, her voice controlled against quivers of rage, as she repeats a story she has now told many times. In September 2003, she recalls, her commander was insisting on a daily basis that she produce information leading to the capture of Saddam Hussein. To speed this process, Baghdad soon received a visit from Maj. Gen. Geoffrey Miller—"the guru" of interrogations, Karpinski calls him—who advised her superiors to "Gitmo-ize" Abu Ghraib: "You have to treat the prisoners like dogs."

Given the Army's version of police procedure, there were more and more dogs to be treated. Former sergeant Javal Davis, a night guard who was sentenced to six months in prison for his role in the photo sessions, explains that the method for uncovering insurgents was to sweep into an area and bring in every able-bodied man for questioning. "Taxicab drivers, welders, bakers. Imagine someone coming to your town and taking all the men in it." Imagine all the men going into Abu Ghraib and never coming out. "What's the release procedure?" Karpinski asks, with fury in her eyes but her voice still in check. "We don't have any resources to provide for the 200 prisoners…and now you're going to give us 1,500 more?"

Lack of food, lack of toilets, lack of adequate space in the cells, for a population that had been hauled in for the explicit purpose of being roughed up. Let's say a tone had been set. And to complete it, Karpinski recalls, she received orders that her guards were not to interfere with the various interrogation staffs—some military, some not—who were busily applying their inexperience. On this latter point, Morris has the testimony of a surprise witness: Tim Dugan, a robust, goateed man of middle years who interrogated prisoners as a private contractor in Abu Ghraib. With the gruffness you'd expect of someone in his profession, Dugan dismisses Military Intelligence as a pack of puppies trying to be wolves. They didn't understand the uselessness of their methods: A man being tortured will say "whatever the hell you want so that the pain stops."

You've heard that before, of course; but the statement gains new force coming from Dugan. You will most likely trust the image he conveys of weighty experience, just as you may read the severity of Karpinski's manner as probity, or interpret Davis's suppressed agitation as a sign of outraged conscience. The habit of moviegoing trains us to make snap judgments like these, discovering meaning in a tilt of the head or a catch in the voice. But if *Standard Operating Procedure* teaches you anything, it's to be cautious when seeking truth from a photograph—or, for that matter, from the snippets of a filmed interview.

This is where *Standard Operating Procedure* becomes problematic, I think—because Morris doesn't want you to apply his lesson in skepticism to the material he shot. Just as he's done in his films from *Gates of Heaven* through *The Fog of War*, he has brought his subjects before the camera to show you the candor, veracity, duplicity or self-delusion written on each one's features. You're meant to judge his people literally at face value—but now, in *Standard Operating Procedure*, he seems to expect you to go further and take some of their words the same way.

You can detect this departure from skepticism in the way *Standard Operating Procedure* sometimes overlays a subject's voice with a reconstruction of the scene that's being narrated. Morris has used such reconstructions before; but in the past they served to complicate the testimony rather than confirm it, the most notable examples being in *The Thin Blue Line*, in which the staged scenes showed contradictory images of the same event. Here, though, there's no critical distance between the voiceover and the conjured-up image. Witness Morris's statements about the evidence, as posted on the film's website. What Karpinski, Dugan, Davis and others alleged before his camera, Morris asserts as fact.

He's right to do so, of course. Independent confirmation in sickening abundance has poured in for Morris's view, most recently in the form of John Yoo's newly released memorandum of March 2003 on behalf of the Justice Department, setting forth for the Pentagon the very standard of conduct that would soon trickle down to Lynndie England: just don't cut off their heads. Many similar documents were readily available to Morris while he was making *Standard Operating Procedure*; but they never entered into the movie, perhaps because England, Harman and the others received no instruction from them. The guards learned how to behave mostly by looking around; and so, by relying for his evidence exclusively on pictures (talking and otherwise), Morris presents you with a challenge like the one these soldiers faced as they tried to draw conclusions based on limited sensory data.

But Morris isn't consistent in presenting his *Introduction to the Phenomenology of the Dungeon*. He ventures beyond what the guards saw, heard and thought by bringing in the contextualizing interviews—though this material, too, is puzzling, when you consider that Morris's portraits contain significantly less visual information than do the Abu Ghraib photos. The snapshots that he questions so rigorously are full of the circumstantial details of their setting, whereas the filmed interviews that he presents as self-evidently reliable show only a succession of isolated individuals—figures without a ground.

So I come back to the alienation effect that Morris practices in *Standard Operating Procedure*. He distances you from what you thought you'd known through the prison photographs; he distances you from the interview subjects, as presented in their undefined space. By means of these estrangements—which include a cunningly macabre musical score (not written by Philip Glass this time but by the far more pop-oriented Danny Elfman)—Morris achieves his stated goal. He creates "a nonfiction horror movie," in which the close analysis of photographs ultimately serves much the same purpose as a scientific discourse by Professor Van Helsing.

Strange ambition. Consider the fact that anyone who cares about this subject has already had the benefit of several years' worth of investigative reporting, as well as two award-winning documentaries—Rory Kennedy's *Ghosts of Abu Ghraib* (2007) and Alex Gibney's *Taxi to the Dark Side* (2007)—that cover much the same territory as *Standard Operating Procedure* but with far less fuss. What does Morris contribute by the addition of atmospheric effects?

As a critic, I am required to ask that question. As a citizen, I will wait to reply, since I don't yet know how audiences will respond to the peculiar emotional tone of *Standard Operating Procedure*. Information, by itself, has failed to arouse a sufficiently large public; exposés have nothing left to lay bare. So let's see what Morris can do with a little art. The methods may be fancy and the date of release a bit late; but if this movie succeeds in horrifying people, its shortcomings will be no more consequential than the awkward framing of the snapshots from Abu Ghraib.

The Nation, May 19, 2008

Full Battle Rattle

As the desert sun beats down on Medina Wasl—its stone-faced houses, its barren souk, its scrawny minaret casting a finger's shadow—filmmakers embedded with a battalion of the First Cavalry ride through the dusty streets, capturing the bad on its way to worse. This is *Full Battle Rattle*, in which Tony Gerber and Jesse Moss have assembled one of the most complete pictures yet to emerge of how an Iraqi town fragments into civil war, given the well-meaning but clumsy nudges of its American occupiers. It is a work of direct cinema, which like all such documentaries demands to be valued for the intense labor that went into it: the weeks of filming, the months of editing. Paradoxically, though, *Full Battle Rattle* may also be the most conveniently made of all records of US military failure in Iraq—because everything you see in it happened in just three weeks, about forty miles outside Barstow, California.

Here, in the Mojave Desert, hundreds of Iraqi-American role players live in Medina Wasl and the dozen other stage-set villages of the National Training Center at Fort Irwin. Motivated by love of their adopted country, housed in a simulation of desperate poverty and equipped with scripted backstories that would be the envy of any Method actor, the performers interact on a round-the-clock basis with Army units that are about to be deployed to Iraq and that have been sent here to find out what it will be like. *Full Battle Rattle* takes you through one such three-week training mission as seen from both sides, with Gerber living in the stage-set Army base and filming the soldiers' activities and Moss living in Medina Wasl and filming its residents. Which of the two producer-directors was responsible for filming the insurgents (played in these exercises by US soldiers rather than Iraqi-born civilians) I don't know; but whoever it was caught such niceties as the whiteboard sign hanging in jihadi headquarters, marked with a helpful reminder to attack the Army base at 4 am.

Like any documentary about putting on a show, *Full Battle Rattle* abounds with mirth-provoking incongruities between the effect aimed for and the means used to achieve it. After a firefight in town—or, rather, a very chaotic game of laser tag—you hear an officer with a bullhorn order, "If you're a casualty, leave your bandage on," while medics rush to the triage station bearing ghastly, mutilated mannequins and assorted plastic body parts. An officer charged with making a jihadi video of an assassination coaches the insurgents to put a little more oomph into their *Allahu akbar!* and reminds the victim, with exasperation, that when he's shot he can't throw out his hands to break the fall. From time to time, when the players need refreshment, an ice cream truck rolls into the main street of Medina Wasl, tinkling its mechanical tune.

It's "surreal comedy," as more than one reviewer characterized *Full Battle Rattle* when it premiered last February at the Berlin Film Festival. Somehow, though, I don't much feel like laughing. The Iraqi role players of Medina Wasl — "deputy mayor" Bassam Kalasho, "shopkeeper" Azhar Cholagh, "deputy police chief" Nagi Moshi — break my heart when they marvel that in the off hours, when they're out of character, they get along beautifully, with no Sunni-Shiite divisions. "For real, we're family," one of them says, boasting of a harmony that scarcely seems possible now in the real Iraq but has been achieved in an imaginary one. For the Army role players, I can feel only respect and sorrow, starting with Lt. Col. Robert McLaughlin, commander of the 5-82 Battalion, who comes into the exercise fully determined to bring peace and prosperity to Medina Wasl. That is his job, and he takes it with the utmost seriousness — though the main lesson he can draw after three weeks' training is that, in reality, he probably won't be able to do it. "Am I a failure?" he asks late in the film, then answers despondently, "Actions speak louder than words." The last we see of McLaughlin, he and his soldiers are back in Texas, at Fort Bliss, getting onto an airplane bound for the real Iraq. Their kids are in costume. It's Halloween.

The Nation, June 26, 2008

Films of the Lebanese Civil War

The Beirut glimpsed retrospectively in Randa Chahal Sabag's 1995 documentary *Our Imprudent Wars* is a city of see-through neighborhoods where the apartment buildings are no more than masonry shells punched through with holes; a city where downtown high-rises slowly vanish within clouds of smoke, which roll up from the streets to engulf them, and the public sculptures—those embodiments of civic aspiration—lift up metal hands that are leprous with bullet scars. To see this place is to wonder how a living city could ever rise here again. To meet the primary witnesses in Sabag's film—notably her sister the political activist, once a leader in the OACL (Communist Action Organization in Lebanon), and her brother the former gunman, instinctively distrustful of politicians but for years willing to fight in their "little wars"—is to wonder how the people of Beirut, no less than the urban fabric, could ever again be made whole.

These dual questions are at the heart of the series "The Calm After the Storm: Making Sense of Lebanon's Civil War," organized by the Film Society of Lincoln Center and ArteEast. A handful of the twenty-one feature-length films in the program date from before the civil war, to give viewers a notion of an earlier Lebanese cinema. A significant number of others were made during the years of fighting. But more than half are postwar pictures, in which a semblance of normality seems to have returned to the present-day cityscape, if not to the people who pass through it. Except for the uncommon number of construction sites, Beirut in these films looks like any traffic-choked Western capital, full of shops and food stalls and neon-lit clubs where young people go searching for one another. But in these films it seems as if there's always a missed connection between the characters, with a hint of something disturbing and irrational lurking in the gap; always a trace of violence, or more than a trace, and the emergence, as if by fate, of a handgun.

Joana Hadjithomas and Khalil Joreige give this postwar tour of Beirut a brooding, melancholic form in *A Perfect Day* (2005): the story of twenty-four outwardly uneventful but inwardly busy hours in the lives of Claudia (Julia Kassar) and her grown son, Malek (Ziad Saad). On this day, with a mixture of dread and numb determination, they at last request that their husband and father be declared legally dead, fifteen years after he disappeared in the civil war. Together, they accept their loss—except that they don't accept it, and they're mostly alone. Claudia goes back almost without interruption to waiting silently in the apartment, listening for her man's return, while Malek leaves her to chase after his obsession: a young woman (Alexandra Kahwagi) who looks to him like the Last Chance, even though she keeps insisting she's through with him.

A Perfect Day keeps Malek in continual movement as he drives back and forth through the city, texts his dismissive lover and occasionally even shows up at a job site. (He is a construction manager, helping to put up some of those new buildings you see everywhere on the skyline.) But this is also a film of inescapable stasis. Though he's a man with a good, strong stubble on his Alexander the Great profile, Malek still lives in his childhood room, sleeping in a narrow bed beneath his schoolboy map of the world. And he sleeps everywhere else, too, being subject to fits of narcolepsy that can abruptly leave him passed out on a concrete bench near the beach or unconscious behind the wheel of his car amid furiously honking traffic. Malek's mother may justifiably accuse him of callousness for abandoning her on this devastating day. To the audience, though, he's just dreamy and distracted, thanks to an incurable drowsiness that seems to seep out of him into the prevailing atmosphere of the movie.

There's a saving humor in the atmosphere, too: in the brusque flirtatiousness of a doctor who is supposed to be treating Malek for sleep apnea but prefers to sneak a cigarette with him, or in the succession of ring tones that Malek idly scrolls through on his mobile phone, each one more apologetic, forlorn or depressed than the last. (He chooses the one titled "Oops.") Graveyard chuckles. They keep you going through a movie that, on the whole, is a mood piece about a dangerous torpor—a postwar condition, evidently, that at the end has Malek driving about in willful blindness while his sleepless mother waits in an armchair, gun in hand, for someone to open the apartment door.

Translate this melancholy into absurdist laughter, and the lassitude into an itchy exasperation, and you've got the mood of another city tour in the series: Michel Kammoun's wryly entertaining *Falafel* (2006). Here the protagonist, Tou (Elie Mitri), is wide awake as he rides his moped through present-day Beirut toward a dance party with his buddies and his heartthrob, Yasmin (Gabrielle Bou Rached). Though he's a scuffling guy without much money, Tou has the hair and beard of a hipster Sufi (the kindness, too) and knows how to shimmy up to a girl with loose-limbed, self-confident charm; and so his chances with Yasmin would be pretty good, if things around him didn't keep getting crazily out of hand. While filling the tank of his moped, he witnesses a kidnapping just outside the gas station. While engaged in a promising chat with Yasmin, he is interrupted by an uproar over his very drunk pal Abboudi (Issam Bou Khaled), who had tried to flatter a woman by grabbing her breasts and is now locked in the bathroom, weeping and apologizing to the world. These incidents are mere inconveniences, though, compared with the precipitating event, in which a well-connected "businessman" gets into a parking lot argument with another of Tou's buddies, takes out a pistol and smashes it against Tou's head.

That's enough to turn easygoing Tou into a moped-riding avenger, roaring through the Beirut night in a blood-red shirt (he's changed for the occasion) until he gets satisfaction—or, rather, until the moped breaks down and he has to walk. Off he trudges, like a Lebanese version of the hero of Martin Scorsese's *After Hours*, through random blunders and confrontations, while his unsteady friends, alarmed, search just as randomly for him. The threat of irreversible violence mounts; and then it dissipates, in fulfillment of a prophecy that had been uttered to Tou earlier that evening in a falafel shop. Imagine, if you will, an antigravitational falafel ball, a falafel ball that alone of its kind can rise above its own deep-fried nature. It's like imagining that one injured and humiliated Lebanese man, out of millions, might miraculously forgo revenge.

Imagine freedom. That's what Kammoun ultimately does in *Falafel*—with enough tartness, and enough of a sense of the fragility of normal life, to make his moment of ground-chickpea whimsy go down easily.

I wish I could say the same for the magical conceits of *The Kite* (2003). This is the final film by Randa Chahal Sabag, which is unfortunate—because she died, tragically, at too young an age, and also because she ought to have finished with something better.

Set on the border between Lebanon and Israel, where members of families have been cut off from one another, *The Kite* is a relentlessly, lifelessly symbolic story about a brave, defiant and beautiful teenager, Lamia (Flavia Bechara), who suffers and triumphs and at last transcends not only borders but death itself. When I compare this fussy stuff to the harsh, probing honesty of Sabag's *Our Imprudent Wars*, I feel as if she had let herself backslide from responsibility to piety. In the documentary, Sabag recorded her sister's disgust at the Lebanese habit (as she saw it) of ascribing their wars to other people, "as if they were fought by Martians." But in *The Kite*, Sabag made her own contribution to Martian-think, locating all violence (and all moral falseness) on the Israeli side of the wire. Yes, I know what the Israeli invasions have done to the south of Lebanon; I know about the cluster bombs, the assaults on civilians and all the rest. I also know an evasion when I see one. When *The Kite*'s leaden thaumaturgy gave out its final clunk, I was glad to see it go—and more convinced than ever that the Middle East is one place in the world where magical thinking should not be encouraged.

But nothing is wished away, and nothing evaded, in Mohamed Soueid's *My Heart Beats Only for Her* (2008), an essay film that is by far the most impressive of the pictures I was able to see in the Lincoln Center series. As wide-ranging and intelligent as a Chris Marker documentary, and as determined to look facts in the face, Soueid's film is on one level a group portrait of revolutionaries in retirement: comfortable, middle-aged men shown talking with pleasure about their years as Fatah militants. On a second level, the film is a fiction told in voiceover, in which a young man named Hassan (a surrogate for Soueid himself) tries to reconstruct the exploits of his late father, Hatem Hatem: film buff, motorcycle enthusiast and Fatah fighter. On yet another level, the film is a critical history, related through archival footage, of Fatah's ideological emulation of the Vietcong, its training in North Vietnam and its determination to make Beirut a second Hanoi. And on a fourth level, *My Heart Beats Only for Her* is a travelogue, taking you from old Hanoi (the Arab dream city of the past) to the Arab dream city of today: Dubai. Indeed, on the evidence of the contemporary footage, Hanoi itself now looks to be running as fast as it can down Dubai's road of shopping malls and spec skyscrapers—and the former militants, taking a break from humming their old battle anthems, admit that there's no resisting real estate development.

Maybe Soueid's interview subjects mourn the passing of their machine-gun days. (As one of them says, in a line that could sum up much of the Lincoln Center series, "I wish I could live in war that went on forever—but where nobody got killed.") Soueid, though, seems to have no regrets, despite his deadpan disdain for the rise of Dubai. Addressing the fictional Hatem Hatem in voiceover and judging what this radical father accomplished through all his fighting, Soueid concludes, "You came closer to Cambodia than Hanoi."

My Heart Beats Only for Her is a challenging, idiosyncratic, utterly personal response to the new normality of Lebanon, and to the horrendous abnormality that still lingers from the past. In its formal and intellectual sophistication, it stands out among the films in "The Calm After the Storm"; but in another way, it is very much a part of the whole. Most of the films in this series are direct evidence in themselves of a society being patched back together, since the film industry (such as it was) may be numbered among all the other elements of Lebanese life that were blasted apart in the wars. Now, against all odds, the cinema has returned but on a different basis, with each film being realized only through the power of individual artistic determination, coupled with a feverish drive for co-production funds.

It's as if all those new towers in Beirut had somehow been put up by artisanal labor, done whenever the architect-contractor happened to have a little money.

The Nation, May 17, 2010

Restrepo

Shot (there's the exact word for you) in 2007—08 in Afghanistan's Korengal Valley, Tim Hetherington and Sebastian Junger's documentary *Restrepo* gives an unadorned, soldier's-eye view of the experiences of a platoon of the 173rd Airborne Brigade, as it patrols the lush and relentlessly hostile landscape, establishes a strategically important but isolated and exposed outpost (just a ring of sandbags on a hilltop at first, plus a barrel in which to burn feces) and comes under fire from all directions, all the time. Intercut with these action scenes are affecting interviews with some of the soldiers, recorded elsewhere after their deployment ended, in which you encounter these men in a reflective mood. But the moments that are more likely to come to mind when you think back on *Restrepo* are the ones of adrenaline-fueled chaos, with both the soldiers and the filmmakers scrambling for their lives.

No one should underestimate the achievement of Hetherington and Junger in bringing back this footage; nor should the implications of their film be overlooked, despite the filmmakers' avowal that they weren't out to make a political statement. The platoon's commanding officer, Capt. Dan Kearney—the sort of smart, solid, responsible soldier you would want in the field—sums up the dilemma of the US campaign against the Taliban when he explains that he's asking the Korengal villagers to push out their own family members. The frustration of the campaign, and its horror, is written on Kearney's face after he calls down a helicopter strike on a supposed Taliban haven and learns that he's inadvertently killed five civilians, young children among them. Soon the radio chatter tells him that the village elders, with whom he'd been meeting regularly, are calling for jihad.

The conclusion you might draw is that the Taliban and their families live in the Korengal Valley, whereas the Americans are just visiting. They set up their temporary outposts at great risk, fight to survive the deployment and then (with undisguised joy and relief) are rotated back home, having "done our job" without necessarily changing much of anything.

You, documentary viewer, are probably just visiting, too. Like the majority of Americans today, you are remote from combat and relatively untouched by it. But because the conflicts in Iraq and Afghanistan are America's first point-and-shoot video wars, you can watch *Gunner Palace*, *Occupation: Dreamland*, *Severe Clear* or now *Restrepo* and dip for a few minutes into the reality of our volunteer soldiers, much as the soldiers dip for a period into the reality of the lands they occupy.

On the principle that it's better to know than not to know, I have to figure that the filmmakers are rendering us a service. But the refrain that runs through all these films — the boastful complaint that civilians just can't understand a soldier's life — might remind us that even with documentarians as brave and committed as Hetherington and Junger, the service is limited.

The Nation, July 12, 2010

Lebanon

After the Israeli tank gunner blasts her apartment, annihilating her husband, her daughter and all that she owns (except for a painting of the Virgin and Child, miraculously left intact on a shattered wall), the Lebanese woman stumbles out of the remains of her building, into the flaming rubble on the street, and begins searching, at once numbly and frantically, for a child she assumes must still exist. The audience watching this scene knows better; and so, too, does the tank gunner, whose telescopic sight provides the only view of the world outside that writer-director Samuel Maoz permits in *Lebanon*. Throughout the course of his film you see either the tank's soldiers, shown in side-lighted close-ups within the murk, or else a variety of strangely depthless images of slaughter, contained within a truncated circle in the center of an otherwise black screen.

These contrasting optics come into confrontation shortly after the desperate mother's dress catches fire. As the scene grinds on horrifically, this woman who already has nothing is stripped bare, left to wander naked and then tossed a blanket to throw over herself. Still, she won't follow the orders of Israeli footsoldiers to stay on the ground. She rises and staggers straight toward the tank, staring directly into its telescopic sight—and this accusatory gaze, encircled in the center of the screen, is intercut with an extreme close-up of the gunner's eye as he watches what you are watching, seeing but not being seen.

From this sample description of *Lebanon*, I hope it will be evident that Maoz's film had both emotional and formal power on its side when it won the top prize at last year's Venice festival. Whether this power is adequate to the subject seems to me a question worth asking, now that *Lebanon* is going into US theatrical release.

To be precise, this is really two questions—one political and the other aesthetic. The first concerns the limitations and biases that one or another viewer might detect in this drama about the 1982 invasion of Lebanon, as experienced by a handful of Israeli soldiers over the course of a little more than twenty-four hours. The second question might seem to be less pressing, being merely artistic; but to my mind it takes precedence, since it asks why a movie would be worth mulling over in the first place.

When I say that *Lebanon* has formal power, I mean that it conforms to a classical model of moviemaking, and of interpreting movies, that is exemplified in the works of Alfred Hitchcock and that was codified by his commentators. Set aside, if you can, the statements that Maoz has given about *Lebanon*'s being his own story, wrenched out therapeutically after almost thirty years of suffering. Maybe so; but the fact remains, his cure has been effected through emulations of *Lifeboat* and *Rear Window*.

In *Lebanon*, as in those pictures, certain basic conditions of moviemaking—such as the constraint of the set or the voyeuristic complicity of the director and audience—no longer function unseen and unremarked in the background but are pushed forward into the plot. Nervous excitement over the events on screen becomes entangled with a potentially critical awareness of one's relationship to the spectacle. To Hitchcock's admirers, and to two or three generations of moviegoers who have absorbed their way of thinking (sometimes without knowing it), this production of a dual consciousness is the sign of intellectual and moral seriousness in a movie.

But why would *Lebanon* need such a sign? This is not a yarn about a snoopy, crotchety Jimmy Stewart who thinks he's discovered a crime. It's a semi-autobiographical portrayal of war. As other Israeli writer-directors have shown, it's possible to make such a film with more than therapeutic intent but without recourse to this particular formalism. In *Kippur*, Amos Gitai used an observational, long-take approach that heightened the reality effect of the film by stretching your sense of time and deliberately draining away momentum. In *Waltz With Bashir*, Ari Folman mongrelized animation and documentary, first-person and third-person narration, to produce a consciousness that wasn't so much dual as fractured and kaleidoscopic. But Maoz, relying on an older and more widely accepted model, has sought to guarantee the probity of his movie by bringing out its movieness. He even adds extra layers of cinematic allusion, sometimes shooting the tank's interior as if it were the slimed-up spaceship in an alien horror movie.

So when the political question gets pushed to the front—does Maoz go too easy on the Israelis, too hard or just hard enough?—the answer ultimately doesn't depend on the information in *Lebanon* that's included or omitted, emphasized or glossed over. You can argue about that for as long as op-eds are written. The Hitchcockian form answers the question by sealing your complicity with the semi-autobiographical gunner. *Lebanon* moves you, over the course of ninety-four minutes, from utter shock at the devastation you see through the gunsight to complete identification with, and pity for, the man who was pulling the trigger.

It's a strong film, complex in many ways, and seems to me to come from a genuinely stricken conscience. But in its formal probity, *Lebanon* turns into a moral dodge.

The Nation, August 30, 2010

This Is My Land... Hebron

The motto of the annual Human Rights Watch Film Festival might have been spoken by Yehuda Shaul, a former Israeli soldier, when he appeared in one of this year's most devastating selections, the documentary *This Is My Land... Hebron*. Not everyone can dedicate his or her life to a cause, Shaul says toward the end of the film, nor is everyone called to be an activist. But "everyone is obligated to stop being silent."

The imperative sounds simple enough, coming from this soft-spoken, teddy-bearish young man. The proof of its difficulty lies in the best films in the series, whose every utterance has manifestly come at a cost.

Directed by Giulia Amati and Stephen Natanson, *This Is My Land... Hebron* puts you in the center of the ancient West Bank city, where 600 or so well-armed Israeli settlers live safeguarded by 2,000 soldiers, who have (in a telling phrase) "sterilized" entire streets by removing the Palestinians. You get to meet some of the remaining residents face to face and hear about how they're hanging on. More alarming, you confront the faces of the settlers, which as often as not are contorted in rage. From the fact that these people do not hesitate to lash out in front of the camera, you understand that they think it normal to hurl curses, threats and stones at the Palestinians, whose besieged homes have in some cases been enclosed by the soldiers in a kind of chain-link cage. Amati and Natanson have done everything possible to present a fair account of this situation; they interview people on both sides and take care to film the settlers' official spokespeople in dignified settings, letting them present their case at length. But fair is not the same as impartial. Like Yehuda Shaul, the filmmakers look on with communicable horror.

The Nation, July 18, 2011

The Gatekeepers

In his absolutely essential documentary *The Gatekeepers*, Dror Moreh has put together a history of Israel's relations with the other people on the land, as seen through unprecedented interviews with six former heads of the Israeli security agency Shin Bet. Illustrated with stunning, often deeply disturbing documentary images and sequences of computer graphics that recall video games (an appropriate choice, now that the security agents mostly sit at computers and push buttons, including triggers), the interviews contain some ideas that *Nation* readers are likely to deplore—such as the permissibility of "extreme interrogation" techniques in cases where there is good reason to believe an attack on civilians is imminent. What's more important by far is the discovery that the heads of the Shin Bet often sound like editorial writers for *The Nation*. Again and again, they say that there is no military solution to a political problem, and that the problem is the neocolonialist occupation of a nation that wants its freedom. "Oh, thank you," groaned a Likudnik sitting behind me in the audience. To which I now add, without the irony: thank you, Dror Moreh.

The Nation, November 12, 2012

The Green Prince

It is possible to say with reasonable certainty that Mosab Hassan Yousef is the eldest son of Sheikh Hassan Yousef, a founder of Hamas and one of its most prominent leaders in the West Bank. We also know that Yousef has denounced Hamas publicly since 2008, when he declared that he had converted to Christianity. He subsequently announced that he had willingly collaborated for a decade with Shin Bet, Israel's domestic security service, starting in the mid-1990s. Yousef first made this claim in a book published in 2010, *Son of Hamas: A Gripping Account of Terror, Betrayal, Political Intrigue, and Unthinkable Choices*. He repeats his story, under a calmer title, in *The Green Prince*, a film that won an audience award at the 2014 Sundance festival and is now going into theatrical release.

One more certainty: the film, written and directed by Nadav Schirman, presents itself as a documentary. Beyond that, things get murky, starting with the question of what, exactly, *The Green Prince* documents.

To be absolutely literal, which I think is a good idea in this case, I would describe the film as a record of Yousef's facial expressions, gestures and tones of voice as he sits in a nondescript room and narrates his story. *The Green Prince* is also an assemblage of existing records: archival images of Sheikh Hassan meeting with people and making speeches in Ramallah, videos of Hamas street demonstrations, news reports from various scenes of bloodshed, and photographs of a younger Yousef in his father's company, dating from childhood through his 20s.

During the latter period, Yousef says, he served as his father's adoring assistant, struggled to protect him from assassination by the Israelis, and also reported to Shin Bet as a matter of conscience and principle on the comings and goings, strategies and operations of Sheikh Hassan's associates. But this account, however gripping, is precisely what *The Green Prince* cannot document.

Yousef has nothing to confirm his story except his own words—and he is, if you believe him, an accomplished liar. There is, of course, no physical evidence to prove the tale, nor is there anyone to confirm this narrative except for the second major character in *The Green Prince*, Gonen Ben Yitzhak, who says in his interview segments that he recruited Yousef and was his handler. A fleshy, broad-faced, grinning man who leans back comfortably in his nondescript room—unlike Yousef, who is slim, long-faced and always leaning in to make a point—Ben Yitzhak tells Schirman's camera that he no longer serves with Shin Bet, which might be true, or not. No one should rush to say who's employed by any intelligence agency, or guess how much fact might be included in any story that one of its present or ostensibly former agents puts out. Taking into account another of the film's admissions against self, we might do well to listen to Ben Yitzhak when he explains that a large part of his job was to manipulate people's minds.

There is simply no way to be sure of when Yousef started to collaborate with the Israelis, the circumstances under which he agreed to work with them, or even whether he was a Shin Bet informer at all. (He has certainly made himself into a propaganda asset for Israel, but he could have accomplished that without actually having spied on his father—he just had to say he did.) Most important of all, we can't be sure of Yousef's motives. He claims he chose to inform against Hamas because he was horrified by the violence it routinely practiced against its own people, and because he considered its tactic of suicide bombing to be nothing but aimless murder. He wanted to save lives, he says, and also stay true to the principles that his father held, or ought to have held.

Could be—but to his credit, Schirman thinks there might be something deeper behind Yousef's declared convictions. In a moment, I'll get to the strange, disturbing way *The Green Prince* digs into this topic. For now, I will merely note that the impossibility of checking Yousef's story has not prevented those in the pro-Netanyahu, anti-Islam camp from taking it at face value. Nor should the story's unverifiability stop people in my camp from positing, however provisionally, that it might be true. The reasonable course, at least when dealing with *The Green Prince*, is to keep doubt in mind but at bay while examining how Schirman tries to make this narrative seem not just plausible but authentic, the better to persuade audiences of something that he and his producers might call the larger truth.

To start, let me consider two aspects of the story that Schirman chooses to minimize. The first is Yousef's conversion to Christianity. In *Son of Hamas*, which was published by a leading evangelical press, this conversion is decisive. A chance introduction to the Gospels—which begins, symbolically enough, outside the Damascus Gate—overthrows Yousef's assumptions about the world and sets his feet on the path of peace. *The Green Prince* downplays this conversion, though, to the point of making it seem as if Yousef found Jesus only after he'd severed his ties with

Shin Bet and relocated to the United States. In this way, Schirman avoids the anti-Koranic polemic of *Son of Hamas*, but he also narrows the focus of the story, confining it to Muslims (a category tacitly assumed to encompass all Palestinians) and Jews (a category presumably encompassing all Israelis).

Schirman further narrows the focus by saying as little as possible about an arguably significant factor in the relationship between Palestinians and Israelis: millions of the former are under military occupation by the latter. Yes, *The Green Prince* acknowledges the existence of checkpoints, patrols, arrests and torture. Early in the film, when Yousef recalls his teenage desire for revenge against any Israeli available, he even speaks of "our pain." But you could not know from *The Green Prince* that this pain is grounded in Israel's relentless official program of annexing land and suppressing people.

To gauge the extent of the omission, you might watch Hany Abu-Assad's *Omar* (2013), an expertly made thriller about a young Palestinian forced into collaboration, or Dror Moreh's *The Gatekeepers* (2012), an exceptional documentary about Shin Bet's role in carrying out Israeli policy. In their different ways, both of these films provide ample context. From *The Green Prince*, you learn only that the Israelis respond to "extremists." Of course, the Israelis have their "extremists" too, as is mentioned in the blandly worded introductory text; but there is no sign in the film of any of those people (let alone their partners in high office), and it's not long before Yousef, in his narrative, has forgotten about wanting revenge against them. Thrown into confusion after seeing the true nature of Hamas, he recalls, Yousef says that he "didn't know what I'm fighting for."

But why was that disillusionment so deep as to move him to switch sides? (He had been driven half-mad by sleep deprivation, Yousef says, but insists that his choice—made after his release from prison—was not coerced.) *The Green Prince* encourages you to speculate about this central question by including little disquisitions from Ben Yitzhak about the art of recruitment, in which he explains that it's necessary to identify and exploit a subject's weaknesses. What Yousef's weaknesses might have been, he never says.

Instead, at a critical point in the narrative—just before Yousef's moment of decision—the film breaks with chronology, introducing a noticeably out-of-place episode from his childhood. When he was 5, Yousef recalls, his father sent him off to harvest olives, so that the boy would feel attached to the land; and there, among friends of the family, Yousef was raped. He could never speak of it to anyone, he says. In his culture, such an admission would have been too shameful.

Like a sleight-of-hand artist forcing a card on a sucker, Schirman uses this story to suggest an entire psychological profile, one that must be full of suppressed rage: against a father who was beyond criticism and yet sent Yousef into this hell; against a family that was blind to what had happened; and even against the olive tree, the ultimate symbol of Palestinian rootedness. Schirman then slips the card back into the deck so that he can produce it with a flourish toward the end of the film, when Yousef speaks of his decision to come forward in 2010 and publicize his alleged work with Shin Bet. That's the only other time the rape is mentioned.

I would say the same thing about this suggested motive that I say about Yousef's story: it might be true. All I know is how Schirman positions the episode, and the effect. He implies that Yousef, in his gut, rejected not just Hamas but an entire "culture" that accepts and perpetuates violence out of a misplaced sense of shame.

With that done, the way is clear for Schirman to advance the larger meaning of the story, as he sees it. Against all odds, Yousef and Ben Yitzhak formed a close and trusting bond. (Never mind that Ben Yitzhak cheerfully speaks of toying with Yousef.) When Yousef was in deep trouble, facing deportation from the United States, Ben Yitzhak stepped forward without authorization (in his account) to testify to Yousef's service in the war against terrorism. Though brought up to hate and fear one another, the two men have proved that Palestinians and Israelis can reach across their lines of division in friendship.

I say, for the last time, that it might be true. As I write these words, though, my heart is not warmed—and not just because Yousef and Ben Yitzhak are opaque figures in the film, who perform rather than reveal their characters. My bigger problem is the report in today's newspaper that Israel and Hamas are both claiming victory in the Gaza war, as they stand over the corpses of the latest 1,500 civilians. Some triumph.

If you want my opinion—and I think anybody writing about *The Green Prince* ought to speak plainly—Yousef is not wrong in the film when he accuses Hamas of being a death cult that has done nothing for the Palestinians except prolong their misery. But Schirman is definitely wrong when he pretends, for the sake of a happy ending, that there is no resistance movement apart from

Hamas and no compelling reason to resist. It's easy enough in *The Green Prince* for a Palestinian and an Israeli to embrace, after one of them has capitulated. Outside the vacuum of this almost fact-free documentary, however, something more than fellow feeling might be needed.

The Nation, September 29, 2014

Whiskey Tango Foxtrot

Disgusted with her dead-end job and fed up with a diffident boyfriend, that overflowing barrel of misbehavior Melissa McCarthy undertakes a radical makeover, shipping out as a war correspondent for Fox News—no experience necessary!—in the fish-out-of-water comedy *What the Fox?!* Hilarity ensues, as the lovable Melissa shoulders another network's cookie-cutter blonde into a ditch, liberates all the women in a Kabul marketplace by tripping over their burkas, panics our troops while also saving them with the woozily aimed blast of a rocket launcher, and at last finds her soul mate (after an alcohol-induced blackout) snoring right in her own bed, in the inert form of freelance photographer Seth Rogen.

I might not respect *What the Fox?!* or own up to having laughed at it, but I would pay to see this film, if someone were to make it. In the case of the actually existing *Whiskey Tango Foxtrot*, I'd be more cautious with my money. Though similar in premise to the imaginary movie, the real *WTF* is less an entertainment than a medicinal product, marketed by Tina Fey with good intentions, considerable valor, and maybe just a little too much self-regard. Her dark eyes set in a level gaze, her frame held taut, Fey looks intent throughout much of the film, as if straining to make the sale: for the character she's playing, for the women of Afghanistan and all the world, but most of all for herself.

One of the few women in show business with the power to develop her own projects—and God bless her for it—Fey is both the star of *Whiskey Tango Foxtrot* and a producer, whose frequent television collaborator Robert Carlock tailored the screenplay to her, based on the memoir *The Taliban Shuffle* by former *Chicago Tribune* reporter Kim Barker. All credit to Fey for betting on the property. As a high-level TV executive remarks in *Whiskey Tango Foxtrot*, Americans don't want to watch the war in Afghanistan— especially if the actress who brings it to them provides only one part comic bumbling to nine parts feminist self-actualization.

But then, Fey has a hedge against her gamble. Barker portrays the war-correspondent lifestyle as a perpetual frat party; and so *Whiskey Tango Foxtrot* can begin in audience-appealing mid-rave, with a neon-hued montage of bongs, bottles, and pogoing bodies swathed in a dense atmosphere of horniness. Despite such high jinks, though, the rough laughter of *The Taliban Shuffle* has mostly fallen silent in a movie that delivers raucousness but little mirth. As for Barker's contextualizing comments about US policy and methods in Afghanistan, they've all but evaporated.

There is a telling exception, which I'll get to. For the most part, though, *Whiskey Tango Foxtrot* treats the war as if it were a geographic feature of Afghanistan, where nature has set forth mountains, deserts, and chaotic bloodshed. The conflict, evidently without beginning or end, also seems to lack any meaning—except that it might bring a small measure of freedom to Afghan women (those who want it) and a combination of adventure, sisterly support (more apparent than real), and career advancement to one particular woman from America.

If that woman reads as both "Kim Barker" and Tina Fey, it's because *Whiskey Tango Foxtrot* is so clearly designed to show what Fey can do beyond comedy. She previously tried playing for something other than laughs in the not-great, not-bad *Admission* (2013), and now she risks straight drama for much longer stretches—very creditably, too. On the upside, she's found an excellent outlet for the qualities that distinguish her comic performances: sharp intelligence and a less-than-optimistic assessment of human nature. Fey is persuasive in scenes that call for Barker to exercise self-control before dangerous idiots and rings entirely true whenever that control lapses, which it does in gradations ranging from impatience and aggravation to righteous indignation and towering rage.

On the downside, the directors of *Whiskey Tango Foxtrot*, Glenn Ficarra and John Requa, have no gradations of their own. They can do well in comedy, as they showed with *Crazy, Stupid, Love* (2011). But when called on to blend Fey's on-edge performance into a story full of unruliness, happy vulgarity, and violence, their solution is to flatten everything. *Whiskey Tango Foxtrot* is a movie with neither highs nor lows. There is not a single moment about which you'd say to a friend, "You've got to see this." The only well-developed motif (this says everything) is a morning ritual of tooth brushing.

Other directors might have done a little better with the material; but I suspect the dullness here is the price of having treated the war as business-as-usual, whether for an American TV reporter who seeks to move up in her profession—standard operating procedure—or for the civilians and combatants who get blown to pieces because, hey, that's Afghanistan.

Here we come to the exception to the movie's lack of context—an attempted exception, I should say. Toward the end, on a visit to a Marine who's been grievously wounded, Fey receives from him the closest thing that *Whiskey Tango Foxtrot* offers in the way of a history.

It's not much: just a list of interventions by major powers, starting with the United States and going back through the Russians to the British. What can a Marine, or by extension an Afghan, do when caught up in this eternal mayhem? "You embrace the suck," the man says with forceful good cheer. "You move the fuck forward. What other choice do we have?"

We could have had Melissa McCarthy, that's what. Compared to the nostrum that *Whiskey Tango Foxtrot* peddles at the end—a mixture of resignation and careerism, packaged as wisdom— McCarthy's loud, rude disobedience is probably a mature choice.

The Nation, March 21, 2016

Atlantis

Atlantis so thoroughly fails the Bechdel Test that its two female characters—the minimum required to pass the assessment—never even meet, let alone converse. Granted, they're educated professionals who talk about their work and not guys. Even so, this film—set in Eastern Ukraine in 2025, "one year after the war"—focuses almost single-mindedly on men, especially those who are no longer in combat but remain in uniform, one way or another. Some keep ready for firefights by donning their old outfits on weekends, driving to a snowy ravine, and shouting their way through target practice—just in case, or because they don't know what else to do with themselves. Others have moldering tatters of fatigues clinging to their bones when they're dug out of mass graves.

This is male cinema, in capital letters—but as written, directed, photographed, and edited by Valentyn Vasyanovych, it's also *real* cinema, made by an artist who has thought about why and how he's showing whatever you see. You're well into the picture, for example, before Vasyanovych stops confining himself to long, static shots, one per scene, and allows more frequent camera movement to begin—or, rather, permits the camera to ride in a truck with his protagonist, the war veteran Sergiy (Andriy Rymaruk), who has taken a part-time job driving down muddy, foggy, mine-infested roads in a grayish nowhere. It's not just that these trips call for traveling shots; it's that Sergiy, in the earlier part of the film, was going nowhere except into himself, furiously, obsessively, but now he is finally looking outward. Or consider the dizzying jumps in scale that Vasyanovych builds into some of his widescreen compositions: setting an apparently minuscule Sergiy in the foreground of the shot, on an apartment building roof that cuts across the frame, while the immense, shadowy jumble of a steel mill looms in the background. How far away is that factory, where Sergiy has been employed? You can't tell. All you know is that it dwarfs him.

And when one of the women at last fulfills the destiny assigned to her from the start, melting into Sergiy as his redemptive squeeze? Even then Vasyanovych keeps his wits about him. The two are in the cab of Sergiy's truck, which has broken down on one of those boggy roads and is being pelted by a downpour. As Katya (Liudmyla Bileka) moves closer to Sergiy, the camera, recording from outside the truck, also begins to move, dollying slowly forward until the torrent on the windshield becomes an impenetrable veil, shielding the kiss from view.

What brought these lovers together? Death. Having lost his job at the steel mill—which suffered one of the two possible fates of factories in this area, demolition or decommission—Sergiy is now driving a small tank truck on alternate weekends, delivering potable water to stations in the former combat zone. He encounters Katya when she flags him down—her van has stalled—and agrees to tow her to the morgue, where she hands over one of the unidentified corpses her volunteer organization disinters. It's not exactly a meet-cute. Katya has to complete some documentation, so Sergiy (like the film's viewer) sticks around for the autopsy. He's helpful, too. Given his experience, he can tell the medical examiners that the method of killing suggests the victim was a captured sniper.

That might be one of the cheerier scenes in *Atlantis*. The action arguably becomes more grim after Sergiy joins the volunteer organization and accompanies Katya to haul seven or eight corpses out of a trench and bag them—Russian soldiers, Ukrainian soldiers, soldiers wearing the rotting insignia of the Donbass militia. Katya takes pity on Sergiy as a first-timer, offering him some scent to dull the stench. And after that, there's yet another mass grave to empty. The autopsies, Katya explains, are the only means by which these people can still tell their stories. Some stories. The best the organization can do, it seems, is erect crosses labeled "Temporarily Non-Identified Defender of Ukraine."

What perversity—apart from the pleasure of recognizing the work of a real filmmaker—makes me feel enthusiasm for this stuff?

At the risk of detracting from the specificity of *Atlantis*, a film so Ukrainian that it is the nation's official submission to the Academy Awards competition, I'll mention two ways in which the movie also speaks to my experience, and maybe yours. First, it's a picture about heavy industry. Remember that? I do, from my youth in the shadow of US Steel, International Harvester, Wisconsin Steel, and more. There's an exhilaration of might about steel mills, a power that's geological in physical scale and elemental in the massive release of flame, steam, fumes, and molten metal. How often do you see that in the movies anymore? How often can you still see it in America? It's vanishing in *Atlantis*, too—foreign owners are abandoning the mill, with the usual blather about there being no other choice, new times are upon us—but for Sergiy and the moviegoer, the hulking majesty remains in sight.

Second, *Atlantis* is about what's left of a landscape after war: not just the pockets of corpses, but the poison. The reason Sergiy has to deliver potable water is because everyone in his part of the world is living not in the 2025 of speculative fiction but in what amounts to the dystopian present. People have fought for this terrain and, in fighting, made it unlivable. *Atlantis* offers you the deep if devastating satisfaction of seeing this truth squarely faced. By showing that Sergiy and Katya persist even so, *Atlantis* might also inspire your own stubborn loyalty to earth that's been scorched, if not by soldiers then by our current warriors of social strife.

If that seems too sentimental, you might think about the alternative chosen by one of Sergiy's combat veteran buddies, who dissolves himself in the smelting bucket. No unsightly remains are left to bury. There's just an extra quart for the slag heap.

Some *Atlantis*.

The Nation, February 24, 2021

A Lover's Alphabet

Aferim!

Ride along, if you will, through the rustic 19th-century world of Radu Jude's *Aferim!*, a place that is nostalgically welcoming for moviegoers who long for wide-screen black-and-white entertainment, but less reassuring for those who contemplate the worldview of its main character, Costandin. Played by the veteran Romanian actor Teodor Corban, he is a Wallachian constable—which is as much as to say, a bounty hunter—with a handlebar mustache, embroidered jacket, and iron-lunged bluster. Costandin endlessly bullies (or, in his mind, instructs) his reedy son and apprentice Ionita (Mihai Comanoiu), extorts bribes on all sides, swills booze, frequents prostitutes, deprecates everyone he encounters (to their faces if they're peasants, behind their backs if they're not), and likes to reminisce about the best times he ever knew: when he was a soldier and killed left and right.

The tale of the pursuit of a runaway slave (Toma Cuzin)—one of the Roma, commonly and dismissively called "crows," who were held as property by the landowners and monks of Wallachia—*Aferim!* is a landscape film of gorgeous variety, which sends Costandin and Ionita riding through mountains, fields, and forests, and a folkloric romp of increasingly grisly tone. The terrain that Costandin and Ionita must negotiate is an obstacle course of stony roads and impassable waterways, the social structure a maze of feudal possessions, and the mentalities a poisonous web spun of spite and ignorance. At first, these low thoughts are so outlandish, and their thinkers so outspoken, that you can laugh at them, as when a priest—one of the film's better-educated characters—improves Costandin's journey by cataloging for him the different inherent vices of all the peoples of Europe. By the time you get to a market, where the bounty hunters catch the cruelest Punch and Judy show you've ever seen, the pervasive brutality is no longer so funny. At the climax, when the slave Carfin falls back into his owner's hands, the violence becomes unspeakable and yet is accepted by everyone—except, it seems, by Costandin, who voices the most tentative and subservient of demurrals before going along like the rest.

And yet, it's not the bloodshed that makes the conclusion of *Aferim!* so horrifying. It's the helpfulness of one of Carfin's fellow slaves, who steps forward to offer the landowner a better tool for his job. Costandin has, as it turns out, the gentlest conscience in the movie.

The Nation, February 22, 2016

Battle in Heaven

Carlos Reygadas's *Battle in Heaven* takes place in a Mexico City of religious processions and flag-raising ceremonies, proliferating highways and improvised market stalls, where the insolent rich literally piss on their servants and the poor ride the subway wearing Aztec Wrestler masks. In explaining why he incorporated such motifs, Reygadas has cited Alfred Hitchcock, who advised that a film set in Holland had better show tulips and windmills. Respect must be paid to convention—all the more so in a film lovingly shot on location, cast with nonprofessional actors who engage in real sex.

The sex bit, even more than the outrageousness of the plot, has raised some clamor against *Battle in Heaven*. Heavy-breasted, myopic, middle-aged Marcos Hernández—a chauffeur in real life—plays the role of a military chauffeur named Marcos, one of whose tasks is to drive around his general's wealthy and stylish daughter Ana (played by Anapola Mushkadiz, who in real life is wealthy and stylish). To make sure he's got your attention, Reygadas begins *Battle in Heaven* with Ana naked on her knees before an equally bare and sweating Marcos. Two perfect tears form in Ana's still-juvenile eyes, as she performs a nonsimulated act in close-up. Marcos, meanwhile, stares ahead with the strained, wooden expression he will wear for most of the movie. You can, of course, watch this scene as a tribute to Warhol's *Blow Job*, following an association that Reygadas all but forces on you. Or you can think about tulips and windmills. Either way, Reygadas is asserting the movieness of the moment and aggressively breaking through it, as he will also do later in a scene of lovemaking between Marcos and his rotund, impassive wife (Bertha Ruiz, who in life as in the movie sells jellies in a subway station).

Reygadas's story, like his sex scenes, merges the materialistic with the fanciful. Throughout the movie, Marcos and his wife bear the guilt of having kidnapped an infant, who died before they could collect the ransom. Since Reygadas refrains from showing either the abduction or the death, and since kidnappers are known to strike frequently in Mexico, there's nothing particularly lurid about this setup. But Reygadas further posits that Ana, like the protagonist of *Belle de Jour*, works in a brothel; that Marcos has the privilege of knowing this secret, and impulsively shares his own secret with her; and that this confidence somehow moves Ana to grant his dream and let him enter her bed. We are now deep into the territory of the unlikely—which Reygadas then denies by venturing on long, nonnarrative forays through the city.

Battle in Heaven takes its dollop of Hitchcock, some Warhol and a lot of Buñuel and mixes them with a large dose of Bresson, posing awkward "models" in tableaux of crime, repentance and maybe redemption. Reygadas steals from the best; but what he steals, he changes into his own. I have warned you about everything—well, almost everything—that you might find exploitative or false. But once Reygadas draws you in to the visionary intensity of *Battle in Heaven*, no warning can shield you.

The Nation, February 27, 2006

Court

Chaitanya Tamhane's astonishing *Court* rides into current view on the long tail of neorealism. Beautifully composed in crisp wide-screen images, paced to ironic effect in calm rhythms, it both exposes the atavistic absurdities of India's judicial system and measures the distance between the lives of Dalits and the lavishness of pop culture. Some of the characters (notably the most privileged) live in a bubble of Bollywood songs. The character who sets off the action, by contrast, adheres to traditional Indian music. He teaches it, promotes it, and is likely to die in jail for having performed it on the street.

Narayan Kamble, "the people's poet," played by the magnificent nonprofessional Vira Sathidar, has been arrested (again) for declaiming his protest verses in the slums, on an improvised stage. This time, the charge is grave: He is accused of having incited a sewer worker to commit suicide. Has he in fact written a song advising sewer workers that their only way out is to kill themselves? "Not yet," he drily tells his questioners, "but I wouldn't mind doing it." Despite this critical gap in his oeuvre, and the absence of any evidence that the sewer worker in question died by his own hand, the state bears down on Kamble with its full prosecutorial apparatus—suborned witnesses, Victorian-era statutes, hallucinatory police reports, impenetrable multilingual jargon—which it does very, very slowly. Month after month, Kamble wastes away in prison (bail being unthinkable for such a serious offense) while his attorney (Vivek Gomber) trudges from court date to court date, sighing with dismay, incredulity, and a carefully maintained pretense of deference.

With a poise that's rare in directors making their first feature, Tamhane delivers both a deadpan satire of a rotten legal system and a nuanced portrayal of the people who inhabit it. Most of the time, he follows the defense lawyer, a marvelously hopeless figure who is as honorable and intelligent as he is portly, lonely, habituated to middle-class ease, and put upon by his parents. (It is characteristic of *Court*'s sense of humor, or despair, that when the lawyer addresses a human-rights conference, his speech is interrupted so that workmen can install a fan on the dais.) But Tamhane also spares time for the lawyer's opponents: the prosecutor (Geetanjali Kulkarni), who has to pull dinner together for her demanding family after a long day of persecuting Dalits, and the judge (Pradeep

Joshi), whose luxurious vacation and unthinking, self-satisfied cruelty are the subject of the film's final scenes.

The judge likes Bollywood tunes. The defense attorney listens to Mozart, hard bop, and cabaret-style bossa nova. The widow of the sewer worker (played by Usha Bane, who in real life is the widow of a sewer worker) doesn't seem to notice music—not even Kamble's folk-based protest songs, which she must have heard but can't remember. Nor does she have patience for the lawyer's well-intentioned offer of a little cash. She won't accept his money, she says—but if he knows of a job, any job at all, she'll take it.

The Nation, August 3, 2015

Django Unchained

Quentin Tarantino knows only two forms of cinematic punctuation—scare quotes and exclamation points—and he uses them both nonstop to produce his "irony!" To his detractors, he's a preening copycat, bombastically frivolous, pedantically vulgar, using the work of older, better filmmakers as his litter box. To his admirers, among whom you may sometimes include me, he's more like a curiously wired electrical transformer, plugged into a main power source of pop moviemaking.

The energy he draws comes from the magnitude of cinema—not so much the dimensions of a big screen (an artifact that is becoming obsolete) as the accumulation of sound and light, part junk pile and part treasure trove, that is the vastness of film history. In Tarantino's best work—which now includes *Django Unchained*—he exaggerates social conflicts to the point that movie culture itself seems to be the only common body of reference large enough to encompass them. Imagine, for example, that racism in America is a monumental fact of centuries-long duration. (A plausible thought.) Older narrative techniques, such as the depiction of an exemplary life, often struggle to convey the tremendous scale of this horror, which extends far beyond any one person's experience; but a film, as Tarantino understands, can express the magnitude at will, pulling images of a multitudinous racism out of 1960s spaghetti westerns and '70s blaxploitation thrillers, Hollywood epics of the silent era and Quentin Tarantino mashups from the recent past.

You might say, in an unkind mood, that Tarantino cares more about the thrills these movies can provide than he does the substance of his story—that he calls up the violence that has haunted the lives of Black Americans, or European Jews, or Uma Thurman, as a mere excuse for satisfying the audience's bloodlust. Judged on a film-by-film basis, this accusation might sometimes stick. But if taken as a principle, which would condemn all gory entertainments as suspect, the argument falls apart, for reasons having to do with the same film history that Tarantino plunders and glorifies.

Throughout this history, dour moralists have fretted that people may confuse the screen with reality, while cynics have never tired of reminding us that "it's only a movie." They're both wrong. Almost from the start—say from the time of Chaplin's *Kid Auto Races at Venice*—audiences have known perfectly well that movies can be a self-referential game. For an equally long period—starting, say, from *The Birth of a Nation* (a film of keen relevance to the subject at hand)—audiences have liked to feel that they're not wasting their time at the movies, and so have admired films in which the game seems to be played for life-and-death stakes. Good popular movies can invite us to recognize them as outsize fantasies, largely concerned with themselves, while at the same time touching on something substantial in our lives—which is what *Django Unchained* is able to do.

It begins with one of those spontaneous confrontations that are a Tarantino specialty, a scene in which a cheerfully self-assured character suddenly initiates and controls a dangerous face-off—made all the more stark in this instance by its taking place in a near void. In the dead of night, in an unpopulated wasteland of the Old West, a line of enslaved Black men is being force-marched through nowhere when an absurd figure materializes out of the darkness. Nattily dressed, elaborately bearded and perched high upon a wagon, from which a large, bobbing sculpture of a tooth protrudes on a spring, the man smilingly introduces not only himself but also his trick horse, Fritz, speaking in an English that is lightly accented but impeccable—though perhaps a little too voluble for the liking of the slave drivers, who are Americans in the brute state, ignorant, monosyllabic and utterly undistinguished. If you've seen a thousand westerns, you've seen these men a thousand times. By contrast, the stranger, the *dentist*—not that he practices dentistry any longer, please excuse the trappings of a former profession—or, to put it more precisely, Dr. King Schultz is clever, European and as individuated as the buoyantly resourceful actor Christoph Waltz can make him. Bang! The figures out of antique cinema are vanquished, clearing the way for Schultz to acquire for his own use one particular slave. This is Django (Jamie Foxx), a man who also appears undistinguished at first—just another shackled wretch, except for a nasty vertical scar over his left eye—but who will soon clean up nicely and eventually prove himself to be "one in 10,000."

In several ways, this stepping out of the ordinary is the theme of *Django Unchained*. Django vengefully escapes being one more piece of chattel; Schultz playfully and profitably exerts his superiority over the mass of crude Americans; and Tarantino once again proves that he can stand above the countless half-forgotten movies from which he borrows. His dramaturgy is more high-handed than theirs (as when he has Schultz reveal to an entire town, with theatrical panache, that he's a bounty hunter), his direction more exuberant (as you can see in the townspeople's reaction, with one woman in the background swooning—normal enough for a movie—but another hopping away on a crutch). Partaking in his creator's nature, Schultz too is a showman of sorts, improvising roles for himself as he goes about collecting bounties and instructing Django, now his apprentice, never to break character.

This method of self-definition through playacting certainly distances Schultz from his surroundings, just as it helps remove Tarantino from both run-of-the-mill cinema and base reality. (The date of the action, 1858, is "two years before the Civil War," according to an introductory title, tipping us off that *Django Unchained* takes place only in the general vicinity of fact.) But distance is not necessarily the same thing as indifference. I think Schultz means exactly what he says when he purchases Django, sealing the deal in blood and crying out with bitter, anachronistic jocularity, "Sold American!" And Django himself clearly speaks from the heart when he claims his first bounty. Watching as a whip-wielding, Bible-toting overseer staggers forward in disbelief with a bullet from the enslaved man's gun lodged in his chest, Django tells him evenly, "I like the way you die." It's as forthright an utterance as John Brown's valedictory statement, "The crimes of this guilty land will never be purged away but with blood," but expressed with grim pleasure—and an anticipation of more to come.

Foxx is a witty actor, though you wouldn't know it from the cold fury of this line reading. Almost until the end of the film, he leaves the humor to Waltz, playing Django as a watchful and deeply determined man—a straight man, you might say, to the joking Schultz.

Gradually, the film itself adopts Django's gravity. In one of its earlier scenes, *Django Unchained* evokes D.W. Griffith's notorious night ride of the Ku Klux Klan (a couple of decades too early, but no matter) and then grants itself the leisure to stop, start the sequence over and this time mock the Klansmen as chatty, bickering dolts, one of whom is so unimpressive under his white sheet that he's played by Jonah Hill. As events progress, though, and Django reveals that his wife (Kerry Washington) was deliberately sold away from him, the two bounty hunters resolve to pause from their moneymaking and try to claim her. This means they have to descend into Mississippi—the name scrolls across the screen in huge, ominous letters—where nothing is all that funny anymore.

The role-playing grows more tense—especially for Django, who must now impersonate a Black slave trader and so make himself the most hated man in the South. The witticisms grow more leaden in this setting, where they are mouthed principally by Calvin Candie (Leonardo DiCaprio), a blandly murderous plantation owner of the sort who is pleased to think himself cultured (he likes to be addressed as "Monsieur Candie," though he speaks no French) and by his Black overseer Stephen (Samuel L. Jackson, made up like Uncle Ben and shouting modern-day ghetto invective), who identifies so thoroughly with his white master that he hovers behind Candie's shoulder at the dinner table, seconding his threats and encouraging them to be redoubled. The tone darkens, and so does the palette, as *Django Unchained* stops being a road movie and gets locked into interiors, and the dominant narrative effect shifts from wide-open surprise to claustrophobic suspense.

These are the outward signs that accompany Tarantino's reliable old trick of introducing the protagonists to their evil doubles. Schultz, who is a sophisticated man and a classic liberal (he intends to own Django for a while, he explains, because he might as well take advantage of the circumstances, but he promises to feel guilty about it), sees himself grotesquely reflected in Candie, who buys and discards people without a qualm and hollowly pretends to refinement. In Stephen, Django faces an even more troubling reflection. The two men are genuinely alike in being tough, wily and unbowed; but even though Django is in full rebellion against slavery, he appears to the world (and temporarily to himself) to be as thorough a collaborator as Stephen. No wonder the situation feels explosive. Django and Schultz stare into their own worst possibilities as they mimic these two men, who may boast of standing out from the ordinary but are, at heart, horribly common.

I could hardly have enjoyed the contest more. My only reservation about *Django Unchained* is that the explosion, when it comes, feels only as satisfying as it has to be—perhaps because the character who exceeds requirements, Schultz, has by this time dropped out of the picture. He's had to; narrative logic demands that Django endure the final trial alone, and yet Schultz's departure reveals how deeply, and strangely, *Django Unchained* has been his movie. Played by the same actor who dominated Tarantino's *Inglourious Basterds* in the role of a Jew-hunting Nazi officer, Schultz is in effect the good German, returned to redeem the impression left by the bad. He is chivalrous toward Django and his wife, attributing this virtue to the inspiration of the Nibelungen Saga. He also rises to a full-throated defense of German culture when a member of the Candie household provides her version of high-class entertainment. "Stop playing Beethoven!" Schultz screams, no longer able to stomach the desecration.

In doing so, he has violated his own rule and broken character. Or, to put it another way, he has evolved as a character, which is something you can't say of Django himself. Over the course of the action, Schultz deepens in his commitments—to what he sees as right, and to the partner he hadn't expected to find—eventually deciding to gamble more than he'd ever bargained for. And how does Django evolve? He changes clothes.

Although Foxx does everything he can to ground Django emotionally (and succeeds), he's playing a man who always wants just one thing, and who practices one steady method—violent self-control—in trying to get it. Such singleness of purpose may arguably be realistic, but it flattens Act IV of *Django Unchained*. Part of Tarantino's achievement is to make nonformulaic films out of movie formulas. The climax of *Django Unchained*, at once bang-up and a letdown, was the moment when I wondered what had interested Tarantino more: the feelings of a Black man fighting his way out of slavery, or the possibility of repurposing Christoph Waltz from *Inglourious Basterds*.

To think that Waltz may have been more important, and that Tarantino couldn't truly dig his way into Foxx's character, is to betray a suspicion that the movie as a whole is an exercise in White Negroism. Having raised that doubt, I now say: let it hang. A charge of inauthenticity was the risk Tarantino took in playing the game of *Django Unchained*. To judge from the payoff coming from the screen, he's won the bet.

The Nation, January 9, 2013

En El Séptimo Día

The immigrant Mexican laborers in Jim McKay's *En el Séptimo Día* pedal around Brooklyn delivering food, clean vegetables in corner delis, mop the floors of porn-video stalls, or hawk cotton candy in Times Square. Those are their days. At night, they cook for each other and then sleep jammed into an apartment that six or seven of them share. Or maybe eight; the guy who finds them jobs and collects the rent is liable at any moment to show up with somebody who just came off the bus from El Paso and will now occupy his own slice of the floor. It's summer 2016, according to a title at the start of the movie—not a good time for immigrants whose papers aren't in order, though not as bad as it was going to get. But the characters in McKay's sparkling fable have things to worry about beyond Immigration and Customs Enforcement. These roommates have formed their own soccer team (the jerseys say "Puebla" but might as well read "Apartment 3B"), and with just one week to go before the league final, they're short a man.

Part De Sica, part Loach, and all Brooklyn, *En el Séptimo Día* is principally the story of José (Fernando Cardona), the apartment's leading scorer and mainstay of the bicycle delivery team at a Sunset Park restaurant that aspires to white tablecloths. Trim, slope-shouldered, and oval-faced, he's everybody's low-key Mr. Reliable: the guy who is last to leave for practice (because he's been in church, praying for the team) and the first to step forward to ease problems with the boss. On Monday, though, José runs into a labor issue he can't negotiate. The restaurant's slick young Anglophone owner (Christopher Gabriel Núñez) tells him with the blandness of unchallengeable authority that he's needed on the coming Sunday, the day of the league final. No substitute or excuse will be accepted—it's show up or lose his job.

Now the team's at risk of being short by two—and Mr. Reliable, who wants to please everyone, doesn't know what to do or how to tell his buddies.

Premised on a single though multilayered workaday problem, filmed on location, and cast almost entirely with nonprofessional performers recruited in Sunset Park, *En el Séptimo Día* plays out day-by-day with the unfussy integrity you'd expect of neorealism. Every detail seems as solid and dependable as José himself, and the actors (an array of vivid, unforced personalities) look and feel at home in whatever they do. But as McKay understands, there's more to neorealism than negativity: the rejection of artifice, the outcry against injustice. The tradition can also affirm the resilience, humor, and even charm of its characters—which *En el Séptimo Día* does so generously that it gave me more pleasure than any film I've seen in a while.

Much of that pleasure comes from sheer visual satisfaction, prompted by the joy that cinematographer Charles Libin finds in every street corner, walk-up apartment, and stretch of public park. When José interrupts his deliveries to phone his lover back in Puebla—his pregnant lover, whom he needs to bring to New York without delay—he tells her something you've been thinking yourself, that it's a beautiful day in the city. José may have paused for this call under a lane of trees near an industrial waterway, but it's the freshest, calmest, most glistening industrial waterway you've ever seen.

To get this kind of cinematography, which releases the inner light of things rather than imposing a vision on them, it helps to have a director with McKay's crisp, self-effacing style. To cite just one of the thousands of decisions he's made: Look at the scene where the members of the soccer team first appear, loaded with gear as they clatter one by one down a staircase in their apartment building. McKay has positioned the camera on the staircase itself, on a low step, to emphasize a sense of narrowness, crowding, and high spirits, as a seemingly endless stream of players pours down from the landing.

The deepest satisfaction of *En el Séptimo Día* comes from these characters, these comrades, as they improvise a piecemeal scheme to rescue their championship hopes and José's self-respect. He has struggled quietly with himself throughout the movie; he has listened to reasonable people advise him that no soccer match is worth his future in the United States with his lover and their child. On the other hand, the people he plays with are more than just teammates; they're his sustainers, his community—and he's really good at this game. When the tension is released at last and the dilemma's put to rest (you can't really call it resolved), McKay does not cheat on the darker implications of the story. But like the rest of the film, the culminating image is radiant: a close-up of José smiling in the soft, late-afternoon light.

En el Séptimo Día has been knocking around the festival circuit for about a year, having started its tour, appropriately enough, at the Brooklyn Academy of Music. It goes into general release in early June, which means you can now watch it without having to search for a special screening. All you'll get is a special experience.

The Nation, July 16, 2018

4 Months, 3 Weeks and 2 Days

I could spot only one moment of levity in Cristian Mungiu's *4 Months, 3 Weeks and 2 Days*; and having neglected to master Romanian, I didn't know why it was funny. It happened early in the film, in a scene where a college student in 1980s Bucharest was made to stand at a hotel reception desk as if she were an accused criminal pleading before the bench, when all she wanted was to rent a room for herself and a friend. "What's your friend called?" the clerk muttered in official displeasure, all the while fussing with her paperwork. "Dragut," the student replied. The clerk looked up sharply: another mark against the defendant. "That's her name," explained the student, with an apologetic shrug. "Dragut."

For all the insight it provided, that last subtitle might have read, "Comic misunderstanding here." So, after the screening, I trolled the Internet and to my delight pulled up an Anglo-Romanian website where young people advise one another on the translation of pickup lines. Who knew? *Dragut* can mean "cute." To the ears of petty authority, the name had sounded insubordinate.

My thanks to Romania's pickup artists, and best wishes for their continued success. I hope, though, that my web informants will be careful. If not, they may be left with an ordeal like the film's remaining 112 minutes.

For this is the story of an illegal abortion—or, more precisely, the story of one long day in the life of that student in the lobby, who risks helping a friend get an illegal abortion and then, under pressure, runs the even greater risk of abandoning her. When summarized, this action might sound like an anecdote. As realized by Mungiu, it's more of a paradox: a brilliant misery, photographed with such wide-eyed clarity, acted with such unwavering conviction and unfolding with such ever-deepening suspense that *4 Months, 3 Weeks and 2 Days* convincingly claimed the Palme d'Or at Cannes last year, followed by a string of other awards and festival invitations. Now the film is at last in theatrical release in the United States, allowing American moviegoers to experience its cool devastation, its calmly observed melodrama—and, most of all, its central character, Otilia (Anamaria Marinca), the helping friend, who's stuck being the strong one in a society that wants her to be powerless.

At the very end, you see Otilia sitting late at night in a restaurant, as shown in one of the film's astonishing wide-screen, deep-focus compositions; and as the shot is held and held, you slowly realize that reflections of car headlights are passing across the image. Posed at a window, Otilia is separated from you by a pane of glass—which I suppose links this scene with the film's opening shot, in which fish are shown swimming inside a little aquarium. Granted, Otilia breaks the symmetry of these first and last images when she finally glances through the glass, toward you; but despite this knowing gesture, she remains a creature on display.

You might think of this, too, as a paradox, since this specimen character, though exposed to the world's curiosity, has spent the entire film in clandestine activity. For late Communist Romania, though, this is no contradiction. In principle there are no secrets, since any lecture-hall monitor or hotel clerk is entitled to know Otilia's business; and in practice there are no secrets, since the whole country runs on illicit exchange, which is hidden in plain view.

Mungiu defines Romanian commerce early in the film, lightly if not with levity, when Otilia goes to buy a few toiletries for the chronically dependent Gabita (Laura Vasiliu) to prepare for her abortion. A decent bar of soap can be acquired in their dorm from a student who also deals in Tic Tacs and pirated videotapes. But decent cigarettes can't be found—even when Otilia tries another dorm room, where the black-market shoppers are shown in a wide band that stretches across the screen, as in one of Tina Barney's big domestic photographs. As you look at this array of people involved in their separate transactions, you see not so much corruption as a normal, daily imposture. Everyone relies on this supposedly nonexistent traffic. Even the juridical desk clerk manages not to notice the fellow who stands a few yards away in her lobby, selling packs of Kents from his overcoat.

It's from this incidental character that Otilia finally scores her cigarettes, in the last innocently dishonest transaction you will see in the film. After that, it's time for her and Gabita to negotiate with the abortionist, Mr. Bebe (Vlad Ivanov), a balding, clenched, leather-jacketed, briefcase-bearing man of about 40, who is officially a criminal but exudes an authority of his own. He, too, is good at disapproval. No sooner does he have Otilia and Gabita locked inside their little hotel room with the oatmeal-colored walls than he begins to lecture them impatiently, with much waving of his open palm. You'd think his hand was a tray, holding out the common sense and superior experience that young women are too dumb to accept.

Unfortunately, he succeeds in educating them.

Wrenching, harrowing, breath-stopping, abysmal: I grasp for words to describe the central sequence of *4 Months* but come up only with analogies. The scene, in its way, is as outrageous as the seduction of the grieving Anne, right over the casket, in *Richard III*; as pitilessly drawn-out, and clinically precise, as the death of Emma Bovary; as quietly, claustrophobically desperate as the breakdown in the elevator in Chantal Akerman's *Jeanne Dielman*. Voices are raised, just once. At one moment only the camera lurches forward, and you find yourself staring into Bebe's hot face. Otherwise, the trap door opens with smooth, slow-motion efficiency, and a very long rope plays out.

And here's the most terrible part of it: once Otilia drops, she just keeps falling. There's no snap, no knowledge that the worst has already happened, because she next leaves Gabita behind, to go into the twilit streets and pretend to participate in ordinary life. She will sit at a table crowded with middle-aged strangers; she will listen to their seemingly endless conversation about potatoes, Easter eggs and the benefits of military conscription. Young people everywhere are driven crazy by such yammerers; but Otilia, in her moral vertigo, needs especially to get away from them and can't. She suffers through a solid eight minutes of their dinner party in a single relentless shot, followed immediately by seven minutes more of painful, one-on-one confrontation, before finally being able to rush back to the hotel. Whatever catastrophe might await her there she will prefer to this normality.

Note the showbiz canniness. For all the formal restraint that Mungiu exercises in this film—a restraint that extends to Marinca's inward-looking, furiously controlled performance and to the deep, steady gaze of Oleg Mutu's cinematography—*4 Months* features the ever-popular devices of a ticking clock, an overbearing villain and a heroine who might as well be tied to the railroad tracks. Sound familiar? These are the same crowd pleasers you find in that other post-Communist prizewinner, Florian Henckel von Donnersmarck's *The Lives of Others*. An evaluation of *4 Months* might as well begin here, with a comparison of the two films' uses of political melodrama.

I think the comparison goes in Mungiu's favor—not only because his style is so much more rigorous and thoughtful but because his melodrama takes place in a world that feels inhabited. Born in Romania in 1968, Mungiu was a student at the time his story takes place. He has even explained, in interviews, that in those days he knew a woman who went through an abortion like this. Out of this experience comes the sense of complicity in *4 Months*—a complicity summed up in Otilia's final glance toward the audience. From *The Lives of Others*, though, you get congratulations. You, Western moviegoer, were never one of those bad, bad Communists; and if you had been, you'd emerge from the movie a good person, as certified by a filmmaker who has imagined East Germany but never lived in it. Thanks for the compliment, but I'll take fear and trembling over flattery.

To get a second standard of judgment, we might look at *4 Months* in the context of other recent movies about abortion. This comparison doesn't take long. Mungiu's film holds up well against Claude Chabrol's exemplary *Une Affaire des Femmes* and Mike Leigh's *Vera Drake*, and as pure filmmaking it towers over Lasse Hallström's *The Cider House Rules*.

That's about it for dramas. As for comedies, I can think only of Alexander Payne's *Citizen Ruth* and Todd Solondz's *Palindromes* (both special cases) before descending to *Knocked Up* and *Juno*. The latter film, I admit, has much to recommend it, but it still conforms to the pattern of contemporary American movies, in which abortion may be contemplated only for the sake of not being performed. Lovable characters come no closer to it than "shmashmortion" (as they say in *Knocked Up*). Mungiu's characters, however, have other things to do than be lovable—an industriousness that's entirely to their credit.

The last remaining comparison would be with the other films in Romania's purported new wave—which is to say, *4 Months* has to pass the *Death of Mr. Lazarescu* test. Here, I think, it falls a little short, for reasons that go back to that absence of levity. Cristi Puiu's *The Death of Mr. Lazarescu* has all the fear and trembling, and all the outrage, of Mungiu's film; but at the same time (to quote a better critic than I, Ben Sonnenberg), "it's as funny as Beckett." It's this doubleness of emotion, far more than the protagonist's allegorical name, that allows everything in *The Death of Mr. Lazarescu* to seem greater than its circumstances. By contrast, what you see is what you get in *4 Months, 3 Weeks and 2 Days*. The film may share some of *Mr. Lazarescu*'s traits—its long takes, its satirical edge—but in the end, it gives you gallows humor without the humor.

What a comfort to have it, though. Romania has produced a film as profoundly affecting and beautifully made as *4 Months, 3 Weeks and 2 Days*, and it's still not the best the country has to offer. For people who take their movies seriously, a quick course in

Romanian might now be necessary—and so is a trip to the theater to see *4 Months*. It may not be *dragut*, but it's awfully good.

The Nation, February 25, 2008

My Golden Days

Arnaud Desplechin's *My Golden Days* (or, as it's known in French, *Trois souvenirs de ma jeunesse*) is a film of mourning: for the parents one might have had but didn't, the siblings who slipped away, the mentor who could not live forever, and above all the first all-consuming love, impossible to have endured without scars and impossible to let go, even after 30 years. Mathieu Amalric, Desplechin's regular on-screen alter ego, plays the protagonist, Paul Dedalus, in the frame story; but most of the action is given to Quentin Dolmaire as the young Paul and Lou Roy-Lecollinet as his siren, victim, and faithful betrayer Esther, so placidly, arrogantly sure of herself and so hopelessly fragile. Stop *My Golden Days* at any moment, and you won't be able to predict what the next shot will be, beyond the certainty that it will be richly, fully alive. Look back at any moment in *My Golden Days* and you will see its connections spread to every other moment. The network is so intricate, while seeming so natural, that it feels as if every other filmmaker compared to Desplechin gives you only one-eighth of a movie.

The Nation, November 9, 2015

The Host

Nothing frightens us more than the dark, said the legendary Hollywood producer Jonathan Shields; so if you're shooting a horror movie, get rid of that extra in the moth-eaten cat suit, turn down the lights and let the encompassing shadows creep up and scare people. Sage advice, if your budget is low and your thrills psychological. And yet, though some dread things really are better left to the imagination, having migrated there from the murkier corners of the heart, others lead public lives and demand to be out in plain view.

Prehistoric beasts awakened by nuclear bombs, hideous colonizers from outer space, birds of a small-town America so blandly pretty that it could kill you: These are monsters from the social order, not the id, and therefore must come into daylight.

So it is with the huge, bellowing, umbrella-fanged, people-eating, humpbacked amphibian marauder that stars in Bong Joon-ho's *The Host*. Give it an audience, and this slithering colossus will perform upside-down back flips while hanging from a bridge, or flourish its tail with teasing, lewd gestures. Making its debut at midday in a popular riverfront park, the showoff runs up and back through the crowd, providing multiple viewing opportunities to the throng that's trying to escape it and offering a marvelous spectacle to commuters riding by on an elevated train. Whether this hyper-steroidal tadpole enjoys giving such a performance, I can't say; but I feel Bong's pleasure in showing it from many ingenious angles, in many acts of exuberant athleticism.

You, too, are expected to take pleasure in the display, which is half the point of devising a coming-out party that's so public in nature, and so uproarious (in both the common and literal senses). The other half of the point is to establish that every resident of Seoul, Korea, knows this monster is abroad. Yet the authorities—which ultimately means the Americans—ignore the obtrusively large threat, preferring to hunt small things: the microbes they insist the beast is spreading and the few hapless, silly humans who are presumably infected.

Not being one to force political interpretations onto a film, I will ignore the obtrusively large allegorical possibilities of this story and just call *The Host* a family movie. Those silly humans are Mr. Park (Byun Hee-bong), the grizzled, old-fashioned proprietor of a concession stand on the Han River esplanade; his three adult children (all of them chronic screw-ups); and his 12-year-old granddaughter, Hyun-seo (Ko A-sung), who scarcely gets to introduce herself to the audience before being swallowed by the monster, plaid middle-school uniform and all.

This engorgement is actually the beginning of Hyun-seo's story, not the end, since she's the functional member of the family. As for her elders, you may judge their abilities by the offerings they place before Hyun-seo's memorial photograph: tokens of failure, all. Aunt Nam-joo (Bae Doo-na), a competitive archer, presents the latest of her bronze medals. Uncle Nam-il (Park Hae-il), once a student radical and now just a ranter, sets down the whiskey bottle he's been guzzling. Father Gang-du (Song Kang-ho), a pudgy, sleepy goofball with dyed blond hair, doesn't have even that much to offer. He's got only tears, plus a used ramen cup filled with coins filched from the concession stand. These are the people on whom Hyun-seo has been forced to rely. Brought together now in an emergency shelter, they weep, wail, get into a four-way wrestling match, collapse onto the floor (in a shot taken from above, the better to show the choreography of the sprawl) and then demand to know what everybody's looking at.

The Host is many things, some of them icky. Above all, though, it is the story of how these slapstick figures rise painfully to the level of competence, and beyond. Somewhere in the soggy atmosphere they traverse, amid the maze of concrete sluiceways and hospital curtains that Bong so cleverly sets up for them, I glimpsed a suggestion that other Koreans, too, ought to become competent, and stop being so accommodating to foreign bodies lodged in their system.

It was just a thought—but a daylight one.

The Nation, March 26, 2007

Inside Man

In an era when most big studio releases lack even a single idea, *Inside Man* has two. One comes from the screenwriter, Russell Gewirtz, who thought up a devilishly clever title and a theme to go with it. The other comes from Universal Pictures and Imagine Entertainment, which could easily have made *Inside Man* from the standard white man's point of view but instead hired Spike Lee to direct. Yes, Lee did a contract job—but that doesn't mean he slapped his coat of paint onto someone else's house. Chronically alert to social divisions in general and the racial divide in partic-ular, Lee heightened the existing tensions between characters and possibly added a few of his own—choices that contributed not just to the style but to the meaning of *Inside Man.*

The theme is spoken directly into the camera at the begin-ning of the film, in close-up, so nobody can later claim that *Inside Man* is merely a bank-heist movie. "Listen closely to what I say," states Clive Owen, calmly but quickly. "Not everyone in a cell is a prisoner." The full import of this adage must not be revealed—although I may be excused for explaining that Owen's character, one Dalton Russell, does in fact rob a bank, in the course of which crime he becomes a prisoner of a sort. He and his crew, disguised as house painters, take hostage a large number of bank employees and customers but then are discovered in mid-robbery by the cops. Russell is surrounded and shut in; but as police detective Keith Frazier (Denzel Washington) begins to understand, this confine-ment may actually be a part of Russell's plan.

I do not think I'm turning *Inside Man* into a Rorschach blot when I say that Frazier, too, is a man in a tight spot, who needs to figure out which of his constraints he ought to embrace. On the personal level, he feels cramped by his lover (who wants to get married) and by her low-life brother, who bunks down just outside the bedroom door. On a professional level, he feels he is routinely put in a box, whether by Internal Affairs (which makes him the first suspect when cash evidence goes missing) or by the average white captain on duty (Willem Dafoe), who sees a Black detective, second grade, and reflexively ignores him. The options for Frazier draw tighter still when a mysterious fixer named Made-leine White (Jodie Foster, dressed in a crisp suit accessorized with a shark's smile) shows up at the crime scene with the mayor in tow to explain that she will be given full co-operation. To do what, only she knows.

Frazier's animosity toward White would not have been so keen, his desire to break rules so pressing, his routine disbelief of people's stories so openly satirical, if he had not been played by Washington, with Lee directing. The combination of actor and director intensifies every aspect of Gewirtz's screenplay, including Frazier's evolving relationship with the increasingly enigmatic bank robber. Thanks to the film's ability to be in two places at once, we see moments that are denied to Frazier—odd events that make Dalton Russell seem surprisingly humane, or even benevolent. When Russell at last shows this side of himself to Frazier, offering him a piece of good advice, the detective responds with instinctive sarcasm; but as the film plays out, we also sense that some understanding has passed between these two men, both of them smart outsiders forced to hole up.

The Nation, April 24, 2006

Joy

Factual in the broadest of strokes, fanciful in detail, David O. Russell's aptly titled *Joy* dramatizes the career of Joy Mangano, inventor and peddler of the Miracle Mop and other useful household items. As a fable of home-workshop tinkering and improbable entrepreneurial riches, this is Preston Sturges material and is mostly handled as such, in a style that's rapid, hectic, and studded with bargain-basement eccentricity. (At this point in his career, Russell even has his equivalent of the Sturges stock company, at a somewhat higher above-the-line cost.) But in tone, *Joy* is far removed from the gleeful cynicism that was so essential to Sturges, or for that matter to Russell himself in *American Hustle*.

Joy is incapable of condescension, in no small part because the heroine's doting grandmother gets to tell the story. You feel that Russell joins her in his respect for Americans who live in tiny, heavily mortgaged houses and shop at big-box stores. He also admires the determination of one of those Americans to make something of herself, even if (or especially because) her tool for doing so is a mop. In many other movies, the means of advancement would have been a kiss. But when the heroine of this Cinderella story—Sleeping Beauty, too—comes face-to-face with Bradley Cooper, Prince Charming in a sport jacket, her mind is not on romance, but rather on 300 feet of continuous cotton loop.

Fortunately, Russell in his sincerity has his thoughts on the cotton and also something more: the possibility of being oneself and connecting authentically with other people, in a society warped by artifice. In other words, *Joy* stars Jennifer Lawrence.

By this point in her astonishing, still-young career, Lawrence has attained a significance of her own in the public's eyes, whether she's shooting arrows in the *Hunger Games* movies, kicking her way through award shows, or giving any journalist with a working microphone a piece of her mind. She's the woman who wins without becoming hardened, the beleaguered yet victorious beauty whose righteous indignation comes with a throaty laugh. It's fair to say that Russell has asked Lawrence to play herself here—but only in the sense that she always rings true, effortlessly and naturally, in everything she does. In *Joy*, this quality turns out to be the key to success.

To show you why, Russell indulges just a little of the wigginess that endeared *I Heart Huckabees* to audiences (well, a few of us), beginning the film with a demonstration of the shooting techniques of soap operas. There's no explanation for this choice; but pay attention anyway, and you'll see how a daytime drama's staging, if viewed from a single head-on perspective, is as crazy as the plot, until it's been transformed by camera placement and editing into an absurdity that audiences can pretend is real. Such tricked-up images, you soon learn, are the stuff of Joy's engulfing nightmares—until she turns them into her launch pad instead, at the film's moment of liftoff, by stepping onto a TV studio's turntable as the first nonprofessional pitchwoman on the QVC channel. The phone calls pour in—because Joy has dared to come forward as herself, a real working mother mopping the floor of a plywood kitchen.

So a mop—the symbol and substance of Joy's subservience—becomes the magic wand that frees her. *Joy* is the tale of one woman's refusal to become a victim of the family that belittles her and the businessmen who are sure they can push her around. For extra fun, it is also a holiday movie—played out mostly in Northeastern slush—in which the heroine at the climax turns her face to the sky and welcomes a fake snowfall. The flakes are scraped out of a machine installed above a shop window; their purpose is to convert a display of toys into a commercial delirium. But the artifice is pretty, the urge to delight children is real, and the woman who gratefully drinks it all in knows herself to be genuine— whether she calls herself Joy or Jennifer Lawrence.

The Nation, January 25, 2016

Kung Fu Hustle

The scene is Shanghai, or Busby Berkeley's dream of it: a Chinese city of the 1930s, teeming on the outskirts with rickety tenement compounds, bustling in its business district with clanging street-cars and plump, humpbacked autos, groaning everywhere under the oppression of the Axe Gang, a chorus of criminals who dance like Fred Astaire and dress like London bankers, except for the hatchets on their belts. As the gangsters jitter and jive in their Art Deco casino—while a docile police chief thumbs through his cash—a montage of well-choreographed mayhem convulses the city. I mean woman-shotgunned-in-the-face, blasted-backward-through-the-air-type mayhem.

"People live in peace," a title explains, "only in the poorest districts, which have nothing to interest the Axe Gang." The camera glides, with 1930s facility, into Pig Sty Alley: four teetering stories of low-ceilinged shops and cramped residences, gathered like a broken-sided box around a courtyard damp with laundry.

Here, a different oppression reigns. The landlord, a would-be lounge lizard, slinks about putting the touch on his tenants, for money if they're men, for the sake of the touch if they're not. Meanwhile his robust wife, her hair permanently rolled up in curlers and a cigarette forever dangling from her lip, reasserts discipline when needed by hurling the landlord out of a second-story window, followed by a skull-denting flowerpot.

Only a loser of the lowest sort would be so stupid as to seek his fortune in Pig Sty Alley. Enter Sing (Stephen Chow): a scrawny fast-talker dressed in clothes assembled from other people's wash lines. He struts into the courtyard pretending to be an Axe Gang member and soon enough, by bluff and swagger, calls down the vengeance of the real gang on Pig Sty Alley. It's Sing's first self-inflicted disaster in *Kung Fu Hustle*.

Thinking of the many more to come—the punctured boasts, the ballooning body parts, the calamities that spark one another like a chain of firecrackers—the synopsizer falls silent. To tell more of the story of *Kung Fu Hustle* is to risk telling all, from the Zither of Doom to the flaming Buddhist Palm, from the flying attack in Toad Style to the explosive Lion's Roar, not excepting the tale of the mute girl with the broken lollipop and the heart-ache of her failed defender, a poor boy pledged to "uphold world peace and fight evil" with instructions from a fifty-cent pamphlet. A mere recital of the plot points would make an entertainment for a winter's night; but since it's spring as I write, let's simply say that *Kung Fu Hustle* gives you something to watch, as today's American pop movies seldom do.

Serving not only as star of the film but as its director, producer and co-writer, the immensely popular Chow (*Shaolin Soccer*) shot *Kung Fu Hustle* on elaborately beautiful sets constructed in and around Shanghai, with a technical crew drawn from the best of Hong Kong's film industry. The cinematographer was the veteran Poon Hang Sang (*Peking Opera Blues*; *A Chinese Ghost Story*), any one of whose crane shots or dolly excursions would be the glory of a Scorsese picture. The production designer was Oliver Wong—a frequent collaborator with Jackie Chan—and the sound engineer was Leung Chi Tat, who has amassed a decade's worth of credits with Wong Kar-Wai. This accumulation of expertise became even more extravagant with the action choreography, for which Chow called on not one but two masters, Yuen Wo Ping (*Crouching Tiger, Hidden Dragon*; *Kill Bill*) and Sammo Hung (*A Touch of Zen*; *Wheels on Meals*).

As this lavish display of pan-Chinese talent unfolds, you get the impression that you're watching a showcase production, like one of those old MGM revues featuring two dozen of the studio's biggest stars—the difference being that Chow has nothing to promote, other than his joy at commanding such riches. He conducts himself in *Kung Fu Hustle* less like a box-office champion than a fan who is especially rapt with admiration for the different generations of performers he has brought together. Deep students of Asian trash cinema will have the pleasure of recognizing them all. More ignorant viewers (including me) will fail to spot them, and so will have the different but equal pleasure of being surprised when a character's disguise falls away to reveal his or her astonishing powers.

I have been told that this theme of disguise goes far back in Chinese culture. For centuries, kung fu masters have figured in folklore and literature as hidden defenders of the poor, often wandering alone, in humble circumstances, to fight against the arrogance of power and the corruptions of officialdom. We recently saw an autumnal version of this myth in Zhang Yimou's *House of Flying Daggers*. Chow, by contrast, looks at kung fu legend with a child's eyes. He believes in the ideals (in a sapheaded, sentimental way) and at the same time sees them as material for a Looney Tune: legs that spin like the Road Runner's, torsos that splat like Wile E. Coyote's. Until close to the end, the comic mood predominates.

Then Chow drops his own shabby disguise to emerge as a shining hero, and the sky opens for him, the evil fall prostrate (or are jammed headfirst into the roof beams), the poor are vindicated and time runs backward, so that innocence may at last be recaptured. Somehow, this climax comes off as sincere—enormously silly, of course, but heartfelt—with Chow himself emerging less as a saint than as a guy who has finally gotten cleaned up and learned the value of hard work.

An unstable yet miraculously coherent mixture of stylized fighting, grotesque comedy, romantic wish fulfillment, deluxe production values and rhetorical appeals to working-class solidarity, *Kung Fu Hustle* may not be the most profound movie you'll see this year but is certainly the only one of its kind. It takes its peculiar place in a now venerable line of Asian films that have reminded us of the simple, kinetic joys that American movies have lost. And although you might suspect Chow of being a little too fond of cinematic artifice, I'm glad to say there's not a whiff of homage when he takes a line here from *Spider-Man*, a line there from *The Matrix* and a whole special-effects sequence from *The Shining*. Chow is working in a tradition that is fully alive, so these are out-and-out thefts.

The Nation, April 18, 2005

Leave No Trace

Bees creep peaceably over the hands of Thomasin McKenzie, the teenage actress cast as the protagonist of Debra Granik's *Leave No Trace*. It's not an editing trick; you see McKenzie's calm, heart-shaped face and unprotected fingers within a single shot, as the bees settle onto her palms and explore. Those same hands also spend a few minutes of screen time cradling a plump bunny and stroking its ears. Rabbits can be nervous creatures, apt to deliver efficient kicks, but this one relaxes into warm lumpishness with McKenzie, despite having Chainsaw as its name.

Set in the verdant world of the American Northwest, *Leave No Trace* begins with close-up views of fecund branches, glistening spiderwebs, and hollows of knee-high ferns, and ends with a panorama, seen from above, of a man disappearing into a mountain thicket. This rustling landscape might not quite pass for a new Eden—one of America's long-favored sites of imagination—but it's nevertheless suffused with a vibrant yet soothing light (thanks to Michael McDonough's cinematography) and seems ready to absorb and shelter, rather than threaten. This is where McKenzie's character, Tom, and her father, Will (Ben Foster), are first seen making their home, without running water, electricity, or fixed walls, in a nature that knows no violence.

A Christmas-tree farm, on the other hand, turns out to be a roaring nightmare of mutilated spruces, crashing loads, and helicopters buzzing down as if for an assault. That's how it seems to Will, anyway, when the State of Oregon decides to civilize him, like some late-30s Huck Finn with PTSD. Having captured him and his daughter in Portland's vast Forest Park, where the two have been living off the land (or is it hiding out?) for an unspecified period of time, the authorities decree that if this family is to remain together, the child must go to school, the parent must earn wages, and both must live in the house that Human Services assigns them, on the farm that jangles Will's nerves and makes him clutch his head. The confinement, the noise, the officiousness masquerading as kindness: They're all intolerable to him, with the helicopters as a special torment, uncannily echoing the choppers that shake him out of sleep at night. What's worst, though, are the hints—given with the tenderness and respect that are the norm between this father and his rapidly maturing daughter—that Tom might like it here.

Co-written with Anne Rosellini, and based on a novel by Peter Rock, *Leave No Trace* is the third film that Granik has made about a woman in extremity—though not the mortal peril that hovered over Vera Farmiga as a recovering addict in *Down to the Bone* (2004), or Jennifer Lawrence as an unwilling intruder into criminal secrets in *Winter's Bone* (2010). In keeping with its vision of an idyllic almost-Eden, *Leave No Trace* generates suspense about Tom's fortunes and signals her moments of defiance almost imperceptibly, with a few words left unspoken or a muttered rejoinder phrased so that her father can take it as acquiescence if he chooses to. *Leave No Trace* is a quiet movie—or, rather, a muffled one. Tom's restiveness is always just below the surface, even when she's offering her habitual "Thank you" to her father (which happens suspiciously often, with perhaps too much meekness) or cheerily complaining that she's hungry (and so reminding him of her growth). In response, her loving father never raises his voice and never lifts a hand in anger, no matter the terrors that he's tamping down.

Foster plays Will with a combination of weariness and patience that is striking for this usually explosive actor. With a bushy beard and close-cropped skull, he keeps his powerful torso a little hunched; his close-set, dangerous eyes are often downcast. The man is so contained within himself that you understand why he can't stand being shut inside a building; and yet he's also given to issuing peremptory commands to Tom, for reasons that seem more tenuous the deeper you get into the movie. As for McKenzie, her piping voice and slim frame don't suggest anything like the inner violence that Will fears and fights against. Instead, matching Foster in subtlety, she embodies an innate steadiness (useful for calming bees and rabbits) that underpins Tom's mounting desire to live outside the forest.

She doesn't want anything as flimsy as romance (a pursuit unknown in any of Granik's movies) or as basic as sex, despite the story's planting of a nice farm boy in her path. If the danger perpetually looming over Tom is the law, the temptation is community. She wants to be free to think her own thoughts (as Will has taught her to say); like other American characters before her, she has approached independence in the green world, and she's known with her father a love that's as pure as it gets—and as isolating. Now, though, the road has taken her among people who are willing to extend their hands and ask nothing in return; and, unlike Will, she feels whole enough to accept and reciprocate.

That's the dilemma: to open up a new life for herself in society, or to blow up her father's old one in the wild.

The choice seems palpable because the characters are, too. You might say that Granik prepared for *Leave No Trace* by making her remarkable documentary *Stray Dog* (2014), a portrait of the Vietnam War veteran, trailer-park manager, makeshift paterfamilias, and recreational motorcyclist Ronnie Hall. With Hall, Granik witnessed the gentleness and commitment to mutual support that can be found in the heartland among no-budget people who have learned to distrust authority. She saw how emotional wounds can persist in combat veterans and learned how these men (they were all men) manage to go on even so, through the understanding they receive and the help they give. When Tom enters a community comparable to Hall's in *Leave No Trace*, she encounters moments of sweetness and generosity that might have seemed sentimental in the hands of another filmmaker. With Granik, they ring true. She knows practical things, such as the character of the faces to put on the screen and how long she can linger on them, and she's also learned a few more important matters, such as the firm allegiance that people can bear to their sense of right and wrong.

Leave No Trace lacks the ferocity that drove Granik's earlier features, as well as a ready hook for audiences; but it offers deeper sorrow and greater hope, as well as a direct line to a substratum of the American imagination. I can think of nothing wrong with it, except for its being Granik's fourth film in 14 years. By contrast, in the time since her breakthrough in *Winter's Bone*, Jennifer Lawrence has found work in 18 pictures, a few of which (when written by David O. Russell) even gave her characters to play. I don't know exactly what Granik might need by way of financing and support so that she, too, can continue to write characters and elevate her actors (as she's done again with McKenzie)—but I wish somebody would give it to her, so she can catch up.

The Nation, June 27, 2018

Munich

In the past, even when Steven Spielberg has concluded a film with a robot boy cuddling up to a corpse, he has pretended to offer a happy ending. He has set his goodbyes in cemeteries—in *Schindler's List* and *Saving Private Ryan*—only to strike a note of fellowship and reconciliation. Just this past summer, he treated the incineration of the entire world as mere prelude to a family hug.

So we might pay attention to Spielberg's *Munich* just because it ends on the word "no," spoken as former colleagues abandon each other on a deserted playground. A chill seems to rise from the choppy river that runs nearby, separating the men from the backdrop of a quietly ominous Manhattan. Their work has cut them off from common humanity, leaving them friendless amid rusted jungle gyms and bare trees, in a place that children have forgotten.

This is some ending for a Spielberg movie, or for that matter any spy thriller, the genre to which *Munich* contributes a crackling example. Outwardly a movie of hardware and logistics, *Munich* takes you step by step through Israel's reprisals for the 1972 massacre at the Munich Olympics. As you would expect from Spielberg, the scale is large, the pace unflagging, the details hypnotically fascinating. But *Munich* is also about the reprisals for the reprisals. ("We're in dialogue now," comments a Mossad officer, with evident satisfaction, after a Palestinian bombing in London answers an Israeli bombing in Paris.) As the spiral of violence swirls downward, *Munich* becomes more and more a movie not of how-to but of loss, sorrow, futility and trepidation—which is to say, it's a first-rate spy thriller with a soul. The unhappy ending is striking for Spielberg, but it flows into the last scene as inevitably as the river itself.

The screenplay, credited to Tony Kushner and Eric Roth, moves quickly from re-creation to dramatization: first the hostage-taking and slaughter in Munich, then the recruitment of young Avner (Eric Bana) to lead a team of Israeli assassins. But "recruitment" may be the wrong word. Although Avner is a grown man, with a regular job and pregnant wife, his elders summon him like a boy. They remind him continually that they knew his father; they demand that he accept an assignment on the basis of blind obedience; they casually strip him of all professional status, so he's reduced to the condition of a kid just starting out in the world; they pay him and his undercover team as if doling out an allowance, and insist on getting receipts: "Whatever you're doing, someone else is paying for it."

Avner is so much in shock at the events in *Munich*—or, perhaps, is so used to being patronized—that he scarcely registers this treatment. In fact, he seems to think his new assignment confirms him as a paterfamilias. He believes he's acting to protect his wife and unborn child; he also behaves like a parent to his assassination team, briefing them over big meals he has cooked himself. But as the shootings and bombings multiply, along with their collateral carnage—Spielberg's direction is meticulous, but the assassins' operations are not—Avner comes to doubt not only the purpose of his mission but also the nature of his most basic relationships, with his elders, his family, his country.

I should now go on to apologize to Eric Bana, an actor I have previously misrepresented as a modern-day Victor Mature. Who would have known, from *The Hulk* and *Troy*, that Bana could so movingly play both sides of Avner's nature, as a man with "a gentle soul and butcher's hands"? Bana shows you how Avner shrugs off the urge to think about his actions, meanwhile registering an intelligence that won't be put off forever. When forced, through a kind of practical joke, to enter into debate with a Palestinian militant, Bana's Avner grows so angry that he almost blows his cover—and part of the reason he's so wild-eyed, you sense, is that he can't entirely shut out what he's hearing.

The image I have just assembled, of Avner and the movie he lives in, is a false one, of course, made by ripping details out of their natural places and collaging them onto a single spot, where they become as exaggerated as a caricature. But I, too, have a purpose in my violence. I want to emphasize that *Munich* has the internal coherence of a work of art. Its politics are inseparable from its narrative themes, its characterizations, even its performances.

This is a point that the film's enemies—the usual gang of hacks, sophists and hirelings—have done their best to ignore. They see that Israeli strongman tactics (and by implication the current Bush war) accomplish nothing in *Munich*, other than to heap misery upon misery; and they interpret this dramatic outcome as if it were a bald political statement, which they condemn. I, on the other hand, applaud *Munich* as a political statement, while recognizing that the film wasn't set up to secure votes, or signatures on petitions, or even cash contributions (other than those made at the box office).

What *Munich* elicits is pity and terror.

The Nation, January 9, 2006

Notre Musique

Michelangelo and Ulysses came home from the war with knap-sacks bulging, bearing the reward for hardships suffered and inflicted. "We promised you the world," the soldiers boasted to their wives. "Here it is"—and onto the kitchen table they spilled a heap of picture postcards.

This scene, from the 1963 *Les Carabiniers*, seems in hind-sight the true starting point for Jean-Luc Godard's art. *Breathless* is immortal, *A Woman Is a Woman* continues to delight, *Le Petit Soldat* forever marks Godard as combative and political; but *Les Carabiniers*, among the early films, most clearly announces "the image" as a primary subject of his work.

Not "images," as you might expect from a maker of moving pictures, but "the image." The wildly assorted photographs that Michelangelo and Ulysses slapped down before their wives resem-bled a primitive travel montage, run so slowly that the frames were visible one by one. This retarding of the flow has become a recurrent device in Godard's late work, starting about fifteen years ago with the series *Histoire(s) du cinéma*. He sometimes makes a point of holding apart the binary elements of filmmaking, shot and reverse shot, rather than letting them merge in the viewer's mind. In place of persistence of vision, he gives you resistance of vision.

In his new film *Notre Musique*—a work of art too tender, sorrowful, gorgeous and profound to be harmed by us critics, with our heavier kind of slowness—Godard demonstrates in person how to pull apart a montage. In a quasi-fictional scene in which he speaks to a small and rather distracted young audience, he holds up a pair of frame enlargements from Howard Hawks's *His Girl Friday*—one of Cary Grant barking into the telephone, the other of Rosalind Russell yakking back—and notes that the two shots, which ostensibly depict warring opposites, are basically identical. ("It proves," he says, "that Hawks didn't know the difference between a man and a woman.") Never mind that this observa-tion, if taken at face value, would be bogus; in *His Girl Friday*, the pictures move and so are not identical at all. But Godard at this moment is not particularly interested in Hawks. He's instructing us in how to read Godard, who thinks in bigger units than most other filmmakers can handle. He treats set-ups, sequences, even whole character arcs as if they were discrete images, to be flashed before you dialectically like shot and reverse shot.

The biggest dialectical opposites in *Notre Musique*, standing symmetrically at either end of the film, are the sequences titled "Hell" and "Heaven." It's the first that reminded me of *Les Carabiniers*, despite the fact that the montage here runs at full speed and beyond.

Godard's "Hell" is a staggering ten minutes of found footage, collected from fiction films and documentaries alike and spliced together with a lifetime's skill to show the horrors of war. Flashes of white light; a quick view of celluloid, colorfully decomposing; the booming attack of a piano's bass notes. A woman's voice says, "And so, in the age of fable, there appeared on earth men armed for extermination." They appear: Civil War soldiers from *The Birth of a Nation* running in from the left of the screen, African warriors from *Zulu* rushing back at them from the right, Crusaders, GIs, samurais, guerrillas, an entire battlefield's worth of medieval figures stabbing clumsily at one another. Fire and smoke erupt skyward from bomb blasts, again and again. Naked, skeletal corpses flop down into a ditch. "Forgive us our trespasses," the voice on the soundtrack prays, "as we forgive others—and no differently." Children beg. On a 1940s street kneels a woman (an accused collaborator?) silently pleading before a man in uniform.

If the Michelangelo and Ulysses of *Les Carabiniers* were right—if an image is a real possession—then this initial, infernal section of *Notre Musique* shows us something we own collectively, as heirs of the twentieth century. God knows, we've paid to receive it. Maybe one picture postcard of this "Hell" was shot on the spot, by a newsreel cameraman, and another was concocted on a movie set by Oliver Stone; but as Godard flips through them, these views add up to a single picture, globally produced, which is highly characteristic of our age and amply deserves the name it gets.

What image of "Heaven," then, have we collectively inherited from the age of moving pictures? One that's far more cryptic, according to Godard. The closing section of *Notre Musique* is gently paced, in counterpoint to the frenzy of "Hell." The basic technique is the tracking shot, not the montage; the colors are those of nature in its freshness—green forest and blue water—and not in decomposition. Perhaps most important, we are now in the company of one identifiable protagonist, a young woman, who wanders past US Marines (alert but pacific) and frolicking nudes and someone reading a French translation of a novel by David Goodis. Settling down by a lakeside, our new Eve bites into an apple, with no apparent ill effect.

Whereas Godard's "Hell" is an image of something dreadfully familiar, made up of horrors that require no further explanation (and that flash by with the speed of television, as if the remote were in the hand of an angry God), his "Heaven" seems truly alien, since it borrows nothing from the celestial fantasies of popular movies, or from the devotional paintings that have given cinema its white robes and golden harps. The kitsch certainties of a *Green Pastures* would have posed a false opposition to Godard's "Hell." The real counterimage must be undecided, and open to the imagination. The lake you see in "Heaven" surely stretches beyond what's visible at the top of the frame, the new Eve's ramble must somehow go on after the apple is bitten, but Godard quietly refrains from showing how either would continue.

This is the neglected legacy of another type of image-making: the mobile, evocative, observational mode that André Bazin praised in his essays half a century ago, and that is still occasionally practiced today, though not by anybody whose films top the weekend box office. Godard's "Heaven" represents, among other things, an abandoned paradise of long takes and unforced meanings—a paradise that remains accessible to anyone who cares to enter, although it's routinely ignored by advertisers, propagandists and popcorn-sellers.

It is also rejected, to a certain degree, by Godard himself. He may respect the cinema of the steady gaze, but in his own perverse way he is a recidivist of montage, always looking to strike up contrasts between shots, or sequences, or character arcs. Between his "Hell" and "Heaven" falls "Purgatory," by far the longest section of *Notre Musique* and the one that's layered most insistently with doubled images.

Set in Sarajevo during a literary conference—a real one, which Godard has in fact attended—"Purgatory" brings together a variety of actual and invented people to sift through the aftermath of war and perhaps imagine (as Spanish author Juan Goytisolo says amid the rubble) a "creative revolution" of a force comparable to that of the negative revolutions that strike all around. As the section title implies, the characters are in a place of transition, where they may find gestures of reconciliation at every turn: interpreters carrying thoughts from one language into another, an engineer (Gilles Pequeux) reconstructing the Old Bridge at Mostar, a young Israeli journalist (played by Sarah Adler) respectfully interviewing the Palestinian poet Mahmoud Darwish in a Holiday Inn.

Not that reconciliation is achieved. The Israeli journalist also wants to talk with the French ambassador (played by Simon Eine)—to hold "just a conversation" with him, about the Palestinians and Israelis—but he refuses. To speak openly, for him, would be to lose the ability to act. Another young Israeli (played by Nade Dieu)—a near-double of the journalist—trails Godard to his lecture in Sarajevo and makes a video of him. She seems to want to unite the word and the act; but she can't do it and still remain in this world.

If this description of "Purgatory" sounds cryptic, please blame me and not Godard. *Notre Musique* is a direct and heartfelt film, by his standards. As usual, he's quotation-mad; but since the authors of the literary texts are now often present on the screen, reciting their own words, the word soup has thinned out considerably. The characters in "Purgatory" are good company (even grizzled old Jean-Luc himself), and the tone is light enough that an impromptu dance can break out at a diplomatic reception. For the people with whom I've discussed *Notre Musique*, only one element seems to weigh down the film: the Indians (George Aguilar and Leticia Gutiérrez). What the hell are they doing in Sarajevo?

Being outsiders, that's what. The Native Americans stick out in *Notre Musique* as bizarre and inexplicable presences—but that's appropriate, since they literally have no place in the discussion. Although they are inextricably bound up with Europeans through their history (much as Palestinians are bound up with Jews), the Indians are shut out, by definition, from something called "European Literary Encounters."

The problem that Godard poses here, as I understand it, is one of recognition. He knows that movie audiences—that is, most people in the developed world—have seldom truly seen an Indian. Instead, they have looked at Wild West projections: images that mirrored their Euro-American authors, as Rosalind Russell mirrors Cary Grant in *His Girl Friday*, and so set up a false opposition, rather than a real dialogue. In much the same way, Palestinians are made into the false mirror image of Jews. ("The world isn't interested in me," Mahmoud Darwish tells his interviewer. "It notices me only because it is interested in you.") The great trial of this "Purgatory," then, is to recognize the other person and not just oneself; to discover a shot and reverse shot that are truly different; to locate the opposite riverbank so we can begin rebuilding the bridge.

Godard tells us nothing new, in other words. Nothing that we can afford to ignore, either, even for one more day.

So I come back at last to Ulysses and Michelangelo—characters who, in Godard's account, always come back anyway. One of them survived battles and monsters and brought home a tale to tell. The other (to quote his sonnet) lived in hell and painted its picture. We know very well what these two characters have to show us of the world; it's our legacy, which we have no good reason to disown.

But if we could slow down the torrent of images—perhaps just by shutting our eyes and thinking for a moment—what new thing might we discover in the gap between the pictures? Godard, though stuck in purgatory, bets there's something more to see in that darkness. And even though Wolfgang Amadeus Mozart is entirely absent from this film (a striking omission, given Godard's lifelong love for his work), there also might be something new out there to hear, a sound we ought to recognize but don't.

Our music.

The Nation, December 20, 2004

Obit

Some people—not everyone, of course, but a large enough group, with members around the world—believe that the ultimate form of recognition is an obituary in *The New York Times*, incontrovertible proof that a life has mattered. If the stiff is famous, the *Times* obit will be instructive and pleasingly nostalgic, filling in details that you didn't know and calling up reminiscences from your own life. If the subject is someone previously unknown, the obituary will bring the excitement of discovery. Obits edify, astonish, refresh, console (after all, you're not the one who's gone), and reaffirm day by day that individuals still count for something, though some more than others. I know quite a few people—my wife, for example, a lively and sociable person with nothing morbid about her—who cheerfully start each day with the *Times* obituary page.

Vanessa Gould's documentary *Obit* shares some of the virtues of this minor literary form and of the writers who practice it at the *Times*. Her film believes in curiosity, anecdote, and concision, the detail that encapsulates and the window that opens onto history. Borrowing from accounts published in the *Times* as well as archival images, Gould entertainingly sums up the achievements of more than a dozen of the departed, while also bringing to life the personalities, opinions, and work habits of another half-dozen people who are with us still: the staff of the *Times*'s obituary department.

It is one of the few such departments that survive in today's newspapers—which is odd, in its way, since the genre is arguably more vital than ever. Margalit Fox, who comes across in her interviews as the most willing theorist on the staff and perhaps its most inventive stylist, proposes that obituaries are now free to be "just as swaggering and rollicking as their subjects." And why not? After the writer has satisfied the minimum requirements—supplying a name, age, and confirmation of the person's passing—the article should have "next to nothing to do with death and absolutely everything to do with the life."

A similar idea, though given different emphasis, comes from the calm and measured Bruce Weber, who is shown working throughout a single day on the obituary of William P. Wilson, John F. Kennedy's television consultant for his presidential debate with Richard Nixon. To tell an engaging story, Weber explains, the article will have to teach a little history to *Times* readers, so he's taking the risk of writing two paragraphs of narrative about the debate before even mentioning Wilson. The headline, Weber says, will take care of the fact that somebody's dead, so he needn't worry about that. All he's got to do after sitting down at his desk in the morning is to interview the widow and gather sources; make himself an instant expert on a topic he's never written about before; give his editor, William McDonald, enough detail to present at the Page 1 meeting at 4 pm; and deliver a first-rate finished article by six. Weber goes to the coffee machine a lot.

Insights like these make *Obit* a remarkably good film about the craft of writing. You learn about news judgment (which is to say, why former Soviet leader Leonid Brezhnev and the guy who invented the Slinky both deserved *Times* obituaries), problems of length ("I don't have time to write it short"), and the challenge of matching style to substance (Paul Vitello, assigned to memorialize the 1960s advertising executive Dick Rich, mulls over verbal equivalents for the images in his subject's best-known TV commercials). Problems specific to the genre also figure into the story. On a good day, Weber says, you come to the office and ask, "Who died?" On a bad day, someone as famous as Robin Williams or Prince dies an hour or two before the print edition closes, and because the death is unexpected, the *Times* has nothing prepared on which to base your article.

Those advance obituaries, more than a thousand of them, are kept with millions of other items in the morgue, which is stored off-site because the sheer weight would "pancake the floors" of the Times Company's skyscraper. So says Jeff Roth, the sole remaining employee at the morgue and one of the film's most demonstrative talkers. A slim, 40-ish fellow who puts on a white shirt and tie to work alone among the file cabinets, Roth may say the most of anyone about institutional change at the *Times*, as the guardian of its yellowing and labyrinthine history. Writers and editors deal with the evolving problems of a digital, 24-hour newsroom; Roth deals with materials that are obsolete but still indispensable, filed in overlapping generations of systems that no one living understands. He sounds perpetually amazed.

I was amazed, too, and often delighted by *Obit*. Now that I've made that recommendation, professional ethics compel me to state that my boss, Katrina vanden Heuvel, is co—executive producer of the film. But I didn't find that out until the closing credits, so you might say it's a dead issue.

The Nation, May 22, 2017

Paterson

Jim Jarmusch's deceptively simple *Paterson* begins with a sense of contentment and then magically sustains this mood through nearly two hours of droll, quotidian soulfulness. Nothing world-shaking happens in the film, but every second of its characters' routines feels rich with meaning, from the moment each day when Paterson (Adam Driver) wakes up in bed with Laura (Golshifteh Farahani), checks his wristwatch, and walks down to the depot to drive a New Jersey Transit bus.

"Poetry does not tamper with the world but moves it," William Carlos Williams wrote in *Spring and All*. The thoughtful young bus driver named Paterson, long of body and face, moves an assortment of people through Paterson, New Jersey—the city of Williams—while mentally composing the next lines of whatever poem he's working on. Reflections of the city's plain-faced downtown move across the surface of the windshield, thanks to one of the film's many miracles of cinematography by Frederick Elmes. The words of each poem move across the screen as Paterson thinks of them. (Jarmusch commissioned the poems from Ron Padgett, who has addressed their humble subjects—a box of matches, for example—with just the right level of skill for a character who is well-read and talented but has no ambition to publish.) When Paterson gets back to his tiny house, where Laura has spent her day painting things in black-and-white patterns and dreaming up dinner recipes, some of them edible, she asks if his new piece is a love poem. It's for you, he tells her, so yes.

Theme and variations, Monday through Friday, with the weekend off to go to the farmers' market and the movies. What is there to love in all this down-at-the-heels normality? Crisp sunlight on red brick, the swerve of a big chassis driving around tight corners, the mysterious tilt of a mailbox skewed on its pole, the casual talk of people who almost never have more than a hundred in cash, and a beautiful recitation by Driver of Williams's plum poem, "This Is Just to Say." This is the world in Jarmusch's *Paterson*. It moves you.

The Nation, January 16, 2017

A Quiet Passion

You might describe it as a counter-séance. *A Quiet Passion*, the eighth feature-length film by Terence Davies, doesn't pretend to recall the skeptical spirit of Emily Dickinson to the land of the living but rather projects you into her departed world, which folds itself almost tangibly around this poet of worldly departures. Everything is odd here: the geometric decorum of family gatherings in the parlor, the formal mode of address mixed with epigrammatic banter, the blanketing hush at evening, the endless play of candlelight and shadow, and most of all the behavior of Dickinson herself. She may put you in mind of a wraith, with her elongated frame and painful trembling, but there's nothing delicate about her: not her refusal to sit in church or kneel in prayer at home, not her crockery-breaking fits of temper, and certainly not her way of thanking the editor of the *Springfield Republican* for having published her work. When he presents himself at her home, she insists on remaining at the top of the stairs, so she can berate him from on high for having altered her punctuation.

You cringe at the affront to a man who seems well-meaning enough, if dim; you ache for the fresh wound that Dickinson has now inflicted on her already enfeebled hopes for literary recognition; but you also understand that this bitter complaint over a few dashes and commas is one more instance of the "rigor" that her devoted sister Vinnie admires in her. Dickinson rejected convention in a spirit not of rampaging freedom but of exactness, the better to leave the reader a trail of meticulously selected pebbles and bleached bones that would lead, by a short but deliberately irregular sequence, to revelation. Davies, too, has been exacting throughout his career, refusing himself the easy norms of exposition and transition; but in his best films (such as *Distant Voices, Still Lives* and *The Long Day Closes*), he's practiced a paradoxically liquid rigor in which each epiphany flows lusciously into the next. In his deep love of Dickinson, Davies has now adapted his smooth and coloristic style into something closer to her jagged tactility, so he can touch on the truth of what he calls *A Quiet Passion*—a title that at first sounds like it belongs on the cover of a less-than-marketable paperback bodice-ripper, but that actually makes a Christ out of Dickinson, who by her suffering and death redeemed all who read.

Of course, there is no plot here. People who let themselves lapse into cliché may speak of an individual's life as a story (or, even worse, a journey), but as Psalm 90 reminds us, there's no more narrative to it than you'd find in a blade of grass. Allow me to recommend, just in passing, the setting of Psalm 90 by Charles Ives, another uncompromising New England artist, whose music Davies has chosen for the end of *A Quiet Passion*. At the movie's climax, Dickinson is lowered into the grave, having been accompanied to it by a geometric cortege, Ives's chilliest orchestral strains, and a soundtrack recitation: "Because I could not stop for Death…" Throughout the rest of the film, while you await this foregone conclusion, you get to see the deaths or distancings of the people Dickinson loves. There's your "story." Nothing else happens of any consequence, except for a few brief shots of the poet scratching at papers in the dead of night and stitching the sheets into tiny booklets by day—but that's everything.

Part of the mystery behind this everything is how a young woman born into the culture of 1830s Amherst could have made herself into the poet Emily Dickinson. The biographies document an education and social circle that were considerably more ample than Davies allows; but he knows these factors cannot explain the transformation (since others drew on the same resources without becoming geniuses), and so he slashes them away. With the concentration on religious bullying that has characterized his films, he begins with the very young Dickinson at Mount Holyoke Female Seminary, where in the face of her evangelizing headmistress's wrath she stands steadfastly alone as the sole self-proclaimed "no-hoper" in her class, confessing neither to an immediate conviction of her sinfulness nor to an aspiration to be saved. Davies does not pretend to show how Dickinson mustered the courage to refuse, in public, demands in which she did not believe. He merely assumes, from the start of the picture, her capacity to say no, then moves on quickly to other moments.

Played in this early part of the film by Emma Bell, Dickinson seems to differ from her sister Vinnie only in the degree of her candor, her more vivid sensitivity, and her desire to be allowed to write poetry in the wee hours, when she won't disturb the household and it won't disturb her. To the question of how this young Emily matures—which is to say, how the lively, clever, and conventionally pretty Emma Bell turns into the intellectually piercing and severe-faced Cynthia Nixon—Davies in effect gives the one-word answer that is faithful to his materialist work: photography.

Davies re-creates a family portrait-sitting session (and in so doing provides one of the film's few moments of levity, when the famously overbearing paterfamilias Edward, played by Keith Carradine, barks at the photographer, "I *am* smiling!"), then dollies in on each image, morphing the subjects one by one into their older selves. As the cliché has it, this is the magic of the movies—but the whole point is that no magic is used. You see only a physical process, which is nevertheless impressive to watch, and which prompts questions—about matters such as the motions of the soul—that are not going to be answered.

Even Dickinson, whose powers of imagination and insight far surpass those of anyone around her, cannot understand how she becomes the person you see in the later part of the film: someone bitter and reclusive, and so judgmental that she's apt to provoke quarrels even with her beloved Vinnie (Jennifer Ehle). Part of the reason for the change, surely, is the long-term effect of the constraints imposed on women, which she feels keenly and does not shy from denouncing. Another reason: Her physical maladies wrack her more and more terribly.

Dickinson's debilitating fits, filmed and acted with impeccable precision, arouse a natural pity and terror in you; meanwhile, her eloquent attacks on male privilege and female submission elicit an almost automatic assent from a 2017 audience. Emotional money in the bank, you might say, well-earned but not mysterious. And yet, despite whatever skepticism you might share with Dickinson and Davies, there is a residual hint of magic in *A Quiet Passion*. You find it in the inexplicable circumstance that Davies's artifice, though blatant, comes to seem less obtrusive as the film goes on, while your engagement with Dickinson's character grows deeper even as she becomes more off-putting.

I'd say your acceptance of the artifice is less a matter of habituation—I never did get used to the arch dialogue—than of your coming to feel how thoroughly the film is steeped in Dickinson's poetry. Early on, for example, when a pious aunt advises Emily not to be afraid of death, you very distinctly hear a fly buzz. Or to take another example: When Emily first holds her newborn nephew (played by the dullest, lumpiest baby the waggish Davies could find), she looks him in the face and coos, "I'm Nobody. Who are you?" As with the passing incidents, so too with the compositions: Davies repeatedly arranges his figures the way Dickinson carves out her stanzas, sculpting the actors into solid, steadily observed groups of two and three.

As for the way Dickinson becomes increasingly compelling, some credit must go to Davies, who has proved himself over the years to be one of the great directors of actresses, but most is emphatically due to the extraordinary Cynthia Nixon. Like any good performer, Nixon knows how to play a subtext. Unlike all but the very best, she can show you layer upon translucent layer, until her character's states of mind take on the clarity and complexity of a polyphonic texture.

When she shouts at the servants, you feel Dickinson's impatience at their clumsiness, recognize her terror at her own sudden infirmity, and see how she blames herself for being physically weak, all at once. When she dares to put one of her little sewn books into the hands of the Rev. Charles Wadsworth, you sense her deep need for intellectual companionship and respect, mingled with fear of being dismissed, reserves of anger (held ready in case of dismissal), and semi-suppressed sexual longing. Nixon gives as detailed, and yet as unaffected, a performance as you could hope to see, even when the words drop away and her acting is entirely physical. During Dickinson's final illness, when she's shaking uncontrollably in bed, it's undecidable whether Nixon is wearing the expression of someone staring in horror or caught up in ecstasy.

This is how materialism and doubt may triumph in poetry, and do triumph in *A Quiet Passion*. You see Nixon's face framed in the crack of a shadowed door—Dickinson is listening with misgivings to a soiree in the parlor below—and the word "stricken" comes to mind, as if to sum up what you're seeing and so allow you to move on. But as Davies holds the shot, and Nixon holds the pose, it becomes obvious that those two explanatory syllables fail the facts that are before you: the skin's pallor, the neck's cords, the grooves running down either side of the nose, the unblinking eyes that stare into nothing. "Stricken" cannot cover all that. You realize, as you do again and again in *A Quiet Passion*, that only the particulars matter—the pebbles and bleached bones, laid out (as they are here) in an order that's made just for them and is just right for this moment.

So teach us to number our days.

The Nation, March 28, 2017

Rust and Bone

To Stéphanie, the character Marion Cotillard plays in Jacques Audiard's thoroughly extraordinary *Rust and Bone*, touch is elemental, visceral, threatening and thrilling. For her amusement, she flirts with men at a dance club in Antibes, sometimes paying with a bloody nose when they escape her control. For her career, she bends brute nature to her will as a trainer of killer whales at the Marineland park. Within the first quarter-hour of the film, Stéphanie goes from a skimpy black dress under the disco lights to a form-fitting wetsuit on the Marineland stage, and it's obvious which type of glamour suits her more. "I like to get them worked up," she says of her men at one point, "but then I get bored"—a statement that you understand she would never make of the whales. In perhaps half a dozen unforgettable shots, Audiard shows you the huge power that seems to dance at the ends of her fingers, leaping and plunging in time with her gestures, while Cotillard (her image expertly cut into scenes of the real, gaudy Marineland spectacle) wordlessly demonstrates Stéphanie's concentrated profession-alism. You might think that nothing could be more intoxicating than such command, until one of her performers fails to respond as anything but a whale, and the water turns dark with something much worse than a nosebleed.

Rust and Bone is the story of how Stéphanie, deprived of both legs by catastrophe, chooses not to collapse into helplessness but instead comes to terms with a new brute—a human one—riding on his strength when she has to and taming him to the degree she can, which she has to admit isn't much.

This new animal in her life is a Belgian boxer known as Ali (Matthias Schoenaerts), who has recently drifted into Antibes dragging along a 5-year-old son he doesn't know how to care for. A pure specimen of cheerful working-class amorality, Ali tends to the kid not because it's right but simply because it's something you do, when you remember to. If feeding the boy requires theft, then Ali will steal. If it requires Ali to work as a security guard and keep others from stealing, that's fine, too. Best of all, though, is to earn a pile of bills, and bring home a toy truck, by surviving a round-robin bare-knuckles tournament held without rules in a gravel parking lot just outside town. Ali wants the money, but at heart he fights for the same uncomplicated reason that he screws when given the opportunity: because it's fun.

This is the man, met by chance, whom Stéphanie calls to help her when she emerges from the hospital—a man who takes her to the beach and without self-consciousness carries her into the water on his back, then makes love to her back in her apartment as if her stumps were perfectly normal. If *Rust and Bone* were a simpler film, cast with a weaker actress in the lead, Stéphanie might have responded to these attentions with gratitude, or a hungry, romantic love. Instead, she emulates Ali and is soon helping him flatten men's noses. He won't dance at her fingertips, as the whales used to do, and when she asks him for a little *délicatesse*, it's painfully clear that she ought to know better. But when Cotillard steps out of her SUV at one of his bouts, the blades of her prostheses exposed beneath her tucked-up trouser legs, none of that matters. She's made herself into the toughest number at the prizefights, and even Ali can see it.

The Nation, December 27, 2012

Spring, Summer, Fall, Winter...and Spring

With its cyclical, Buddhist narrative, *Spring, Summer, Fall, Winter...and Spring* will strike some moviegoers as profound and others as profoundly clichéd. A rustic temple floats on a pond, cupped in the mountains of rural Korea; and there, in the springtime, a hermit monk (Oh Young-soo) watches and guides his child apprentice. Years pass; and one summer, when a young woman comes to the temple to be healed of an undefined malaise, the apprentice (now a young man) feels the first overpowering stirrings of desire. Autumn, some ten years later, finds the former apprentice emotionally ravaged and the old monk ready for death. You may imagine for yourself the meanings that attach to winter and the return of spring.

Archetype, or stereotype? The more curmudgeonly among us may notice that in this ninth feature film by Korea's prolific Kim Ki-duk, the wheel of sin and expiation, death and rebirth, sometimes seems a little creaky. But because Kim is willing to bet his whole movie on a single stunning last shot—a summing up of the abundant natural beauty in the film, rendered so intense that the world seems to return your gaze, as if it were a single great eye— *Spring, Summer* is likely to win over even the most determinedly antispiritual moviegoer.

Kim's first career was as a painter; but the painter's eye accounts for only part of the elegance and charm of the film, and none of its sly humor. For example, Kim knows the trick of framing a shot with an architectural element—the elaborately carved wood panels of a gate, which magically swing open at the beginning of each season, or the doorway that separates the main room of the temple from its sleeping quarters. Coupled with the gracefulness of these images, though, is a sense of what you might call the ceremonial absurd. Both the gate and the doorway are freestanding, without walls; they mark points of entry that are entirely arbitrary. In a similar spirit, the older monk's teachings sometimes take on the character of practical jokes, which grow more serious as the seasons turn. Even in autumn, when the apprentice is desperately agitated, having dragged the world's violence (and its modernity) back to the lake, the old monk is capable of writing down for his student an entire *sutra*, using as a pen the tail of a remarkably patient cat. Kim's inventiveness seems to me entirely cinematic—and not only in managing such physical details but also in guiding the performances, especially during the summertime romance between the eager, accident-prone, caterpillar-browed young monk (Kim Young-min) and the demure city girl (Ha Yeo-jin) who remains disdainful until she's not.

Other actors who turn in good performances include a frog, some snakes, a waterfall and a tree that stands in the lake. Under Kim's quietly assured direction, they all become animated — which is to say, he gives them a soul. Without that quality, the film would perhaps amount to little more than a package tour. (Take a vacation from your real problems in life! Get five seasons of Buddhism, complete with landscapes and sex, for just $10, popcorn not included.) With that quality, *Spring, Summer* is a living, breathing pleasure.

The Nation, April 26, 2004

Thirst

No other film this summer has made me so thrilled to be in a theater as Park Chan-wook's *Thirst*. I say this as a confession—because a morally aware adult with responsible tastes cannot excuse, let alone indulge, the feral pleasures set loose in this movie. At least I have company in my guilt. One of the film's two main protagonists feels as awful as I do about participating in the experience. The other has the time of her life, or undeath.

Recognized by scholarly viewers as a modern-dress Korean adaptation of Émile Zola's *Thérèse Raquin*—whatever—*Thirst* is in fact many things: a tale of adultery and murder, a drama of Catholic spirituality, a thriller about medical science gone awry, a satire on provincial life (the hours clacked away in mah-jongg games, the years sighed out in claustrophobic shops and their upstairs apartments). But *Thirst* is always and above all a vampire movie, and as such it provides the best opportunity yet for the director of *Oldboy* and *Lady Vengeance* to express his lavish, grotesque and gleeful talent for bloodletting.

The star of this delirium is Song Kang-ho, who was so delightfully loose-jointed when playing the bleached-blond hero-despite-himself of Bong Joon-ho's *The Host* but here moves initially with heavy care, as if each gesture cost him pain from an inner wound. As Sang-hyun, a young hospital chaplain, he suffers from the death all around him, from the apparent futility of his efforts to aid the dying and from a spirit of renunciation that is perhaps too complete. Aspiring to martyrdom—or is it suicide?—Sang-hyun volunteers to be a research patient in an African clinic, where doctors are seeking a cure for a deadly virus that (strangely enough) infects only missionaries. He awaits the agony in his cell, playing Bach's "*Ich habe genug*" on the recorder; breaks out in pustules; hemorrhages profusely; and then dies on the operating table while receiving a blood transfusion—only to revive.

Still swaddled in bandages to hide the pustules, so he looks more like the Invisible Man than a vampire, Sang-hyun returns to Korea and resumes his hospital duties, now with the additional shame of being popularly thought to be a saint whose prayers have special efficacy. No one has ever survived the virus. How he survived it, and on what terms, does not become clear to him until the full moon, when he is suddenly overcome by a wash of red on the screen, the echoes of energetic copulation on the soundtrack and a flickering montage of wildlife imagery, intercut with pictures of a bandaged Jesus on the cross. By the time the fit passes, Sang-hyun understands that his body cries out for blood—a few swigs of which do wonders for that embarrassing skin problem.

One deeply carnal craving is bad enough for a priest with a perpetually heavy conscience. But a desire even worse than blood lust comes over Sang-hyun next, when chance reintroduces him to an old grammar school acquaintance—a scrawny, grinning, snot-nosed mama's boy—and the man's apparently abject wife, Tae-ju (Kim Ok-vin). She is gorgeous, in a delicate-featured yet pouty way—and also glum, fragile, put-upon and somnambulistic, all of which goes right to Sang-hyun's heart. He doesn't realize that Tae-ju's sleepwalking is actually a conscious ritual of escape, carried out regularly after she practices the best angle for shoving scissors into her husband's snoring mouth. Sang-hyun knows only that Tae-ju, like him, is a lonely creature of the night. He sees nothing wrong with rescuing her (as he imagines it) on one of her nocturnal forays, lifting her off the pavement with his more-than-human strength, then lowering her bare feet into the protection of his worn-out shoes. Charity covers the first physical contact. The contact after that won't be covered at all.

New love, as everyone knows, often brings people shock as well as joy—but rarely a shock so indelible as the one that Chan-wook now puts on the screen, when Tae-ju finds her priest lying on the floor beside a hospital bed, making illicit use of a rerouted IV line. New love also brings a moment when one partner or the other takes command of the exhilaration—but rarely in such a bravura manner as Chan-wook invents for this couple. Standing with Sang-hyun on a rooftop several floors above street level, Tae-ju asks whether he's able to jump down. In response, he wordlessly gathers her in his arms and leaps into the night air, his cassock billowing behind him—at which point you get a close-up of Tae-ju as Sang-hyun would see her, laughing wildly at the magic he has put at her disposal.

By the next time Chan-wook stages a scene on the rooftops, much later in *Thirst*, Tae-ju will have gained that terrible magic for herself, and Sang-hyun will be leaping after her from building to building, horrified at what he's done both for her and to her. But she will not be horrified. Unlike her priest, whose vampirism only sharpens the bite of conscience, Tae-ju will revel in being a predator. If she were not undead, you would think the life force overflowed in her. As for responsible, remorseful, self-restrained

Sang-hyun, you'd say his heart was all the more sick with desire for being fastened to an animal that won't die.

This contrasting development between Tae-ju and Sang-hyun has distressed some viewers, who have resisted being carried away by the flood of Chan-wook's images. According to A.O. Scott in his impeccably judicious review in the *New York Times*, "The difference between the lovers is indicative of the film's queasy, quasi-misogynist ideas about eros and ethics." But with due respect for a critic I admire, I will argue that Chan-wook's supposed misogyny is visible only if you're looking at *Thirst* with one eye—the eye that identifies with Sang-hyun. Look with both eyes at once so you also identify with Tae-ju, and you not only lose the misogyny but gain some depth perception.

Tae-ju is, admittedly, a reprehensible character; but that doesn't mean she hasn't suffered, and it doesn't mean she's wrong to reject being a victim. *Thirst* takes the trouble to show her wasting away at work in her mother-in-law's airless kimono shop, and dragging through interminable nights of social boredom in the equally suffocating apartment. While Sang-hyun has been swaddled in bandages, Tae-ju's owners (you can scarcely call them family) have kept her as immobile as a corpse in its winding sheet—so it's no surprise that her pretended sleepwalking is actually a sprint through the deserted streets. She doesn't just have to get out; she has to *move*. And if she eventually gains the ability to move like no mortal being, that's not her doing but Sang-hyun's. The vampire priest has needed her badly enough to give her power but then, in his anguished, mopey way, can't accept the reality that power is what this woman needs. Depending on which eye you're looking with, that makes him either a morally aware adult or a hypocrite.

Thirst is hardly the first film to play this double game with the audience; but it plays the game beautifully and with a brio that requires no apology. You might look for it on the one out-of-the-way screen where it still lingers in your town, its title now shrunk to insignificance amid the newspaper ads, its reflected light washing nightly across empty seats. Secrets are best savored in dark, hidden places.

The Nation, August 31, 2009

Uncut Gems

Joyously, programmatically icky and utterly obsessive about the way certain white Americans are obsessed with African American athletes, Benny and Josh Safdie's *Uncut Gems* is the story of a middle-aged merchant in New York's diamond district and his manic pursuit of various big scores. Sometimes the hustle involves paying an accomplice to steer NBA players to his claustrophobic shop, where he flogs gaudy wristwatches. Sometimes the play is to pile one more risky sports bet onto his pyramid of losses, hoping to hit before the goons catch up. Grandest of all is the scheme to auction an opal-encrusted rock he has just had smuggled to him from Ethiopia in the intestines of an iced fish.

According to the merchant, Howard Ratner (Adam Sandler, furnished with a dyed-black goatee and ratlike prosthetic teeth, a bejeweled ear stud, and a high-roller's leather jacket), the rock is worth a million dollars. But consider the anatomical vehicle through which the piece entered the country, the views the Safdies have given us of the geological bowels in which Ethiopian miners labor and bleed, and the way the film has introduced Howard through a live video feed of his colonoscopy—right up the business end. This character is not just running toward the biggest stack of cash he can grab. Something in his guts keeps him running away from the certainty of death.

A holiday movie of sorts, if you accept that the celebration is Passover, *Uncut Gems*, like the Safdies' previous *Good Time*, is a street-smart New York film about chasing around on an adrenaline high with time running out—a film full of breaking glass, rasping security-door buzzers, and pursuers with the mugs of concentration camp guards, presided over by a "crazy Jew" (in the words of his NBA wrangler) who seems to think he'll die if his patter drops below 90 miles an hour. Characters crowd one another, the camera (in the masterly hands of Darius Khondji) crowds the characters, and the music by Daniel Lopatin occasionally breaks into a gamelan-inspired clatter to remind everyone to hurry the funk up.

It's a movie that wrings sadistic humor out of a doorman's routine question about whether anything's in the trunk of Howard's car (there was indeed an earlier load, and it was unfortunate) and builds suspense out of moments so small as a walk to the end of the driveway with the garbage cans. The standard response in this pitiless movie to the statement "I feel like an asshole" is "You are." The appropriate way for Howard to thank his girlfriend for tattooing his name on her ass is to wail, "You can't even get buried with me now."

Is there a purpose to this marathon of sleaze, in which your pace may lag behind the tireless Safdies'? Does *Uncut Gems* show you anything beyond the universality of exploitation? I would argue that Howard, as embodied by Sandler with complete, fearless conviction, is an idiosyncratic but meaningful example of the American entrepreneur: in this case a physically unimpressive man enamored of the majesty of basketball stars, a highly cerebral man with no better use for his brain than to figure the angles, a Jewish family man who would pawn his wife and a Torah scroll for a hot night in a casino. The point is, this irredeemable character is human—and with furious cunning, the Safdies get you to feel for him in his rush toward the end.

The Nation, December 12, 2019

Vera Drake

Set in London in 1950, Mike Leigh's new film *Vera Drake* is the story of a wife, mother and cleaning woman (Imelda Staunton) who is always waddling cheerfully up the staircases of dingy brick apartment compounds, sometimes to serve tea to a handicapped neighbor and sometimes to perform an abortion. The word for her method, I believe, is "dodgy." Vera forces soapy water up her patients' bodies, explaining that in a day or so the bleeding will come. Then she leaves, providing nothing in the way of postoperative care beyond a sincere smile and a reassuring pat. Given the state of English law in 1950 and her patients' resources, it's as good as these women can get. If Vera could give more, we have no doubt she'd do it.

Always humming little tunes, always puffing busily and keeping her chin up, Vera initially seems, in Staunton's performance, like some hard-working family's beloved little dog, no longer young but still bright-eyed and eager to please. This raises a question: Does Leigh like Vera?

I'm sure he prefers her to the rich women she serves, who come off like unfunny stick figures, lacking the sensitive, lifelike modeling that a Ken Loach, say, might have given them. But to say that Leigh despises one class is not to say he admires another. Early in the film, he has Vera and her family engage in a long, detailed conversation about the recent war, one purpose of which is to establish a cozy sense of English solidarity. Generous, uncomplaining Vera is a ridiculously improbable character, unless you see her as exemplifying the belief that we're all in this together, and we'll pull each other through.

That, more than the harm done by anti-abortion laws, is the real subject of the movie: the chummy ethos that animates Vera. As far as Leigh is concerned, it's a worldview fit for idiots.

Look at how dull a character Vera is, when she's at liberty and helping others. Look at how she becomes more compelling, and the film much more interesting, as soon as she's arrested and her suffering begins. (You know, of course, she's going to be nabbed. You wait for it, and wait.) It's not just that Staunton's tears are varied, while her smiles are not. The difference is that consciousness begins to light up in dim Vera, the consciousness that her abundant kindness can be fatal.

You can take the film at face value as an exposé of the bad old days, in which case it plays like a one-block-long trip down a one-way street—or take it as an act of termitelike subversion, in which Leigh calls up a popular conception of English virtue so he can gnaw away at it from inside.

The Nation, November 1, 2004

The World

Jia Zhangke established his reputation with three remarkable films—*Xiao Wu* (1997), *Platform* (2000) and *Unknown Pleasures* (2002)—all of which were rapturously received at international festivals but are known in China only through bootleg DVDs. Made without government approval, these films officially do not exist and therefore cannot be shown. For his latest picture, though, Jia secured the right stamps in Beijing and Shanghai to go with his funding from Tokyo and Paris. His countrymen can at last watch one of his films.

And what will they see in *The World*? A fun-house reflection of the filmmaker's situation, and theirs, as globalized yet wholly isolated.

Jia's characters in *The World* are fictional workers at an actually existing theme park outside Beijing: a place with reduced-scale models of the Eiffel Tower, St. Peter's, the New York skyline (with Twin Towers still standing), the Taj Mahal. See the World Without Leaving Beijing! reads a billboard on the property, selling people their own constraint as a form of entertainment. Tao (Zhao Tao), a dancer in the theme park's gaudy shows, and her boyfriend Taisheng (Chen Taishen), a security guard, are free-moving enough to have made it here from their rural birthplace in Shanxi, but it's clear they're not getting any farther. They may take the park's video "magic carpet ride"; they may sit in the facsimile of a passenger jet, where Tao sometimes plays a flight attendant to help visitors imagine the wonders of air travel; but their real world will remain the workers' maze of underground corridors and dressing rooms, where faint echoes of music and applause filter in from above.

I can see I'm in danger of insisting too much on the film's social critique, and so making *The World* into castor oil. It's anything but. Jia's patient observational style makes plenty of room for humor and incongruity—as when his characters carry on an argument in front of a camel, tethered forlornly next to the theme-park Pyramids, or when they get so excited by the miracle of text messaging that they visualize the calls as psychedelic cartoons. Jia's art can also open up the most devastating sorrow, sprung from nothing fancier than a chance meeting in a washroom or a few words scrawled on a cigarette wrapper.

Emotionally, *The World* is as full as any movie you're going to see—and it has something to say, by the way, about the situation of a billion or so people, for whom modernity is a growing pressure, a bitter fantasy, a show to be played for a little money.

The Nation, July 18, 2005

Ex Machina

While waiting like everybody else to see *Mad Max: Fury Road*, I went searching for interim thrills from the kind of movie that grosses tens of millions of dollars and found what I wanted in Alex Garland's *Ex Machina*.

It's the story of a reclusive Internet gazillionaire (Oscar Isaac), a young coder (Domhnall Gleeson) plucked from obscurity and summoned to his mountain lair, and the gazillionaire's new robot (Alicia Vikander), which he's built to have a fully self-conscious mind (maybe) in a va-va-voom body. The coder's job is to decide whether the robot, named Ava, has true intelligence; but soon you start to wonder whether the Internet genius can be trusted—or Ava, for that matter.

Ex Machina is worth watching just as an exercise in suspense, creepy high-tech production design (the house is a cross between a *2001* spaceship and Superman's Fortress of Solitude), and excellent acting (high-powered from Isaac, nuanced from Gleeson and Vikander). It's of special interest, though, as part of a recent cinematic trend, in which men become attracted to, and perhaps victimized by, nonhuman things that appear to be women. *Ex Machina* can't live up to the very best film of this type, Jonathan Glazer's astonishing *Under the Skin*; but it adds to the evidence that the Mechanical Bride, as we've known her from *Tales of Hoffmann* through *Metropolis*, has definitively changed. Men still think they want her for sex; but as she—it—surpasses them, what they're really hoping for is a parting moment of pity.

The Nation, June 8, 2015

The Young Karl Marx

"Yes, that's it!" Karl cries to Friedrich as they reel, very drunkenly, through an alley in Paris on the first night of their bromance. "Until now, philosophers interpreted the world. But it must be transformed!" At this stage of intoxication, guys like Seth Rogen and James Franco might have had the sudden, giggling inspiration, if transported back to the 19th century, to borrow that sweet phaeton they'd spotted in an archduke's driveway and take it for a trot through the Bois de Boulogne. Not Karl and Friedrich: They come up with the *Theses on Feuerbach*.

So it goes in *The Young Karl Marx*, an improbably lush and deadpan-funny epic about a pair of two-fisted materialists and the bodacious babes who loved them, as they brawled and rollicked their way toward writing *The Communist Manifesto*. ("We must deliver it by February first! Only five weeks!") Directed by Raoul Peck on the heels of his triumphant *I Am Not Your Negro*, and co-written by him with the perpetually waggish Pascal Bonitzer (who has helped the likes of Raul Ruiz and Jacques Rivette invent unexpected gifts), *The Young Karl Marx* is to the best of my knowledge something new, both in buddy comedies and romantic costume adventures: the story of a scheme to shoulder aside the leaders of the League of the Just and rededicate the organization to a bold new movement, marrying descriptive sociology to post-Hegelian theory!

Lantern-jawed August Diehl plays Marx, with a scraggly beard on his face and indignation forever burning in his deep-set eyes. Stefan Konarske, last seen as a space officer in *Valerian and the City of a Thousand Planets*, brings a touch of sulky, pretty-boy glamour to the role of Engels. (Always chafing under the burden of his father's money; always flinching at the expectation that Marx will bring it up again.) As Jenny von Westphalen, Vicky Krieps is as assertive as she was in *Phantom Thread* (the old order, she declares, will crumble!), though not to the point of serving her husband Karl an untrustworthy mushroom omelet. She just gives him a forgiving kiss and the reassurance that he must leave her behind in chilly Brussels with a newborn child, if the revolution needs him in London. (To be fair, this happens long before Engels would write *The Origin of the Family, Private Property, and the State*.) As for Engels's soul mate Mary Burns, Hannah Steele gives her the full Maureen O'Hara firebrand performance. John Ford would be smiling somewhere, if he were a communist and knew how to smile.

You get all this, plus horses, candles, drawing rooms, cobblestone streets, dark Satanic mills, and multiple debates with the ever-forgiving anarchist Pierre-Joseph Proudhon (Olivier Gourmet), photographed in approximately the same palette that cinematographer Kolja Brandt previously used for *Young Goethe in Love* (aka *Goethe!*).

Believing as I do that the best of all social programs, gendered pronouns aside, is "From each according to his abilities, to each according to his needs," I am delighted to receive the improbable gift of *The Young Karl Marx*. That said, I'm a little worried that Peck might take this movie more seriously than I do. Although he clearly wants to entertain, he does not signal a desire like Iannucci's to make you laugh—that's your choice—and at the end presents a heroic montage of communism's march through the decades. Faced with that finale, I have to say that one of my abilities is a capacity to make distinctions, and one of my needs is for a fair historical accounting. So, while I insist that communism get credit for its role in the international labor movement and the struggle against colonialism, I also think that Peck's montage ought to have included a few less celebratory images: Soviet tanks on the streets of Budapest and Prague, let's say, or starving Chinese peasants slaving over backyard steel foundries, or the rogues' gallery from *The Death of Stalin*. Despite that lapse, Peck has, as with *Lumumba*, proved that he has a skill for historical epics. Now that it's streaming, will you enjoy watching it? Very possibly, if you've got enough nerdiness to thrill at seeing Marx and Engels respond to Proudhon's *The Philosophy of Poverty* with *The Poverty of Philosophy*. Is the whole thing kind of silly? Yes, but maybe not quite enough. Will it inspire the masses to take up the *Manifesto* anew? Now, *that's* funny.

The Nation, April 23, 2018

Zodiac

Because the much praised *Zodiac* is concerned with the desire to impose order, and with our perpetual failure to do so, you might say it's something like a Kubrick film, though realized with an empathy that Kubrick disdained. Because of this theme, maybe you'll also excuse the lateness of my review. Like *Zodiac*'s characters, I tried to control circumstances—press screening schedules, deadlines, the kids' bedtimes—and like them, I screwed up.

Now I can offer only a tardy echo: *Zodiac* is, as everyone says, an unusually complex and ambitious true-crime story, and (more important) a deeply engaging study of three obsessed men.

Or four, if you count the title character: the serial killer who announced himself to the San Francisco newspapers in 1969, issued a string of communiqués and taunts (some in code), terrorized the region, disappeared, reappeared and has never been conclusively identified. As a crime story, *Zodiac* is utterly inconclusive (unlike, say, *Dirty Harry*, which based its plot in part on this case). You don't get any answers—just the satisfaction of riding along with people who are caught up in this mystery.

They are two professionals and an amateur: police inspector Dave Toschi (Mark Ruffalo), newspaper police reporter Paul Avery (Robert Downey Jr.) and editorial cartoonist Robert Graysmith (Jake Gyllenhaal), an overgrown Eagle Scout and puzzle enthusiast known in the newsroom as Retard. Once the initial murders are out of the way—the film deliberately front-loads its violence— *Zodiac* settles into the story of these men and their intertwined, ever accelerating downward spirals.

Zodiac is a long movie, but one with a steadily quickening pace. The longer you watch the film, the more absorbing it becomes— which is enough to set it apart. What I really like about *Zodiac*, though, is that it is neither the usual product (a producer-driven marketing ploy dressed up like a movie) nor the usual alternative (the latest auteurist masterpiece by director David Fincher). *Zodiac* is Fincher's film, certainly; but it also belongs to screenwriter James Vanderbilt, cinematographer Harris Savides and the entire cast. For a change, the major studios have given us a whole movie. Just like old times.

The Nation, April 23, 2007

Index

Sticking Place Books (stickingplacebooks.com) is a New York-based publisher specializing in cinema, offering inter-view books, memoirs, critical and historical studies, screen-plays, and essay collections. Our titles include:

Lessons with Kiarostami. Edited by Paul Cronin

In the Shadow of Trees: The Collected Poetry of Abbas Kiarostami

Still Film Crazy (After All These Years) by Patrick McGilligan

It's Only a Movie by Bruce Joel Rubin

Three Visionary Screenplays by Bruce Joel Rubin

Playing Among the Stars: Conversations with Damien Chazelle by Nathan Réra

The Magic Eye: The Cinema of Stanley Kubrick by Neil Hornick

A Shared Cinema: Conversations with Michael Ciment by N. T. Bihn

The Naughty Bits: What the Censors Wouldn't Let You See in Hollywood's Most Famous Movies by Nat Segaloff

Mexico: The Aztec Account of the Conquest by Werner Herzog

Werner Herzog/Rogue Filmmaker by David LaRocca

De Palma on De Palma: Conversations with Samuel Blumenfeld and Laurent Vachaud

Publication as Autobiography: Occasional and Forsaken Texts— and Endangered Cinema Species by Scott MacDonald

Filmmakers Thinking by Adrian Martin

Secret Cinema: The Rise and Fall of the Blue Movie by John Baxter

Casualties of War: An Investigation by Nathan Réra

Hollywood on the Tiber by Hank Kaufman and Gene Lerner

I Loved Movies… But: Conversations with Joseph McBride
  by Danny Peary

A Reluctant Film Critic by Gerald Peary

The Zen of the Director by Peter Markham

Adventures in Auteurism: A Crusade for the Criminally Neglected
  by Daniel Kremer

Persistence of Vision: A Collection of Film Criticism
  Edited by Joseph McBride

Writings and Relics 1990–95 by Michael Almereyda

The Autobiography of Jane Brakhage by Jane Wodening
  With P. Adams Sitney and David E. James

The Curse of Queen Kelly by Pamela Hutchinson

Lost Screenplays of the 1970s by Jim McBride

My Lunches with Henry Jaglom by Daniel Kremer

Bender's L.A. by Michael Elias

My Strange Love: Selected Film Reviews and Essays, 2001–2021
  by Stuart Klawans

Dentists with Guns by David Mamet

Late Style in Film by Collin Brinkmann

Dressing the Story by Debra McGuire

Metafiction by David LaRocca

The Most Important Art by Ian Christie

Two Screenplays by Eve Babitz and Michael Elias

All That Black by Cristiana Astori

Night Moves: Twenty-four letters
by Dominic Lash and David R J Stent

Body Parts & Zero Tolerance by Alex Cox and Rudy Wurlitzer